Frontispiece to the 1698 folio edition of
The Aeneid of Virgil.

THE AENEID OF VIRGIL

THE
AENEID
OF
VIRGIL

TRANSLATED BY JOHN DRYDEN

EDITED, WITH AN INTRODUCTION AND NOTES,
BY ROBERT FITZGERALD

THE MACMILLAN COMPANY, NEW YORK
Collier-Macmillan Limited, London

Library of Congress Catalog Card Number: 65-16929

First Printing

ACKNOWLEDGMENT

The editor wishes to acknowledge the cooperation
of The Clarendon Press, Oxford, in allowing him to use
The Works of Virgil, Translated by John Dryden,
as the basis of this text of the *Aeneid.*

The Macmillan Company, New York
Collier-Macmillan Canada, Ltd., Toronto, Ontario
Printed in the United States of America

CONTENTS

5

CONTENTS

INTRODUCTION

THE VERSION OF *The Aeneid* that we might have had in English
poetry was never written. By this I do not mean merely that there is
no complete *Aeneid* in English as good as Gavin Douglas' *Eneados*
in Scots of the fifteenth century; I mean that during two periods,
very roughly from 1570 to 1650 and from 1800 to 1880, someone
might have done justice to the poem, but no one did. It is easy to
conceive an *Aeneid* by Keats, who had read Virgil in school and
whose power over language resembled Virgil's, or by the Tennyson
of *Milton* and *Ulysses*. From these poets and their century, however,
we do not have even any partial attempts that are really memorable.
From Tudor times we do; an English *Aeneid* of the sixteenth century
exists in fragments, so to speak, or potentially. It can be so present
to the imagination that we can almost reconstruct it or make a
composite. There is the dignity and sonority of Surrey:

> "O Queen, it is thy will
> I should renew a woe cannot be told,
> How that the Greeks did spoil and overthrow
> The Phrygian wealth and wailful realm of Troy. . . ."

And there is the motley splendor and kick of Stanyhurst:

> Now manhood and garbroyles I chaunt, and martial horror.
> I blaze that captayne first from Troy cittye repairing
> Like wandring pilgrim too famosed Italie trudging
> And coast of Lavyn; soust with tempestuus hurlwynd . . . .

And the élan of Marlowe:

> Not moved at all, but smiling at his tears,
> This butcher whilst his hands were yet held up,
> Treading upon his breast, struck off his hands . . .

7

Spenser, an avowed Virgilian, could have made an admirable *Aeneid*. But the poet most capable of the full Virgilian range was probably John Milton. Suppose that on his return from Italy around 1640 Milton had taken up Virgil and had spent the next years not in controversy but in retirement, translating the *Aeneid*. Our literature would have been handsomely—and very usefully—enlarged. Just as Marvell wrote the one truly Horatian ode in English, Milton might have written the one truly Virgilian long poem.

It was John Dryden, however, who produced the English *Aeneid*; and at the time he did so neither he nor any other Englishmen, it seems, could manage, except briefly, the kind of poetry required. They were too interested in improving on it. I do not say this entirely in malice, but with some sympathy for the criterion of "sense" and with respect for the cultivated and sometimes noble energy of Dryden's writing. If anyone then living could have done a great *Aeneid*, Dryden could. He was not narrowly a man of his time in the way Rochester was, for example. He admired and drew upon Spenser, Shakespeare and Jonson. He appreciated Donne's *Satires*, and the Metaphysical poets contributed something to his style. But after the Restoration in 1660 urbanity and abstraction overcame English letters, and Dryden himself wanted an English Academy, on the order of the French, to "purify" the language of poetry. In the exploration of the physical world the Royal Society, of which Dryden as Poet Laureate was a nominal member, had succeeded Raleigh and Drake. Likewise in poetry, discussion and wit now flourished at a certain remove from discovery and experience.

If we think only of prosody, it may appear that the blank verse masters, Shakespeare and Milton, had exhausted one great form for generations. It is certainly impressive and odd that long before the end of the seventeenth century the rhymed couplet had swept the field in English verse. We might imagine that the couplet itself diminished the range of poetry, but in fact pentameter couplets had been used by Douglas for his *Eneados* and by Chapman for his *Odyssey*. An *Aeneid* in blank verse would not necessarily have been any better than in couplets like these:

> Buskins of shells all silvered usèd she,
> And brancht with blushing corall to the knee;

> Where sparrows pearcht, of hollow pearl and gold,
> Such as the world would wonder to behold . . .

or these:

> When Evening grey doth rise, I fetch my round
> Over the mount, and all this hallow'd ground,
> And early ere the odorous breath of morn
> Awakes the slumbring leaves, or tassel'd horn
> Shakes the high thicket, haste I all about,
> Number my ranks, and visit every sprout
> With puissant words, and murmurs made to bless,
> But else in deep of night when drowsiness
> Hath lockt up mortal sense, then listen I
> To the celestial Sirens harmony,
> That sit upon the nine enfolded sphears,
> And sing to those that hold the vital shears,
> And turn the adamantine spindle round,
> On which the fate of gods and men is wound.

In fact, each of these examples could be called Virgilian: Marlowe's
for the image and sound and Milton's for the running syntax and
resourceful diction, culminating in his superb "adamantine spindle."

Dryden's predicament, then, was not that of being enslaved by the
rhymed couplet; it was the enslavement of the couplet itself by a certain style. The example of the French Alexandrine had had much to
do with tidying and balancing the English couplet, though Dryden
himself remarked on the variety that the alternation of masculine and
feminine endings gave the French couplets and on the lightness that
made the French language fall easily into logical symmetries. He
realized that the genius of his own language might be cramped by
them, but they charmed him and his contemporaries, and in place
of greater touchstones Dryden was fond of quoting Denham's lines
on the Thames:

> O could I flow like thee, and make thy stream
> My great example, as it is my theme!
> Though deep, yet clear, though gentle, yet not dull,
> Strong without rage, without ore-flowing full.

He was also fond of alluding to Waller as the man who taught
smoothness to English numbers, by which he meant rhyming without

wrenching the natural order of words, disposed as in "the negligence of prose." It is perhaps a revealing phrase. Engaged as he was in breaking ground for English criticism and in developing English critical prose, Dryden in practice wanted the discursive merits, a little negligence included, in verse as well.

At any rate, a new realm of possibilities had opened for English poets to explore, and we know the refinement to which in due course Pope would bring the couplet. But now another fact comes in for consideration: before this couplet became "heroic," its chief triumph was in satire. Dryden wrote *Absalom and Achitophel* and *Mac Flecknoe* in his prime, years before he thought of translating the *Aeneid*. Another way of putting this is to say that his couplet was mock heroic first. The satires owe their savor partly to a deliberate use of epic convention or allusion for topical burlesque. In *Mac Flecknoe*, for example, there are a number of lines that parody well known passages in Virgil:

> At his right hand our young Ascanius sate,
> Rome's other hope, and pillar of the State.
> His brows thick fogs, instead of glories, grace,
> And lambent dullness played around his face . . .

The pleasure given by this sort of thing was about all anyone wanted of the heroic under Charles II, apart from theatrical heroics, another genre. Could a style so ingeniously employed in making fun of epic be effectively used for epic? The same sequence occurred and the same question arises a generation later in the case of Pope, who wrote *The Rape of the Lock* before he translated Homer.

In 1689, under William and Mary, Dryden, a Jacobite and a Catholic, lost his Laureateship and his income and faced relative adversity. Among various shifts to support himself, he gave thought again to writing a heroic poem, an enterprise that his former royal patrons had not encouraged. He must have realized that by this time it was beyond him; even for the translation of Virgil, upon which at length he settled, he doubted his powers and his poetic means. Insofar as chief among these means was the couplet trained in verse satire, it is curious to see him dragging his favorite Virgil into a discourse on satire that he prefaced to a book of translations of Persius and Juvenal in 1692. Noting Martial's remark that Virgil could have written better lyrics than Horace, Dryden went Martial one better: "Virgil," he said, "could have written sharper satires than either Horace or Juvenal, if he would have employed his talent that way." As evidence, he supplied a well-chosen quotation from the Third Eclogue. The notion of Virgil as a satirist has the elation of some great figure of speech, a sublime chiasmus, when proposed by the author of *Mac Flecknoe* just before he girds himself for the *Aeneid*.

Before Dryden, the art of translation had been a gentleman's diversion or a scribbler's piece work, but Dryden's Virgil was a business venture, a writing project of a distinctly modern kind. He arranged for it and eventually signed a contract with his Fleet Street Printer, Tonson; and in a letter of December 12th, 1693, he said: "I propose to do it by subscription, having an hundred and two brass cuts, with the coats of arms of the subscriber to each cut; and every subscriber to pay five guineas, half in hand, besides another inferior subscription of two guineas for the rest, whose names are only written in a catalogue printed with the book."

This may not have been the first publishing enterprise of the kind, but it was the most ambitious and successful until then ever carried out in England. One hundred and one subscribers were found for the "brass cuts"—deplorable engravings of neoclassic statuary—and three hundred fifty-one gentlemen paid two guineas to be enrolled in the "catalogue," or list. Thus the total amount subscribed appears to have been 1,229 pounds 8 shillings. Besides his share of this, Dryden received gifts from the three noble patrons to whom he dedicated, respectively, the *Pastorals*, the *Georgics*, and the *Aeneid*—"that no opportunity of profit might be lost," as Dr. Johnson observed more than eighty years later. According to a recent estimate,* the poet's income can be reckoned at about 1,600 pounds, or 400 pounds a year if divided equally among the four years—1694, 1695, 1696 and 1697—spent on the labor.

It probably came down to little more than three working years, as he himself counted it, for besides time lost to affairs or illness he took two months off to do a prose version of du Fresnoy's Latin poem,

* By William Frost, in *Dryden and the Art of Translation* (Yale, 1955).

De Arte Graphica, and a preface for it. If we suppose Dryden to have worked 1,000 full days on his Virgil, he must have turned out an average of at least sixteen lines, or eight couplets, a day, for his *Aeneid* alone runs to 13,700 lines (for 9,896 Latin lines), and the *Pastorals* and *Georgics*, some of which he had only to revise, come to 4,358 lines more.

It seems that all England, or at any rate all Englishmen who had paid their guineas, awaited the result with impatience, if not with anxiety; the poet later complained that some grew clamorous. According to Johnson, "the nation considered its honor as interested in the event." Since Dryden felt under great pressure of time, his friends and admirers helped him as they could. Noblemen invited him to work at their country houses; a young barrister made him a gift of the principal annotated editions of Virgil; Addison, at twenty-four, undertook to write the prose "arguments" for the various Books; and Congreve, at twenty-seven, did Dryden the considerable favor of checking his *Aeneid* against the Latin text.

At the end of these exertions Tonson was able to bring out, in July, 1697, in the pomp of folio, "The WORKS of VIRGIL: containing His PASTORALS, GEORGICS, AND AENEIS. Translated into English Verse; By Mr. DRYDEN / Adorn'd with a Hundred Sculptures," etc. A few corrections and changes were made and a missing couplet supplied in a second folio edition in 1698. Dryden had been sixty-two when he undertook the translation; he was sixty-six when it was published. It was the longest sustained labor of his life. By his own account, his health suffered from application to it, and in any case he had but three more years to live. Although he may for a time have felt some hopes of royal recognition from their Protestant Majesties, he had refused to seek King William's favor and had resigned himself to his position as a veteran of a repudiated party and a vanished court—a court with whose vices he felt unfairly associated. He renounced satire, "for who gives physic to the great when uncalled?" and produced his Virgil as both a demonstration of his independence and a means of maintaining it. In his "Postscript to the Reader," he wrote:

> What Virgil wrote in the vigor of his age, in plenty and at ease, I have undertaken to translate in my declining years: struggling with wants, oppressed with sickness, curbed in my genius, liable to be mis-

construed in all I write; and my judges, if they are not very equitable, already prejudiced against me, by the lying character which has been given them of my morals. Yet steady to my principles, and not dispirited with my afflictions, I have, by the blessing of God on my endeavors, overcome all difficulties; and, in some measure, acquitted myself of the debt which I owed the public, when I undertook this work. In the first place therefore, I thankfully acknowledge to the Almighty Power, the assistance he has given me in the beginning, the prosecution, and conclusion of my present studies, which are more happily performed than I could have promised to myself, when I labored under such discouragements. For, what I have done, imperfect as it is, for want of health and leisure to correct it, will be judged in after ages, and possibly in the present, to be no dishonor to my native country . . .

He was quite right. Few subscribers were disappointed, and the eighteenth century immensely appreciated Dryden's *Aeneid*. Pope called it "the most noble and spirited translation that I know in any language." There is no doubt that it gave Pope the idea for his own enterprise with the *Iliad* some fifteen years later. The heroic couplet had had the heroic thrust upon it by Dryden. We cannot call ourselves acquainted with English poetry in his age and in the next unless we have read his translation, and it is still fascinating to see his mind at play over his great original.

Whatever the incongruities between the two poets, between the shy perfectionist of Latin verse in his Parthenopean villa and the able Restoration wit in his coffee house, the fact remains that few English writers have ever known or admired Virgil as Dryden did. Amid the pages of flattery, interested pleading and neoclassic aesthetics in Dryden's prefaces, we come upon nothing more genuine—and nothing more perceptive within a certain range—than his frequent references to Virgil. To some extent, of course, it was an interest that he shared with the age itself. Writers for whom Latin was still a living language knew what it was to make Latin verses and in this sense knew what Virgil had been doing. Aspects of the Virgilian lingered in their imaginations and took life again even in their candlelit theaters: Racine's *Andromaque* was first performed in 1667 and Purcell's

Dido and Aeneas in 1689. Still, Dryden's devotion was remarkable. It began early and lasted all his life.

During 1665 and 1666, when London was being visited first by plague and then by the Great Fire, Dryden worked in Wiltshire on his Dialogue *Essay of Dramatic Poesy* and on a long poem, *Annus Mirabilis*. In the Dialogue he touched on Virgil as the "pattern of elaborate writing" and as Ovid's superior in restraint. In his preface to *Annus Mirabilis* he declared that Virgil had been his master in this poem, as, in a sense, anyone could see from the fact that some thirty passages in it were direct imitations or echoes. For example:

> All hands employed, the royal work grows warm,
> Like laboring bees on a long summer's day . . .

It is a baroque poem, in which Virgil as a pattern of elaborate writing served him only too well, but Dryden's critical remarks on Virgil are another matter. "We see the objects he presents us with in their native figures, in their proper motions; but so we see them, as our own eyes could never have beheld them so beautiful in themselves . . . the very sound of his words have often somewhat that is connatural to the subject . . ." Not only is this just, but the concluding remark is far from commonplace even now.

In his subsequent prose, Dryden refers often enough to Virgil to give us the impression that the text lay open on his table for thirty years. He praised "the divine Virgil" more frequently even than he did Waller's contribution to English numbers. His last insights appear to have come, naturally enough, during his work on the translation. One, particularly valuable, he found a place for in his preface to *De Arte Graphica* in 1695. "Virgil knew how to rise by degrees in his expressions; Statius was in his towering heights at the first stretch of his pinions." In the course of his long dedicatory preface to the *Aeneid* Dryden wrote with a craftsman's interest in Virgil's style. He had compared Virgil and Ovid years before, to Ovid's disadvantage, and now touched again on this subject. Speaking of French poets, he said: "The turn on thoughts and words is their chief talent, but the epic poem is too stately to receive those little ornaments. . . . Virgil is never frequent in those turns, like Ovid, but much more sparing of them in his Aeneis than in his Pastorals and Georgics.

> Ignoscenda quidem, scirent si ignoscere Manes.

That turn is beautiful indeed, but he employs it in the story of Orpheus and Eurydice, not in his great poem. I have used that licence in his Aeneis sometimes: but I own it as my fault. 'Twas given to those who understand no better . . ."

As we read Dryden's *Aeneid*, we may find this passage recurring to us fairly often; it becomes a nice question, in fact, how much weight to give to the last sentence. Another passage of special interest in the light of the translation itself is that in which he remarks on "the sober retrenchments of his [Virgil's] sense, which always leaves somewhat to gratify our imagination, on which it may enlarge at pleasure . . ."

Of formal criticism, analysis of Virgil's composition in the large, Dryden had little to offer beyond a discussion of standard topics of neoclassic criticism (the relative greatness of heroic poetry and tragedy, piety versus valor as the virtue of the epic hero, the behavior of Aeneas toward Dido, the debt of Virgil to Homer, the elapsed time of the main action, etc.) that no longer seem to us of the greatest interest. He did notice that extended epic similes were introduced by Virgil after, not before, the crest of an action, and took as his example the one in Book I in which Neptune is likened to a respected Roman official calming a mob. A modern critic would not fail to see something thematic in this first simile of the *Aeneid*, but notions of that sort could not occur to Dryden. He wondered, oddly enough, why Virgil allowed Aeneas to be wounded toward the end of the poem—an episode that is not only obviously dramatic but makes for epic symmetry: the just prince's disablement balanced against that of the cruel exile, Mezentius, as the death of Pallas is balanced by that of Lausus. We hear nothing from Dryden of Virgil's architectonics and depth of suggestion, nor of the quality of his imagination—so supreme and terrifying when the Fury in the form of a small bird beats around Turnus' head in the final combat, so forced and awkward when Aeneas' ships are transformed into sea-nymphs and we are troubled for a moment by an image of nereids on that scale.

As to Virgil's way with language, however, I do not know any happier descriptions than Dryden's. "His words are not only chosen, but the places in which he ranks them, for the sound. He who removes them from the station wherein their master set them spoils the harmony. What he says of the Sibyl's prophecies may be as properly applied to every word of his: they must be read in order as they lie; the least breath discomposes them; and somewhat of their divinity is lost . . . he is like ambergris, a rich perfume, but of so close and glutinous a body that it must be opened with inferior scents of musk or civet, or the sweetness will not be drawn out into another language. . . . What modern language, or what poet, can express the majestic beauty of this one verse amongst a thousand others?

> aude, hospes, contemnere opes, et te quoque dignum
> finge deo.

For my part, I am lost in the admiration of it: I contemn the world when I think on it, and myself when I translate it."

Conscious as he was of the inferiority of his "coarse English," Dryden strove undaunted to correct it as well as he could. "I have endeavored," he said, "to follow the example of my master: and am the first Englishman, perhaps, who made it his design to copy him in his numbers [metrical excellence], his choice of words, and his placing them for the sweetness of the sound. On this last consideration I have shunned the caesura [elision]. . . . For where that is used, it gives a roughness to the verse, of which we can have little need, in a language which is over-stocked with consonants. Such is not the Latin, where the vowels and consonants are mixed in proportion to each other." His tentative claim for himself may recall a wicked remark of Swift's to the effect that people would not have been so aware of Dryden's merit as a playwright if he had not told them of it so often in his prefaces. But it is true and highly pertinent that English is overstocked with consonants, while in Latin vowels and consonants are in better proportion.

With respect to diction, the translator knew from Horace that Virgil's secret lay in the placement of words and their subtle stress upon one another, a mutual energizing of words within a line or passage to achieve that "majesty in the midst of plainness" that Dryden so admired. The difficulty of rendering such effects is rather simplified in his account of it. In practice, he said, "I found the difficulty of translation growing on me in every succeeding Book. For Virgil, above all poets, had a stock, which I may call inexhaustible, of figurative, elegant, and sounding words. . . . Virgil called upon me in every line for some new word: and I paid so long, that I was almost bankrupt. So that the latter end must needs be more burdensome than the beginning or the middle. And consequently the Twelfth Aeneid cost me double the time of the first and second. What had become of me if Virgil had taxed me with another Book?"

Dryden's opinion of what a translation should be had already been expressed at some length in various essays, beginning with his preface to *Ovid's Epistles* in 1680. No part of Dryden's criticism seemed more important or more definitive to Pope and Johnson. It has been rejected by some later critics, to whom scientific scholarship and historical study have made differences of language and culture appear more nearly absolute, but it has continued to be the premise of poet-translators, including Ezra Pound. ("The best trans. is into the language the author wd. have used had he been writing in the translator's language.") In his preface to the *Aeneid* Dryden restated it. "The way I have taken is not so strait as Metaphrase [word for word] nor so loose as Paraphrase: Some things too I have omitted, and sometimes have added of my own. Yet the omissions, I hope, are but of circumstances [incidentals] and such as would have no grace in English; and the additions, I also hope, are easily deduced from Virgil's sense. . . . I have endeavored to make Virgil speak such English as he would himself have spoken, if he had been born in England, and in this present age . . ."

There was nothing wrong with Dryden's command of Latin. It was better than ours is likely to be, and has been well defended* against imputations of ignorance. He used the latest edition of Virgil, prepared in 1675 by the French editor Charles de la Rue (Carolus Ruaeus) for the Dauphin of France (*in usum serenissimi Delphini*), one of a series referred to by Dryden as "the Dolphins." This presented to him on every page not only the best text available in his time but also a Latin prose paraphrase, or *interpretatio*, and notes. Dryden generally stuck to Ruaeus' interpretation and followed it in many of his expansions, but he occasionally insisted on his own interpretation and at least once left untranslated a line that baffled him

* By J. McG. Bottkol in *Modern Philology*, Vol. XI, No. 3, February, 1943.

in Ruaeus—though he later found a better reading in an edition by the Dutch scholar Nicolas Heinsius.

As he worked with all possible speed, Dryden used all possible aids to composition, including such previous translations as he could lay his hands on. He does not appear to have known the Scots translation by Gavin Douglas; he made no reference to Surrey's version (1574) of Books I and II nor to Stanyhurst's version (1582) of Books I through IV. He had the Italian translation by Caro (1581) and the French translation by Segrais (1668); he had Denham's version (1636) of Book II, Waller and Godolphin's version (1658) of Book IV, and Ogilby's version (1649) of the whole poem. He also received from Paris, in manuscript, a translation by the Jacobite Earl of Lauderdale, completed before his death in 1695 but unpublished until 1718. Dryden drew on all of these for rhymes, phrases, and even for lines. He took five lines of Denham and acknowledged taking one; from Lauderdale he plundered freely, taking about 800 lines with improvements or at least minor changes and about 200 lines without change and without acknowledgement. We would call this plagiarism, but an ambiguous reference to Lauderdale in Dryden's preface may indicate that that nobleman had consented to it, perhaps because on another occasion he had printed a great many lines of Dryden as his own. Dryden admitted his debt somewhat disingenuously by saying that "having his manuscript in my hands, I consulted it as often as I doubted of my author's sense."

It is plain from Dryden's own remarks that he felt the inadequacy of his verse and his diction. To break the monotony of his couplets he resorted to triplets and Alexandrines, often in combination. This provided what could be called momentary relief, but did not suffice in the long run. In certain Books, III for example, the habit of the closed couplet so hobbled the movement of his narrative that he himself seems to have become bored with it, and in the following Books we find him trying more successfully to make verse paragraphs beginning within one couplet and ending within a later one.

He also tried to extend his resources of language. The effort was not constant enough to save him from the curse of a number of poeticisms that were even then clichés. Reiteration does not convince us that shades were so frequently dusky, bosoms manly, seas briny, gore purple, night sable, skies vaulted and rent by shrieks—to name only a few. One recourse from this sort of thing would have been to look again at shades, bosoms, seas, gore, night, skies etc., but this would have been asking too much not only of Dryden but of the age. The role of vocabulary in poetry can be slightly misconceived, and Dryden slightly misconceived it. The "store of words" he found so inexhaustible in Virgil was first of all *copia* of imagination and feeling, and Dryden matched it best—as on occasion he did match it—from the same sources, not by using new words and Latinisms.

"He was no lover of labor," observed Johnson. "What he thought sufficient, he did not stop to make better; and allowed himself to leave many parts unfinished, in confidence that the good lines would overbalance the bad." This would be fair enough if it took account of Dryden's haste, probably as much to blame for his faults as aversion to labor. A number of his bad lines were doubly bad in that they introduced literal absurdities into Virgil's narrative. In Book I, 302 sqq., we hear that after the intervention of Mercury

> ponunt ferocia Poeni
> corda volente deo; in primis regina quietum
> accepit in Teucros animum et mentem benignam. . . .

The Carthaginians and their queen, so the Latin says, were put in a benignant mood toward the approaching Trojans. In Dryden, 414 sqq.,

> The surly murmurs of the people cease,
> And, as the Fates required, they give the peace.
> The Queen herself suspends the rigid laws. . . .

But at that point the Queen took no such action, and when later the Trojans appeared, they petitioned her to do so. In Book II, 52–3, a spear is hurled at the Wooden Horse:

> stetit illa tremens, uteroque recusso
> insonuere cavae gemitumque dedere cavernae. . . .

It stuck trembling, and from the blow in the belly the hollow interior gave a resounding groan. In Dryden, 68–9:

> The sides transpierced return a rattling sound
> And groans of Greeks enclosed come issuing through the wound.

Apart from the padded "come issuing," this misrepresents the situation to the point of farce. If any Greek had been heard groaning, the Horse would have had a short career. So it goes, too frequently, throughout the poem.

Faults of this kind were not necessary, and it may seem to us that they could have been corrected by a moment's thought. They betray the haste of the translator. But more than this, they suggest that Dryden did not really value fidelity in such particulars as we do. Though in theory he understood that his task was to do so and liked to think that he had, he did not consistently enter into the mind of the original artist to the point of seeing, hearing and feeling the scenes that Virgil created. Most often he wished rather to make a literary artifact answering to another literary artifact, and this satisfied the taste of his contemporaries. Up to a point, of course, they were right. The *Aeneid* is not a realistic work of art. Nevertheless, Dryden himself had noted of Virgil that "we see the objects he presents us with," and this therefore was one of the qualities of Virgil that he must have hoped to emulate. If his failures mattered less to his own age than they do to ours, so much the worse for his age.

Minor effects of haste are occasional eccentricities like "herds of wolves" in VII, 21, or tangled syntax, as in VII, 92:

> This plant, Latinus, when his town he walled
> Then found, and from the tree Laurentum called . . .

or X, 752:

> The holy coward fell: and forced to yield,
> The prince stood o'er the priest . . .

or fatal asyndeton, as in XII, 414:

> And struck the gentle youth, extended on the ground,

meaning that he hit and felled him. Again, we are inclined to ask why Dryden could not have reworked lines like these, if not for the first edition then for the second. Johnson appears to have been struck by the fact that he did not do so. "What he had once written, he dismissed from his thoughts; and I believe there is no example found of any correction or improvement made by him after publication."

Johnson may be excused for thinking so, but in fact he was wrong about this. Dryden "bestowed nine entire days" on corrections for the edition of 1698. These are usually of a spelling, a single word, sometimes of a phrase or a line, and hardly ever represent an attempt to rewrite a passage or to revise it substantially. If, however, we look at certain parts of the *Aeneid* that Dryden had already done years before for a literary miscellany, *Sylvae* (1684), we find a few revisions of longer passages. At least one of these is worth close attention. For lines 459–61 of Book V, the earlier version had:

> A lion's hide, amazing to behold,
> Ponderous with bristles, and with paws of gold,
> He gave the youth. . . .

Ten years later Dryden wrote:

> . . . and from among the spoils he draws
> (Ponderous with shaggy mane, and golden paws)
> A lion's hide. . . .

Here several admirable motives were at work: to abandon the padding phrase, to let the syntax float and carry through the couplet, and to strengthen the image and "feel" of the lion's hide. The line in parentheses is masterful and typical of Dryden at his best. This revision shows what the poet might have done if he had been able, or had wished, to take his whole translation as a draft and to spend another three years rewriting it.

Dryden's good lines are often very good indeed, and they occur frequently enough to keep the reader on the alert for the next one. He was capable of lyric beauty:

> With branches we the fanes adorn . . .

> Not her own star confessed a light so clear . . .

> And rent away with ease the lingering gold . . .

But more often his peculiar excellence lay in a whiplike power of statement, swift and flexible but weighted:

> His holy fillets the blue venom blots . . .

> And on the shaded ocean rushed the night . . .

> See! Pallas, of her snaky buckler proud . . .

> While the fierce riders clattered on their shields . . .

Lines like these may not "overbalance" the inferior ones, but they check the effect of them and contribute enormously to the vigor of the translation. So does Dryden's syntactical ingenuity within the couplet. Those "turns" that he regarded as Ovidian are indeed Ovidian in the sense that Ovid did them to death, but they are not quite so sparse in Virgil as Dryden suggested; in fact they occur here and there very naturally in the compact Latin (*nostro doluisti saepe dolore . . . una salus victis nullam sperare salutem*). Virgil was perhaps deliberately sparing of them, but Dryden certainly was not. Often they too give an effect of swiftness and concision:

> Through such a train of woes if I should run,
> The day would sooner than the tale be done . . .

> . . . All combine to leave the state
> Who hate the tyrant, or who fear his hate . . .

The truth is that structure of this kind had already become an essential characteristic of the couplet style that Dryden bequeathed to Pope. Dryden probably could not have translated Virgil or anyone else without "that licence" that he owned as a fault. What he meant by saying " 'Twas given to those who understand no better," I am not sure, unless this is a unique reflection on the taste of his readers— surely not those who got their coats of arms on the brass cuts? Every so often, no doubt, it is chiefly interesting as a trick, a rhetorician's amusement:

> Her cheeks the blood, her hand the web, forsakes. . . .

There is also the point that since Dryden's wit in his satires depends partly on the balanced, antithetical style, the more we find of that style in his Virgil, the more we are reminded of the satires. We are reminded of them also by Dryden's gusto in many passages:

> . . . a thirsty soul,
> He took the challenge, and embraced the bowl . . .

> . . . the bleating lambs
> Securely swig the dug beneath the dams. . . .

Then there are moments when we perceive a tone of decided burlesque, as in the episode of Hercules and Cacus in Book VIII, or in this couplet given to Turnus in Book XI (658–9) on the subject of human fortunes:

> Some, raised aloft, come tumbling down amain;
> Then fall so hard, they bound and rise again.

That, I think, was for the boys in school. In general, though, Dryden's touches of the satiric gave variety to his style and kept it from being unrelievedly high-flown. Certain couplets seem to have come straight out of *Absalom and Achitophel*, and are none the worse for that:

> But cautious in the field, he shunned the sword:
> A close-caballer, and tongue-valiant lord.

In the altercation between Drances, so characterized, and Turnus in Book XI, Dryden was able to use the gift for verse debate that he had exercised for years in writing for the Restoration stage.

The attitude conveyed by Virgil's whole narrative of the war in Latium is cumulative and very complex. The way in which time and again violence gets out of hand, by malign force overcoming the will of peaceful leaders, makes us think that the iron of the Roman civil wars had entered into the poet. His laments for slain princes are overdone to the point of bathos. Slaughter interests him, of course, as a challenge to description, but he does not have Homer's even-handed and rather superhuman gaiety about battle. Dryden could scarcely equal Virgil's massive effect of tragic ambiguity, but for all his heartiness he, who had lived through Cromwell's time and Monmouth's, looked with a reserve of his own on the heroic convention. In an occasional turn of phrase he implies it:

> The champion's chariot next is seen to roll,
> Besmeared with hostile blood, and honorably foul. . . .

That is neither heroic nor Virgilian, but it has edge and character, and a sophisticated civilization stands behind it.

These notes will perhaps have suggested how Dryden's *Aeneid* suffered from being a rush job and yet how brilliantly he brought it off. No one else, with no matter how much time, has yet achieved a version as variously interesting and as true to the best style of a later age as his was to his own. He allowed himself a complacent sentence or two about it, but the final judgment expressed in his Dedication was severe: "I have done great wrong to Virgil in the whole translation: want of time, the inferiority of our language, the inconvenience of rhyme, and all the other excuses I have made, may alleviate my fault, but cannot justify the boldness of my undertaking. What avails it me to acknowledge freely that I have been unable to do him right in any line?"

Too severe.

THE AENEID OF VIRGIL

BOOK I

THE ARGUMENT

The Trojans, after a seven years' voyage, set sail for Italy, but are overtaken by a dreadful storm, which Aeolus raises at Juno's request. The tempest sinks one ship, and scatters the rest. Neptune drives off the winds, and calms the sea. Aeneas, with his own ship and six more, arrives safe at an African port. Venus complains to Jupiter of her son's misfortunes. Jupiter comforts her, and sends Mercury to procure him a kind reception among the Carthaginians. Aeneas, going out to discover the country, meets his mother in the shape of a huntress, who conveys him in a cloud to Carthage, where he sees his friends whom he thought lost, and receives a kind entertainment from the queen. Dido, by a device of Venus, begins to have a passion for him, and after some discourse with him, desires the history of his adventures since the siege of Troy, which is the subject of the two following books.

ARMS and the man I sing, who, forced by Fate,
And haughty Juno's unrelenting hate,
Expelled and exiled, left the Trojan shore.
Long labors, both by sea and land, he bore,
And in the doubtful war, before he won   5
The Latian realm, and built the destined town;
His banished gods restored to rites divine;
And settled sure succession in his line,
From whence the race of Alban fathers come,
And the long glories of majestic Rome.   10

9. *Alban*: of Alba Longa, the city in Latium of which Aeneas' immediate descendants were to be kings. More of this in Book VI, 1035.

O muse! the causes and the crimes relate;
What goddess was provoked, and whence her hate;
For what offense the queen of heaven began
To persecute so brave, so just a man;
Involved his anxious life in endless cares,   15
Exposed to wants, and hurried into wars!
Can heavenly minds such high resentment show,
Or exercise their spite in human woe?
   Against the Tiber's mouth, but far away,
An ancient town was seated on the sea—   20
A Tyrian colony—the people made
Stout for the war, and studious for their trade:
Carthage the name—beloved by Juno more
Than her own Argos, or the Samian shore.
Here stood her chariot; here, if heaven were kind,   25
The seat of awful empire she designed.
Yet she had heard an ancient rumor fly
(Long cited by the people of the sky),
That times to come should see the Trojan race
Her Carthage ruin, and her towers deface;   30
Nor thus confined, the yoke of sovereign sway
Should on the necks of all the nations lay.
She pondered this, and feared it was in fate;
Nor could forget the war she waged of late,
For conquering Greece, against the Trojan state,   35
Besides, long causes working in her mind,
And secret seeds of envy, lay behind:
Deep graven in her heart, the doom remained
Of partial Paris, and her form disdained;
The grace bestowed on ravished Ganymed,   40
Electra's glories, and her injured bed.
Each was a cause alone; and all combined
To kindle vengeance in her haughty mind.
For this, far distant from the Latian coast,
She drove the remnants of the Trojan host;   45

24. The temple of Juno (Hera) at Samos was famous in antiquity.
39–41. *Paris*: Trojan prince and shepherd, who awarded Venus (Aphrodite) the prize of beauty over Juno and Minerva (Athena). Ganymedes, son of Tros, had been carried off by an eagle to be cupbearer to Jove (Zeus). Electra, one of Jove's mortal mistresses, bore him Dardanus, ancestor of the Trojans.

And seven long years the unhappy wandering train
Were tossed by storms, and scattered through the main.
Such time, such toil, required the Roman name,
Such length of labor for so vast a frame!
   Now scarce the Trojan fleet, with sails and oars, 50
Had left behind the fair Sicilian shores,
Entering with cheerful shouts the watery reign,
And plowing frothy furrows in the main;
When, lab'ring still with endless discontent,
The queen of heaven did thus her fury vent: 55
   "Then am I vanquished? must I yield? (said she)
And must the Trojans reign in Italy?
So Fate will have it; and Jove adds his force;
Nor can my power divert their happy course.
Could angry Pallas, with revengeful spleen, 60
The Grecian navy burn, and drown the men?
She, for the fault of one offending foe,
The bolts of Jove himself presumed to throw:
With whirlwinds from beneath she tossed the ship,
And bare exposed the bosom of the deep: 65
Then—as an eagle gripes the trembling game—
The wretch, yet hissing with her father's flame,
She strongly seized, and, with a burning wound
Transfixed, and naked on a rock she bound.
But I, who walk in awful state above, 70
The majesty of heaven, the sister-wife of Jove,
For length of years my fruitless force employ
Against the thin remains of ruined Troy!
What nations now to Juno's power will pray,
Or offerings on my slighted altars lay?" 75
   Thus raged the goddess; and with fury fraught,
The restless regions of the storms she sought,
Where, in a spacious cave of living stone,
The tyrant Aeolus, from his airy throne,

---

60 sqq. On the night of the sack of Troy Ajax, son of Oileus (not the greater
Ajax, son of Telamon), raped the Trojan princess Cassandra in the temple of
Minerva. The goddess revenged herself on the homeward-bound Greeks with a
storm in which Ajax and others were lost.
   76. *loca feta furentibus Austris* . . . : It is the regions that are "fraught."
Dryden's syntax barely permits this but in effect transfers the "fraught" to Juno.

With power imperial curbs the struggling winds,   80
And sounding tempests in dark prisons binds:
This way, and that, the impatient captives tend,
And, pressing for release, the mountains rend.
High in his hall the undaunted monarch stands,
And shakes his scepter, and their rage commands;   85
Which did he not, their unresisted sway
Would sweep the world before them in their way;
Earth, air, and seas, through empty space would roll,
And heaven would fly before the driving soul.
In fear of this, the father of the gods   90
Confined their fury to those dark abodes,
And locked them safe within, oppressed with mountain loads:
Imposed a king with arbitrary sway,
To loose their fetters, or their force allay;
To whom the suppliant queen her prayers addressed,   95
And thus the tenor of her suit expressed:
"O Aeolus!—for to thee the king of heaven
The power of tempests and of winds has given;
Thy force alone their fury can restrain,
And smooth the waves, or swell the troubled main—   100
A race of wandering slaves, abhorred by me,
With prosperous passage cut the Tuscan sea:
To fruitful Italy their course they steer,
And, for their vanquished gods design new temples there.
Raise all thy winds; with night involve the skies;   105
Sink or disperse my fatal enemies!
Twice seven—the charming daughters of the main,
Around my person wait, and bear my train:
Succeed my wish, and second my design;
The fairest, Deiopeia, shall be thine,   110
And make thee father of a happy line."
    To this the god: " 'Tis yours, O queen! to will
The work, which duty binds me to fulfill.
These airy kingdoms, and this wide command,
Are all the presents of your bounteous hand: 115

89. *soul*: Latin *anima* means breath or wind before spirit or soul.
102. *Tuscan*: for Tyrrhenum, the sea west of Italy.

Yours is my sovereign's grace; and as your guest,
I sit with gods at their celestial feast.
Raise tempests at your pleasure, or subdue;
Dispose of empire, which I hold from you."
    He said, and hurled against the mountain side   120
His quivering spear, and all the god applied.
The raging winds rush through the hollow wound,
And dance aloft in air, and skim along the ground;
Then, settling on the sea, the surges sweep,
Raise liquid mountains, and disclose the deep.   125
South, East, and West, with mixed confusion roar,
And roll the foaming billows to the shore.
The cables crack; the sailors' fearful cries
Ascend; and sable night involves the skies;
And heaven itself is ravished from their eyes.   130
Loud peals of thunder from the poles ensue;
Then flashing fires the transient light renew;
The face of things a frightful image bears,
And present death in various forms appears.
Struck with unusual fright, the Trojan chief,   135
With lifted hands and eyes, invokes relief;
And, "Thrice and four times happy those (he cried),
That under Ilian walls, before their parents, died!
Tydides, bravest of the Grecian train!
Why could not I by that strong arm be slain,   140
And lie by noble Hector on the plain,
Or great Sarpedon; in those bloody fields,
Where Simoïs rolls the bodies and the shields
Of heroes, whose dismembered hands yet bear
The dart aloft, and clench the pointed spear?"   145
    Thus while the pious prince his fate bewails,
Fierce Boreas drove against his flying sails,
And rent the sheets: the raging billows rise,
And mount the tossing vessel to the skies;

139. *Tydides*: Diomedes, son of Tydeus.
144–5. Dryden made these two lines of *virum . . . fortia corpora . . .* "Strong bodies of warriors."

Nor can the shivering oars sustain the blow: 150
The galley gives her side, and turns her prow;
While those astern, descending down the steep,
Through gaping waves behold the boiling deep.
Three ships were hurried by the southern blast,
And on the secret shelves with fury cast.   155
Those hidden rocks the Ausonian sailors knew:
They called them Altars, when they rose in view,
And showed their spacious backs above the flood.
Three more, fierce Eurus in his angry mood,
Dashed on the shallows of the moving sand,   160
And in mid-ocean left them moored a-land.
Orontes' bark, that bore the Lycian crew,
(A horrid sight!) e'en in the hero's view,
From stem to stern by waves was overborne.
The trembling pilot, from his rudder torn,   165
Was headlong hurled: thrice round, the ship was tossed,
Then bulged at once, and in the deep was lost;
And here and there above the waves were seen
Arms, pictures, precious goods, and floating men.
The stoutest vessel to the storm gave way,   170
And sucked through loosened planks the rushing sea.
Ilioneus was her chief: Aletes old,
Achates faithful, Abas young and bold,
Endured not less: their ships, with gaping seams,
Admit the deluge of the briny streams.   175
   Meantime imperial Neptune heard the sound
Of raging billows breaking on the ground.
Displeased, and fearing for his watery reign,
He reared his awful head above the main,
Serene in majesty,—then rolled his eyes   180
Around the space of earth, and seas, and skies.

   156. *Ausonian*: Italian.
   159. *Eurus*: the East wind.
   167. *bulged*: He may have meant "bilged"—i.e., struck and stove in the
bilge or bottom.
   169. *pictures*: for *tabulae*, "planks."
   171. *accipiunt inimicum imbrem* . . . : Dryden did not render the suggestion
of troops pouring through a broken wall.

He saw the Trojan fleet dispersed, distressed,
By stormy winds and wintry heaven oppressed.
Full well the god his sister's envy knew,
And what her aims and what her arts pursue.   185
He summoned Eurus and the western blast,
And first an angry glance on both he cast,
Then thus rebuked: "Audacious winds! from whence
This bold attempt, this rebel insolence?
Is it for you to ravage seas and land,   190
Unauthorized by my supreme command?
To raise such mountains on the troubled main?
Whom I—but first 'tis fit the billows to restrain;
And then you shall be taught obedience to my reign.
Hence! to your lord my royal mandate bear—   195
The realms of ocean and the fields of air
Are mine, not his. By fatal lot to me
The liquid empire fell, and trident of the sea.
His power to hollow caverns is confined:
There let him reign the jailor of the wind,   200
With hoarse commands his breathing subjects call,
And boast and bluster in his empty hall."
He spoke; and while he spoke, he smoothed the sea,
Dispelled the darkness, and restored the day.
Cymothoë, Triton, and the sea-green train   205
Of beauteous nymphs, the daughters of the main,
Clear from the rocks the vessels with their hands:
The god himself with ready trident stands,
And opes the deep, and spreads the moving sands;
Then heaves them off the shoals.—Where'er he guides   210
His finny coursers, and in triumph rides,
The waves unruffle, and the sea subsides.
As, when in tumults rise the ignoble crowd,
Mad are their motions, and their tongues are loud;
And stones and brands in rattling volleys fly,   215
And all the rustic arms that fury can supply:

193. *Whom I: Quos ego.* Neptune begins a threat and breaks it off, something the rhetoricians called Aposiopesis, or Supervention of Abrupt Silence.

If then some grave and pious man appear,
They hush their noise, and lend a listening ear:
He soothes with sober words their angry mood,
And quenches their innate desire of blood: 220
So, when the father of the flood appears,
And o'er the seas his sovereign trident rears,
Their fury falls: he skims the liquid plains,
High on his chariot, and, with loosened reins,
Majestic moves along, and awful peace maintains.   225
The weary Trojans ply their shattered oars
To nearest land, and make the Libyan shores.
    Within a long recess there lies a bay:
An island shades it from the rolling sea,
And forms a port secure for ships to ride: 230
Broke by the jutting land, on either side,
In double streams the briny waters glide,
Betwixt two rows of rocks: a sylvan scene
Appears above, and groves for ever green:
A grot is formed beneath, with mossy seats,   235
To rest the Nereïds, and exclude the heats.
Down through the crannies of the living walls,
The crystal streams descend in murmuring falls.
No halsers need to bind the vessels here,
Nor bearded anchors; for no storms they fear.   240
Seven ships within this happy harbor meet,
The thin remainders of the scattered fleet.
The Trojans, worn with toils, and spent with woes,
Leap on the welcome land, and seek their wished repose.
    First, good Achates, with repeated strokes   245
Of clashing flints, their hidden fire provokes:
Short flame succeeds: a bed of withered leaves
The dying sparkles in their fall receives:
Caught into life, in fiery fumes they rise,
And, fed with stronger food, invade the skies.   250
The Trojans, dropping wet, or stand around
The cheerful blaze, or lie along the ground.

    251-2. *or . . . or*: either . . . or.

Some dry their corn infected with the brine,
Then grind with marbles, and prepare to dine.
    Aeneas climbs the mountain's airy brow,   255
And takes a prospect of the seas below,
If Capys thence, or Antheus, he could spy,
Or see the streamers of Caïcus fly.
No vessels were in view; but, on the plain,
Three beamy stags command a lordly train   260
Of branching heads: the more ignoble throng
Attend their stately steps, and slowly graze along.
He stood; and, while secure they fed below,
He took the quiver and the trusty bow
Achates used to bear: the leaders first   265
He laid along, and then the vulgar pierced;
Nor ceased his arrows, till the shady plain
Seven mighty bodies with their blood distain.
For the seven ships he made an equal share,
And to the port returned triumphant from the war.   270
The jars of generous wine (Acestes' gift,
When his Trinacrian shores the navy left)
He set abroach, and for the feast prepared,
In equal portions with the ven'son shared.
Thus while he dealt it round, the pious chief   275
With cheerful words allayed the common grief:—
"Endure, and conquer! Jove will soon dispose
To future good, our past and present woes.
With me, the rocks of Scylla you have tried;
The inhuman Cyclops, and his den, defied.   280
What greater ills hereafter can you bear?
Resume your courage, and dismiss your care:
An hour will come, with pleasure to relate
Your sorrows past, as benefits of fate.

254. *marbles*: stones.
260. *beamy*: A "beam" was a stag's horn. Dryden used the same word to mean "bright" (Book VIII) and "massive" (Book XII).
272. *Trinacrian*: Sicilian.
283–4. *forsan et haec olim meminisse iuvabit*: Dryden dropped the *forsan*, "perhaps."

Through various hazards and events, we move   285
To Latium, and the realms foredoomed by Jove.
Called to the seat (the promise of the skies)
Where Trojan kingdoms once again may rise,
Endure the hardships of your present state;
Live, and reserve yourselves for better fate."   290
   These words he spoke, but spoke not from his heart;
His outward smiles concealed his inward smart.
The jolly crew, unmindful of the past,
The quarry share, their plenteous dinner haste.
Some strip the skin; some portion out the spoil;   295
The limbs, yet trembling, in the caldrons boil;
Some on the fire the reeking entrails broil.
Stretched on the grassy turf, at ease they dine,
Restore their strength with meat, and cheer their souls with wine.
Their hunger thus appeased, their care attends   300
The doubtful fortune of their absent friends:
Alternate hopes and fears their minds possess,
Whether to deem them dead, or in distress.
Above the rest, Aeneas mourns the fate
Of brave Orontes, and the uncertain state   305
Of Gyas, Lycus, and of Amycus.
The day, but not their sorrows, ended thus.
   When from aloft, almighty Jove surveys
Earth, air, and shores, and navigable seas:
At length, on Libyan realms he fixed his eyes: 310
Whom, pondering thus on human miseries,
When Venus saw, she with a lowly look,
Not free from tears, her heavenly sire bespoke:
"O king of gods and men! whose awful hand
Disperses thunder on the seas and land;   315
Disposes all with absolute command;
How could my pious son thy power incense?
Or what, alas! is vanished Troy's offense?
Our hope of Italy not only lost;
On various seas by various tempests tossed,   320

309. *navigable seas: mare velivolum,* "the sail-winged sea." Carolus Ruaeus
(Charles de la Rue), editor of the text used by Dryden, supplied the commonplace interpretation.

But shut from every shore, and barred from every coast.
You promised once, a progeny divine,
Of Romans, rising from the Trojan line,
In after-times should hold the world in awe,
And to the land and ocean give the law.   325
How is your doom reversed, which eased my care
When Troy was ruined in that cruel war!
Then fates to fates I could oppose; but now,
When fortune still pursues her former blow,
What can I hope? What worse can still succeed?   330
What end of labors has your will decreed?
Antenor, from the midst of Grecian hosts
Could pass secure, and pierce the Illyrian coasts:
Where, rolling down the steep, Timavus raves,
And through nine channels disembogues his waves.   335
At length he founded Padua's happy seat,
And gave his Trojans a secure retreat:
There fixed their arms, and there renewed their name;
And there in quiet rules, and crowned with fame.
But we, descended from your sacred line,   340
Entitled to your heaven and rites divine,
Are banished earth, and, for the wrath of one,
Removed from Latium, and the promised throne.
Are these our scepters? these our due rewards?
And is it thus that Jove his plighted faith regards?"   345
    To whom the father of the immortal race,
Smiling, with that serene indulgent face
With which he drives the clouds and clears the skies—
First gave a holy kiss; then thus replies:
"Daughter, dismiss thy fears: to thy desire,   350
The fates of thine are fixed, and stand entire.
Thou shalt behold thy wished Lavinian walls;
And, ripe for heaven, when fate Aeneas calls,
Then shalt thou bear him up, sublime, to me:
No counsels have reversed my firm decree.   355
And, lest new fears disturb thy happy state,
Know, I have searched the mystic rolls of fate:

334. *Timavus*: the River Reca, at the head of the Adriatic.
352. *Lavinian*: Lavinia, daughter of King Latinus, was to marry Aeneas.
Lavinium was to be their city.

Thy son (nor is the appointed season far)
In Italy shall wage successful war:
Shall tame fierce nations in the bloody field;   360
And sovereign laws impose, and cities build;
Till, after every foe subdued, the sun
Thrice through the signs his annual race shall run.
This is his time prefixed. Ascanius then,
Now called Iülus, shall begin his reign.   365
He, thirty rolling years the crown shall wear;
Then from Lavinium shall the seat transfer,
And with hard labor, Alba-longa build:
The throne with his succession shall be filled,
Three hundred circuits more: then shall be seen   370
Ilia the fair, a priestess and a queen,
Who, full of Mars, in time, with kindly throes,
Shall at a birth two goodly boys disclose.
The royal babes a tawny wolf shall drain:
Then Romulus his grandsire's throne shall gain,   375
Of martial towers the founder shall become,
The people Romans call, the city Rome.
To them no bounds of empire I assign,
Nor term of years to their immortal line.
E'en haughty Juno, who, with endless broils,   380
Earth, seas, and heaven, and Jove himself, turmoils,
At length atoned, her friendly power shall join,
To cherish and advance the Trojan line.
The subject world shall Rome's dominion own,
And, prostrate, shall adore the nation of the gown.   385
  An age is ripening in revolving fate,
When Troy shall overturn the Grecian state,
And sweet revenge her conquering sons shall call,
To crush the people that conspired her fall.

365. *Iülus*: The Emperor Augustus belonged of course to the Julian family, whose name Virgil here "traces" to Aeneas' son.

374. The Latin here more probably means that Romulus wore the hide of the she-wolf that nursed him.

378–9. Famous lines: *his ego nec metas rerum nec tempora pono,/ imperium sine fine dedi.*

385. *gown*: toga.

Then Caesar from the Julian stock shall rise,   390
Whose empire ocean, and whose fame the skies
Alone shall bound; whom, fraught with eastern spoils,
Our heaven, the just reward of human toils,
Securely shall repay with rights divine;
And incense shall ascend before his sacred shrine.   395
Then dire debate, and impious war, shall cease,
And the stern age be softened into peace:
Then banished Faith shall once again return,
And Vestal fires in hallowed temples burn;
And Remus, with Quirinus shall sustain   400
The righteous laws, and fraud and force restrain.
Janus himself before his fane shall wait,
And keep the dreadful issues of his gate
With bolts and iron bars: within remains
Imprisoned Fury, bound in brazen chains: 405
High on a trophy raised, of useless arms,
He sits, and threats the world with vain alarms."
    He said, and sent Cyllenius with command
To free the ports, and ope the Punic land
To Trojan guests; lest, ignorant of fate,   410
The queen might force them from her town and state.
Down from the steep of heaven Cyllenius flies,
And cleaves with all his wings the yielding skies.
Soon on the Libyan shore descends the god,
Performs his message, and displays his rod.   415
The surly murmurs of the people cease;
And, as the fates required, they give the peace.
The queen herself suspends the rigid laws,
The Trojans pities, and protects their cause.
    Meantime, in shades of night Aeneas lies: 420
Care seized his soul, and sleep forsook his eyes.
But when the sun restored the cheerful day,
He rose, the coast and country to survey,

400. *Quirinus*: originally the local god of the Sabines on the Quirinal Hill,
later identified with Romulus.
408. *Cyllenius*: Mercury (Hermes).
411. *The queen*: Dido.

Anxious and eager to discover more.
It looked a wild uncultivated shore: 425
But, whether human kind, or beasts alone
Possessed the new-found region, was unknown.
Beneath a ledge of rocks his fleet he hides:
Tall trees surround the mountain's shady sides:
The bending brow above, a safe retreat provides.   430
Armed with two pointed darts, he leaves his friends,
And true Achates on his steps attends.
Lo! in the deep recesses of the wood,
Before his eyes his goddess mother stood:
A huntress in her habit and her mien;   435
Her dress, a maid, her air, confessed a queen.
Bare were her knees, and knots her garments bind;
Loose was her hair, and wantoned in the wind;
Her hand sustained a bow; her quiver hung behind.
She seemed a virgin of the Spartan blood: 440
With such array Harpalycë bestrode
Her Thracian courser, and outstripped the rapid flood.
"Ho! strangers! have you lately seen (she said),
One of my sisters, like myself arrayed,
Who crossed the lawn, or in the forest strayed?   445
A painted quiver at her back she bore;
Varied with spots, a lynx's hide she wore;
And at full cry pursued the tusky boar."
    Thus Venus: thus her son replied again:
"None of your sisters have we heard or seen,   450
O virgin! or what other name you bear
Above that style—O more than mortal fair!
Your voice and mien celestial birth betray.
If, as you seem, the sister of the day,
Or one at least of chaste Diana's train,   455
Let not an humble suppliant sue in vain;
But tell a stranger, long in tempests tossed,
What earth we tread, and who commands the coast?

441. *Harpalycë*: a Thracian warrior-princess.
451. *O—quam te memorem, virgo?*
454. *sister of the day*: *Phoebi soror*: Apollo's sister Diana (Artemis).

Then on your name shall wretched mortals call,
And offered victims at your altars fall." 460
　"I dare not (she replied) assume the name
Of goddess, or celestial honors claim;
For Tyrian virgins bows and quivers bear,
And purple buskins o'er their ankles wear.
Know, gentle youth, in Libyan lands you are 465
A people rude in peace, and rough in war.
The rising city, which from far you see,
Is Carthage, and a Tyrian colony.
Phoenician Dido rules the growing state;
Who fled from Tyre, to shun her brother's hate. 470
Great were her wrongs, her story full of fate;
Which I will sum in short. Sichaeus, known
For wealth, and brother to the Punic throne,
Possessed fair Dido's bed; and either heart
At once was wounded with an equal dart. 475
Her father gave her, yet a spotless maid:
Pygmalion then the Tyrian scepter swayed—
One who contemned divine and human laws:
Then strife ensued, and cursèd gold the cause.
The monarch, blinded with desire of wealth, 480
With steel invades his brother's life by stealth;
Before the sacred altar made him bleed,
And long from her concealed the cruel deed.
Some tale, some new pretense, he daily coined
To soothe his sister, and delude her mind. 485
　At length, in dead of night, the ghost appears
Of her unhappy lord: the specter stares,
And, with erected eyes, his bloody bosom bares.
The cruel altars, and his fate, he tells,
And the dire secret of his house reveals; 490
Then warns the widow, with her household gods,
To seek a refuge in remote abodes.
Last, to support her in so long a way,
He shows her where his hidden treasure lay.

---

488. *erected eyes: ora modis attolens pallida miris*, "in strange ways lifting up his pale visage." Virgil took this substantially from Lucretius, Book I, 123.

Admonished thus, and seized with mortal fright,   495
The queen provides companions of her flight:
They meet, and all combine to leave the state,
Who hate the tyrant, or who fear his hate.
They seize a fleet, which ready rigged they find;
Nor is Pygmalion's treasure left behind.   500
The vessels, heavy laden, put to sea
With prosperous winds: a woman leads the way.
I know not, if by stress of weather driven,
Or was their fatal course disposed by Heaven:
At last they landed, where from far, your eyes   505
May view the turrets of new Carthage rise:
There, bought a space of ground, which (Byrsa call
From the bull's hide) they first enclosed, and wall
But whence are you? what country claims your birth?
What seek you, strangers, on our Libyan earth?"   510
   To whom, with sorrow streaming from his eyes,
And deeply sighing, thus her son replies:
"Could you with patience hear, or I relate,
O nymph! the tedious annals of our fate,
Through such a train of woes if I should run,   515
The day would sooner than the tale be done.
From ancient Troy, by force expelled, we came—
If you by chance have heard the Trojan name.
On various seas by various tempests tossed,
At length we landed on your Libyan coast.   520
The good Aeneas am I called—a name,
While Fortune favored, not unknown to fame.
My household gods, companions of my woes,
With pious care I rescued from our foes.
To fruitful Italy my course was bent;   525
And from the king of heaven is my descent.
With twice ten sail I crossed the Phrygian sea;
Fate and my mother-goddess led my way.

---

521. "Virgil makes Aeneas a bold avower of his own virtue:
             Sum pius Aeneas, fama super aethera notus;
which in the civility of our poets is the character of a Fanfaron. . . ."—Dryden:
An Essay of Dramatic Poesy.
   526. *the king of heaven*: Aeneas' maternal grandfather.

Scarce seven, the thin remainders of my fleet,
From storms preserved, within your harbor meet.   530
Myself distressed, an exile, and unknown,
Debarred from Europe, and from Asia thrown,
In Libyan deserts wander thus alone."
    His tender parent could no longer bear,
But, interposing, sought to soothe his care.   535
"Whoe'er you are—not unbeloved by Heaven,
Since on our friendly shore your ships are driven—
Have courage: to the gods permit the rest,
And to the queen expose your just request.
Now take this earnest of success for more: 540
Your scattered fleet is joined upon the shore;
The winds are changed, your friends from danger free;
Or I renounce my skill in augury.
Twelve swans behold in beauteous order move,
And stoop with closing pinions from above;   545
Whom late the bird of Jove had driven along,
And through the clouds pursued the scattering throng:
Now, all united in a goodly team,
They skim the ground, and seek the quiet stream.
As they, with joy returning, clap their wings,   550
And ride the circuit of the skies in rings:
Not otherwise your ships, and every friend,
Already hold the port, or with swift sails descend.
No more advice is needful; but pursue
The path before you, and the town in view."   555
    Thus having said, she turned, and made appear
Her neck refulgent, and dishevelled hair,
Which, flowing from her shoulders, reached the ground,
And widely spread ambrosial scents around.
In length of train descends her sweeping gown;   560
And by her graceful walk, the queen of love is known.
The prince pursued the parting deity
With words like these: "Ah! whither do you fly?
Unkind and cruel! to deceive your son
In borrowed shapes, and his embrace to shun: 565
Never to bless my sight but thus, unknown;
And still to speak in accents not your own."

Against the goddess these complaints he made,
But took the path, and her commands obeyed.
They march obscure; for Venus kindly shrouds   570
With mists their persons, and involves in clouds,
That, thus unseen, their passage none might stay,
Or force to tell the causes of their way.
This part performed, the goddess flies sublime,
To visit Paphos, and her native clime;   575
Where garlands, ever green and ever fair,
With vows are offered, and with solemn prayer:
A hundred altars in her temples smoke:
A thousand bleeding hearts her power invoke.
    They climb the next ascent, and, looking down,   580
Now at a nearer distance view the town.
The prince with wonder sees the stately towers
(Which late were huts, and shepherds' homely bowers),
The gates and streets; and hears from every part
The noise and busy concourse of the mart.   585
The toiling Tyrians on each other call,
To ply their labor: some extend the wall;
Some build the citadel; the brawny throng
Or dig, or push unwieldy stones along.
Some for their dwellings choose a spot of ground,   590
Which, first designed, with ditches they surround.
Some laws ordain; and some attend the choice
Of holy senates, and elect by voice.
Here some design a mole, while others there
Lay deep foundations for a theater,   595
From marble quarries mighty columns hew,
For ornaments of scenes, and future view.
Such is their toil, and such their busy pains,
As exercise the bees in flowery plains,
When winter past, and summer scarce begun,   600
Invites them forth to labor in the sun;
Some lead their youth abroad, while some condense
Their liquid store, and some in cells dispense:
Some at the gate stand ready to receive
The golden burden, and their friends relieve: 605

579. I.e., no "blood sacrifices" except these. Dryden's wit, not Virgil's.

All, with united force, combine to drive
The lazy drones from the laborious hive.
With envy stung, they view each other's deeds:
The fragrant work with diligence proceeds.
"Thrice happy you, whose walls already rise!"   610
Aeneas said, and viewed, with lifted eyes,
Their lofty towers: then entering at the gate,
Concealed in clouds (prodigious to relate),
He mixed, unmarked, among the busy throng,
Borne by the tide, and passed unseen along.   615
    Full in the center of the town there stood,
Thick set with trees, a venerable wood:
The Tyrians, landing near this holy ground,
And digging here, a prosperous omen found:
From under earth a courser's head they drew,   620
Their growth and future fortune to foreshow:
This fated sign their foundress Juno gave,
Of a soil fruitful, and a people brave.
Sidonian Dido here with solemn state
Did Juno's temple build, and consecrate;   625
Enriched with gifts, and with a golden shrine;
But more the goddess made the place divine.
On brazen steps the marble threshold rose,
And brazen plates the cedar beams inclose:
The rafters are with brazen coverings crowned;   630
The lofty doors on brazen hinges sound.
What first Aeneas in this place beheld,
Revived his courage, and his fears expelled.
For, while expecting there the queen, he raised
His wondering eyes, and round the temple gazed,   635
Admired the fortune of the rising town,
The striving artists, and their art's renown—
He saw, in order painted on the wall,
Whatever did unhappy Troy befall:
The wars that fame around the world had blown,   640
All to the life, and every leader known.

613. *prodigious*: magical or miraculous.
620. *courser*: a war horse.

There Agamemnon, Priam here, he spies,
And fierce Achilles, who both kings defies.
He stopped, and weeping said: "O friend, e'en here
The monuments of Trojan woes appear!   645
Our known disasters fill e'en foreign lands:
See there, where old unhappy Priam stands!
E'en the mute walls relate the warrior's fame,
And Trojan griefs the Tyrians' pity claim."
    He said—(his tears a ready passage find)   650
Devouring what he saw so well designed;
And with an empty picture fed his mind:
For there he saw the fainting Grecians yield,
And here the trembling Trojans quit the field,
Pursued by fierce Achilles through the plain,   655
On his high chariot driving o'er the slain.
The tents of Rhesus next his grief renew,
By their white sails betrayed to nightly view;
And wakeful Diomede, whose cruel sword
The sentries slew, nor spared their slumbering lord; 660
Then took the fiery steeds, ere yet the food
Of Troy they taste, or drink the Xanthian flood.
Elsewhere, he saw where Troïlus defied
Achilles, and unequal combat tried;
Then, where the boy disarmed, with loosened reins, 665
Was by his horses hurried o'er the plains,
Hung by the neck and hair, and dragged around:
The hostile spear, yet sticking in his wound,
With tracks of blood inscribed the dusty ground.
    Meantime the Trojan dames, oppressed with woe, 670
To Pallas' fane in long procession go,
In hopes to reconcile their heavenly foe:
They weep; they beat their breasts; they rend their hair,
And rich embroidered vests for presents bear;
But the stern goddess stands unmoved with prayer. 675

    649. This translates the well known *sunt lacrimae rerum*, etc., by specifying
whose *lacrimae* for whose *res*. It is difficult to deny Dryden's dramatic rightness
and good sense. But Virgil's line also sings and mourns.
    669. Virgil's spear writes in the dust like a stylus; the "tracks of blood" are
Dryden's.

Thrice round the Trojan walls Achilles drew
The corpse of Hector, whom in fight he slew.
Here Priam sues; and there, for sums of gold,
The lifeless body of his son is sold.
So sad an object, and so well expressed,   680
Drew sighs and groans from the grieved hero's breast,
To see the figure of his lifeless friend,
And his old sire his helpless hands extend.
Himself he saw amidst the Grecian train,
Mixed in the bloody battle on the plain.   685
And swarthy Memnon in his arms he knew,
His pompous ensigns, and his Indian crew.
Penthesilea there, with haughty grace,
Leads to the wars an Amazonian race:
In their right hands a pointed dart they wield;   690
The left, for ward, sustains the lunar shield.
Athwart her breast a golden belt she throws,
Amidst the press alone provokes a thousand foes,
And dares her maiden arms to manly force oppose.

Thus while the Trojan prince employs his eyes,   695
Fixed on the walls with wonder and surprise,
The beauteous Dido, with a numerous train,
And pomp of guards, ascends the sacred fane.
Such on Eurotas' banks, or Cynthus' height,
Diana seems; and so she charms the sight,   700
When in the dance the graceful goddess leads
The choir of nymphs, and overtops their heads.
Known by her quiver, and her lofty mien,
She walks majestic, and she looks their queen:
Latona sees her shine above the rest,   705
And feeds with secret joy her silent breast.
Such Dido was; with such becoming state,
Amidst the crowd, she walks serenely great.
Their labor to her future sway she speeds,
And passing with a gracious glance proceeds;   710

692. *aurea subnectens exsertae cingula mammae*: "a golden baldrick passing under one bare breast," i.e., like a sling passing over the other, and so "athwart" it.
705. *Latona*: Leto, mother of Apollo and Diana.

Then mounts the throne, high placed before the shrine:
In crowds around the swarming people join.
She takes petitions, and dispenses laws,
Hears and determines every private cause;
Their tasks in equal portions she divides,   715
And, where unequal, there by lot decides.
    Another way by chance Aeneas bends
His eyes, and unexpected sees his friends,
Antheus, Sergestus brave, Cloanthus strong,
And at their backs a mighty Trojan throng,   720
Whom late the tempest on the billows tossed,
And widely scattered on another coast.
The prince, unseen, surprised with wonder stands,
And longs, with joyful haste, to join their hands;
But, doubtful of the wished event, he stays,   725
And from the hollow cloud his friends surveys,
Impatient, till they told their present state,
And where they left their ships, and what their fate,
And why they came, and what was their request:
For these were sent commissioned by the rest,   730
To sue for leave to land their sickly men,
And gain admission to the gracious queen.
Entering, with cries they filled the holy fane;
Then thus, with lowly voice, Ilioneus began:
"O queen! indulged by favor of the gods   735
To found an empire in these new abodes;
To build a town; with statutes to restrain
The wild inhabitants beneath thy reign:
We wretched Trojans, tossed on every shore,
From sea to sea, thy clemency implore!   740
Forbid the fires our shipping to deface:
Receive the unhappy fugitives to grace,
And spare the remnant of a pious race!
We come not with design of wasteful prey,
To drive the country, force the swains away: 745
Nor such our strength, nor such is our desire:
The vanquished dare not to such thoughts aspire.

A land there is, Hesperia named of old—
The soil is fruitful, and the men are bold
(The Oenotrians held it once)—by common fame   750
Now called Italia, from the leader's name.
To that sweet region was our voyage bent,
When winds and every warring element
Disturbed our course, and, far from sight of land
Cast our torn vessels on the moving sand.   755
The sea came on; the South, with mighty roar,
Dispersed and dashed the rest upon the rocky shore.
Those few you see, escaped the storm, and fear
(Unless you interpose) a shipwreck here.
What men, what monsters, what inhuman race,   760
What laws, what barbarous customs of the place,
Shut up a desert shore to drowning men,
And drive us to the cruel seas again!
If our hard fortune no compassion draws,
Nor hospitable rights, nor human laws,   765
The gods are just, and will revenge our cause.
    Aeneas was our prince: a juster lord,
Or nobler warrior, never drew a sword:
Observant of the right, religious of his word.
If yet he lives, and draws this vital air,   770
Nor we, his friends, of safety shall despair,
Nor you, great queen, these offices repent,
Which he will equal, and perhaps augment.
We want not cities, nor Sicilian coasts,
Where king Acestes Trojan lineage boasts.   775
Permit our ships a shelter on your shores,
Refitted from your woods with planks and oars,
That, if our prince be safe, we may renew
Our destined course, and Italy pursue.
But if, O best of men! the Fates ordain   780
That thou art swallowed in the Libyan main,

748. *Hesperia*: Hesperus is the Greek evening star, so a Hesperian is an evening land, or a western one, for Greeks or Trojans. Italus is supposed to have been a chief of the Oenotrians there.
769. Dryden's exegesis of *pius*.

And if our young Iülus be no more,
Dismiss our navy from your friendly shore,
That we to good Acestes may return,
And with our friends our common losses mourn."   785
   Thus spoke Ilioneus: the Trojan crew
With cries and clamors his request renew.
The modest queen awhile, with downcast eyes,
Pondered the speech, then briefly thus replies:
"Trojans! dismiss your fears: my cruel fate,   790
And doubts attending an unsettled state,
Force me to guard my coast from foreign foes.
Who has not heard the story of your woes,
The name and fortune of your native place,
The fame and valor of the Phrygian race?   795
We Tyrians are not so devoid of sense,
Nor so remote from Phoebus' influence.
Whether to Latian shores your course is bent,
Or, driven by tempests from your first intent,
You seek the good Acestes' government,   800
Your men shall be received, your fleet repaired,
And sail, with ships of convoy for your guard:
Or, would you stay, and join your friendly powers
To raise and to defend the Tyrian towers,
My wealth, my city, and myself, are yours.   805
And would to heaven, the storm you felt would bring
On Carthaginian coasts your wandering king.
My people shall, by my command, explore
The ports and creeks of every winding shore,
And towns, and wilds, and shady woods, in quest   810
Of so renowned, and so desired a guest."
   Raised in his mind the Trojan hero stood,
And longed to break from out his ambient cloud:
Achates found it, and thus urged his way:
"From whence, O goddess-born, this long delay?   815
What more can you desire, your welcome sure,
Your fleet in safety, and your friends secure?
One only wants; and him we saw in vain
Oppose the storm, and swallowed in the main.

Orontes in his fate our forfeit paid: 820
The rest agrees with what your mother said."
　　Scarce had he spoken, when the cloud gave way;
The mists flew upward, and dissolved in day.
The Trojan chief appeared in open sight,
August in visage, and serenely bright.   825
His mother-goddess, with her hands divine,
Had formed his curling locks, and made his temples shine,
And given his rolling eyes a sparkling grace,
And breathed a youthful vigor on his face;
Like polished ivory, beauteous to behold,   830
Or Parian marble, when enchased in gold:
Thus radiant from the circling cloud he broke;
And thus with manly modesty he spoke:
"He whom you seek am I; by tempests tossed,
And saved from shipwreck on your Libyan coast   835
Presenting, gracious queen, before your throne,
A prince that owes his life to you alone:
Fair majesty! the refuge and redress
Of those whom fate pursues, and wants oppress!
You, who your pious offices employ   840
To save the relics of abandoned Troy;
Receive the shipwrecked on your friendly shore;
With hospitable rites relieve the poor;
Associate in your town a wandering train,
And strangers in your palace entertain.   845
What thanks can wretched fugitives return,
Who, scattered through the world in exile mourn?
The gods (if gods to goodness are inclined:
If acts of mercy touch their heavenly mind),
And, more than all the gods, your generous heart,   850
Conscious of worth, requite its own desert!
In you this age is happy, and this earth;
And parents more than mortal gave you birth.
While rolling rivers into seas shall run,
And round the space of heaven the radiant sun;   855
While trees the mountain-tops with shades supply,
Your honor, name, and praise, shall never die.

Whate'er abode my fortune has assigned,
Your image shall be present in my mind."
Thus having said, he turned with pious haste,   860
And joyful his expecting friends embraced:
With his right hand Ilioneus he graced,
Sergestus with his left; then to his breast
Cloanthus and the noble Gyas pressed;
And so by turns descended to the rest.   865
   The Tyrian queen stood fixed upon his face,
Pleased with his motions, ravished with his grace;
Admired his fortunes, more admired the man;
Then re-collected stood, and thus began:
"What fate, O goddess-born! what angry powers   870
Have cast you shipwrecked on our barren shores?
Are you the great Aeneas, known to fame,
Who from celestial seed your lineage claim?
The same Aeneas, whom fair Venus bore
To famed Anchises on the Idaean shore?   875
It calls into my mind, though then a child,
When Teucer came, from Salamis exiled,
And sought my father's aid, to be restored:
My father, Belus, then with fire and sword
Invaded Cyprus, made the region bare,   880
And, conquering, finished the successful war.
From him the Trojan siege I understood,
The Grecian chiefs, and your illustrious blood.
Your foe himself the Dardan valor praised,
And his own ancestry from Trojans raised.   885
Enter, my noble guest! and you shall find,
If not a costly welcome, yet a kind:
For I myself, like you, have been distressed,
Till Heaven afforded me this place of rest:

   868. *admired*: wondered at.
   877. *Teucer*: exiled by his father, Telamon, for not having avenged his
brother, Ajax, who killed himself at Troy when the arms of Achilles were awarded
to Odysseus rather than to himself. Belus (a word that meant "lord" in Phoenician and is found in the Old Testament as Baal) helped him found a new
Salamis on Cyprus.

Like you, an alien in a land unknown,   890
I learn to pity woes so like my own."
   She said, and to the palace led her guest;
Then offered incense, and proclaimed a feast.
Nor yet less careful for her absent friends,
Twice ten fat oxen to the ships she sends: 895
Besides a hundred boars, a hundred lambs,
With bleating cries, attend their milky dams;
And jars of generous wine, and spacious bowls
She gives, to cheer the sailors' drooping souls.
Now purple hangings clothe the palace walls,   900
 And sumptuous feasts are made in splendid halls:
On Tyrian carpets, richly wrought, they dine;
With loads of massy plate the sideboards shine,
And antique vases all of gold, embossed
(The gold itself inferior to the cost   905
Of curious work), where on the sides were seen
The fights and figures of illustrious men,
From their first founder to the present queen.
   The good Aeneas, whose paternal care
Iülus' absence could no longer bear,   910
Dispatched Achates to the ships in haste,
To give a glad relation of the past,
And, fraught with precious gifts, to bring the boy,
Snatched from the ruins of unhappy Troy.
A robe of tissue, stiff with golden wire;   915
An upper vest, once Helen's rich attire,
From Argos by the famed adult'ress brought,
With golden flowers and winding foliage wrought:
Her mother Leda's present, when she came
To ruin Troy, and set the world on flame;   920
The scepter Priam's eldest daughter bore,
Her orient necklace, and the crown she wore
Of double texture, glorious to behold:
One order set with gems, and one with gold.

891. *Non ignara mali miseris succurrere disco.*
915. *golden wire*: gold thread.

Instructed thus, the wise Achates goes,   925
And, in his diligence, his duty shows.
    But Venus, anxious for her son's affairs,
New counsels tries, and new designs prepares:
That Cupid should assume the shape and face
Of sweet Ascanius, and the springhtly grace;   930
Should bring the presents, in her nephew's stead,
And in Eliza's veins the gentle poison shed:
For much she feared the Tyrians, double-tongued:
And knew the town to Juno's care belonged.
These thoughts by night her golden slumbers broke;   935
And thus, alarmed, to wingèd Love she spoke:
"My son, my strength, whose mighty power alone
Controls the Thunderer on his awful throne!
To thee thy much-afflicted mother flies,
And on thy succor and thy faith relies.   940
Thou knowest, my son, how Jove's revengeful wife
By force and fraud, attempts thy brother's life;
And often hast thou mourned with me his pains.
Him Dido now with blandishment detains;
But I suspect the town where Juno reigns.   945
For this, 'tis needful to prevent her art,
And fire with love the proud Phoenician's heart—
A love so violent, so strong, so sure,
That neither age can change, nor art can cure.
How this may be performed, now take my mind: 950
Ascanius, by his father is designed
To come with presents laden, from the port,
To gratify the queen, and gain the court.
I mean to plunge the boy in pleasing sleep,
And, ravished, in Idalian bowers to keep,   955
Or high Cythera, that the sweet deceit
May pass unseen, and none prevent the cheat.
Take thou his form and shape. I beg the grace
But only for a night's revolving space:
Thyself a boy, assume a boy's dissembled face;   960

932. *Eliza*: Elissa, as Dido is called in Book IV, 146.
955. *Idalian*: on Mount Ida.
956. *high Cythera*: the island off whose shore Venus was born.

That when, amidst the fervor of the feast,
The Tyrian hugs and fonds thee on her breast,
And with sweet kisses in her arms constrains,
Thou mayest infuse thy venom in her veins."
The god of love obeys, and sets aside   965
His bow and quiver, and his plumy pride:
He walks Iülus in his mother's sight,
And in the sweet resemblance takes delight.
   The goddess then to young Ascanius flies,
And in a pleasing slumber seals his eyes: 970
Lulled in her lap, amidst a train of Loves,
She gently bears him to her blissful groves;
Then with a wreath of myrtle crowns his head,
And softly lays him on a flowery bed.
   Cupid meantime assumed his form and face,   975
Following Achates with a shorter pace,
And brought the gifts. The queen already sat
Amidst the Trojan lords, in shining state,
High on a golden bed: her princely guest
Was next her side; in order sat the rest.   980
Then canisters with bread are heaped on high:
The attendants water for their hands supply,
And, having washed, with silken towels dry.
Next fifty handmaids in long order bore
The censers, and with fumes the gods adore;   985
Then youths and virgins, twice as many, join
To place the dishes, and to serve the wine.
The Tyrian train, admitted to the feast,
Approach, and on the painted couches rest.
All on the Trojan gifts with wonder gaze,   990
But view the beauteous boy with more amaze;
His rosy-colored cheeks, his radiant eyes,
His motions, voice, and shape, and all the god's disguise;
Nor pass unpraised the vest and veil divine,
Which wandering foliage and rich flowers entwine.   995

   980. *strato super discumbitur ostro*: Dryden's note: "This, I confess, is im-
properly translated, and according to the modern fashion of sitting at table. But
the ancient custom of lying on beds had not been understood by the unlearned
reader."

But far above the rest, the royal dame
(Already doomed to love's disastrous flame),
With eyes insatiate, and tumultuous joy,
Beholds the presents, and admires the boy.
The guileful god about the hero, long,   1000
With children's play, and false embraces, hung;
Then sought the queen: she took him to her arms
With greedy pleasure, and devoured his charms.
Unhappy Dido little thought, what guest,
How dire a god she drew so near her breast.   1005
But he, not mindless of his mother's prayer,
Works in the pliant bosom of the fair,
And molds her heart anew, and blots her former care.
The dead is to the living love resigned;
And all Aeneas enters in her mind.   1010
    Now, when the rage of hunger was appeased,
The meat removed, and every guest was pleased,
The golden bowls with sparkling wine are crowned,
And through the palace cheerful cries resound.
From gilded roofs depending lamps display   1015
Nocturnal beams, that emulate the day.
A golden bowl, that shone with gems divine,
The queen commanded to be crowned with wine—
The bowl that Belus used, and all the Tyrian line.
Then, silence through the hall proclaimed, she spoke: 1020
"O hospitable Jove! we thus invoke
With solemn rites, thy sacred name and power:
Bless to both nations this auspicious hour!
So may the Trojan and the Tyrian line
In lasting concord from this day combine.   1025
Thou, Bacchus, god of joys and friendly cheer,
And gracious Juno, both, be present here!
And you, my lords of Tyre, your vows address
To heaven with mine, to ratify the peace."
The goblet then she took, with nectar crowned   1030
(Sprinkling the first libations on the ground),

1021. *hospitable*: god of hospitality.

And raised it to her mouth with sober grace,
Then, sipping, offered to the next in place.
'Twas Bitias whom she called—a thirsty soul:
He took the challenge, and embraced the bowl,   1035
With pleasure swilled the gold, nor ceased to draw
Till he the bottom of the brimmer saw.
The goblet goes around: Iöpas brought
His golden lyre, and sung what ancient Atlas taught—
The various labors of the wandering moon,   1040
And whence proceed the eclipses of the sun;
The original of men and beasts; and whence
The rains arise, and fires their warmth dispense,
And fixed and erring stars dispose their influence;
What shakes the solid earth; what cause delays   1045
The summer nights, and shortens winter days.
With peals of shouts the Tyrians praise the song;
Those peals are echoed by the Trojan throng.
The unhappy queen with talk prolonged the night,
And drank large drafts of love with vast delight: 1050
Of Priam much inquired, of Hector more;
Then asked what arms the swarthy Memnon wore,
What troops he landed on the Trojan shore:
The steeds of Diomede varied the discourse,
And fierce Achilles, with his matchless force: 1055
At length, as Fate and her ill stars required,
To hear the series of the war desired.
"Relate at large, my godlike guest (she said),
The Grecian stratagems, the town betrayed:
The fatal issue of so long a war,   1060
Your flight, your wanderings, and your woes declare:
For, since on every sea, on every coast,
Your men have been distressed, your navy tossed,
Seven times the sun has either tropic viewed,
The winter banished, and the spring renewed."   1065

1040. Probably a tribute to Lucretius. There is another in the *Second
Georgic*, 475 sqq., from which in fact the lines translated in Dryden's 1045–6
are taken.

⎧⎩⎨⎫

BOOK II

THE ARGUMENT

Aeneas relates how the city of Troy was taken, after a ten years' siege, by the treachery of Sinon, and the stratagem of a wooden horse. He declares the fixed resolution he had taken not to survive the ruin of his country, and the various adventures he met with in the defense of it. At last, having been before advised by Hector's ghost, and now by the appearance of his mother Venus, he is prevailed upon to leave the town, and settle his household gods in another country. In order to [do] this, he carries off his father on his shoulders, and leads his little son by the hand, his wife following him behind. When he comes to the place appointed for the general rendezvous, he finds a great confluence of people, but misses his wife, whose ghost afterwards appears to him, and tells him the land which was designed for him.

ALL were attentive to the godlike man,
When from his lofty couch he thus began:
"Great queen, what you command me to relate,
Renews the sad remembrance of our fate:
An empire from its old foundations rent,   5
And every woe the Trojans underwent;
A peopled city made a desert place;
All that I saw, and part of which I was;
Not e'en the hardest of our foes could hear,
Nor stern Ulysses tell, without a tear.   10
And now the latter watch of wasting night,
And setting stars, to kindly rest invite.

8. *et quorum pars magna fui* . . . : So Tennyson, in *Ulysses*: "I am a part of all that I have met."

But since you take such interest in our woe,
And Troy's disastrous end desire to know,
I will restrain my tears, and briefly tell   15
What in our last and fatal night befell.
　By destiny compelled, and in despair,
The Greeks grew weary of the tedious war,
And by Minerva's aid, a fabric reared,
Which like a steed of monstrous height appeared: 20
The sides were planked with pine: they feigned it made
For their return, and this the vow they paid.
Thus they pretend; but in the hollow side,
Selected numbers of their soldiers hide:
With inward arms the dire machine they load;   25
And iron bowels stuff the dark abode.
In sight of Troy lies Tenedos, an isle
(While Fortune did on Priam's empire smile)
Renowned for wealth; but since, a faithless bay,
Where ships exposed to wind and weather lay.   30
There was their fleet concealed. We thought, for Greece,
Their sails were hoisted, and our fears release.
The Trojans, cooped within their walls so long,
Unbar their gates, and issue in a throng
Like swarming bees, and with delight survey   35
The camp deserted, where the Grecians lay:
The quarters of the several chiefs they showed:
Here Phoenix, here Achilles, made abode;
Here joined the battles; there the navy rode.
Part on the pile their wondering eyes employ—   40
The pile by Pallas raised to ruin Troy.
Thymoetes first ('tis doubtful whether hired,
Or so the Trojan destiny required)
Moved that the ramparts might be broken down,
To lodge the monster fabric in the town.   45
But Capys, and the rest of sounder mind,
The fatal present to the flames designed,
Or to the watery deep: at least to bore
The hollow sides, and hidden frauds explore.

　22. *vow*: votive offering.

The giddy vulgar, as their fancies guide,   50
With noise say nothing, and in parts divide.
Laocoön, followed by a numerous crowd,
Ran from the fort, and cried from far, aloud:
'O wretched countrymen! what fury reigns?
What more than madness has possessed your brains?   55
Think you the Grecians from your coasts are gone?
And are Ulysses' arts no better known?
This hollow fabric either must inclose
Within its blind recess, our secret foes;
Or 'tis an engine raised above the town   60
To overlook the walls, and then to batter down.
Somewhat is sure designed by fraud or force:
Trust not their presents, nor admit the horse.'
Thus having said, against the steed he threw
His forceful spear, which, hissing as it flew,   65
Pierced through the yielding planks of jointed wood.
And trembling in the hollow belly stood.
The sides, transpierced, return a rattling sound;
And groans of Greeks inclosed come issuing through the wound.
And had not Heaven the fall of Troy designed,   70
Or had not men been fated to be blind,
Enough was said and done t' inspire a better mind.
Then had our lances pierced the treacherous wood,
And Ilian towers and Priam's empire stood.

Meantime, with shouts, the Trojan shepherds bring   75
A captive Greek in bands, before the king—
Taken, to take—who made himself their prey
To impose on their belief, and Troy betray:
Fixed on his aim, and obstinately bent
To die undaunted, or to circumvent.   80
About the captive, tides of Trojans flow;
All press to see, and some insult the foe.
Now hear how well the Greeks their wiles disguised:
Behold a nation in a man comprised!

63. Dryden compresses out of existence the well known *timeo Danaos et dona ferentes*, "I fear the Greeks even when they bear gifts."

69. *gemitumque dedere cavernae*: "the interior hollows gave a groan." No Greeks were heard on this occasion.

76. *bands*: bonds.

Trembling the miscreant stood: unarmed and bound,   85
He stared, and rolled his haggard eyes around,
Then said, 'Alas! what earth remains, what sea,
Is open to receive unhappy me?
What fate a wretched fugitive attends,
Scorned by my foes, abandoned by my friends?'   90
He said, and sighed, and cast a rueful eye:
Our pity kindles, and our passions die.
We cheer the youth to make his own defense,
And freely tell us what he was, and whence:
What news he could impart we long to know,   95
And what to credit from a captive foe.
   His fear at length dismissed, he said, 'Whate'er
My fate ordains, my words shall be sincere;
I neither can nor dare my birth disclaim;
Greece is my country, Sinon is my name: 100
Though plunged by Fortune's power in misery,
'Tis not in Fortune's power to make me lie.
If any chance has hither brought the name
Of Palamedes, not unknown to fame,
Who suffered from the malice of the times,   105
Accused and sentenced for pretended crimes,
Because these fatal wars he would prevent:
Whose death the wretched Greeks too late lament.
Me, then a boy, my father, poor and bare
Of other means, committed to his care,   110
His kinsman and companion in the war.
While fortune favored, while his arms support
The cause, and ruled the counsels of the court,
I made some figure there; nor was my name
Obscure, nor I without my share of fame.   115
But when Ulysses, with fallacious arts,
Had made impression in the people's hearts,
And forged a treason in my patron's name
(I speak of things too far divulged by fame),
My kinsman fell. Then I, without support,   120
In private mourned his loss, and left the court.
Mad as I was, I could not bear his fate
With silent grief, but loudly blamed the state,

And cursed the direful author of my woes.—
'Twas told again; and hence my ruin rose.   125
I threatened, if indulgent Heaven once more
Would land me safely on my native shore,
His death with double vengeance to restore.
This moved the murderer's hate; and soon ensued
The effects of malice from a man so proud.   130
Ambiguous rumors through the camp he spread,
And sought, by treason, my devoted head;
New crimes invented; left unturned no stone,
To make my guilt appear, and hide his own;
Till Calchas was by force and threatening wrought—   135
But why—why dwell I on that anxious thought?
If on my nation just revenge you seek.
(And 'tis to appear a foe, to appear a Greek);
Already you my name and country know:
Assuage your thirst of blood, and strike the blow: 140
My death will both the kingly brothers please,
And set insatiate Ithacus at ease.'
This fair unfinished tale, these broken starts,
Raised expectations in our longing hearts,
Unknowing as we were in Grecian arts.   145
His former trembling once again renewed,
With acted fear, the villain thus pursued:
'Long had the Grecians (tired with fruitless care
And wearied with an unsuccessful war)
Resolved to raise the siege, and leave the town;   150
And had the gods permitted, they had gone.
But oft the wintry seas, and southern winds,
Withstood their passage home, and changed their minds,
Portents and prodigies their souls amazed;
But most, when this stupendous pile was raised;   155
Then flaming meteors, hung in air, were seen,
And thunders rattled through a sky serene.
Dismayed, and fearful of some dire event,
Eurypylus, to inquire their fate, was sent.

142. *Ithacus*: the Ithacan, Ulysses, of course.

He from the gods this dreadful answer brought: 160
"O Grecians, when the Trojan shores you sought,
Your passage with a virgin's blood was bought:
So must your safe return be bought again,
And Grecian blood once more atone the main."
The spreading rumor round the people ran;   165
All feared, and each believed himself the man.
Ulysses took the advantage of their fright;
Called Calchas, and produced in open sight;
Then bade him name the wretch, ordained by fate
The public victim, to redeem the state.   170
Already some presaged the dire event,
And saw what sacrifice Ulysses meant.
For twice five days, the good old seer withstood
The intended treason, and was dumb to blood,
Till, tired with endless clamors and pursuit   175
Of Ithacus, he stood no longer mute,
But, as it was agreed, pronounced that I
Was destined by the wrathful gods to die.
All praised the sentence, pleased the storm should fall
On one alone, whose fury threatened all.   180
The dismal day was come; the priests prepare
Their leavened cakes, and fillets for my hair.
I followed nature's laws, and must avow,
I broke my bonds, and fled the fatal blow.
Hid in a weedy lake all night I lay,   185
Secure of safety when they sailed away.
But now, what further hopes for me remain
To see my friends, or native soil again;
My tender infants, or my careful sire,
Whom they, returning, will to death require;   190
Will perpetrate on them their first design,
And take the forfeit of their heads for mine?
Which, O! if pity mortal minds can move,
If there be faith below, or gods above,
If innocence and truth can claim desert,   195
Ye Trojans, from an injured wretch avert!'

False tears true pity move: the king commands
To loose his fetters, and unbind his hands;
Then adds these friendly words: 'Dismiss thy fears;
Forget the Greeks; be mine as thou wert theirs;   200
But truly tell, was it for force or guile,
Or some religious end, you raised the pile?'
Thus said the king. He, full of fraudful arts,
This well invented tale for truth imparts:
'Ye lamps of heaven! (he said, and lifted high   205
His hands, now free) Thou venerable sky!
Inviolable powers, adored with dread!
Ye fatal fillets, that once bound this head!
Ye sacred altars, from whose flames I fled!
Be all of you adjured; and grant I may   210
Without a crime, the ungrateful Greeks betray,
Reveal the secrets of the guilty state,
And justly punish whom I justly hate!
But you, O king! preserve the faith you gave,
If I to save myself, your empire save.   215
The Grecian hopes, and all the attempts they made,
Were only founded on Minerva's aid.
But from the time when impious Diomede,
And false Ulysses, that inventive head,
Her fatal image from the temple drew,   220
The sleeping guardians of the castle slew,
Her virgin statue with their bloody hands
Polluted, and profaned her holy bands;
From thence the tide of fortune left their shore,
And ebbed much faster than it flowed before: 225
Their courage languished, as their hopes decayed;
And Pallas, now averse, refused her aid.
Nor did the goddess doubtfully declare
Her altered mind, and alienated care.
When first her fatal image touched the ground,   230
She sternly cast her glaring eyes around,

220. *Her . . . image*: a statue, the Palladium, which Diomede and Ulysses stole from Minerva's temple on the citadel of Troy.
223. *her holy bands*: white wool fillets worn by the statue in token of the goddess's virginity.

That sparkled as they rolled, and seemed to threat:
Her heavenly limbs distilled a briny sweat.
Thrice from the ground she leaped, was seen to wield
Her brandished lance, and shake her horrid shield. 235
Then Calchas bade our host for flight prepare,
And hope no conquest from the tedious war,
Till first they sailed for Greece; with prayers besought
Her injured power, and better omens brought.
And now their navy ploughs the watery main, 240
Yet soon expect it on your shores again,
With Pallas pleased; as Calchas did ordain.
But first, to reconcile the blue-eyed maid
For her stolen statue and her tower betrayed,
Warned by the seer, to her offended name 245
We raised and dedicate this wondrous frame,
So lofty, lest through your forbidden gates
It pass, and intercept our better fates:
For, once admitted there, our hopes are lost;
And Troy may then a new Palladium boast: 250
For so religion and the gods ordain,
That, if you violate with hands profane
Minerva's gift, your town in flames shall burn;
(Which omen, O ye gods, on Graecia turn!)
But if it climb, with your assisting hands, 255
The Trojan walls, and in the city stands;
Then Troy shall Argos and Mycenae burn,
And the reverse of fate on us return.'
   With such deceits he gained their easy hearts,
Too prone to credit his perfidious arts. 260
What Diomede, nor Thetis' greater son,
A thousand ships, nor ten years' siege, had done—
False tears and fawning words the city won.
   A greater omen, and of worse portent,
Did our unwary minds with fear torment, 265
Concurring to produce the dire event.
Laocoön, Neptune's priest by lot that year,
With solemn pomp then sacrificed a steer;

243. *blue-eyed maid*: Minerva; the epithet is from Homer, not from Virgil.

When (dreadful to behold!) from sea we spied
Two serpents, ranked abreast, the seas divide,   270
And smoothly sweep along the swelling tide.
Their flaming crests above the waves they show;
Their bellies seem to burn the seas below;
Their speckled tails advance to steer their course,
And on the sounding shore the flying billows force.   275
And now the strand, and now the plain, they held:
Their ardent eyes with bloody streaks were filled;
Their nimble tongues they brandished as they came,
And licked their hissing jaws, that sputtered flame.
We fled amazed; their destined way they take,   280
And to Laocoön and his children make:
And first around the tender boys they wind,
Then with their sharpened fangs their limbs and bodies grind.
The wretched father, running to their aid
With pious haste, but vain, they next invade: 285
Twice round his waist their winding volumes rolled;
And twice about his gasping throat they fold.
The priest thus doubly choked—their crests divide,
And towering o'er his head in triumph ride.
With both his hands he labors at the knots;   290
His holy fillets the blue venom blots;
His roaring fills the flitting air around.
Thus, when an ox receives a glancing wound,
He breaks his bands, the fatal altar flies,
And with loud bellowings breaks the yielding skies.   295
Their tasks performed, the serpents quit their prey,
And to the tower of Pallas make their way:
Couched at her feet they lie, protected there
By her large buckler, and protended spear.
    Amazement seizes all: the general cry   300
Proclaims Laocoön justly doomed to die,
Whose hand the will of Pallas had withstood,
And dared to violate the sacred wood.

---

270. *Two serpents*: no doubt representing Agamemnon and Menelaus, chiefs
of the Greek army.
299. The statue is either the Palladium, restored to its place, or another
effigy of Minerva.

All vote to admit the steed; that vows be paid,
And incense offered, to the offended maid.   305
A spacious breach is made: the town lies bare:
Some hoisting-levers, some the wheels prepare,
And fasten to the horse's feet: the rest
With cables haul along the unwieldy beast.
Each on his fellow for assistance calls: 310
At length, the fatal fabric mounts the walls,
Big with destruction. Boys with chaplets crowned,
And choirs of virgins, sing and dance around.
Thus raised aloft, and then descending down,
It enters o'er our heads, and threats the town.   315
O sacred city, built by hands divine!
O valiant heroes of the Trojan line!
Four times he struck: as oft the clashing sound
Of arms was heard, and inward groans rebound.
Yet mad with zeal, and blinded with our fate,   320
We haul along the horse in solemn state;
Then place the dire portent within the tower.
Cassandra cried, and cursed the unhappy hour;
Foretold our fate; but, by the god's decree,
All heard, and none believed the prophecy.   325
With branches we the fanes adorn, and waste
In jollity the day ordained to be the last.
    Meantime the rapid heavens rolled down the light,
And on the shaded ocean rushed the night:
Our men, secure, nor guards nor sentries held;   330
But easy sleep their weary limbs compelled.
The Grecians had embarked their naval powers
From Tenedos, and sought our well-known shores,
Safe under covert of the silent night,
And guided by the imperial galley's light;   335

318. *he struck: substitit,* translated "it stuck" by Sir John Denham. Dryden, following Denham's translation here as elsewhere in Book II, may have wanted to improve on it by suggesting a ship on a reef.

319. *inward groans:* the groans are Dryden's contribution, as in line 69 were the groaning Greeks.

334. *tacitae per amica silentia lunae:* "through the friendly stillnesses of the silent moon." Perhaps Dante derived from this his famous phrase, *dove il Sol tace* (*Inferno,* I, 60). It does not mean "in the dark of the moon."

When Sinon, favored by the partial gods,
Unlocked the horse, and oped his dark abodes;
Restored to vital air our hidden foes,
Who joyful from their long confinement rose.
Thessander bold, and Sthenelus their guide,   340
And dire Ulysses, down the cable slide:
Then Thoas, Athamas, and Pyrrhus, haste;
Nor was the Podalirian hero last,
Nor injured Menelaus, nor the famed
Epeus, who the fatal engine framed.   345
A nameless crowd succeed; their forces join
To invade the town, oppressed with sleep and wine.
Those few they find awake, first meet their fate;
Then to their fellows they unbar the gate.
'Twas in the dead of night, when sleep repairs   350
Our bodies, worn with toils, our minds, with cares,
When Hector's ghost before my sight appears:
A bloody shroud he seemed, and bathed in tears;
Such as he was, when, by Pelides slain,
Thessalian coursers dragged him o'er the plain.   355
Swoln were his feet, as when the thongs were thrust
Through the bored holes: his body black with dust:
Unlike that Hector who returned from toils
Of war, triumphant in Aeacian spoils;
Or him, who made the fainting Greeks retire,   360
And launched against their navy Phrygian fire.
His hair and beard stood stiffened with his gore;
And all the wounds he for his country bore
Now streamed afresh, and with new purple ran.
I wept to see the visionary man,   365
And, while my trance continued, thus began:
'O light of Trojans, and support of Troy,
Thy father's champion, and thy country's joy!

343. *the Podalirian hero*: Machaon, a Greek medic. Ruaeus, in a note, made
him a brother of Podalirius, a son of Asclepius.
354. *Pelides*: Achilles, son of Peleus.
359. *Aeacian spoils*: the armor of Achilles, stripped by Hector from Patroclus.
Aeacus was Achilles' grandfather.

O, long expected by thy friends! from whence
Art thou so late returned for our defense?   370
Do we behold thee, wearied as we are
With length of labors, and with toils of war?
After so many funerals of thy own,
Art thou restored to thy declining town?
But say, what wounds are these? what new disgrace   375
Deforms the manly features of thy face?'
  To this, the specter no reply did frame,
But answered to the cause for which he came;
And, groaning from the bottom of his breast,
This warning, in these mournful words, expressed: 380
'O goddess-born! escape, by timely flight,
The flames and horrors of this fatal night.
The foes already have possessed the wall:
Troy nods from high, and totters to her fall.
Enough is paid to Priam's royal name,   385
More than enough to duty and to fame.
If by a mortal hand my father's throne
Could be defended, 'twas by mine alone.
Now Troy to thee commends her future state,
And gives her gods companions of thy fate;   390
From their assistance, happier walls expect,
Which wand'ring long, at last thou shalt erect.'
He said, and brought me, from their blest abodes,
The venerable statues of the gods;
With ancient Vesta from the sacred choir,   395
The wreaths and relics of the immortal fire.
  Now peals of shouts came thundering from afar,
Cries, threats, and loud laments, and mingled war:
The noise approaches, though our palace stood
Aloof from streets, encompassed with a wood.   400
Louder, and yet more loud, I hear the alarms
Of human cries, distinct, and clashing arms.
Fear broke my slumbers; I no longer stay,
But mount the terrace, thence the town survey,
And hearken, what the frightful sounds convey.   405

Thus, when a flood of fire by wind is borne,
Crackling it rolls, and mows the standing corn;
Or deluges, descending on the plains,
Sweep o'er the yellow year, destroy the pains
Of lab'ring oxen, and the peasant's gains;   410
Unroot the forest oaks, and bear away
Flocks, folds, and trees, an undistinguished prey.
The shepherd climbs the cliff, and sees from far
The wasteful ravage of the watery war.

Then Hector's faith was manifestly cleared;   415
And Grecian frauds in open light appeared.
The palace of Deïphobus ascends
In smoky flames, and catches on his friends'.
Ucalegon's burns next: the seas are bright
With splendor not their own, and shine with Trojan light.   420
New clamors and new clangors now arise,
The sound of trumpets mixed with fighting cries.
With frenzy seized, I run to meet the alarms,
Resolved on death, resolved to die in arms,
But first to gather friends, with them to oppose   425
(If fortune favored) and repel the foes:
Spurred by my courage, by my country fired
With sense of honor, and revenge inspired.

Panthus, Apollo's priest, a sacred name,
Had 'scaped the Grecian swords and passed the flame.   430
With relics laden, to my doors he fled,
And by the hand his tender grandson led.
'What hope, O Panthus! whither can we run?
Where make a stand? and what may yet be done?'
Scarce had I said, when Panthus, with a groan: 435
'Troy is no more, and Ilium was a town!
The fatal day, the appointed hour is come,
When wrathful Jove's irrevocable doom
Transfers the Trojan state to Grecian hands.
The fire consumes the town, the foe commands;   440
And armed hosts, an unexpected force,
Break from the bowels of the fatal horse.

436. *fuimus Troes, fuit Ilium* . . . : An expressive Roman use of the perfect
tense. "We've had it," equally expressive, would be heard in a later war.

Within the gates, proud Sinon throws about
The flames; and foes, for entrance press without,
With thousand others, whom I fear to name, 445
More than from Argos or Mycenae came.
To several posts their parties they divide:
Some block the narrow streets, some scour the wide,
The bold they kill, the unwary they surprise;
Who fights finds death, and death finds him who flies. 450
The warders of the gate but scarce maintain
The unequal combat, and resist in vain.'
    I heard; and heaven, that well-born souls inspires,
Prompts me, through lifted swords and rising fires,
To run, where clashing arms and clamor calls, 455
And rush undaunted to defend the walls.
Ripheus and Iphitus by my side engage;
For valor one renowned, and one for age.
Dymas and Hypanis by moonlight knew
My motions and my mien, and to my party drew; 460
With young Choroebus, who by love was led
To win renown, and fair Cassandra's bed;
And lately brought his troops to Priam's aid,
Forewarned in vain by the prophetic maid;
Whom when I saw resolved in arms to fall, 465
And that one spirit animated all,
'Brave souls! (said I) but brave, alas! in vain;
Come, finish what our cruel fates ordain:
You see the desperate state of our affairs;
And Heaven's protecting powers are deaf to prayers. 470
The passive gods behold the Greeks defile
Their temples, and abandon to the spoil
Their own abodes: we, feeble few, conspire
To save a sinking town, involved in fire.
Then let us fall, but fall amidst our foes: 475
Despair of life the means of living shows.'
So bold a speech encouraged their desire
Of death, and added fuel to their fire.

450. A line more Ovidian than Virgilian, and all Dryden's.
476. *una salus victis nullam sperare salutem:* "for the vanquished the one
safety is to hope for none."

As hungry wolves, with raging appetite,
Scour through the fields, nor fear the stormy night: 480
Their whelps at home expect the promised food,
And long to temper their dry chaps in blood:
So rushed we forth at once: resolved to die,
Resolved, in death, the last extremes to try,
We leave the narrow lanes behind, and dare   485
The unequal combat in the public square:
Night was our friend; our leader was despair.
What tongue can tell the slaughter of that night?
What eyes can weep the sorrows and affright?
An ancient and imperial city falls;   490
The streets are filled with frequent funerals;
Houses and holy temples float in blood;
And hostile nations make a common flood.
Not only Trojans fall; but, in their turn,
The vanquished triumph, and the victors mourn.   495
Ours take new courage from despair and night.
Confused the fortune is, confused the fight.
All parts resound with tumults, plaints, and fears;
And grisly death in sundry shapes appears.

Androgeos fell among us, with his band,   500
Who thought us Grecians newly come to land.
'From whence (said he), my friends, this long delay?
You loiter, while the spoils are borne away:
Our ships are laden with the Trojan store;
And you, like truants, come too late ashore.'   505
He said, but soon corrected his mistake,
Found by the doubtful answers which we make.
Amazed, he would have shunned the unequal fight;
But we, more numerous, intercept his flight.
As when some peasant in a bushy brake   510
Has with unwary footing pressed a snake,
He starts aside, astonished, when he spies
His rising crest, blue neck, and rolling eyes.
So, from our arms, surprised Androgeos flies
In vain; for him and his we compass round,   515

491. *frequent funerals*: corpses everywhere.

Possessed with fear, unknowing of the ground,
And of their lives an easy conquest found.
Thus fortune on our first endeavor smiled.
   Choroebus then, with youthful hopes beguiled,
Swol'n with success, and of a daring mind,   520
This new invention fatally designed
'My friends (said he), since fortune shows the way,
'Tis fit we should the auspicious guide obey;
For what has she these Grecian arms bestowed,
But their destruction, and the Trojans' good?   525
Then change we shields, and their devices bear:
Let fraud supply the want of force in war.
They find us arms.' This said, himself he dressed
In dead Androgeos' spoils, his upper vest,
His painted buckler, and his plumy crest.   530
Thus Ripheus, Dymas, all the Trojan train,
Lay down their own attire, and strip the slain.
Mixed with the Greeks, we go with ill presage,
Flattered with hopes to glut our greedy rage;
Unknown, assaulting whom we blindly meet,   535
And strew with Grecian carcases, the street.
Thus while their straggling parties we defeat,
Some to the shore and safer ships retreat;
And some, oppressed with more ignoble fear,
Remount the hollow horse, and pant in secret there.   540
   But ah! what use of valor can be made,
When heaven's propitious powers refuse their aid?
Behold the royal prophetess, the fair
Cassandra, dragged by her disheveled hair;
Whom not Minerva's shrine, nor sacred bands,   545
In safety could protect from sacrilegious hands.
On heaven she cast her eyes, she sighed, she cried—
'Twas all she could—her tender arms were tied.
So sad a sight Choroebus could not bear;
But, fired with rage, distracted with despair,   550
Amid the barbarous ravishers he flew:

529. *his upper vest*: for the rhyme.

Our leader's rash example we pursue.
But storms of stones, from the proud temple's height
Pour down, and on our battered helms alight:
We from our friends received this fatal blow,   555
Who thought us Grecians, as we seemed in show.
They aim at the mistaken crests, from high;
And ours beneath the ponderous ruin lie.
Then, moved with anger and disdain, to see
Their troops dispersed, the royal virgin free,   560
The Grecians rally, and their powers unite,
With fury charge us, and renew the fight.
The brother-kings with Ajax join their force,
And the whole squadron of Thessalian horse.
        Thus, when the rival winds their quarrel try,   565
Contending for the empire of the sky,
South, East, and West, on airy coursers borne:
The whirlwind gathers, and the woods are torn:
Then Nereus strikes the deep: the billows rise,
And, mixed with ooze and sand, pollute the skies.   570
The troops we squandered first, again appear
From several quarters, and inclose the rear.
They first observe, and to the rest betray
Our different speech: our borrowed arms survey.
Oppressed with odds, we fall; Choroebus first,   575
At Pallas' altar, by Peneleus pierced.
Then Ripheus followed, in the unequal fight;
Just of his word, observant of the right:
Heaven thought not so. Dymas their fate attends,
With Hypanis, mistaken by their friends.   580
Nor, Panthus, thee thy miter nor the bands
Of awful Phoebus, saved from impious hands.
Ye Trojan flames! your testimony bear,
What I performed and what I suffered there;
No sword avoiding in the fatal strife,   585
Exposed to death, and prodigal of life.

    579. *Heaven thought not so: dis aliter visum.* Dante reproved this melancholy
touch by putting Ripheus in his *Paradiso* (XX, 68).

Witness ye heavens! I live not by my fault:
I strove to have deserved the death I sought.
But when I could not fight, and would have died;
Borne off to distance by the growing tide,   590
Old Iphitus and I were hurried thence,
With Pelias, wounded, and without defense.
New clamors from the invested palace ring:
We run to die, or disengage the king.
So hot the assault, so high the tumult rose,   595
While ours defend, and while the Greeks oppose,
As all the Dardan and Argolic race
Has been contracted in that narrow space;
Or, as all Ilium else were void of fear,
And tumult, war, and slaughter, only there.   600
Their targets in a tortoise cast, the foes,
Secure advancing, to the turrets rose:
Some mount the scaling ladders; some, more bold,
Swerve upwards, and by posts and pillars hold:
Their left hand grips their bucklers in the ascent,   605
While with the right they seize the battlement.
From the demolished towers, the Trojans throw
Huge heaps of stones, that, falling, crush the foe:
And heavy beams and rafters from the sides
(Such arms their last necessity provides!)   610
And gilded roofs, come tumbling from on high,
The marks of state and ancient royalty.
The guards below, fixed in the pass, attend
The charge, undaunted, and the gate defend.
Renewed in courage with recovered breath,   615
A second time we ran to tempt our death,
To clear the palace from the foe, succeed
The weary living, and revenge the dead.
    A postern-door, yet unobserved and free,
Joined by the length of a blind gallery,   620
To the king's closet led (a way well known
To Hector's wife, while Priam held the throne—
Through which she brought Astyanax, unseen,
To cheer his grandsire, and his grandsire's queen).

Through this we pass, and mount the tower, from whence   625
With unavailing arms the Trojans make defense.
From this the trembling king had oft descried
The Grecian camp, and saw their navy ride.
Beams from its lofty height with swords we hew,
Then, wrenching with our hands, the assault renew,   630
And where the rafters on the columns meet,
We push them headlong with our arms and feet.
The lightning flies not swifter than the fall;
Nor thunder louder than the ruined wall:
Down goes the top at once: the Greeks beneath   635
Are piecemeal torn, or pounded into death.
Yet more succeed, and more to death are sent:
We cease not from above, nor they below relent.
    Before the gate stood Pyrrhus, threatening loud,
With glittering arms conspicuous in the crowd.   640
So shines, renewed in youth, the crested snake
Who slept the winter in a thorny brake,
And casting off his slough when spring returns,
Now looks aloft, and with new glory burns,
Restored with poisonous herbs; his ardent sides   645
Reflect the sun; and, raised on spires, he rides
High o'er the grass: hissing he rolls along,
And brandishes by fits his forky tongue.
Proud Periphas, and fierce Automedon,
His father's charioteer, together run   650
To force the gate: the Scyrian infantry
Rush on in crowds, and the barred passage free.
Entering the court, with shouts the skies they rend,
And flaming firebrands to the roofs ascend.
Himself, among the foremost, deals his blows,   655
And with his axe repeated strokes bestows
On the strong doors: then all their shoulders ply,
Till from the posts the brazen hinges fly.
He hews apace: the double bars at length
Yield to his axe, and unresisted strength.   660

    639. Pyrrhus: Neoptolemus, Achilles' son.

A mighty breach is made; the rooms concealed,
Appear, and all the palace is revealed:
The halls of audience, and of public state,
And where the lonely queen in secret sat.
 Armed soldiers now by trembling maids are seen,   665
With not a door, and scarce a space between.
The house is filled with loud laments and cries;
And shrieks of women rend the vaulted skies.
The fearful matrons run from place to place,
And kiss the thresholds, and the posts embrace.   670
The fatal work inhuman Pyrrhus plies;
And all his father sparkles in his eyes.
No bars nor fighting guards his force sustain:
The bars are broken, and the guards are slain.
In rush the Greeks, and all the apartments fill;   675
Those few defendants whom they find, they kill.
Not with so fierce a rage, the foaming flood
Roars when he finds his rapid course withstood,
Bears down the dams with unresisted sway,
And sweeps the cattle and the cots away.   680
These eyes beheld him when he marched between
The brother-kings: I saw the unhappy queen,
The hundred wives, and where old Priam stood,
To stain his hallowed altar with his blood.
The fifty nuptial beds (such hopes had he,   685
So large a promise of a progeny),
The posts of plated gold, and hung with spoils.
Fell the reward of the proud victor's toils.
Where'er the raging fire had left a space,
The Grecians enter, and possess the place.   690
 Perhaps you may of Priam's fate inquire.
He, when he saw his regal town on fire,
His ruined palace, and his entering foes,
On every side, inevitable woes:
In arms disused invests his limbs, decayed   695
Like them with age: a late and useless aid.

670. *And kiss the thresholds*: These prostrations were not imagined by Virgil.

His feeble shoulders scarce the weight sustain:
Loaded, not armed, he creeps along with pain,
Despairing of success, ambitious to be slain!
Uncovered but by heaven, there stood in view   700
An altar: near the hearth a laurel grew,
Doddered with age, whose boughs encompass round
The household gods, and shade the holy ground.
Here Hecuba, with all her helpless train
Of dames, for shelter sought, but sought in vain.   705
Driven like a flock of doves along the sky,
Their images they hug, and to their altars fly.
The queen, when she beheld her trembling lord,
And hanging by his side a heavy sword:
'What rage (she cried) has seized my husband's mind?   710
What arms are these, and to what use designed?
These times want other aids! Were Hector here,
E'en Hector now in vain, like Priam, would appear.
With us, one common shelter thou shalt find,
Or in one common fate with us be joined.'   715
She said, and with a last salute embraced
The poor old man, and by the laurel placed.
Behold! Polites, one of Priam's sons,
Pursued by Pyrrhus, there for safety runs.
Through swords and foes, amazed and hurt, he flies   720
Through empty courts, and open galleries.
Him Pyrrhus, urging with his lance, pursues,
And often reaches, and his thrusts renews.
The youth, transfixed, with lamentable cries
Expires before his wretched parents' eyes: 725
Whom gasping at his feet when Priam saw,
The fear of death gave place to Nature's law;
And, shaking more with anger than with age:
'The gods (said he) requite thy brutal rage!
(As sure they will, barbarian, sure they must,   730
If there be gods in heaven, and gods be just)

---

702. *Doddered*: According to Kinsley, "dottard" meant a decayed trunk in
Northamptonshire; to "dod" meant to lop. The first meaning is obviously pref-
erable here.

Who takest in wrongs an insolent delight;
With a son's death to infect a father's sight.
Not he, whom thou and lying fame conspire
To call thee his—not he, thy vaunted sire   735
Thus used my wretched age: the gods he feared,
The laws of nature and of nations heard.
He cheered my sorrows, and, for sums of gold,
The bloodless carcase of my Hector sold;
Pitied the woes a parent underwent,   740
And sent me back in safety from his tent.'
    This said, his feeble hand a javelin threw,
Which, fluttering, seemed to loiter as it flew:
Just, and but barely, to the mark it held,
And faintly tinkled on the brazen shield.   745
    Then Pyrrhus thus: 'Go thou from me to fate,
And to my father my foul deeds relate.
Now die!' With that he dragged the trembling sire,
Sliddering through clottered blood and holy mire
(The mingled paste his murdered son had made),   750
Hauled from beneath the violated shade,
And on the sacred pile the royal victim laid.
His right hand held his bloody falchion bare;
His left he twisted in his hoary hair;
Then, with a speeding thrust his heart he found: 755
The lukewarm blood came rushing through the wound,
And sanguine streams distained the sacred ground.
Thus Priam fell, and shared one common fate
With Troy in ashes, and his ruined state:
He, who the scepter of all Asia swayed,   760
Whom monarchs like domestic slaves obeyed!
On the bleak shore now lies the abandoned king,
A headless carcase, and a nameless thing!
    Then, not before, I felt my curdled blood
Congealed with fear; my hair with horror stood: 765

734–5. I.e., you are no true son of the hero who showed me mercy.
  763. In a footnote Dryden acknowledged taking this line from Denham, from who he also took lines 274, 318, 351, 442 and 514. It is one of Virgil's mysterious great moments, suggesting to us the defaced and broken sculpture of antiquity.

My father's image filled my pious mind,
Lest equal years might equal fortune find.
Again I thought on my forsaken wife,
And trembled for my son's abandoned life.
I looked about, but found myself alone,   770
Deserted at my need! My friends were gone!
Some spent with toil, some with despair oppressed
Leaped headlong from the heights; the flames consumed the rest.
Thus, wandering in my way without a guide,
The graceless Helen in the porch I spied   775
Of Vesta's temple; there she lurked alone;
Muffled she sat, and what she could, unknown;
But by the flames that cast their blaze around,
That common bane of Greece and Troy I found:
For Ilium burnt, she dreads the Trojan sword;   780
More dreads the vengeance of her injured lord:
E'en by those gods who refuged her, abhorred.
Trembling with rage, the strumpet I regard,
Resolved to give her guilt the due reward.
'Shall she triumphant sail before the wind,   785
And leave in flames unhappy Troy behind?
Shall she her kingdom and her friends review,
In state attended with a captive crew,
While unrevenged the good old Priam falls,
And Grecian fires consume the Trojan walls?   790
For this the Phrygian fields and Xanthian flood
Were swelled with bodies, and were drunk with blood!
'Tis true, a soldier can small honor gain,
And boast no conquest from a woman slain;
Yet shall the fact not pass without applause,   795
Of vengeance taken in so just a cause.
The punished crime shall set my soul at ease,
And murmuring manës of my friends appease.'
    Thus while I rave, a gleam of pleasing light
Spread o'er the place; and, shining heavenly bright,   800
My mother stood revealed before my sight

798. *manës*: shades.

(Never so radiant did her eyes appear;
Not her own star confessed a light so clear):
Great in her charms, as when on gods above
She looks, and breathes herself into their love.   805
She held my hand, the destined blow to break;
Then from her rosy lips began to speak:
'My son! from whence this madness, this neglect
Of my commands, and those whom I protect?
Why this unmanly rage? Recall to mind   810
Whom you forsake, what pledges leave behind.
Look if your helpless father yet survive,
Or if Ascanius or Creüsa live.
Around your house the greedy Grecians err;
And these had perished in the nightly war   815
But for my presence, and protecting care.
Not Helen's face, nor Paris, was in fault;
But by the gods was this destruction brought.
Now cast your eyes around, while I dissolve
The mists and films that mortal eyes involve,   820
Purge from your sight the dross, and make you see
The shape of each avenging deity.
Enlightened thus, my just commands fulfill,
Nor fear obedience to your mother's will.
Where yon disordered heap of ruin lies,   825
Stones rent from stones—where clouds of dust arise,—
Amid that smother, Neptune holds his place,
Below the wall's foundation drives his mace,
And heaves the building from the solid base.
Look! where in arms, imperial Juno stands,   830
Full in the Scaean gate, with loud commands
Urging on shore the tardy Grecian bands.
See! Pallas, of her snaky buckler proud,
Bestrides the tower, refulgent through the cloud:
See! Jove new courage to the foe supplies,   835
And arms against the town the partial deities.
Haste hence, my son! this fruitless labor end:
Haste! where your trembling spouse and sire attend:
Haste! and a mother's care your passage shall befriend.'

She said, and swiftly vanished from my sight,   840
Obscure in clouds, and gloomy shades of night.
  I looked, I listened! dreadful sounds I hear;
And the dire forms of hostile gods appear,
Troy sunk in flames I saw (nor could prevent),
And Ilium from its old foundations rent—   845
Rent like a mountain-ash, which dared the winds,
And stood the sturdy strokes of laboring hinds.
About the roots the cruel axe resounds;
The stumps are pierced with oft-repeated wounds:
The war is felt on high; the nodding crown   850
Now threats a fall, and throws the leafy honors down.
To their united force it yields, though late,
And mourns with mortal groans the approaching fate:
The roots no more their upper load sustain;
But down she falls, and spreads a ruin through the plain.   855
  Descending thence, I 'scape through foes and fire:
Before the goddess, foes and flames retire.
Arrived at home, he, for whose only sake,
Or most for his, such toils I undertake—
The good Anchises—whom, by timely flight,   860
I purposed to secure on Ida's height—
Refused the journey, resolute to die,
And add his funerals to the fate of Troy,
Rather than exile and old age sustain.
'Go you, whose blood runs warm in every vein.   865
Had heaven decreed that I should life enjoy,
Heaven had decreed to save unhappy Troy.
'Tis, sure, enough, if not too much, for one,
Twice to have seen our Ilium overthrown.
Make haste to save the poor remaining crew;   870
And give this useless corpse a long adieu.
These weak old hands suffice to stop my breath:
At least the pitying foes will aid my death,
To take my spoils, and leave my body bare:
As for my sepulcher, let Heaven take care.   875

  876. *my celestial wife*: Venus, of course.

'Tis long since I, for my celestial wife
Loathed by the gods, have dragged a lingering life;
Since every hour and moment I expire,
Blasted from heaven by Jove's avenging fire.'
This oft repeated, he stood fixed to die: 880
Myself, my wife, my son, my family,
Entreat, pray, beg, and raise a doleful cry—
'What! will he still persist, on death resolve,
And in his ruin all his house involve?'
He still persists his reasons to maintain;   885
Our prayers, our tears, our loud laments are vain.
   Urged by despair, again I go to try
The fate of arms, resolved in fight to die.
What hope remains, but what my death must give?
'Can I without so dear a father, live?   890
You term it prudence, what I baseness call:
Could such a word from such a parent fall?
If fortune please, and so the gods ordain,
That nothing should of ruined Troy remain,
And you conspire with fortune to be slain;   895
The way to death is wide, the approaches near;
For soon relentless Pyrrhus will appear,
Reeking with Priam's blood—the wretch who slew
The son (inhuman) in the father's view;
And then the sire himself to the dire altar drew.   900
O goddess mother! give me back to fate;
Your gift was undesired, and came too late.
Did you, for this, unhappy me convey
Through foes and fires, to see my house a prey!
Shall I my father, wife, and son, behold   905
Weltering in blood, each others' arms infold?
Haste! gird my sword, though spent and overcome;
'Tis the last summons to receive our doom.
I hear thee, fate! and I obey thy call!
Not unrevenged the foe shall see my fall.   910
Restore me to the yet unfinished fight:
My death is wanting to conclude the night.'

   912. All Dryden's.

Armed once again, my glittering sword I wield,
While the other hand sustains my weighty shield;
And forth I rush to seek the abandoned field.   915
I went; but sad Creüsa stopped my way,
And 'cross the threshold in my passage lay,
Embraced my knees, and, when I would have gone,
Showed me my feeble sire, and tender son.
'If death be your design—at least (said she)   920
Take us along, to share your destiny.
If any further hopes in arms remain,
This place, these pledges of your love, maintain.
To whom do you expose your father's life,
Your son's, and mine, your now forgotten wife?'   925
    While thus she fills the house with clamorous cries,
Our hearing is diverted by our eyes:
For, while I held my son, in the short space
Betwixt our kisses and our last embrace,
(Strange to relate!) from young Iülus' head   930
A lambent flame arose, which gently spread
Around his brows, and on his temples fed.
Amazed, with running water we prepare
To quench the sacred fire, and slake his hair;
But old Anchises, versed in omens, reared   935
His hands to heaven, and this request preferred:
'If any vows, almighty Jove, can bend
Thy will, if piety can prayers commend;
Confirm the glad presage which thou art pleased to send.'
Scarce had he said, when on our left we hear   940
A peal of rattling thunder roll in air:
There shot a streaming lamp along the sky,
Which on the wingèd lightning seemed to fly;
From o'er the roof the blaze began to move,
And, trailing, vanished in the Idean grove.   945
It swept a path in heaven, and shone a guide,
Then in a steaming stench of sulfur died.
    The good old man with suppliant hands implored
The gods' protection, and their star adored.
'Now, now (said he), my son, no more delay!   950
I yield, I follow where heaven shows the way.

Keep (O my country gods!) our dwelling place,
And guard the relic of this Trojan race,
This tender child!—These omens are your own;
And you can yet restore the ruined town.   955
At least accomplish what your signs foreshow:
I stand resigned, and am prepared to go.'
   He said; the crackling flames appear on high,
And driving sparkles dance along the sky;
With Vulcan's rage the rising winds conspire,   960
And near our palace roll the flood of fire.
'Haste, my dear father! ('tis no time to wait)
And load my shoulders with a willing freight.
Whate'er befalls, your life shall be my care;
One death, or one deliverance we will share.   965
My hand shall lead our little son; and you,
My faithful consort, shall our steps pursue.
Next, you my servants, heed my strict commands:
Without the walls a ruined temple stands,
To Ceres hallowed once: a cypress nigh   970
Shoots up her venerable head on high,
By long religion kept: there bend your feet;
And in divided parties let us meet.
Our country gods, the relics, and the bands,
Hold you, my father, in your guiltless hands: 975
In me 'tis impious, holy things to bear,
Red as I am with slaughter, new from war,
Till in some living stream I cleanse the guilt
Of dire debate, and blood in battle spilt.'
Thus, ordering all that prudence could provide,   980
I clothe my shoulders with a lion's hide
And yellow spoils; then, on my bending back,
The welcome load of my dear father take;
While on my better hand Ascanius hung,
And with unequal paces tripped along.   985
Creüsa kept behind: by choice we stray
Through every dark and every devious way.
I, who so bold and dauntless, just before,
The Grecian darts and shock of lances bore,

974. *bands*: fillets.

At every shadow now, am seized with fear,   990
Not for myself, but for the charge I bear;
Till, near the ruined gate arrived at last,
Secure, and deeming all the danger past,
A frightful noise of trampling feet we hear.
My father, looking through the shades with fear,   995
Cried out, 'Haste, haste, my son! the foes are nigh;
Their swords and shining armor I descry.'
Some hostile god, for some unknown offense,
Had sure bereft my mind of better sense;
For, while through winding ways I took my flight,   1000
And sought the shelter of the gloomy night,
Alas! I lost Creüsa: hard to tell
If by her fatal destiny she fell,
Or weary sat, or wandered with affright;
But she was lost for ever to my sight.   1005
I knew not, or reflected, till I meet
My friends at Ceres' now-deserted seat.
We met: not one was wanting; only she
Deceived her friends, her son, and wretched me.
What mad expressions did my tongue refuse?   1010
Whom did I not of gods or men accuse?
This was the fatal blow, that pained me more
Than all I felt from ruined Troy before.
    Stung with my loss, and raving with despair,
Abandoning my now-forgotten care,   1015
Of counsel, comfort, and of hope bereft,
My sire, my son, my country gods, I left.
In shining armor once again I sheath
My limbs, not feeling wounds, nor fearing death;
Then headlong to the burning walls I run,   1020
And seek the danger I was forced to shun.
I tread my former tracks, through night explore
Each passage, every street I crossed before.
All things were full of horror and affright,
And dreadful e'en the silence of the night.   1025
Then to my father's house I make repair,
With some small glimpse of hope to find her there.

Instead of her, the cruel Greeks I met:
The house was filled with foes, with flames beset.
Driven on the wings of winds, whole sheets of fire   1030
Through air transported, to the roofs aspire.
From thence to Priam's palace I resort,
And search the citadel, and desert court.
Then, unobserved, I pass by Juno's church:
A guard of Grecians had possessed the porch;   1035
There Phoenix and Ulysses watch the prey;
And thither all the wealth of Troy convey:
The spoils which they from ransacked houses brought;
And golden bowls from burning altars caught;
The tables of the gods, the purple vests,   1040
The people's treasure, and the pomp of priests.
A rank of wretched youths, with pinioned hands,
And captive matrons, in long order stands.
Then, with ungoverned madness, I proclaim
Through all the silent streets Creüsa's name: 1045
Creüsa still I call: at length she hears,
And sudden, through the shades of night, appears—
Appears, no more Creüsa, nor my wife,
But a pale specter, larger than the life.
Aghast, astonished, and struck dumb with fear   1050
I stood: like bristles rose my stiffened hair.
Then thus the ghost began to soothe my grief:
'Nor tears, nor cries, can give the dead relief.
Desist, my much-loved lord, to indulge your pain;
You bear no more than what the gods ordain.   1055
My fates permit me not from hence to fly;
Nor he, the great controller of the sky.
Long wand'ring ways for you the powers decree:
On land, hard labors, and a length of sea.
Then, after many painful years are past,   1060
On Latium's happy shore you shall be cast;
Where gentle Tiber from his bed beholds
The flowery meadows, and the feeding folds.
There, end your toils, and there your fates provide
A quiet kingdom, and a royal bride: 1065

There Fortune shall the Trojan line restore;
And you for lost Creüsa weep no more.
Fear not that I shall watch, with servile shame,
The imperious looks of some proud Grecian dame;
Or, stooping to the victor's lust, disgrace   1070
My goddess-mother, or my royal race.
And now, farewell! the parent of the gods
Restrains my fleeting soul in her abodes.
I trust our common issue to your care.'
She said, and gliding passed unseen in air.   1075
I strove to speak; but horror tied my tongue;
And thrice about her neck my arms I flung,
And thrice deceived, on vain embraces hung:
Light as an empty dream at break of day,
Or as a blast of wind, she rushed away.   1080
   Thus having passed the night in fruitless pain,
I to my longing friends return again
(Amazed the augmented number to behold,
Of men and matrons mixed, of young and old):
A wretched exiled crew together brought,   1085
With arms appointed, and with treasure fraught,
Resolved, and willing, under my command
To run all hazards both of sea and land.
The Morn begun, from Ida, to display
Her rosy cheeks; and Phosphor led the day: 1090
Before the gates the Grecians took their post,
And all pretense of late relief was lost.
I yield to Fate, unwillingly retire,
And, loaded, up the hill convey my sire."

1071. *my goddess-mother*: Venus, her mother-in-law.
1072. *the parent of the Gods*: Cybele, worshiped in Phrygia and on the
Trojan Mount Ida, and identified with Gea, the Earth.
1090. *Phosphor*: Dryden uses the Greek word for the Latin Lucifer, the
Morning Star.

BOOK III

THE ARGUMENT

Aeneas proceeds in his relation: he gives an account of the fleet with which he sailed, and the success of his first voyage to Thrace. From thence he directs his course to Delos, and asks the oracle what place the gods had appointed for his habitation. By a mistake of the oracle's answer, he settles in Crete. His household gods give him the true sense of the oracle in a dream. He follows their advice, and makes the best of his way for Italy. He is cast on several shores, and meets with very surprising adventures, till at length he lands on Sicily, where his father Anchises dies. This is the place which he was sailing from, when the tempest rose, and threw him upon the Carthaginian coast.

"WHEN Heaven had overturned the Trojan state
And Priam's throne, by too severe a fate;
When ruined Troy became the Grecian's prey,
And Ilium's lofty towers in ashes lay;
Warned by celestial omens, we retreat,   5
To seek in foreign lands a happier seat.
Near old Antandros, and at Ida's foot,
The timber of the sacred groves we cut,
And build our fleet—uncertain yet to find
What place the gods for our repose assigned.   10
Friends daily flock; and scarce the kindly spring
Began to clothe the ground, and birds to sing,

---

7. *Ida's foot.* There are two Mount Idas. One is on Crete and Jove was said to have been born there (line 145). The other is a range in South Phrygia in Trojan country.

When old Anchises summoned all to sea:
The crew, my father and the Fates obey.
With sighs and tears I leave my native shore,   15
And empty fields, where Ilium stood before.
My sire, my son, our less and greater gods,
All sail at once, and cleave the briny floods.

Against our coast appears a spacious land,
Which once the fierce Lycurgus did command   20
(Thracia the name—the people bold in war—
Vast are their fields, and tillage is their care),
A hospitable realm while Fate was kind,
With Troy in friendship and religion joined.
I land with luckless omens; then adore   25
Their gods, and draw a line along the shore:
I lay the deep foundations of a wall,
And Aenos, named from me, the city call.
To Dionaean Venus vows are paid,
And all the powers that rising labors aid;   30
A bull on Jove's imperial altar laid.
Not far, a rising hillock stood in view.
Sharp myrtles on the sides, and cornels grew.
There, while I went to crop the sylvan scenes,
And shade our altar with their leafy greens,   35
I pulled a plant (with horror I relate
A prodigy so strange, and full of fate),
The rooted fibres rose, and from the wound,
Black bloody drops distilled upon the ground.
Mute and amazed, my hair with terror stood;   40
Fear shrunk my sinews, and congealed my blood.
Manned once again, another plant I try;
That other gushed with the same sanguine dye.
Then fearing guilt for some offense unknown,
With prayers and vows the Dryads I atone,   45
With all the sisters of the woods, and most
The god of arms, who rules the Thracian coast—

19. *Against*: opposite, as in Book I, 19.
29. *Dionaean*. Dionë was the mother of Venus.
47. *The god of arms*: Mars (Ares) who when embarrassed in the *Odyssey*
(VIII, 361) retreated to Thrace.

That they, or he, these omens would avert,
Release our fears, and better signs impart.
Cleared, as I thought, and fully fixed at length 50
To learn the cause, I tugged with all my strength:
I bent my knees against the ground: once more
The violated myrtle ran with gore.
Scarce dare I tell the sequel: from the womb
Of wounded earth, and caverns of the tomb, 55
A groan, as of a troubled ghost, renewed
My fright, and then these dreadful words ensued:
'Why dost thou thus my buried body rend?
O! spare the corpse of thy unhappy friend!
Spare to pollute thy pious hands with blood: 60
The tears distill not from the wounded wood;
But every drop this living tree contains,
Is kindred blood, and ran in Trojan veins.
O! fly from this unhospitable shore,
Warned by my fate; for I am Polydore! 65
Here loads of lances; in my blood embrued,
Again shoot upward, by my blood renewed.'
　My faltering tongue and shivering limbs declare
My horror, and in bristles rose my hair.
When Troy with Grecian arms was closely pent, 70
Old Priam, fearful of the war's event,
This hapless Polydore to Thracia sent:
Loaded with gold, he sent his darling far
From noise and tumults, and destructive war:
Committed to the faithless tyrant's care; 75
Who, when he saw the power of Troy decline,
Forsook the weaker, with the strong to join:
Broke every bond of nature and of truth,
And murdered, for his wealth, the royal youth.
O sacred hunger of pernicious gold! 80
What bands of faith can impious lucre hold?
Now, when my soul had shaken off her fears,
I call my father, and the Trojan peers—

66. *loads of lances*: *telorum seges*. Virgil suggests a "crop" of them.
80. *sacred*: *sacra*, which can also mean accursed, and does here.

Relate the prodigies of heaven—require
What he commands, and their advice desire.   85
All vote to leave that execrable shore,
Polluted with the blood of Polydore;
But, ere we sail, his funeral rites prepare;
Then to his ghost, a tomb and altars rear.
In mournful pomp the matrons walk the round,   90
With baleful cypress and blue fillets crowned,
With eyes dejected, and with hair unbound.
Then bowls of tepid milk and blood we pour,
And thrice invoke the soul of Polydore.

   Now, when the raging storms no longer reign,   95
But southern gales invite us to the main,
We launch our vessels, with a prosperous wind,
And leave the cities and the shores behind.

   An island in the Aegaean main appears:
Neptune and watery Doris claim it theirs.   100
It floated once, till Phoebus fixed the sides
To rooted earth; and now it braves the tides.
Here, borne by friendly winds, we come ashore,
With needful ease our weary limbs restore,
And the Sun's temple and his town adore.   105

   Anius, the priest and king, with laurel crowned,
His hoary locks with purple fillets bound,
Who saw my sire the Delian shore ascend,
Came forth with eager haste to meet his friend:
Invites him to his palace; and in sign   110
Of ancient love, their plighted hands they join.
Then to the temple of the god I went,
And thus, before the shrine, my vows present:
'Give, O Thymbraeus! give a resting place
To the sad relics of the Trojan race: 115
A seat secure, a region of their own,
A lasting empire, and a happier town.
Where shall we fix? where shall our labors end?
Whom shall we follow, and what fate attend?

   99. *An island*: Delos.
   100. *Doris*: *nereidum matri*, mother of the nereids.
   114. *Thymbraeus*: Apollo.

Let not my prayers a doubtful answer find;   120
But in clear auguries unveil thy mind.'
Scarce had I said: he shook the holy ground,
The laurels, and the lofty hills around;
And from the tripos rushed a bellowing sound.
Prostrate we fell; confessed the present god,   125
Who gave this answer from his dark abode:
'Undaunted youths! go, seek that mother earth
From which your ancestors derive their birth.
The soil that sent you forth, her ancient race,
In her old bosom shall again embrace.   130
Through the wide world the Aeneian house shall reign,
And children's children shall the crown sustain.'
Thus Phoebus did our future fates disclose;
A mighty tumult, mixed with joy, arose.
All are concerned to know what place the god   135
Assigned, and where determined our abode.
My father, long revolving in his mind
The race and lineage of the Trojan kind,
Thus answered their demands: 'Ye princes! hear
Your pleasing fortune, and dispel your fear.   140
The fruitful isle of Crete, well known to fame,
Sacred of old to Jove's imperial name,
In the mid-ocean lies, with large command;
And on its plains a hundred cities stand.
Another Ida rises there; and we   145
From thence derive our Trojan ancestry.
From thence, as 'tis divulged by certain fame,
To the Rhoetean shores old Teucer came;
There fixed, and there the seat of empire chose,
Ere Ilium and the Trojan towers arose.   150
In humble vales they built their soft abodes;
Till Cybele, the mother of the gods,
With tinkling cymbals charmed the Idean woods.
She secret rites and ceremonies taught,
And to the yoke the savage lions brought.   155

124. *the tripos*: A seat with three legs, used by the priestess at the oracle of
Apollo at Delphi. Here it simply means an oracular shrine.
148. *Rhoetean*: Trojan.

Let us the land which Heaven appoints, explore;
Appease the winds, and seek the Gnossian shore.
If Jove assists the passage of our fleet,
The third propitious dawn discovers Crete.'
Thus having said, the sacrifices, laid   160
On smoking altars, to the gods he paid:
A bull to Neptune, an oblation due,
Another bull to bright Apollo, slew:
A milk-white ewe, the western winds to please,
And one coal-black, to calm the stormy seas.   165
Ere this, a flying rumor had been spread,
That fierce Idomeneus from Crete was fled,
Expelled and exiled; that the coast was free
From foreign or domestic enemy.

We leave the Delian ports, and put to sea;   170
By Naxos, famed for vintage, make our way;
Then green Donysa pass; and sail in sight
Of Paros' isle, with marble quarries white.
We pass the scattered isles of Cyclades,
That, scarce distinguished, seem to stud the seas.   175
The shouts of sailors double near the shores;
They stretch their canvas, and they ply their oars.
'All hands aloft! for Crete! for Crete!' they cry,
And swiftly through the foamy billows fly.
Full on the promised land at length we bore,   180
With joy descending on the Cretan shore.
With eager haste a rising town I frame,
Which from the Trojan Pergamus I name:
The name itself was grateful:—I exhort
To found their houses, and erect a fort.   185
Our ships are hauled upon the yellow strand:
The youth begin to till the labored land;
And I myself new marriages promote,
Give laws; and dwellings I divide by lot:

159. *discovers*: reveals.
178. *All hands aloft*: Dryden liked nautical terms, but all hands did not go
aloft in the sailing ships of antiquity.

When rising vapors choke the wholesome air,   190
And blasts of noisome winds corrupt the year:
The trees, devouring caterpillars burn:
Parched was the grass, and blighted was the corn:
Nor 'scape the beasts; for Sirius, from on high
With pestilential heat infects the sky: 195
My men—some fall, the rest in fevers fry.
Again my father bids me seek the shore
Of sacred Delos, and the god implore,
To learn what end of woes we might expect,
And to what clime our weary course direct.   200
   'Twas night, when every creature void of cares,
The common gift of balmy slumber shares:
The statues of my gods (for such they seemed—
Those gods whom I from flaming Troy redeemed),
Before me stood, majestically bright,   205
Full in the beams of Phoebe's entering light.
Then thus they spoke, and eased my troubled mind:
'What from the Delian god thou goest to find,
He tells thee here, and sends us to relate.
Those powers are we, companions of thy fate,   210
Who from the burning town by thee were brought,
Thy fortune followed, and thy safety wrought.
Through seas and lands as we thy steps attend,
So shall our care thy glorious race befriend.
An ample realm for thee thy fates ordain,   215
A town, that o'er the conquered world shall reign.
Thou, mighty walls for mighty nations build;
Nor let thy weary mind to labors yield:
But change thy seat; for not the Delian god
Nor we, have given thee Crete for our abode.   220
A land there is, Hesperia called of old,
(The soil is fruitful, and the natives bold—
The Oenotrians held it once), by later fame
Now called Italia, from the leader's name.

191. *the year*: crops, as in Book II, 409.
206. *Phoebe*: A name for Diana (Artemis) and the moon.

Iäsius there, and Dardanus, were born: 225
From thence we came, and thither must return.
Rise, and thy sire with these glad tidings greet:
Search Italy; for Jove denies thee Crete.'
    Astonished at their voices and their sight,
(Nor were they dreams but visions of the night;   230
I saw, I knew their faces, and descried
In perfect view, their hair with fillets tied)
I started from my couch: a clammy sweat
On all my limbs, and shivering body, sat.
To heaven I lift my hands with pious haste,   235
And sacred incense in the flames I cast.
Thus to the gods their perfect honors done,
More cheerful to my good old sire I run,
And tell the pleasing news. In little space
He found his error of the double race,   240
Not, as before he deemed, derived from Crete;
No more deluded by the doubtful seat;
Then said: 'O son, turmoiled in Trojan fate!
Such things as these Cassandra did relate.
This day revives within my mind, what she   245
Foretold of Troy renewed in Italy,
And Latian lands: but who could then have thought
That Phrygian gods to Latium should be brought;
Or who believed what mad Cassandra taught?
Now let us go where Phoebus leads the way.'   250
    He said; and we with glad consent obey;
Forsake the seat; and, leaving few behind,
We spread our sails before the willing wind.
Now from the sight of land our galleys move,
With only seas around, and skies above;   255
When o'er our heads descends a burst of rain,
And night with sable clouds involves the main;
The ruffling winds the foamy billows raise;
The scattered fleet is forced to several ways;

    225. *Iäsius*: Born like Dardanus (Book I, 41) to Jupiter and Electra, mi-
grated with him from Italy to Asia Minor, where Dardanus married the daughter
of Teucrus (198). The Trojans, their descendants, were thus Teucrians or
Dardanians.

The face of heaven is ravished from our eyes;   260
And in redoubled peals the roaring thunder flies.
Cast from our course, we wander in the dark;
No stars to guide, no point of land to mark.
E'en Palinurus no distinction found
Betwixt the night and day; such darkness reigned around.   265
Three starless nights the doubtful navy strays
Without distinction, and three sunless days:
The fourth renews the light; and from our shrouds
We view a rising land, like distant clouds;
The mountain tops confirm the pleasing sight,   270
And curling smoke ascending from their height.
The canvas falls; their oars the sailors ply;
From the rude strokes the whirling waters fly.

At length I land upon the Strophades,
Safe from the danger of the stormy seas.   275
Those isles are compassed by the Ionian main;
The dire abode where the foul Harpies reign,
Forced by the wingèd warriors to repair
To their old homes, and leave their costly fare.
Monsters more fierce, offended Heaven ne'er sent   280
From hell's abyss, for human punishment:
With virgin-faces, but with wombs obscene,
Foul paunches, and with ordure still unclean;
With claws for hands, and looks for ever lean.

We landed at the port, and soon beheld   285
Fat herds of oxen graze the flowery field;
And wanton goats without a keeper strayed.
With weapons we the welcome prey invade;
Then call the gods for partners of our feast,
And Jove himself, the chief invited guest.   290
We spread the tables on the greensward ground;
We feed with hunger, and the bowls go round;
When from the mountain-tops, with hideous cry,
And clattering wings, the hungry Harpies fly:

264. *Palinurus*: the helmsman of Aeneas' ship.
277. *Harpies*: "snatchers," in Homer were storm winds, in Apollonius Rhodius they took the form they have here. Sent to torment King Phineus in Thrace, they were driven to the Strophades by two of the Argonauts.

They snatch the meat, defiling all they find,   295
And parting, leave a loathsome stench behind.
Close by a hollow rock, again we sit,
New-dress the dinner, and the beds refit,
Secure from sight, beneath a pleasing shade,
Where tufted trees a native arbor made.   300
Again the holy fires on altars burn;
And once again the ravenous birds return,
Or from the dark recesses where they lie,
Or from another quarter of the sky:
With filthy claws their odious meal repeat,   305
And mix their loathsome ordures with their meat.
  I bid my friends for vengeance then prepare,
And with the hellish nation wage the war.
They, as commanded, for the fight provide,
And in the grass their glittering weapons hide;   310
Then, when along the crooked shore we hear
Their clattering wings, and saw the foes appear,
Misenus sounds a charge: we take the alarm,
And our strong hands with swords and bucklers arm.
In this new kind of combat, all employ   315
Their utmost force, the monsters to destroy—
In vain:—the fated skin is proof to wounds;
And from their plumes the shining sword rebounds.
At length rebuffed, they leave their mangled prey,
And their stretched pinions to the skies display.   320
Yet one remained—the messenger of fate:
High on a craggy cliff Celaeno sat,
And thus her dismal errand did relate:
'What! not contented with our oxen slain,
Dare you with heaven an impious war maintain,   325
And drive the Harpies from their native reign?
Heed therefore what I say; and keep in mind
What Jove decrees, what Phoebus has designed,
And I, the Furies' queen, from both relate—
You seek the Italian shores: foredoomed by fate,   330
The Italian shores are granted you to find,
And a safe passage to the port assigned.

But know, that, ere your promised walls you build,
My curses shall severely be fulfilled.
Fierce famine is your lot: for this misdeed,   335
Reduced to grind the plates on which you feed.'
She said, and to the neighboring forest flew.
Our courage fails us, and our fears renew.
Hopeless to win by war, to prayers we fall,
And on the offended Harpies humbly call,   340
And (whether gods or birds obscene they were)
Our vows, for pardon and for peace, prefer.
But old Anchises, offering sacrifice,
And lifting up to heaven his hands and eyes,
Adored the greater gods—'Avert (said he)   345
These omens! render vain this prophecy,
And from the impending curse a pious people free.'
    Thus having said, he bids us put to sea.
We loose from shore our halsers, and obey,
And soon with swelling sails pursue our watery way.   350
Amidst our course, Zacynthian woods appear;
And next by rocky Neritos we steer:
We fly from Ithaca's detested shore,
And curse the land which dire Ulysses bore.
At length Leucate's cloudy top appears,   355
And the Sun's temple, which the sailor fears.
Resolved to breathe awhile from labor past,
Our crooked anchors from the prow we cast,
And joyful to the little city haste.
Here, safe beyond our hopes, our vows we pay   360
To Jove, the guide and patron of our way.
The customs of our country we pursue,
And Trojan games on Actian shores renew.

336. *to grind*: to eat; *ambesas . . . absumere mensas*, "to gnaw around and consume your trenchers." A prophecy fulfilled in Book VII, 159 sqq.

351 sqq. Virgil names all the islands of Ulysses' kingdom, Doulichion, Samë, Zacynthus and Ithaca, which he also calls Neritos, the name of its principal mountain.

363. *Actian*. Actium is not in fact on the island of Leucas but north of it on the mainland. Augustus had instituted quinquennial games there in memory of the great victory described in Book VIII, 897 sqq.

Our youth their naked limbs besmear with oil,
And exercise the wrestlers' noble toil: 365
Pleased to have sailed so long before the wind,
And left so many Grecian towns behind.
   The sun had now fulfilled his annual course,
And Boreas on the seas displayed his force:
I fixed upon the temple's lofty door   370
The brazen shield which vanquished Abas bore:
The verse beneath, my name and action speaks:
'These arms Aeneas took from conquering Greeks.'
Then I command to weigh: the seamen ply
Their sweeping oars: the smoking billows fly.   375
The sight of high Phaeacia soon we lost,
And skimmed along Epirus' rocky coast.
Then to Chaonia's port our course we bend,
And, landed, to Buthrotus' heights ascend.
Here wondrous things were loudly blazed by Fame: 380
How Helenus revived the Trojan name,
And reigned in Greece; that Priam's captive son
Succeeded Pyrrhus in his bed and throne;
And fair Andromache, restored by fate,
Once more was happy in a Trojan mate.   385
I leave my galleys riding in the port,
And long to see the new Dardanian court.
   By chance, the mournful queen, before the gate,
Then solemnized her former husband's fate.
Green altars, raised of turf, with gifts she crowned;   390
And sacred priests in order stand around,
And thrice the name of hapless Hector sound.
The grove itself resembles Ida's wood;
And Simoïs seemed the well-dissembled flood.

371. *Abas*: an early king of Argos. Homer does not mention him as vanquished by Aeneas, but by other accounts a wonderworking shield of his hung in
the temple of Juno at Argos.
   376. *Phaeacia*: Corcyra, or Corfu.
   380 sqq. Racine derived his play, *Andromache*, from this story. Andromache,
Hector's wife, became Pyrrhus' prize at Troy. Helenus, a seer and son of Priam,
was also taken prisoner by Pyrrhus. Homer refers to Achilles' son as ruling over
the Myrmidons in his father's Thessalian kingdom (*Odyssey*, Book IV) but here
he is in Epirus, furnishing an ancestor, no doubt, for that king who won a
"Pyrrhic" victory over the Romans in 279 B.C.

But when, at nearer distance, she beheld   395
My shining armor and my Trojan shield,
Astonished at the sight, the vital heat
Forsakes her limbs, her veins no longer beat:
She faints, she falls, and scarce recovering strength,
Thus, with a faltering tongue, she speaks at length: 400
'Are you alive, O goddess-born! (she said)
Or, if a ghost, then where is Hector's shade?'
At this she cast a loud and frightful cry.
With broken words I made this brief reply:
'All of me that remains, appears in sight;   405
I live; if living be to loathe the light—
No phantom; but I drag a wretched life;
My fate resembling that of Hector's wife.
What have you suffered since you lost your lord?
By what strange blessing are you now restored?   410
Still are you Hector's? or is Hector fled,
And his remembrance lost in Pyrrhus' bed?'
With eyes dejected, in a lowly tone,
After a modest pause, she thus begun:
'O only happy maid of Priam's race,   415
Whom death delivered from the foe's embrace!
Commanded on Achilles' tomb to die,
Not forced, like us, to hard captivity,
Or in a haughty master's arms to lie.
In Grecian ships, unhappy we were borne,   420
Endured the victor's lust, sustained the scorn:
Thus I submitted to the lawless pride
Of Pyrrhus, more a handmaid than a bride.
Cloyed with possession, he forsook my bed,
And Helen's lovely daughter sought to wed;   425
Then, me to Trojan Helenus resigned,
And his two slaves in equal marriage joined;
Till young Orestes, pierced with deep despair,
And longing to redeem the promised fair,

425. *Helen's lovely daughter*: Hermionë.
429. *the promised fair*: Hermionë.
430. *Before Apollo's altar*: retribution, since Pyrrhus had killed Priam at the
altar (Book II, 746 sqq.)

Before Apollo's altar slew the ravisher.   430
By Pyrrhus' death the kingdom we regained:
At least one half with Helenus remained.
Our part, from Chaon, he Chaonia calls;
And names, from Pergamus, his rising walls.
But you, what fates have landed on our coast?   435
What gods have sent you, or what storms have tossed?
Does young Ascanius life and health enjoy,
Saved from the ruins of unhappy Troy?
O! tell me how his mother's loss he bears,
What hopes are promised from his blooming years,   440
How much of Hector in his face appears?'
She spoke; and mixed her speech with mournful cries;
And fruitless tears came trickling from her eyes.
At length her lord descends upon the plain,
In pomp, attended with a numerous train;   445
Receives his friends, and to the city leads,
And tears of joy amidst his welcome sheds.
Proceeding on, another Troy I see,
Or in less compass, Troy's epitome.
A rivulet by the name of Xanthus ran;   450
And I embrace the Scaean gate again.
My friends in porticoes were entertained;
And feasts and pleasures through the city reigned.
The tables filled the spacious hall around;
And golden bowls with sparkling wine were crowned.   455
Two days we passed in mirth, till friendly gales,
Blown from the south, supplied our swelling sails;
Then to the royal seer I thus began:
'O thou who knowest beyond the reach of man,
The laws of heaven, and what the stars decree;   460
Whom Phoebus taught unerring prophecy,
From his own tripod, and his holy tree—
Skilled in the winged inhabitants of air,
What auspices their notes and flights declare—
O! say—(for all religious rights portend   465
A happy voyage, and a prosperous end;

And every power and omen of the sky
Direct my course for destined Italy;
But only dire Celaeno, from the gods,
A dismal famine fatally forebodes)—   470
O! say, what dangers I am first to shun,
What toils to vanquish, and what course to run.'
  The prophet first with sacrifice adores
The greater gods; their pardon then implores;
Unbinds the fillet from his holy head;   475
To Phoebus, next, my trembling steps he led,
Full of religious doubts and awful dread.
Then, with his god possessed, before the shrine
These words proceeded from his mouth divine:
'O goddess-born! (for heaven's appointed will,   480
With greater auspices of good than ill,
Foreshows thy voyage, and thy course directs;
Thy fates conspire, and Jove himself protects),
Of many things, some few I shall explain,
Teach thee to shun the dangers of the main,   485
And how at length the promised shore to gain.
The rest, the fates from Helenus conceal,
And Juno's angry power forbids to tell.
First then, that happy shore that seems so nigh,
Will far from your deluded wishes fly: 490
Long tracts of seas divide your hopes from Italy.
For you must cruise along Sicilian shores,
And stem the currents with your struggling oars;
Then round the Italian coast your navy steer;
And, after this, to Circe's island veer;   495
And last, before your new foundations rise,
Must pass the Stygian lake, and view the nether skies.
Now mark the signs of future ease and rest;
And bear them safely treasured in thy breast.
When, in the shady shelter of a wood,   500
And near the margin of a gentle flood,
Thou shalt behold a sow upon the ground,
With thirty sucking young encompassed round

(The dam and offspring white as falling snow);
These, on thy city shall their name bestow;   505
And there, shall end thy labors and thy woe.
Nor let the threatened famine fright thy mind;
For Phoebus will assist; and Fate the way will find.
Let not thy course to that ill coast be bent,
Which fronts from far the Epirian continent: 510
Those parts are all by Grecian foes possessed.
The savage Locrians here the shores infest:
There fierce Idomeneus his city builds,
And guards with arms the Salentinian fields;
And on the mountain's brow Petilia stands,   515
Which Philoctetes with his troops commands.
E'en when thy fleet is landed on the shore,
And priests with holy vows the gods adore,
Then with a purple veil involve your eyes,
Lest hostile faces blast the sacrifice.   520
These rites and customs to the rest commend,
That to your pious race they may descend.
    When, parted hence, the wind that ready waits
For Sicily, shall bear you to the straits:
Where proud Pelorus opes a wider way,   525
Tack to the larboard, and stand off to sea:
Veer starboard sea and land. The Italian shore
And fair Sicilia's coast were one, before
An earthquake caused the flaw: the roaring tides
The passage broke, that land from land divides;   530
And, where the lands retired, the rushing ocean rides
Distinguished by the straits, on either hand,
Now rising cities in long order stand,
And fruitful fields:—so much can time invade
The moldering work, that beauteous Nature made.   535

505. *their name*: rather, its name. Alba Longa would be the city, founded by
Ascanius after thirty years (the number of piglets in the farrow). *Alba*, white,
is Virgil's adjective for sow and farrow.
    511. *Those parts*: South Italy, Magna Graecia, was not in fact colonized by
Greeks until centuries after the Trojan War.
    519. *involve your eyes*: The Romans veiled their heads during prayer and
sacrifice.
    525. *a wider way*: The Straits of Messina appear to widen as you approach.

Far on the right, her dogs foul Scylla hides:
Charybdis roaring on the left presides,
And in her greedy whirlpool sucks the tides,
Then spouts them from below: with fury driven,
The waves mount up, and wash the face of heaven.   540
But Scylla from her den, with open jaws,
The sinking vessel in her eddy draws,
Then dashes on the rocks.—A human face,
And virgin bosom, hide her tail's disgrace:
Her parts obscene below the waves descend,   545
With dogs inclosed, and in a dolphin end.
'Tis safer, then, to bear aloof to sea,
And coast Pachynus, though with more delay,
Than once to view misshapen Scylla near,
And the loud yell of watery wolves to hear.   550
   Besides, if faith to Helenus be due,
And if prophetic Phoebus tell me true,
Do not this precept of your friend forget,
Which therefore more than once I must repeat
Above the rest, great Juno's name adore;   555
Pay vows to Juno; Juno's aid implore.
Let gifts be to the mighty queen designed;
And mollify with prayers her haughty mind.
Thus, at the length, your passage shall be free,
And you shall safe descend on Italy.   560
   Arrived at Cumae, when you view the flood
Of black Avernus, and the sounding wood,
The mad prophetic Sibyl you shall find,
Dark in a cave, and on a rock reclined.
She sings the fates, and in her frantic fits,   565
The notes and names, inscribed, to leaves commits.
What she commits to leaves, in order laid,
Before the cavern's entrance are displayed:
Unmoved they lie; but, if a blast of wind
Without, or vapors issue from behind,   570
The leaves are borne aloft in liquid air,
And she resumes no more her museful care;

546. *With dogs inclosed*: pregnant with predatory fish.

Nor gathers from the rocks her scattered verse,
Nor sets in order what the winds disperse.
Thus, many not succeeding, most upbraid   575
The madness of the visionary maid,
And with loud curses leave the mystic shade.
   Think it not loss of time awhile to stay,
Though thy companions chide thy long delay;
Though summoned to the seas; though pleasing gales   580
Invite thy course, and stretch thy swelling sails;
But beg the sacred priestess to relate
With willing words, and not to write, thy fate.
The fierce Italian people she will show,
And all thy wars, and all thy future woe;   585
And what thou may'st avoid, and what must undergo.
She shall direct thy course, instruct thy mind,
And teach thee how the happy shores to find.
This is what heaven allows me to relate:
Now part in peace; pursue thy better fate,   590
And raise, by strength of arms, the Trojan state.'
   This when the priest with friendly voice declared,
He gave me license, and rich gifts prepared:
Bounteous of treasure, he supplied my want
With heavy gold, and polished elephant;   595
Then Dodonaean caldrons put on board;
And every ship with sums of silver stored.
A trusty coat of mail to me he sent,
Thrice chained with gold, for use and ornament;
The helm of Pyrrhus added to the rest,   600
That flourished with a plume and waving crest.
Nor was my sire forgotten, nor my friends;
And large recruits he to my navy sends:
Men, horses, captains, arms, and warlike stores;
Supplies new pilots, and new sweeping oars.   605
Meantime, my sire commands to hoist our sails,
Lest we should lose the first auspicious gales.

   595. *elephant*: ivory.
   596. *caldrons*: to serve as gongs. They were hung from the sacred oaks at
Dodona, the ancient shrine of Jove in Epirus.

The prophet blessed the parting crew, and last,
With words like these, his ancient friend embraced:
'Old happy man, the care of gods above!   610
Whom heavenly Venus honored with her love,
And twice preserved thy life when Troy was lost;
Behold from far the wished Ausonian coast!
There land; but take a larger compass round;
For that, before, is all forbidden ground.   615
The shore that Phoebus has designed for you,
At farther distance lies, concealed from view.
Go happy hence, and seek your new abodes,
Blessed in a son, and favored by the gods;
For I with useless words prolong your stay,   620
When southern gales have summoned you away.'
    Nor less the queen our parting thence deplored,
Nor was less bounteous than her Trojan lord.
A noble present to my son she brought,
A robe with flowers on golden tissue wrought: 625
A Phrygian vest; and loads with gifts beside
Of precious texture, and of Asian pride.
'Accept (she said) these monuments of love,
Which in my youth with happier hands I wove:
Regard these trifles for the giver's sake: 630
'Tis the last present Hector's wife can make.
Thou call'st my lost Astyanax to mind:
In thee, his features and his form I find;
His eyes so sparkled with a lively flame;
Such were his motions; such was all his frame;   635
And ah! had heaven so pleased, his years had been the same.'
    With tears I took my last adieu, and said:
'Your fortune, happy pair, already made,
Leaves you no further wish. My different state,
Avoiding one, incurs another fate.   640
To you a quiet seat the gods allow:
You have no shores to search, no seas to plow;
Nor fields of flying Italy to chase—
Deluding visions and a vain embrace!

You see another Simoïs, and enjoy   645
The labors of your hands, another Troy,
With better auspice than her ancient towers;
And less obnoxious to the Grecian powers.
If e'er the gods whom I with vows adore,
Conduct my steps to Tiber's happy shore: 650
If ever I ascend the Latian throne,
And build a city I may call my own:
As both of us our birth from Troy derive;
So let our kindred lines in concord live;
And both in acts of equal friendship strive.   655
Our fortunes, good or bad, shall be the same:
The double Troy shall differ but in name:
That what we now begin, may never end,
But long to late posterity descend.'
    Near the Ceraunian rocks our course we bore—   660
The shortest passage to the Italian shore.
Now had the sun withdrawn his radiant light,
And hills were hid in dusky shades of night:
We land, and, on the bosom of the ground,
A safe retreat and a bare lodging found.   665
Close by the shore we lay; the sailors keep
Their watches, and the rest securely sleep.
The night, proceeding on with silent pace,
Stood in her noon, and viewed with equal face
Her steepy rise, and her declining race.   670
Then wakeful Palinurus rose, to spy
The face of heaven, and the nocturnal sky;
And listened every breath of air to try;
Observes the stars, and notes their sliding course,
The Pleiads, Hyads, and their watery force;   675
And both the Bears is careful to behold,
And bright Orion, armed with burnished gold.
Then, when he saw no threatening tempest nigh,
But a sure promise of a settled sky,

    660. *Ceraunian rocks*: a ridge in Epirus at the narrowest part of the Adriatic.
    675. *watery force*: *pluvias*; Virgil derives Hyades from the Greek verb "to rain."

He gave the sign to weigh: we break our sleep,   680
Forsake the pleasing shore, and plow the deep.
  And now the rising morn with rosy light
Adorns the skies, and puts the stars to flight;
When we from far, like bluish mists, descry
The hills, and then the plains, of Italy.   685
Achates first pronounced the joyful sound;
Then 'Italy!' the cheerful crew rebound.
My sire Anchises crowned a cup with wine,
And, offering, thus implored the powers divine:
'Ye gods, presiding over lands and seas,   690
And you, who raging winds and waves appease,
Breathe on our swelling sails a prosperous wind,
And smooth our passage to the port assigned.'
The gentle gales their flagging force renew;
And now the happy harbor is in view.   695
Minerva's temple then salutes our sight,
Placed, as a landmark, on the mountain's height.
We furl our sails, and turn the prows to shore:
The curling waters round the galleys roar.
The land lies open to the raging east,   700
Then, bending like a bow, with rocks compressed,
Shuts out the storms; the wind and waves complain,
And vent their malice on the cliffs in vain.
The port lies hid within; on either side,
The towering rocks the narrow mouth divide.   705
The temple, which aloft we viewed before,
To distance flies, and seems to shun the shore.
  Scarce landed, the first omens I beheld
Were four white steeds, that cropped the flowery field.
'War, war is threatened from this foreign ground   710
(My father cried), where warlike steeds are found.
Yet since reclaimed, to chariots they submit,
And bend to stubborn yokes, and champ the bit,
Peace may succeed to war.'—Our way we bend
To Pallas, and the sacred hill ascend;   715

685. *hills . . . plains*: keeping the Latin order, that in which each came into
view on the horizon.

There, prostrate, to the fierce virago pray,
Whose temple was the landmark of our way.
Each with a Phrygian mantle veiled his head,
And all commands of Helenus obeyed;
And pious rites to Grecian Juno paid.   720
  These dues performed, we stretch our sails and stand
To sea, forsaking that suspected land.
From hence Tarentum's bay appears in view,
For Hercules renowned, if fame be true.
Just opposite, Lacinian Juno stands;   725
Caulonian towers, and Scylacaean strands
For shipwrecks feared. Mount Aetna thence we spy,
Known by the smoky flames which cloud the sky.
Far off we hear the waves with surly sound
Invade the rocks, the rocks their groans rebound.   730
The billows break upon the sounding strand,
And roll the rising tide, impure with sand.
Then thus, Anchises, in experience old:
' 'Tis that Charybdis which the seer foretold,
And those the promised rocks! Bear off to sea!'   735
With haste the frighted mariners obey.
First Palinurus to the larboard veered;
Then all the fleet by his example steered.
To heaven aloft on ridgy waves we ride,
Then down to hell descend, when they divide;   740
And thrice our galleys knocked the stony ground,
And thrice the hollow rocks return the sound,
And thrice we saw the stars that stood with dews around.
The flagging winds forsook us, with the sun;
And, wearied, on Cyclopean shores we run.   745
  The port, capacious and secure from wind,
Is to the foot of thundering Aetna joined.
By turns a pitchy cloud she rolls on high;
By turns hot embers from her entrails fly,
And flakes of mountain flames, that lick the sky.   750

725. *Just opposite*: at the west end of the Gulf of Tarentum.
743. *with dews*: with spray rather; *rorantia vidimus astra*: "we saw the stars
dripping."

Oft from her bowels massy rocks are thrown,
And shivered by the force, come piecemeal down:
Oft liquid lakes of burning sulfur flow,
Fed from the fiery springs that boil below.
Enceladus, they say, transfixed by Jove,   755
With blasted limbs came tumbling from above;
And where he fell, the avenging father drew
This flaming hill, and on his body threw.
As often as he turns his weary sides,
He shakes the solid isle, and smoke, the heavens hides.   760
In shady woods we pass the tedious night,
Where bellowing sounds and groans our souls affright,
Of which no cause is offered to the sight;
For not one star was kindled in the sky;
Nor could the moon her borrowed light supply;   765
For misty clouds involved the firmament:
The stars were muffled, and the moon was pent.
   Scarce had the rising sun the day revealed;
Scarce had his heat the pearly dews dispelled;
When from the woods there bolts, before our sight,   770
Somewhat betwixt a mortal and a sprite,
So thin, so ghastly meager, and so wan,
So bare of flesh, he scarce resembled man.
This thing, all tattered, seemed from far to implore
Our pious aid, and pointed to the shore.   775
We look behind; then view his shaggy beard:
His clothes were tagged with thorns, and filth his limbs besmeared;
The rest, in mien, in habit, and in face,
Appeared a Greek: and such indeed he was.
He cast on us, from far, a frightful view,   780
Whom soon for Trojans and for foes he knew:
Stood still, and paused; then all at once began
To stretch his limbs, and trembled as he ran.
Soon as approached, upon his knees he falls,
And thus with tears and sighs for pity calls: 785
'Now, by the powers above, and what we share
From nature's common gift, this vital air,

755. *Enceladus, they say*: Most of them say Typhoeus, another giant.

O Trojans, take me hence! I beg no more;
But bear me far from this unhappy shore.
'Tis true I am a Greek, and further own,   790
Among your foes besieged the imperial town.
For such demerits if my death be due,
No more for this abandoned life I sue:
This only favor let my tears obtain,
To throw me headlong in the rapid main: 795
Since nothing more than death my crime demands,
I die content, to die by human hands.'
　　He said; and on his knees my knees embraced:
I bade him boldly tell, his fortune past,
His present state, his lineage, and his name,   800
The occasion of his fears, and whence he came.
The good Anchises raised him with his hand;
Who thus encouraged, answered our demand:
'From Ithaca, my native soil, I came
To Troy; and Achaemenides my name.   805
Me my poor father with Ulysses sent;
(O! had I stayed, with poverty content!)
But, fearful for themselves, my countrymen
Left me forsaken in the Cyclop's den.
The cave, though large, was dark; the dismal floor   810
Was paved with mangled limbs and putrid gore.
Our monstrous host, of more than human size
Erects his head and stares within the skies:
Bellowing, his voice, and horrid is his hue.
Ye gods, remove this plague from mortal view!   815
The joints of slaughtered wretches are his food;
And for his wine, he quaffs the streaming blood.
These eyes beheld, when with his spacious hand
He seized two captives of our Grecian band;
Stretched on his back, he dashed against the stones   820
Their broken bodies, and their crackling bones:
With spouting blood the purple pavement swims,
While the dire glutton grinds the trembling limbs.
　　Not unrevenged Ulysses bore their fate,
Nor thoughtless of his own unhappy state;   825

809. This eyewitness account corroborates the *Odyssey*, Book IX.

For, gorged with flesh, and drunk with human wine,
While fast asleep the giant lay supine
(Snoring aloud, and belching from his maw
His indigested foam, and morsels raw);
We pray, we cast the lots, and then surround   830
The monstrous body stretched along the ground.
Each, as he could approach him, lends a hand
To bore his eye-ball with a flaming brand.
Beneath his frowning forehead lay his eye;
For only one did the vast frame supply—   835
But that a globe so large, his front it filled,
Like the sun's disk, or like a Grecian shield.
The stroke succeeds; and down the pupil bends.
This vengeance followed for our slaughtered friends.
But haste, unhappy wretches! haste to fly!   840
Your cables cut, and on your oars rely!
Such, and so vast as Polypheme appears,
A hundred more this hated island bears:
Like him, in caves they shut their woolly sheep;
Like him, their herds on tops of mountains keep;   845
Like him, with mighty strides they stalk from steep to steep.
And now three moons their sharpened horns renew,
Since thus in woods and wilds, obscure from view,
I drag my loathsome days with mortal fright,
And in deserted caverns lodge by night.   850
Oft from the rocks a dreadful prospect see
Of the huge Cyclops, like a walking tree:
From far I hear his thundering voice resound,
And trampling feet that shake the solid ground.
Cornels and savage berries of the wood,   855
And roots and herbs have been my meager food.
While all around my longing eyes I cast,
I saw your happy ships appear at last.
On those I fixed my hopes, to these I run:
'Tis all I ask, this cruel race to shun: 860
What other death you please, yourselves bestow.'
Scarce had he said, when on the mountain's brow,
We saw the giant shepherd stalk before
His following flock, and leading to the shore:

A monstrous bulk, deformed, deprived of sight;   865
His staff a trunk of pine, to guide his steps aright.
His ponderous whistle from his neck descends;
His woolly care their pensive lord attends:
This only solace his hard fortune sends.
Soon as he reached the shore and touched the waves,   870
From his bored eye the gutt'ring blood he laves:
He gnashed his teeth and groaned: through seas he strides;
And scarce the topmost billows touched his sides.
    Seized with a sudden fear, we run to sea,
The cables cut, and silent haste away;   875
The well-deserving stranger entertain;
Then, buckling to the work, our oars divide the main.
The giant hearkened to the dashing sound;
But, when our vessels out of reach he found,
He strided onward, and in vain essayed   880
The Ionian deep, and durst no farther wade.
With that he roared aloud: the dreadful cry
Shakes earth and air and seas; the billows fly
Before the bellowing noise to distant Italy,
The neighboring Aetna trembling all around,   885
The winding caverns echo to the sound.
    His brother Cyclops hear the yelling roar,
And rushing down the mountains, crowd the shore.
We saw their stern distorted looks, from far,
And one-eyed glance, that vainly threatened war—   890
A dreadful council! with their heads on high
(The misty clouds about their foreheads fly)
Not yielding to the towering tree of Jove,
Or tallest cypress of Diana's grove.
New pangs of mortal fear our minds assail;   895
We tug at every oar, and hoist up every sail,
And take the advantage of the friendly gale.
Forewarned by Helenus, we strive to shun
Charybdis' gulf, nor dare to Scylla run.

865. monstrum horrendum, informe, ingens, cui lumen ademptum.
867. His ponderous whistle: de collo fistula pendet, a half-line printed in
Ruaeus' edition, but rejected by modern editors.

An equal fate on either side appears: 900
We, tacking to the left, are free from fears;
For, from Pelorus' point, the north arose,
And drove us back where swift Pantagias flows.
His rocky mouth we pass; and make our way
By Thapsus, and Megara's winding bay.   905
This passage Achaemenides had shown,
Tracing the course which he before had run.
    Right o'er against Plemmyrium's watery strand,
There lies an isle, once called the Ortygian land.
Alpheüs, as old fame reports, has found   910
From Greece a secret passage under ground;
By love to beauteous Arethusa led;
And, mingling here, they roll in the same sacred bed.
As Helenus enjoined, we next adore
Diana's name, protectress of the shore.   915
With prosperous gales we pass the quiet sounds
Of still Helorus, and his fruitful bounds.
Then, doubling cape Pachynus, we survey
The rocky shore extended to the sea.
The town of Camarine from far we see,   920
And fenny lake, undrained by Fate's decree.
In sight of the Geloan fields we pass,
And the large walls, where mighty Gela was;
Then Agragas, with lofty summits crowned,
Long for the race of warlike steeds renowned.   925
We passed Selinus, and the palmy land;
And widely shun the Lilybaean strand,
Unsafe, for secret rocks and moving sand.
At length on shore the weary fleet arrived,
Which Drepanum's unhappy port received.   930
Here, after endless labors (often tossed

902. *the north*: wind.
908 sqq. The promontory of Plemmyrium and the island of Ortygia enclose
the harbor of Syracuse. On the island is the fountain Arethusa, named for a
nymph pursued by the river Alpheüs, who is supposed to have run undersea from
the Peloponneus to mingle with her. Between Syracuse and Drepanum (now
Trapani) the Trojans pass other places that were made notable long before
Roman times by Greek colonies on the south shore of Sicily.

By raging storms, and driven on every coast),
My dear, dear father, spent with age, I lost—
Ease of my cares, and solace of my pain,
Saved through a thousand toils, but saved in vain!   935
The prophet, who my future woes revealed,
Yet this, the greatest and the worse, concealed;
And dire Celaeno, whose foreboding skill
Denounced all else, was silent of this ill.
This my last labor was. Some friendly god   940
From thence conveyed us to your blest abode."
    Thus, to the listening queen, the royal guest
His wandering course and all his toils expressed;
And here concluding, he retired to rest.

BOOK IV

THE ARGUMENT

Dido discovers to her sister her passion for Aeneas, and her thoughts of marrying him. She prepares a hunting match for his entertainment. Juno, by Venus's consent, raises a storm which separates the hunters, and drives Aeneas and Dido into the same cave, where their marriage is supposed to be completed. Jupiter despatches Mercury to Aeneas, to warn him from Carthage. Aeneas secretly prepares for his voyage. Dido finds out his design, and, to put a stop to it, makes use of her own and her sister's entreaties, and discovers all the variety of passions that are incident to a neglected lover. When nothing would prevail upon him, she contrives her own death, with which this book concludes.

But anxious cares already seized the queen;
She fed within her veins a flame unseen:
The hero's valor, acts, and birth, inspire
Her soul with love, and fan the secret fire.
His words, his looks, imprinted in her heart,   5
Improve the passion, and increase the smart.
Now, when the purple morn had chased away
The dewy shadows, and restored the day,
Her sister first with early care she sought,
And thus in mournful accents eased her thought: 10
"My dearest Anna! what new dreams affright
My laboring soul! what visions of the night
Disturb my quiet, and distract my breast
With strange ideas of our Trojan guest!
His worth, his actions, and majestic air,   15
A man descended from the gods, declare.

Fear ever argues a degenerate kind:
His birth is well asserted by his mind.
Then, what he suffered, when by fate betrayed!
What brave attempts for falling Troy he made!   20
Such were his looks, so gracefully he spoke,
That, were I not resolved against the yoke
Of hapless marriage—never to be cursed
With second love, so fatal was my first—
To this one error I might yield again;   25
For, since Sichaeus was untimely slain,
This only man is able to subvert
The fixed foundations of my stubborn heart.
And, to confess my frailty, to my shame,
Somewhat I find within, if not the same,   30
Too like the sparkles of my former flame.
But first let yawning earth a passage rend,
And let me through the dark abyss descend—
First let avenging Jove, with flames from high,
Drive down this body to the nether sky,   35
Condemned with ghosts in endless night to lie—
Before I break the plighted faith I gave!
No! he who had my vows, shall ever have;
For, whom I loved on earth, I worship in the grave."

   She said: the tears ran gushing from her eyes,   40
And stopped her speech. Her sister thus replies:
"O dearer than the vital air I breathe!
Will you to grief your blooming years bequeath,
Condemned to waste in woes your lonely life,
Without the joys of mother or of wife?   45
Think you these tears, this pompous train of woe,
Are known or valued by the ghosts below?
I grant, that, while your sorrows yet were green,
It well became a woman, and a queen,
The vows of Tyrian princes to neglect;   50
To scorn Iärbas and his love reject;
With all the Libyan lords of mighty name:
But will you fight against a pleasing flame?

   51. *Iärbas*: a Libyan suitor.

This little spot of land, which heaven bestows,
On every side is hemmed with warlike foes: 55
Gaetulian cities here are spread around,
And fierce Numidians there your frontiers bound:
Here lies a barren waste of thirsty land,
And there the Syrtes raise the moving sand:
Barcaean troops besiege the narrow shore;   60
And from the sea Pygmalion threatens more.
Propitious heaven, and gracious Juno, lead
This wandering navy to your needful aid:
How will your empire spread, your city rise,
From such a union, and with such allies!   65
Implore the favor of the powers above;
And leave the conduct of the rest to love.
Continue still your hospitable way,
And still invent occasions of their stay,
Till storms and winter winds shall cease to threat,   70
And planks and oars repair their shattered fleet."
    These words, which from a friend and sister came
With ease resolved the scruples of her fame,
And added fury to the kindled flame.
Inspired with hope, the project they pursue;   75
On every altar sacrifice renew;
A chosen ewe of two years old they pay
To Ceres, Bacchus, and the god of day.
Preferring Juno's power (for Juno ties
The nuptial knot, and makes the marriage joys),   80
The beauteous queen before her altar stands,
And holds the golden goblet in her hands.
A milk-white heifer she with flowers adorns,
And pours the ruddy wine betwixt her horns;
And, while the priests with prayer the gods invoke,   85
She feeds their altars with Sabaean smoke;
With hourly care the sacrifice renews,
And anxiously the panting entrails views.
What priestly rites, alas! what pious art,
What vows avail to cure a bleeding heart?   90

    79. *Preferring: ante omnes,* above all.

A gentle fire she feeds within her veins,
Where the soft god secure in silence reigns.
　Sick with desire, and seeking him she loves,
From street to street the raving Dido roves.
So, when the watchful shepherd, from the blind,   95
Wounds with a random shaft the careless hind,
Distracted with her pain she flies the woods,
Bounds o'er the lawn, and seeks the silent floods—
With fruitless care; for still the fatal dart
Sticks in her side, and rankles in her heart.   100
And now she leads the Trojan chief along
The lofty walls, amidst the busy throng;
Displays her Tyrian wealth, and rising town,
Which love, without his labor makes his own.
This pomp she shows, to tempt her wandering guest: 105
Her faltering tongue forbids to speak the rest.
When day declines and feasts renew the night,
Still on his face she feeds her famished sight;
She longs again to hear the prince relate
His own adventures, and the Trojan fate.   110
He tells it o'er and o'er; but still in vain;
For still she begs to hear it once again.
The hearer on the speaker's mouth depends;
And thus the tragic story never ends.
　Then, when they part, when Phoebe's paler light   115
Withdraws, and falling stars to sleep invite,
She last remains; when every guest is gone,
Sits on the bed he pressed, and sighs alone;
Absent, her absent hero sees and hears;
Or in her bosom young Ascanius bears,   120
And seeks the father's image in the child,
If love by likeness might be so beguiled.
　Meantime the rising towers are at a stand;
No labors exercise the youthful band,
Nor use of arts, nor toils of arms they know: 125
The mole is left unfinished to the foe;
The mounds, the works, the walls neglected lie,
Short of their promised height, that seemed to threat the sky.

But when imperial Juno, from above,
Saw Dido fettered in the chains of Love, 130
Hot with the venom which her veins inflamed;
And by no sense of shame to be reclaimed;
With soothing words to Venus she begun:
"High praises, endless honors, you have won,
And mighty trophies, with your worthy son! 135
Two gods a silly woman have undone!
Nor am I ignorant, you both suspect
This rising city which my hands erect:
But shall celestial discord never cease?
'Tis better ended in a lasting peace. 140
You stand possessed of all your soul desired;
Poor Dido with consuming love is fired.
Your Trojan with my Tyrian let us join;
So Dido shall be yours, Aeneas mine—
One common kingdom, one united line. 145
Eliza shall a Dardan lord obey,
And lofty Carthage for a dower convey."
Then Venus (who her hidden fraud descried,
Which would the scepter of the world misguide
To Libyan shores) thus artfully replied: 150
"Who, but a fool, would wars with Juno choose,
And such alliance and such gifts refuse;
If fortune with our joint desires comply?
The doubt is all from Jove, and destiny;
Lest he forbid, with absolute command, 155
To mix the people in one common land—
Or will, the Trojan and the Tyrian line
In lasting leagues, and sure succession, join.
But you, the partner of his bed and throne,
May move his mind: my wishes are your own." 160
"Mine (said imperial Juno) be the care:
Time urges now:—to perfect this affair
Attend my counsel, and the secret share.
    When next the sun his rising light displays,
And gilds the world below with purple rays, 165

146. *Eliza: Elissa:* Dido.

The queen, Aeneas, and the Tyrian court,
Shall to the shady woods, for sylvan game, resort.
There, while the huntsmen pitch their toils around,
And cheerful horns, from side to side, resound,
A pitchy cloud shall cover all the plain   170
With hail, and thunder, and tempestuous rain:
The fearful train shall take their speedy flight,
Dispersed, and all involved in gloomy night:
One cave a grateful shelter shall afford
To the fair princess and the Trojan lord.   175
I will myself the bridal bed prepare,
If you, to bless the nuptials, will be there;
So shall their loves be crowned with due delights;
And Hymen shall be present at the rites."
The queen of love consents, and closely smiles   180
At her vain project, and discovered wiles.

     The rosy morn was risen from the main;
And horns and hounds awake the princely train:
They issue early through the city gate,
Where the more wakeful huntsmen ready wait,   185
With nets, and toils, and darts, beside the force
Of Spartan dogs, and swift Massylian horse.
The Tyrian peers and officers of state,
For the slow queen, in antechambers wait:
Her lofty courser, in the court below   190
(Who his majestic rider seems to know),
Proud of his purple trappings, paws the ground;
And champs the golden bit, and spreads the foam around.
The queen at length appears: on either hand,
The brawny guards in martial order stand.   195
A flowered cymar with golden fringe she wore,
And at her back a golden quiver bore;
Her flowing hair a golden caul restrains;
A golden clasp the Tyrian robe sustains.
Then young Ascanius, with a sprightly grace   200
Leads on the Trojan youth to view the chase.

     180. *closely*: privately.
     196. *cymar*: a chlamys, or short cloak.
     198. *caul*: a snood.

But far above the rest in beauty shines
The great Aeneas, when the troop he joins;
Like fair Apollo, when he leaves the frost
Of wintry Xanthus, and the Lycian coast;   205
When to his native Delos he resorts,
Ordains the dances, and renews the sports;
Where painted Scythians, mixed with Cretan bands,
Before the joyful altars join their hands:
Himself, on Cynthus walking, sees below   210
The merry madness of the sacred show.
Green wreaths of bays his length of hair inclose;
A golden fillet binds his awful brows;
His quiver sounds.—Not less the prince is seen
In manly presence, or in lofty mien.   215
   Now had they reached the hills, and stormed the seat
Of savage beasts, in dens, their last retreat.
The cry pursues the mountain goats; they bound
From rock to rock, and keep the craggy ground:
Quite otherwise the stags, a trembling train   220
In herds unsingled, scour the dusty plain,
And a long chase, in open view maintain.
The glad Ascanius, as his courser guides,
Spurs through the vale, and these and those outrides.
His horse's flanks and sides are forced to feel   225
The clanking lash, and goring of the steel.
Impatiently he views the feeble prey,
Wishing some nobler beast to cross his way;
And rather would the tusky boar attend,
Or see the tawny lion downward bend.   230
   Meantime, the gathering clouds obscure the skies;
From pole to pole the forky lightning flies;
The rattling thunders roll; and Juno pours
A wintry deluge down, and sounding showers.

205. Apollo's oracle at Patara in Lycia was near the mouth of the Xanthus.
208. *Scythians*: pilgrims from the Far North.
226. *clanking*: Dryden liked the word, but the choice is inscrutable here.
230. *bend*: The expression "to bend one's steps" is still not quite obsolete.
233. *rattling*: The word meant something more thunderous to Dryden than
it does to us.

The company, dispersed, to coverts ride,   235
And seek the homely cots, or mountain's hollow side.
The rapid rains, descending from the hills,
To rolling torrents raise the creeping rills.
The queen and prince, as love or fortune guides,
One common cavern in her bosom hides,   240
Then first the trembling earth the signal gave;
And flashing fires enlighten all the cave:
Hell from below, and Juno from above,
And howling nymphs, were conscious to their love.
From this ill-omened hour, in time arose   245
Debate and death, and all succeeding woes.
    The queen, whom sense of honor could not move,
No longer made a secret of her love,
But called it marriage; by that specious name
To veil the crime, and sanctify the shame.   250
    The loud report through Libyan cities goes.
Fame, the great ill, from small beginnings grows—
Swift from the first; and every moment brings
New vigor to her flights, new pinions to her wings.
Soon grows the pigmy to gigantic size;   255
Her feet on earth, her forehead in the skies.
Enraged against the gods, revengeful Earth
Produced her, last of the Titanian birth:
Swift is her walk, more swift her wingèd haste:
A monstrous phantom, horrible and vast.   260
As many plumes as raise her lofty flight;
So many piercing eyes enlarge her sight;
Millions of opening mouths to fame belong,
And every mouth is furnished with a tongue;
And round, with listening ears the flying plague is hung.   265
She fills the peaceful universe with cries
No slumbers ever close her wakeful eyes.
By day, from lofty towers her head she shows,
And spreads through trembling crowds disastrous news;

244. *howling: ulularunt*, a word used of wolves in Book VII.
258. *Titanian birth*: of the race of giants, challengers of the Olympian gods.

With court informers, haunts, and royal spies;   270
Things done, relates; not done, she feigns, and mingles truth
    with lies.
Talk is her business; and her chief delight
To tell of prodigies, and cause affright.
She fills the people's ears with Dido's name,
Who, lost to honor and the sense of shame,   275
Admits into her throne and nuptial bed
A wandering guest, who from his country fled.
Whole days with him she passes in delights;
And wastes in luxury long winter nights,
Forgetful of her fame, and royal trust,   280
Dissolved in ease, abandoned to her lust.
   The goddess widely spreads the loud report,
And flies at length to king Iärbas' court.
When first possessed with this unwelcome news,
Whom did he not of men and gods accuse?   285
This prince, from ravished Garamantis born,
A hundred temples did with spoils adorn
In Ammon's honor, his celestial sire;
A hundred altars fed with wakeful fire;
And, through his vast dominions, priests ordained,   290
Whose watchful care these holy rites maintained.
The gates and columns were with garlands crowned,
And blood of victim beasts enriched the ground.
   He, when he heard a fugitive could move
The Tyrian princess, who disdained his love,   295
His breast with fury burned, his eyes with fire—
Mad with despair, impatient with desire—
Then on the sacred altars pouring wine,
He thus with prayers implored his sire divine:
"Great Jove! propitious to the Moorish race,   300
Who feast on painted beds, with offerings grace
Thy temples, and adore thy power divine
With blood of victims, and with sparkling wine;
Seest thou not this! or do we fear in vain
Thy boasted thunder, and thy thoughtless reign?   305

271. This unusual verse is a "fourteener" with seven stresses.

Do thy broad hands the forky lightnings lance?
Thine are the bolts, or the blind work of chance?
A wandering woman builds within our state,
A little town, bought at an easy rate;
She pays me homage—(and my grants allow   310
A narrow space of Libyan lands to plow);
Yet, scorning me, by passion blindly led,
Admits a banished Trojan to her bed!
And now this other Paris, with his train
Of conquered cowards, must in Afric reign!   315
(Whom, what they are, their looks and garb confess,
Their locks with oil perfumed, their Lydian dress.)
He takes the spoil, enjoys the princely dame;
And I, rejected I, adore an empty name!"

   His vows, in haughty terms, he thus preferred,   320
And held his altar's horns: the mighty Thunderer heard,
Then cast his eyes on Carthage, where he found
The lustful pair in lawless pleasure drowned,
Lost in their loves, insensible of shame,
And both forgetful of their better fame.   325
He calls Cyllenius; and the god attends;
By whom this menacing command he sends:
"Go, mount the western winds, and cleave the sky;
Then, with a swift descent, to Carthage fly:
There find the Trojan chief, who wastes his days   330
In slothful riot and inglorious ease,
Nor minds the future city, given by fate.
To him this message from my mouth relate:
Nor so fair Venus hoped, when twice she won
Thy life with prayers; nor promised such a son.   335
Her's was a hero, destined to command
A martial race, and rule the Latian land;
Who should his ancient line from Teucer draw;
And on the conquered world impose the law.
If glory cannot move a mind so mean,   340
Nor future praise from fading pleasure wean,
Yet why should he defraud his son of fame,
And grudge the Romans their immortal name?

   338. *Teucer*: Teucrus.

What are his vain designs? what hopes he more
From his long lingering on a hostile shore,   345
Regardless to redeem his honor lost,
And for his race to gain the Ausonian coast?
Bid him with speed the Tyrian court forsake;
With this command the slumbering warrior wake."
   Hermes obeys; with golden pinions binds   350
His flying feet, and mounts the western winds:
And, whether o'er the seas or earth he flies,
With rapid force they bear him down the skies.
But first he grasps within his awful hand
The mark of sovereign power, his magic wand;   355
With this he draws the ghosts from hollow graves;
With this he drives them down the Stygian waves;
With this he seals in sleep the wakeful sight,
And eyes, though closed in death, restores to light.
Thus armed, the god begins his airy race,   360
And drives the racking clouds along the liquid space;
Now sees the top of Atlas, as he flies,
Whose brawny back supports the starry skies:
Atlas, whose head with piney forests crowned,
Is beaten by the winds, with foggy vapors bound.   365
Snows hide his shoulders: from beneath his chin
The founts of rolling streams their race begin:
A beard of ice on his large breast depends:
Here, poised upon his wings, the god descends.
Then, rested thus, he from the towering height   370
Plunged downward with precipitated flight:
Lights on the seas, and skims along the flood.
As water-fowl, who seek their fishy food,
Less, and yet less, to distant prospect show;
By turns they dance aloft, and dive below: 375
Like these, the steerage of his wings he plies,
And near the surface of the water flies;
Till, having passed the seas, and crossed the sands,
He closed his wings, and stooped on Libyan lands;

   362. *Atlas*: Mount Atlas in North Africa is far west of Carthage; a direct
flight from Olympus would not cross it.
   376. *steerage*: for *remigium alarum*, "rowing of wings"—a Virgilian phrase
but one found elsewhere, not here.

Where shepherds once were housed in homely sheds,   380
Now towers, within the clouds advance their heads.
  Arriving there, he found the Trojan prince
New ramparts raising for the town's defense.
A purple scarf, with gold embroidered o'er
(Queen Dido's gift), about his waist he wore;   385
A sword, with glittering gems diversified,
For ornament, not use, hung idly by his side.
Then thus, with wingèd words, the god began
(Resuming his own shape): "Degenerate man!
Thou woman's property! what mak'st thou here,   390
These foreign walls and Tyrian towers to rear?—
Forgetful of thy own! All-powerful Jove,
Who sways the world below and heaven above,
Has sent me down with this severe command:
What means thy lingering in the Libyan land?   395
If glory cannot move a mind so mean,
Nor future praise from flitting pleasure wean,
Regard the fortunes of thy rising heir:
The promised crown let young Ascanius wear,
To whom the Ausonian scepter, and the state   400
Of Rome's imperial name, is owed by fate."
So spoke the god; and, speaking, took his flight
Involved in clouds; and vanished out of sight.
  The pious prince was seized with sudden fear:
Mute was his tongue, and upright stood his hair.   405
Revolving in his mind the stern command,
He longs to fly, and loathes the charming land.
What should he say, or how should he begin?
What course, alas! remains, to steer between
The offended lover and the powerful queen?   410
This way, and that, he turns his anxious mind;
And all expedients tries, and none can find.
Fixed on the deed, but doubtful of the means;
After long thought, to this advice he leans:
Three chiefs he calls, commands them to repair   415
The fleet, and ship their men, with silent care.
Some plausible pretense he bids them find,
To color what in secret he designed.

Himself, meantime, the softest hours would choose,
Before the love-sick lady heard the news,   420
And move her tender mind, by slow degrees
To suffer what the sovereign power decrees:
Jove will inspire him, when, and what to say.
They hear with pleasure, and with haste obey.
   But soon the queen perceives the thin disguise: 425
(What arts can blind a jealous woman's eyes?)
She was the first to find the secret fraud,
Before the fatal news was blazed abroad:
Love the first motions of the lover hears,
Quick to presage, and e'en in safety fears.   430
Nor impious Fame was wanting, to report
The ships repaired, the Trojans' thick resort,
And purpose to forsake the Tyrian court.
Frantic with fear, impatient of the wound,
And impotent of mind, she roves the city round.   435
Less wild the Bacchanalian dames appear,
When, from afar, their nightly god they hear,
And howl about the hills, and shake the wreathy spear.
At length she finds the dear perfidious man;
Prevents his formed excuse, and thus began: 440
"Base and ungrateful! could you hope to fly,
And undiscovered 'scape a lover's eye?
Nor could my kindness your compassion move,
Nor plighted vows, nor dearer bands of love?
Or is the death of a despairing queen   445
Not worth preventing, though too well foreseen?
E'en when the wintry winds command your stay,
You dare the tempests, and defy the sea.
False as you are, suppose you were not bound
To lands unknown, and foreign coasts to sound;   450
Were Troy restored, and Priam's happy reign,
Now durst you tempt, for Troy, the raging main?
See, whom you fly! am I the foe you shun?
Now, by those holy vows, so late begun,

426. *quis fallere possit amantem:* "who can deceive a woman in love?"
   438. *the wreathy spear:* a thyrsus was a staff twined with ivy and vine-shoots, carried by Bacchantes.

By this right hand (since I have nothing more   455
To challenge, but the faith you gave before),
I beg you by these tears too truly shed,
By the new pleasures of our nuptial bed;
If ever Dido, when you most were kind,
Were pleasing in your eyes, or touched your mind;   460
By these my prayers, if prayers may yet have place,
Pity the fortunes of a falling race!
For you I have provoked a tyrant's hate,
Incensed the Libyan and the Tyrian state,
For you alone, I suffer in my fame,   465
Bereft of honor, and exposed to shame!
Whom have I now to trust, ungrateful guest?
(That only name remains of all the rest!)
What have I left? or whither can I fly?
Must I attend Pygmalion's cruelty,   470
Or, till Iärbas shall in triumph lead
A queen that proudly scorned his proffered bed?
Had you deferred, at least, your hasty flight,
And left behind some pledge of our delight;
Some babe to bless the mother's mournful sight;   475
Some young Aeneas to supply your place,
Whose features might express his father's face;
I should not then complain to live bereft
Of all my husband, or be wholly left."
    Here paused the queen. Unmoved he holds his eyes,   480
By Jove's command; nor suffered love to rise
Though heaving in his heart; and thus at length replies:
"Fair queen, you never can enough repeat
Your boundless favors, or I own my debt;
Nor, can my mind forget Eliza's name   485
While vital breath inspires this mortal frame.
This only let me speak in my defense—
I never hoped a secret flight from hence,
Much less pretended to the lawful claim
Of sacred nuptials, or a husband's name.   490
For, if indulgent heaven would leave me free,
And not submit my life to fate's decree,

My choice would lead me to the Trojan shore,
Those relics to review, their dust adore;
And Priam's ruined palace to restore.   495
But now the Delphian oracle commands,
And fate invites me to the Latian lands.
That is the promised place to which I steer;
And all my vows are terminated there.
If you, a Tyrian and a stranger born,   500
With walls and towers a Libyan town adorn,
Why may not we—like you, a foreign race—
Like you, seek shelter in a foreign place?
As often as the night obscures the skies
With humid shades, or twinkling stars arise,   505
Anchises' angry ghost in dreams appears,
Chides my delay, and fills my soul with fears;
And young Ascanius justly may complain,
Defrauded of his fate and destined reign.
E'en now the herald of the gods appeared—   510
Waking I saw him, and his message heard.
From Jove he came commissioned, heavenly bright
With radiant beams, and manifest to sight
(The sender and the sent I both attest):
These walls he entered, and those words expressed.   515
Fair queen, oppose not what the gods command:
Forced by my fate, I leave your happy land."
    Thus while he spoke, already she began
With sparkling eyes to view the guilty man;
From head to foot surveyed his person o'er;   520
Nor longer these outrageous threats forbore:
"False as thou art, and more than false, forsworn!
Not sprung from noble blood, nor goddess born,
But hewn from hardened entrails of a rock!
And rough Hyrcanian tigers gave thee suck!   525
Why should I fawn? what have I worse to fear?
Did he once look, or lend a listening ear,
Sighed when I sobbed, or shed one kindly tear?

496. *the Delphian oracle*: in fact the oracle at Delos (Book III, 208 sqq.)
525. *Hyrcanian*: of the region south of the Caspian Sea.

All, symptoms of a base ungrateful mind,
So foul, that which is worse, 'tis hard to find.   530
Of man's injustice why should I complain?
The gods, and Jove himself, behold in vain
Triumphant treason: yet no thunder flies;
Nor Juno views my wrongs with equal eyes:
Faithless is earth, and faithless are the skies!   535
Justice is fled, and truth is now no more!
I saved the shipwrecked exile on my shore:
With needful food his hungry Trojans fed:
I took the traitor to my throne and bed.
Fool that I was! 'tis little to repeat   540
The rest: I stored and rigged his ruined fleet.
I rave, I rave! a god's command he pleads,
And makes heaven accessory to his deeds.
Now Lycian lots, and now the Delian god,
Now Hermes is employed from Jove's abode,   545
To warn him hence; as if the peaceful state
Of heavenly powers were touched with human fate!
But go! thy flight no longer I detain—
Go! seek thy promised kingdom through the main!
Yet, if the heavens will hear my pious vow,   550
The faithless waves, not half so false as thou,
Or secret sands, shall sepulchers afford
To thy proud vessels, and their perjured lord!
Then shalt thou call on injured Dido's name:
Dido shall come in a black sulfury flame,   555
When death has once dissolved her mortal frame—
Shall smile to see the traitor vainly weep:
Her angry ghost, arising from the deep,
Shall haunt thee waking, and disturb thy sleep!
At least my shade thy punishment shall know;   560
And fame shall spread the pleasing news below."
    Abruptly here she stops; then turns away
Her loathing eyes, and shuns the sight of day.
Amazed he stood, revolving in his mind
What speech to frame, and what excuse to find.   565

    555. *in a black sulfury flame: sequar atris ignibus absens.* More probably she
conceives of her avenging spirit as a Fury carrying "black fires," or "infernal
torches," like the ghost of Clytemnestra in line 684.

Her fearful maids their fainting mistress led,
And softly laid her on her ivory bed.
　　But good Aeneas, though he much desired
To give that pity which her grief required
(Though much he mourned, and labored with his love);   570
Resolved at length, obeys the will of Jove:
Reviews his forces: they with early care
Unmoor their vessels, and for sea prepare.
The fleet is soon afloat, in all its pride;
And well-caulked galleys in the harbor ride.   575
Then oaks for oars they felled; or, as they stood,
Of its green arms despoiled the growing wood,
Studious of flight. The beach is covered o'er
With Trojan bands, that blacken all the shore:
On every side are seen, descending down,   580
Thick swarms of soldiers laden, from the town.
Thus, in battalia, march embodied ants,
Fearful of winter, and of future wants,
T" invade the corn, and to their cells convey
The plundered forage of their yellow prey.   585
The sable troops, along the narrow tracks,
Scarce bear the weighty burden on their backs:
Some set their shoulders to the ponderous grain;
Some guard the spoil; some lash the lagging train;
All ply their several tasks, and equal toil sustain.   590
　　What pangs the tender breast of Dido tore,
When, from the tower, she saw the covered shore,
And heard the shouts of sailors from afar,
Mixed with the murmurs of the watery war!
All-powerful Love! what changes canst thou cause   595
In human hearts, subjected to thy laws!
Once more her haughty soul the tyrant bends
To prayers and mean submissions she descends.
No female arts or aids she left untried,
Nor counsels unexplored, before she died.   600
　　"Look, Anna! look! the Trojans crowd to sea;
They spread their canvas, and their anchors weigh;

582. *battalia*: plural of battalion.
　　　embodied: in a body.

The shouting crew their ships with garlands bind,
Invoke the sea-gods, and invite the wind.
Could I have thought this threatening blow so near,   605
My tender soul had been forewarned to bear.
But do not you my last request deny;
With yon perfidious man your interest try;
And bring me news, if I must live or die.
You are his favorite; you alone can find   610
The dark recesses of his inmost mind;
In all his trusted secrets you have part,
And know the soft approaches to his heart.
Haste then, and humbly seek my haughty foe;
Tell him, I did not with the Grecians go,   615
Nor did my fleet against his friends employ,
Nor swore the ruin of unhappy Troy,
Nor moved with hands profane his father's dust:
Why should he then reject a suit so just?
Whom does he shun? and whither would he fly?   620
Can he this last, this only prayer deny?
Let him at least his dangerous flight delay,
Wait better winds, and hope a calmer sea.
The nuptials he disclaims, I urge no more:
Let him pursue the promised Latian shore.   625
A short delay is all I ask him now—
A pause of grief, an interval from woe;
Till my soft soul be tempered to sustain
Accustomed sorrows, and inured to pain.
If you in pity grant this one request,   630
My death shall glut the hatred of his breast."
    This mournful message pious Anna bears,
And seconds with her own, her sister's tears:
But all her arts are still employed in vain:
Again she comes, and is refused again.   635
His hardened heart nor prayers nor threat'nings move;
Fate and the god, had stopped his ears to love.
    As, when the winds their airy quarrel try,
Justling from every quarter of the sky;
This way and that the mountain oak they bend;   640
His boughs they shatter, and his branches rend;

With leaves and falling mast they spread the ground;
The hollow valleys echo to the sound;
Unmoved, the royal plant their fury mocks,
Or, shaken, clings more closely to the rocks: 645
Far as he shoots his towering head on high,
So deep in earth his fixed foundations lie.
No less a storm the Trojan hero bears;
Thick messages and loud complaints he hears,
And bandied words, still beating on his ears. 650
Sighs, groans, and tears, proclaim his inward pains;
But the firm purpose of his heart remains.
　　The wretched queen, pursued by cruel Fate,
Begins at length the light of heaven to hate;
And loathes to live. Then dire portents she sees, 655
To hasten on the death her soul decrees—
Strange to relate! for when, before the shrine
She pours in sacrifice the purple wine,
The purple wine is turned to putrid blood;
And the white offered milk, converts to mud. 660
This dire presage, to her alone revealed,
From all, and e'en her sister, she concealed.
A marble temple stood within the grove,
Sacred to death, and to her murdered love;
That honored chapel she had hung around 665
With snowy fleeces, and with garlands crowned.
Oft, when she visited this lonely dome,
Strange voices issued from her husband's tomb:
She thought she heard him summon her away,
Invite her to his grave, and chide her stay. 670
Hourly 'tis heard, when with a boding note
The solitary screech-owl strains her throat,
And on a chimney's top, or turret's height,
With songs obscene, disturbs the silence of the night.
Besides, old prophecies augment her fears; 675
And stern Aeneas in her dreams appears,
Disdainful as by day: she seems, alone,
To wander in her sleep, through ways unknown,

642. *mast*: acorns.

Guideless and dark; or, in a desert plain
To seek her subjects, and to seek in vain—   680
Like Pentheus, when, distracted with his fear
He saw two suns, and double Thebes, appear;
Or mad Orestes, when his mother's ghost
Full in his face infernal torches tossed,
And shook her snaky locks: he shuns the sight,   685
Flies o'er the stage, surprised with mortal fright:
The Furies guard the door, and intercept his flight.
    Now, sinking underneath a load of grief,
From death alone she seeks her last relief:
The time and means resolved within her breast,   690
She to her mournful sister thus addressed
(Dissembling hope, her cloudy front she clears,
And a false vigor in her eyes appears):
"Rejoice! (she said) instructed from above,
My lover I shall gain, or lose my love.   695
Nigh rising Atlas, next the falling sun,
Long tracts of Aethiopian climates run:
There, a Massylian priestess I have found,
Honored for age, for magic arts renowned.
The Hesperian temple was her trusted care;   700
'Twas she supplied the wakeful dragon's fare:
She, poppy seeds in honey taught to steep:
Reclaimed his rage, and soothed him into sleep:
She watched the golden fruit. Her charms unbind
The chains of love, or fix them on the mind: 705
She stops the torrents, leaves the channel dry,
Repels the stars, and backward bears the sky.
The yawning earth rebellows to her call;
Pale ghosts ascend; and mountain ashes fall.
Witness ye gods, and thou, my better part,   710
How loth I am to try this impious art!
Within the secret court, with silent care,
Erect a lofty pile, exposed in air:

    681. *Pentheus*: king of Thebes, resisted the cult of Bacchus and was torn to
pieces by Bacchantes. Virgil was thinking of Euripides' *Bacchae*.
    700. The tree bearing golden apples, a gift of Gea (Earth) to Juno on her
marriage to Jove, was guarded far in the west by the Hesperides (Daughters of
Evening) and by a dragon.

Hang on the topmost part, the Trojan vest,
Spoils, arms, and presents, of my faithless guest.   715
Next, under these, the bridal bed be placed,
Where I my ruin in his arms embraced.
All relics of the wretch are doomed to fire;
For so the priestess and her charms require."
   Thus far she said, and further speech forbears.   720
A mortal paleness in her face appears:
Yet the mistrustless Anna could not find
The secret funeral in these rites designed;
Nor thought so dire a rage possessed her mind.
Unknowing of a train concealed so well,   725
She feared no worse than when Sichaeus fell;
Therefore obeys. The fatal pile they rear
Within the secret court, exposed in air,
The cloven holms and pines are heaped on high:
And garlands on the hollow spaces lie: 730
Sad cypress, vervain, yew, compose the wreath;
And every baleful green denoting death.
The queen, determined to the fatal deed,
The spoils and sword he left, in order spread,
And the man's image on the nuptial bed.   735
  And now (the sacred altars placed around)
The priestess enters, with her hair unbound,
And thrice invokes the powers below the ground.
Night, Erebus, and Chaos, she proclaims,
And threefold Hecate, with her hundred names,   740
And three Dianas: next, she sprinkles round
With feigned Avernian drops, the hallowed ground;
Culls hoary simples, found by Phoebe's light,
With brazen sickles reaped at noon of night;
Then mixes baleful juices in the bowl,   745
And cuts the forehead of a new-born foal,
Robbing the mother's love. The destined queen
Observes, assisting at the rites obscene:

   740. *threefold Hecate*: the same as the "three Dianas," a trinity composed
of Luna, Diana, Hecate. Hecate was infernal, favored in witchcraft. The "hundred names," transposed by Dryden, belonged not to her but to the "powers
below the ground": *ter centum ore tonat deos.*

A leavened cake in her devoted hands
She holds; and next the highest altar stands: 750
One tender foot was shod, her other bare;
Girt was her gathered gown, and loose her hair.
Thus dressed, she summoned with her dying breath
The heavens and planets conscious of her death,
And every power, if any rules above,   755
Who minds or who revenges injured love.
  'Twas dead of night, when weary bodies close
Their eyes in balmy sleep, and soft repose:
The winds no longer whisper through the woods;
Nor murmuring tides disturb the gentle floods.   760
The stars in silent order moved around;
And Peace, with downy wings was brooding on the ground.
The flocks and herds, and particolored fowl
Which haunt the woods or swim the weedy pool,
Stretched on the quiet earth, securely lay,   765
Forgetting the past labors of the day.
All else, of Nature's common gift partake:
Unhappy Dido was alone awake:
Nor sleep nor ease the furious queen can find:
Sleep fled her eyes, as quiet fled her mind.   770
Despair, and rage, and love, divide her heart;
Despair and rage had some, but love the greater part.
  Then thus she said within her secret mind:
"What shall I do? what succor can I find?
Become a suppliant to Iärbas' pride,   775
And take my turn to court, and be denied?
Shall I with this ungrateful Trojan go,
Forsake an empire, and attend a foe?
Himself I refuged, and his train relieved—
'Tis true—but am I sure to be received?   780
Can gratitude in Trojan souls have place?
Laomedon still lives in all his race!
Then shall I seek alone the churlish crew,
Or with my fleet their flying sails pursue?
What force have I but those, whom scarce before   785
I drew reluctant from their native shore?

782. *Laomedon*: a king of Troy who defrauded Apollo and Neptune
(Poseidon) of their wages for building the city's walls.

Will they again embark at my desire,
Once more sustain the seas, and quit their second Tyre?
Rather with steel thy guilty breast invade,
And take the fortune thou thyself hast made. 790
Your pity, sister, first seduced my mind;
Or seconded too well what I designed.
These dear-bought pleasures had I never known:
Had I continued free, and still my own
(Avoiding love), I had not found despair, 795
But shared with savage beasts the common air:
Like them, a lonely life I might have led;
Not mourned the living, nor disturbed the dead."
These thoughts she brooded in her anxious breast.—
On board, the Trojan found more easy rest. 800
Resolved to sail, in sleep he passed the night;
And ordered all things for his early flight.
   To whom, once more the wingèd god appears:
His former youthful mien and shape he wears;
And with this new alarm invades his ears: 805
"Sleep'st thou, O goddess-born? and canst thou drown
Thy needful cares, so near a hostile town,
Beset with foes; nor hear'st the western gales
Invite thy passage, and inspire thy sails?
She harbors in her heart a furious hate 810
(And thou shalt find the dire effects too late),
Fixed on revenge, and obstinate to die.—
Haste swiftly hence, while thou hast power to fly!
The sea with ships will soon be covered o'er,
And blazing firebrands kindle all the shore. 815
Prevent her rage, while night obscures the skies;
And sail before the purple morn arise.
Who knows what hazards thy delay may bring?
Woman's a various and a changeful thing!"
Thus, Hermes in the dream; then took his flight 820
Aloft in air, unseen, and mixed with night.
   Twice warned by the celestial messenger,
The pious prince arose with hasty fear;

816. *Prevent*: forestall.
819. *varium et mutabile semper / femina* . . .

Then roused his drowsy train without delay:
"Haste to your banks! your crooked anchors weigh,   825
And spread your flying sails, and stand to sea!
A god commands! he stood before my sight,
And urged us once again to speedy flight.
O sacred power! what power soe'er thou art,
To thy blessed orders I resign my heart.   830
Lead thou the way; protect thy Trojan bands;
And prosper the design thy will commands."
He said; and, drawing forth his flaming sword,
His thundering arm divides the many-twisted cord.
An emulating zeal inspires his train: 835
They run; they snatch; they rush into the main.
With headlong haste they leave the desert shores,
And brush the liquid seas with laboring oars.

   Aurora now had left her saffron bed,
And beams of early light the heavens o'erspread;   840
When, from a tower, the queen, with wakeful eyes,
Saw day point upward from the rosy skies.
She looked to seaward; but the sea was void,
And scarce in ken the sailing ships descried.
Stung with despite, and furious with despair,   845
She struck her trembling breast, and tore her hair.
"And shall the ungrateful traitor go (she said),
My land forsaken, and my love betrayed?
Shall we not arm? not rush from every street,
To follow, sink, and burn, his perjured fleet?   850
Haste! haul my galleys out! pursue the foe!
Bring flaming brands! set sail, and swiftly row!
What have I said? Where am I? Fury turns
My brain; and my distempered bosom burns.
Then, when I gave my person and my throne,   855
This hate, this rage, had been more timely shown.
See now the promised faith, the vaunted name,
The pious man, who, rushing through the flame,

   854. The next line in Dryden's text of Virgil was *infelix Dido, nunc te fata impia tangunt*. Dryden did not translate it, he said, because he "doubted of the sense," thinking it inconsistent with line 997. Later, it seems, he found *fata* "reasonably altered" in N. Heinsius' 1676 edition (as in most later ones) to *facta*. The sense is, "now your impious acts are coming home to you."

Preserved his gods, and to the Phrygian shore
The burden of his feeble father bore!   860
I should have torn him piecemeal—strewed in floods
His scattered limbs, or left exposed in woods:
Destroyed his friends, and son; and from the fire
Have set the reeking boy before the sire!
Events are doubtful, which on battle wait;   865
Yet where's the doubt, to souls secure of fate?
My Tyrians, at their injured queen's command,
Had tossed their fires amid the Trojan band:
At once extinguished all the faithless name;
And I myself, in vengeance of my shame,   870
Had fall'n upon the pile, to mend the funeral flame.
Thou Sun, who view'st at once the world below!
Thou Juno, guardian of the nuptial vow!
Thou Hecate, hearken from thy dark abodes!
Ye Furies, fiends, and violated gods!   875
All powers invoked with Dido's dying breath,
Attend her curses, and avenge her death!
If so the Fates ordain, and Jove commands,
The ungrateful wretch should find the Latian lands,
Yet let a race untamed, and haughty foes,   880
His peaceful entrance with dire arms oppose:
Oppressed with numbers in the unequal field,
His men discouraged, and himself expelled,
Let him for succor sue from place to place,
Torn from his subjects, and his son's embrace.   885
First, let him see his friends in battle slain,
And their untimely fate lament in vain:
And when at length, the cruel war will cease,
On hard conditions may he buy his peace;
Nor let him then enjoy supreme command;   890
But fall, untimely, by some hostile hand;
And lie unburied on the barren sand!
These are my prayers, and this my dying will;
And you, my Tyrians, every curse fulfill:

882 sqq. Charles I is said to have opened on this passage in Virgil when he
consulted the *sortes Virgilianae* in the Bodleian Library at Oxford.

Perpetual hate and mortal wars proclaim   895
Against the prince, the people, and the name.
These grateful offerings on my grave bestow;
Nor league, nor love, the hostile nations know!
Now, and from hence in every future age,
When rage excites your arms, and strength supplies the rage,   900
Rise some avenger of our Libyan blood;
With fire and sword pursue the perjured brood:
Our arms, our seas, our shores, opposed to theirs;
And the same hate descend on all our heirs!"
   This said, within her anxious mind she weighs   905
The means of cutting short her odious days.
Then to Sichaeus' nurse she briefly said
(For, when she left her country, her's was dead),
"Go, Barce, call my sister. Let her care
The solemn rites of sacrifice prepare;   910
The sheep, and all the atoning offerings, bring;
Sprinkling her body from the crystal spring
With living drops: then let her come; and thou,
With sacred fillets bind thy hoary brow.
Thus will I pay my vows to Stygian Jove,   915
And end the cares of my disastrous love;
Then cast the Trojan image on the fire;
And, as that burns, my passion shall expire."
   The nurse moves onward with officious care,
And all the speed her aged limbs can bear.   920
But furious Dido, with dark thoughts involved,
Shook at the mighty mischief she resolved.
With livid spots distinguished was her face;
Red were her rolling eyes, and discomposed her pace:
Ghastly she gazed; with pain she drew her breath;   925
And nature shivered at approaching death.
   Then swiftly to the fatal place she passed,
And mounts the funeral pile with furious haste;
Unsheaths the sword the Trojan left behind
(Not for so dire an enterprise designed).   930
But when she viewed the garments loosely spread,
Which once he wore, and saw the conscious bed,

She paused, and with a sigh, the robes embraced;
Then on the couch her trembling body cast,
Repressed her ready tears, and spoke her last: 935
"Dear pledges of my love, while heaven so pleased,
Receive a soul, of mortal anguish eased.
My fatal course is finished; and I go,
A glorious name, among the ghosts below.
A lofty city by my hands is raised; 940
Pygmalion punished, and my lord appeased.
What could my fortune have afforded more,
Had the false Trojan never touched my shore?"
Then kissed the couch; and "Must I die (she said),
And unrevenged? 'tis doubly to be dead! 945
Yet e'en this death with pleasure I receive:
On any terms, 'tis better than to live.
These flames, from far, may the false Trojan view;
These boding omens his base flight pursue!"
She said, and struck: deep entered in her side 950
The piercing steel, with reeking purple dyed.
Clogged in the wound the cruel weapon stands;
The spouting blood came streaming on her hands.
    Her sad attendants saw the deadly stroke,
And with loud cries the sounding palace shook. 955
Distracted, from the fatal sight they fled,
And through the town the dismal rumor spread.
First from the frighted court the yell began;
Redoubled, thence from house to house it ran:
The groans of men, with shrieks, laments, and cries 960
Of mixing women, mount the vaulted skies.
Not less the clamor, than if—ancient Tyre,
Or the new Carthage, set by foes on fire—
The rolling ruin, with their loved abodes,
Involved the blazing temple of their gods. 965
    Her sister hears: and furious with despair,
She beats her breast, and rends her yellow hair;
And, calling on Eliza's name aloud,
Runs breathless to the place, and breaks the crowd,
"Was all that pomp of woe for this prepared, 970
These fires, this funeral pile, these altars reared?

Was all this train of plots contrived (said she),
All, only to deceive unhappy me?
Which is the worst? Didst thou in death pretend
To scorn thy sister, or delude thy friend?   975
Thy summoned sister and thy friend had come:
One sword had served us both, one common tomb:
Was I to raise the pile, the powers invoke,
Not to be present at the fatal stroke?
At once thou hast destroyed thyself and me,   980
Thy town, thy senate, and thy colony!
Bring water! bathe the wound; while I in death
Lay close my lips to hers, and catch the flying breath."
This said, she mounts the pile with eager haste,
And in her arms the gasping queen embraced;   985
Her temples chafed; and her own garments tore
To stanch the streaming blood, and cleanse the gore.
Thrice Dido tried to raise her drooping head,
And, fainting, thrice fell groveling on the bed:
Thrice oped her heavy eyes, and saw the light;   990
But, having found it, sickened at the sight,
And closed her lids at last in endless night.
    Then Juno, grieving that she should sustain
A death so lingering, and so full of pain,
Sent Iris down to free her from the strife   995
Of laboring nature, and dissolve her life.
For, since she died not doomed by heaven's decree,
Or her own crime, but human casualty,
And rage of love that plunged her in despair,
The Sisters had not cut the topmost hair,   1000
Which Proserpine and they can only know;
Nor made her sacred to the shades below.
Downward the various goddess took her flight,
And drew a thousand colors from the light.
Then stood above the dying lover's head,   1005
And said: "I thus devote thee to the dead:
This offering to the infernal gods I bear."
Thus while she spoke, she cut the fatal hair:
The struggling soul was loosed, and life dissolved in air.

    1003. *various*: in hue, being the rainbow.

BOOK V

THE ARGUMENT

Aeneas, setting sail from Africa, is driven by a storm on the coasts of
Sicily, where he is hospitably received by his friend Acestes, king of part
of the island, and born of Trojan parentage. He applies himself to celebrate the memory of his father with divine honors, and accordingly insti-
tutes funeral games, and appoints prizes for those who should conquer in
them. While these ceremonies were performing, Juno sends Iris to persuade the Trojan women to burn the ships, who upon her instigation set
fire to them; which burned four, and would have consumed the rest, had
not Jupiter by a miraculous shower extinguished it. Upon this, Aeneas, by
the advice of one of his generals, and a vision of his father, builds a city
for the women, old men, and others, who were either unfit for war, or
weary of the voyage, and sails for Italy. Venus procures of Neptune a safe
voyage for him and all his men, excepting only his pilot Palinurus, who
was unfortunately lost.

MEANTIME the Trojan cuts his watery way,
Fixed on his voyage, through the curling sea;
Then, casting back his eyes, with dire amaze,
Sees on the Punic shore the mountain blaze:
The cause unknown; yet his presaging mind   5
The fate of Dido from the fire divined.
He knew the stormy souls of womankind;
What secret springs their eager passions move,
How capable of death for injured love.
Dire auguries from hence the Trojans draw;   10
Till neither fires nor shining shores they saw.
   Now seas and skies their prospects only bound:
An empty space above, a floating field around.

But soon the heavens with shadows were o'erspread;
A swelling cloud hung hovering o'er their head: 15
Livid it looked—the threatening of a storm;
Then night and horror ocean's face deform.
The pilot, Palinurus, cried aloud:
"What gusts of weather from that gathering cloud
My thoughts presage! Ere yet the tempest roars,   20
Stand to your tackle, mates, and stretch your oars;
Contract your swelling sails, and luff to wind."
The frighted crew perform the task assigned.
Then, to his fearless chief, "Not heaven (said he),
Though Jove himself should promise Italy,   25
Can stem the torrent of this raging sea.
Mark, how the shifting winds from west arise,
And what collected night involves the skies!
Nor can our shaken vessels live at sea,
Much less against the tempest force their way: 30
'Tis fate diverts our course, and fate we must obey.
Not far from hence, if I observed aright
The southing of the stars, and polar light,
Sicilia lies, whose hospitable shores
In safety we may reach, with struggling oars."   35
Aeneas then replied: "Too sure I find,
We strive in vain against the seas and wind:
Now shift your sails: what place can please me more
Than what you promise, the Sicilian shore,
Whose hallowed earth Anchises' bones contains,   40
And where a prince of Trojan lineage reigns."
The course resolved, before the western wind
They scud amain, and make the port assigned.
    Meantime Acestes, from a lofty stand,
Beheld the fleet descending on the land;   45
And, not unmindful of his ancient race,
Down from the cliff he ran, with eager pace,
And held the hero in a strict embrace.
Of a rough Libyan bear, the spoils he wore,
And either hand a pointed javelin bore.   50

33. Fixed stars of course are seen further southward as a ship sails north; the altitude of the Pole Star increases.

His mother was a dame of Dardan blood;
His sire Crinisus, a Sicilian flood.
He welcomes his returning friends ashore
With plenteous country cates, and homely store.
  Now, when the following morn had chased away   55
The flying stars, and light restored the day,
Aeneas called the Trojan troops around,
And thus bespoke them from a rising ground:
"Offspring of heaven, divine Dardanian race!
The sun, revolving through the ethereal space,   60
The shining circle of the year has filled,
Since first this isle my father's ashes held:
And now the rising day renews the year—
A day for ever sad, for ever dear.
This would I celebrate with annual games,   65
With gifts on altars piled, and holy flames,
Though banished to Gaetulia's barren sands,
Caught on the Grecian seas, or hostile lands:
But, since this happy storm our fleet has driven
(Not, as I deem, without the will of heaven)   70
Upon these friendly shores and flowery plains,
Which hide Anchises and his blest remains;
Let us with joy perform his honors due,
And pray for prosperous winds, our voyage to renew—
Pray, that in towns and temples of our own,   75
The name of great Anchises may be known;
And yearly games may spread the god's renown.
Our sports, Acestes, of the Trojan race,
With royal gifts ordained, is pleased to grace:
Two steers on every ship the king bestows: 80
His gods and ours shall share your equal vows.
Besides, if, nine days hence, the rosy morn
Shall with unclouded light the skies adorn,
That day with solemn sports I mean to grace:
Light galleys on the seas shall run a watery race: 85

52. *flood*: river.
54. *cates*: victuals.
65. *annual games*: the Parentalia, held every February at Rome in honor of
the dead, were said by Ovid (*Fasti*, Book II, 543) to have been instituted by
Aeneas in honor of Anchises.

Some shall in swiftness for the goal contend,
And others try the twanging bow to bend:
The strong, with iron gauntlets armed, shall stand
Opposed in combat on the yellow sand.
Let all be present at the games prepared;   90
And joyful victors wait the just reward.
But now assist the rites with garlands crowned."
He said, and first his brows with myrtle bound.
Then Helymus, by his example led,
And old Acestes, each adorned his head;   95
Thus young Ascanius, with a sprightly grace,
His temples tied, and all the Trojan race.
    Aeneas then advanced amidst the train,
By thousands followed through the flowery plain,
To great Anchises' tomb; which when he found,   100
He poured to Bacchus, on the hallowed ground
Two bowls of sparkling wine, of milk two more,
And two (from offered bulls) of purple gore.
With roses then the sepulcher he strowed,
And thus, his father's ghost bespoke aloud: 105
"Hail, O ye holy manës! hail again,
Paternal ashes, now revived in vain!
The gods permitted not, that you with me
Should reach the promised shores of Italy,
Or Tiber's flood—what flood soe'er it be."   110
Scarce had he finished, when, with speckled pride,
A serpent from the tomb began to glide;
His hugy bulk on seven high volumes rolled;
Blue was his breadth of back, but streaked with scaly gold:
Thus riding on his curls, he seemed to pass   115
A rolling fire along, and singe the grass.
More various colors through his body run,
Than Iris when her bow imbibes the sun.
Betwixt the rising altars, and around,
The sacred monster shot along the ground;   120
With harmless play amidst the bowls he passed,

113. *volumes*: coils.
115. *curls*: coils.

And with his lolling tongue assayed the taste:
Thus fed with holy food, the wondrous guest
Within the hollow tomb retired to rest.
The pious prince, surprised at what he viewed,   125
The funeral honors with more zeal renewed;
Doubtful if this the place's genius were,
Or guardian of his father's sepulcher.
Five sheep, according to the rites, he slew;
As many swine, and steers of sable hue;   130
New generous wine he from the goblets poured;
And called his father's ghost, from hell restored.
The glad attendants in long order come,
Offering their gifts at great Anchises' tomb.
Some add more oxen; some divide the spoil;   135
Some place the chargers on the grassy soil;
Some blow the fires, and offered entrails broil.
    Now came the day desired. The skies were bright
With rosy luster of the rising light:
The bordering people, roused by sounding fame   140
Of Trojan feasts and great Acestes' name,
The crowded shore with acclamations fill;
Part to behold, and part to prove their skill.
And first the gifts in public view they place,
Green laurel wreaths, and palm, the victors' grace.   145
Within the circle, arms and tripods lie,
Ingots of gold and silver heaped on high,
And vests embroidered, of the Tyrian dye.
The trumpet's clangor then the feast proclaims;
And all prepare for their appointed games.   150
Four galleys first, which equal rowers bear,
Advancing, in the watery lists appear.
The speedy Dolphin, that outstrips the wind,
Bore Mnestheus, author of the Memmian kind:
Gyas the vast Chimaera's bulk commands,   155
Which rising like a towering city stands:

127-8. *genius* . . . *Or guardian: genius* or *famulus,* that is, either the tutelary
deity of the place or the "familiar" of the dead.
154 sqq. *Memmian kind* . . . *Sergian race* . . . *Cluentius:* Roman families.

Three Trojans tug at every laboring oar;
Three banks in three degrees the sailors bore;
Beneath their sturdy strokes the billows roar.
Sergestus, who began the Sergian race   160
In the great Centaur, took the leading place:
Cloanthus on the sea-green Scylla stood;
From whom Cluentius draws his Trojan blood.
    Far in the sea, against the foaming shore,
There stands a rock: the raging billows roar   165
Above his head in storms; but when 'tis clear,
Uncurl their ridgy backs, and at his foot appear.
In peace, below, the gentle waters run;
The cormorants, above, lie basking in the sun.
On this the hero fixed an oak in sight,   170
The mark to guide the mariners aright.
To bear with this, the seamen stretch their oars;
Then round the rock they steer, and seek the former shores.
The lots decide their place. Above the rest,
Each leader shining in his Tyrian vest: 175
The common crew, with wreaths of poplar boughs
Their temples crown, and shade their sweaty brows:
Besmeared with oil, their naked shoulders shine:
All take their seats, and wait the sounding sign.
They grip their oars; and every panting breast   180
Is raised by turns with hope, by turns with fear depressed.
The clangor of the trumpet gives the sign;
At once they start, advancing in a line;
With shouts the sailors rend the starry skies;
Lashed with their oars, the smoky billows rise;   185
Sparkles the briny main, and the vexed ocean fries.
Exact in time, with equal strokes they row:
At once the brushing oars and brazen prow
Dash up the sandy waves, and ope the depths below.
Not fiery coursers, in a chariot-race,   190
Invade the field with half so swift a pace:
Not the fierce driver with more fury lends
The sounding lash, and ere the stroke descends,
Low to the wheels his pliant body bends.

The partial crowd their hopes and fears divide,   195
And aid with eager shouts, the favored side.
Cries, murmurs, clamors, with a mixing sound,
From woods to woods, from hills to hills rebound.
    Amidst the loud applauses of the shore,
Gyas outstripped the rest, and sprung before: 200
Cloanthus, better manned, pursued him fast;
But his o'er-masted galley checked his haste.
The Centaur and the Dolphin brush the brine
With equal oars, advancing in a line:
And now the mighty Centaur seems to lead,   205
And now the speedy Dolphin gets ahead:
Now board to board the rival vessels row;
The billows lave the skies, and ocean groans below.
They reached the mark. Proud Gyas and his train
In triumph rode, the victors of the main: 210
But, steering round, he charged his pilot: "Stand
More close to shore, and skim along the sand!
Let others bear to sea." Menoetes heard;
But secret shelves too cautiously he feared,
And, fearing, sought the deep; and still aloof he steered.   215
With louder cries the captain called again:
"Bear to the rocky shore, and shun the main!"
He spoke, and speaking, at his stern he saw
The bold Cloanthus near the shelvings draw.
Betwixt the mark and him the Scylla stood,   220
And in a closer compass plowed the flood.
He passed the mark; and, wheeling, got before:
Gyas blasphemed the gods, devoutly swore,
Cried out for anger, and his hair he tore.
Mindless of others' lives (so high was grown   225
His rising rage), and careless of his own,
The trembling dotard to the deck he drew,
And hoisted up, and overboard he threw:
This done, he seized the helm; his fellows cheered;
Turned short upon the shelves, and madly steered.   230
    Hardly his head the plunging pilot rears,
Clogged with his clothes, and cumbered with his years:

Now drooping wet, he climbs the cliff with pain.
The crowd that saw him fall, and float again,
Shout from the distant shore; and loudly laughed,   235
To see his heaving breast disgorge the briny draught.
The following Centaur, and the Dolphin's crew,
Their vanished hopes of victory renew;
While Gyas lags, they kindle in the race,
To reach the mark. Sergestus takes the place;   240
Mnestheus pursues; and, while around they wind,
Comes up, not half his galley's length behind;
Then on the deck amidst his mates, appeared,
And thus their drooping courages he cheered:
"My friends, and Hector's followers heretofore,   245
Exert your vigor; tug the laboring oar;
Stretch to your strokes, my still-unconquered crew,
Whom from the flaming walls of Troy I drew.
In this our common interest, let me find
That strength of hand, that courage of the mind,   250
As when you stemmed the strong Malean flood;
And o'er the Syrtes' broken billows rowed.
I seek not now the foremost palm to gain;
Though yet—but, ah! that haughty wish is vain!
Let those enjoy it whom the gods ordain.   255
But to be last, the lags of all the race!—
Redeem yourselves and me from that disgrace."
Now, one and all, they tug amain; they row
At the full stretch, and shake the brazen prow.
The sea beneath them sinks; their laboring sides   260
Are swelled, and sweat runs guttering down in tides.
Chance aids their daring with unhoped success:
Sergestus, eager, with his beak to press
Betwixt the rival galley and the rock,
Shuts up the unwieldy Centaur in the lock.   265
The vessel struck; and, with the dreadful shock
Her oars she shivered, and her head she broke.

251. *Malean flood*: currents are strong off Cape Malea, the southerly tip of
the Peloponnesus.

The trembling rowers from their banks arise,
And, anxious for themselves, renounce the prize.
With iron poles they heave her off the shores;   270
And gather from the sea their floating oars.
The crew of Mnestheus, with elated minds,
Urge their success, and call the willing winds;
Then ply their oars, and cut their liquid way
In larger compass, on the roomy sea.   275
As, when the dove her rocky hold forsakes,
Roused in a fright, her sounding wings she shakes;
The cavern rings with clattering; out she flies,
And leaves her callow care, and cleaves the skies:
At first she flutters; but at length she springs   280
To smoother flight, and shoots upon her wings:
So Mnestheus in the Dolphin cuts the sea;
And, flying with a force, that force assists his way.
Sergestus in the Centaur soon he passed,
Wedged in the rocky shoals, and sticking fast.   285
In vain the victor he with cries implores,
And practices to row with shattered oars.
Then Mnestheus bears with Gyas and outflies:
The ship, without a pilot, yields the prize.
Unvanquished Scylla now alone remains: 290
Her he pursues; and all his vigor strains.
Shouts from the favoring multitude arise;
Applauding Echo to the shouts replies:
Shouts, wishes, and applause, run rattling through the skies.
These clamors with disdain the Scylla heard;   295
Much, grudged the praise, but more, the robbed reward:
Resolved to hold their own, they mend their pace;
All obstinate to die, or gain the race.
Raised with success, the Dolphin swiftly ran;
For they can conquer, who believe they can.   300
Both urge their oars; and fortune both supplies
(And both perhaps had shared an equal prize);
When to the seas Cloanthus holds his hands,
And succor from the watery powers demands:

"Gods of the liquid realms on which I row!   305
If, given by you, the laurel bind my brow,
(Assist to make me guilty of my vow!)
A snow-white bull shall on your shores be slain;
His offered entrails cast into the main,
And ruddy wine, from golden goblets thrown,   310
Your grateful gift and my return shall own."
The choir of nymphs, and Phorcus, from below,
With virgin Panopea, heard his vow;
And old Portunus, with his breadth of hand,
Pushed on and sped the galley to the land.   315
Swift as a shaft, or wingèd wind, she flies,
And, darting to the port, obtains the prize.
    The herald summons all, and then proclaims
Cloanthus conqueror of the naval games.
The prince with laurel, crowns the victor's head;   320
And three fat steers are to his vessel led
(The ship's reward); with generous wine beside,
And sums of silver, which the crew divide.
The leaders are distinguished from the rest;
The victor honored with a nobler vest,   325
Where gold and purple strive in equal rows,
And needlework its happy cost bestows.
There, Ganymede is wrought with living art,
Chasing through Ida's groves the trembling hart;
Breathless he seems, yet eager to pursue;   330
When from aloft descends, in open view
The bird of Jove, and, sousing on his prey,
With crooked talons bears the boy away.
In vain, with lifted hands and gazing eyes,
His guards behold him soaring through the skies;   335
And dogs pursue his flight, with imitated cries.
    Mnestheus, the second victor was declared:
And, summoned there, the second prize he shared.

312–13. *Phorcus, Panopea*: sea deities.
314. *Portunus*: god of ports.
332. *sousing*: diving.

A coat of mail, which brave Demoleus bore,
More brave Aeneas from his shoulders tore,   340
In single combat on the Trojan shore.
This was ordained for Mnestheus to possess—
In war for his defense, for ornament in peace.
Rich was the gift, and glorious to behold,
But yet so ponderous with its plates of gold,   345
That scarce two servants could the weight sustain:
Yet, loaded thus, Demoleus o'er the plain
Pursued and lightly seized the Trojan train.
The third, succeeding to the last reward,
Two goodly bowls of massy silver shared,   350
With figures prominent, and richly wrought,
And two brass caldrons from Dodona brought.
    Thus all, rewarded by the hero's hands,
Their conquering temples bound with purple bands.
And now Sergestus, clearing from the rock,   355
Brought back his galley shattered with the shock.
Forlorn she looked, without an aiding oar,
And, hooted by the vulgar, made to shore.
As when a snake, surprised upon the road,
Is crushed athwart her body by the load   360
Of heavy wheels; or with a mortal wound
Her belly bruised, and trodden to the ground—
In vain, with loosened curls, she crawls along;
Yet, fierce above, she brandishes her tongue;
Glares with her eyes, and bristles with her scales,   365
But, groveling in the dust, her parts unsound she trails.
So slowly to the port the Centaur tends,
But, what she wants in oars, with sails amends.
Yet, for his galley saved, the grateful prince
Is pleased the unhappy chief to recompense: 370
Pholoe, the Cretan slave, rewards his care,
Beauteous herself, with lovely twins as fair.
    From thence his way the Trojan hero bent
Into the neighboring plain, with mountains pent,
Whose sides were shaded with surrounding wood.   375
Full in the midst of this fair valley, stood

A native theater, which, rising slow
By just degrees, o'erlooked the ground below.
High on a sylvan throne the leader sat;
A numerous train attend in solemn state.   380
Here those, that in the rapid course delight,
Desire of honor, and the prize, invite.
The rival runners without order stand;
The Trojans, mixed with the Sicilian band.
First Nisus, with Euryalus, appears—   385
Euryalus a boy of blooming years,
With sprightly grace and equal beauty crowned—
Nisus, for friendship to the youth, renowned.
Diores next, of Priam's royal race,
Then Salius, joined with Patron, took their place;   390
(But Patron in Arcadia had his birth,
And Salius, his from Acarnanian earth;)
Then two Sicilian youths—the names of these
Swift Helymus, and lovely Panopes
(Both jolly huntsmen, both in forests bred,   395
And owning old Acestes for their head),
With several others of ignobler name,
Whom time has not delivered o'er to fame.
    To these the hero thus his thoughts explained,
In words which general approbation gained: 400
"One common largess is for all designed
(The vanquished and the victor shall be joined):
Two darts of polished steel and Gnossian wood,
A silver-studded axe, alike bestowed.
The foremost three have olive wreaths decreed   405
The first of these obtains a stately steed
Adorned with trappings; and the next in fame,
The quiver of an Amazonian dame,
With feathered Thracian arrows well supplied:
A golden belt shall gird his manly side,   410
Which with a sparkling diamond shall be tied.
The third this Grecian helmet shall content."
He said. To their appointed base they went;

With beating hearts the expected sign receive,
And, starting all at once, the barrier leave. 415
Spread out, as on the wingèd winds, they flew,
And seized the distant goal with greedy view.
Shot from the crowd, swift Nisus all o'er-passed;
Nor storms, nor thunder, equal half his haste.
The next, but, though the next, yet far disjoined, 420
Came Salius; and Euryalus behind;
Then Helymus, whom young Diores plied,
Step after step, and almost side by side,
His shoulders pressing—and, in longer space,
Had won, or left at least a dubious race. 425
   Now, spent, the goal they almost reach at last,
When eager Nisus, hapless in his haste,
Slipped first, and, slipping, fell upon the plain,
Soaked with the blood of oxen newly slain.
The careless victor had not marked his way; 430
But, treading where the treacherous puddle lay,
His heels flew up; and on the grassy floor
He fell, besmeared with filth and holy gore.
Not mindless then, Euryalus, of thee,
Nor of the sacred bonds of amity, 435
He strove the immediate rival's hope to cross,
And caught the foot of Salius as he rose:
So Salius lay extended on the plain:
Euryalus springs out, the prize to gain,
And leaves the crowd:—applauding peals attend 440
The victor to the goal, who vanquished by his friend.
Next Helymus; and then Diores came,
By two misfortunes made the third in fame.
   But Salius enters, and, exclaiming loud
For justice, deafens and disturbs the crowd; 445
Urges his cause may in the court be heard;
And pleads the prize is wrongfully conferred.
But favor for Euryalus appears;
His blooming beauty, with his tender years,
Had bribed the judges for the promised prize; 450
Besides, Diores fills the court with cries,

Who vainly reaches at the last reward,
If the first palm on Salius be conferred.
Then thus the prince: "Let no disputes arise:
Where Fortune placed it, I award the prize.   455
But Fortune's errors give me leave to mend,
At least to pity my deserving friend."
He said, and, from among the spoils, he draws
(Ponderous with shaggy mane and golden paws)
A lion's hide: to Salius this he gives: 460
Nisus with envy sees the gift, and grieves.
"If such rewards to vanquished men are due
(He said), and falling is to rise by you,
What prize may Nisus from your bounty claim,
Who merited the first rewards and fame?   465
In falling, both an equal fortune tried;
Would Fortune for my fall so well provide!"
With this he pointed to his face, and showed
His hands and all his habit smeared with blood.
The indulgent father of the people smiled,   470
And caused to be produced an ample shield,
Of wondrous art, by Didymaon wrought,
Long since from Neptune's bars in triumph brought.
This given to Nisus, he divides the rest,
And equal justice in his gifts expressed.   475
    The race thus ended, and rewards bestowed,
Once more the prince bespeaks the attentive crowd:
"If there be here, whose dauntless courage dare
In gauntlet fight, with limbs and body bare,
His opposite sustain in open view,   480
Stand forth the champion, and the games renew.
Two prizes I propose, and thus divide—
A bull with gilded horns, and fillets tied,
Shall be the portion of the conquering chief:
A sword and helm shall cheer the loser's grief."   485
    Then haughty Dares in the lists appears:
Stalking he strides, his head erected bears:
His nervous arms the weighty gauntlet wield;
And loud applauses echo through the field.

Dares alone in combat used to stand   490
The match of mighty Paris, hand to hand;
The same, at Hector's funerals, undertook
Gigantic Butes, of the Amycian stock,
And, by the stroke of his resistless hand,
Stretched the vast bulk upon the yellow sand.   495
Such Dares was; and such he strode along,
And drew the wonder of the gazing throng.
His brawny back and ample breast he shows;
His lifted arms around his head he throws,
And deals, in whistling air, his empty blows.   500
His match is sought; but, through the trembling band,
Not one dares answer to the proud demand.
Presuming of his force, with sparkling eyes
Already he devours the promised prize.
He claims the bull with aweless insolence,   505
And, having seized his horns, accosts the prince:
"If none my matchless valor dares oppose,
How long shall Dares wait his dastard foes?
Permit me, chief, permit without delay,
To lead this uncontended gift away."   510
The crowd assents, and, with redoubled cries,
For the proud challenger demands the prize.
   Acestes, fired with just disdain, to see
The plain usurped without a victory,
Reproached Entellus thus, who sat beside,   515
And heard and saw, unmoved, the Trojan's pride:
"Once, but in vain, a champion of renown,
So tamely can you bear the ravished crown,
A prize in triumph borne before your sight,
And shun for fear the danger of the fight?   520
Where is your Eryx now, the boasted name,
The god who taught your thundering arm the game?
Where now your baffled honor? where the spoil
That filled your house, and fame that filled our isle?"
Entellus thus: "My soul is still the same,   525
Unmoved with fear, and moved with martial fame;

But my chill blood is curdled in my veins;
And scarce the shadow of a man remains.
Oh! could I turn to that fair prime again,
That prime, of which this boaster is so vain,   530
The brave, who this decrepit age defies,
Should feel my force, without the promised prize."
He said; and, rising at the word, he threw
Two ponderous gauntlets down in open view—
Gauntlets, which Eryx wont in fight to wield,   535
And sheath his hands with, in the listed field.
With fear and wonder seized, the crowd beholds
The gloves of death, with seven distinguished folds
Of tough bull hides; the space within is spread
With iron, or with loads of heavy lead.   540
Dares himself was daunted at the sight,
Renounced his challenge, and refused to fight.
Astonished at their weight, the hero stands,
And poised the ponderous engines in his hands.
"What had your wonder (said Entellus) been,   545
Had you the gauntlets of Alcides seen,
Or viewed the stern debate on this unhappy green!
These, which I bear, your brother Eryx bore,
Still marked with battered brains and mingled gore.
With these he long sustained the Herculean arm;   550
And these I wielded while my blood was warm,
This languished frame while better spirits fed,
Ere age unstrung my nerves, or time o'er-snowed my head,
But if the challenger these arms refuse,
And cannot wield their weight, or dare not use;   555
If great Aeneas and Acestes join
In his request, these gauntlets I resign;
Let us with equal arms perform the fight;
And let him leave to fear, since I resign my right."
This said, Entellus for the strife prepares;   560
Stripped of his quilted coat, his body bares:

546. *Alcides*: Hercules.
548. *brother Eryx*: son of Venus and the Argonaut, Butes.
559. *leave to fear*: leave off being afraid.

Composed of mighty bones and brawn, he stands,
A goodly towering object on the sands.
    Then just Aeneas equal arms supplied,
Which round their shoulders to their wrists they tied.   565
Both on the tiptoe stand, at full extent,
Their arms aloft, their bodies inly bent;
Their heads from aiming blows they bear afar;
With clashing gauntlets then provoke the war.
One on his youth and pliant limbs relies;   570
One on his sinews, and his giant size.
The last is stiff with age, his motion slow;
He heaves for breath; he staggers to and fro;
And clouds of issuing smoke his nostrils loudly blow.
Yet equal in success, they ward, they strike;   575
Their ways are different, but their art alike.
Before, behind, the blows are dealt; around
Their hollow sides the rattling thumps resound
A storm of strokes, well meant, with fury flies,
And errs about their temples, ears, and eyes—   580
Nor always errs; for oft the gauntlet draws
A sweeping stroke along the crackling jaws.
Heavy with age, Entellus stands his ground.
But with his warping body wards the wound.
His hand and watchful eye keep even pace;   585
While Dares traverses, and shifts his place,
And, like a captain who beleaguers round
Some strong-built castle on a rising ground,
Views all the approaches with observing eyes;
This and that other part in vain he tries,   590
And more on industry than force relies.
With hands on high, Entellus threats the foe;
But Dares watched the motion from below,
And slipped aside, and shunned the long-descending blow.
Entellus wastes his forces on the wind,   595
And, thus deluded of the stroke designed,

565. *et paribus palmas amborum innexuit armis*: "he [Aeneas] bound their
hands with identical armor." The cestus was of bull's hide, weighted with lead,
tied around the forearm and back of the hand. It did not extend from shoulder
to wrist.

Headlong and heavy fell: his ample breast,
And weighty limbs, his ancient mother pressed.
So falls a hollow pine, that long had stood
On Ida's height, or Erymanthus' wood,   600
Torn from the roots. The differing nations rise;
And shouts and mingled murmurs rend the skies.
Acestes runs with eager haste, to raise
The fallen companion of his youthful days.
Dauntless he rose, and to the fight returned;   605
With shame his glowing cheeks, his eyes with fury, burned.
Disdain and conscious virtue fired his breast;
And with redoubled force his foe he pressed.
He lays on load with either hand, amain,
And headlong drives the Trojan o'er the plain;   610
Nor stops, nor stays; nor rest nor breath allows;
But storms of strokes descend about his brows,
A rattling tempest, and a hail of blows.
But now the prince, who saw the wild increase
Of wounds, commands the combatants to cease,   615
And bounds Entellus' wrath, and bids the peace.
   First to the Trojan, spent with toil, he came,
And soothed his sorrow for the suffered shame.
"What fury seized my friend? The gods (said he),
To him propitious, and averse to thee,   620
Have given his arm superior force to thine.
'Tis madness to contend with strength divine."
The gauntlet-fight thus ended, from the shore
His faithful friends unhappy Dares bore:
His mouth and nostrils poured a purple flood;   625
And pounded teeth came rushing with his blood.
Faintly he staggered through the hissing throng,
And hung his head, and trailed his legs along.
The sword and casque are carried by his train;
But with his foe the palm and ox remain.   630
   The champion, then, before Aeneas came,
Proud of his prize, but prouder of his fame:

600. *Erymanthus*: a mountain in Arcadia.

"O goddess-born, and you, Dardanian host,
Mark with attention, and forgive my boast:
Learn what I was, by what remains! and know,   635
From what impending fate you saved my foe."
Sternly he spoke; and then confronts the bull;
And, on his ample forehead aiming full,
The deadly stroke, descending, pierced the skull.
Down drops the beast, nor needs a second wound,   640
But sprawls in pangs of death, and spurns the ground.
Then thus: "In Dares' stead I offer this.
Eryx! accept a nobler sacrifice:
Take the last gift my withered arms can yield:
Thy gauntlets I resign, and here renounce the field."   645
    This done, Aeneas orders, for the close,
The strife of archers, with contending bows.
The mast, Sergestus' shattered galley bore,
With his own hands he raises on the shore.
A fluttering dove upon the top they tie,   650
The living mark at which their arrows fly.
The rival archers in a line advance,
Their turn of shooting to receive from chance:
A helmet holds their names: the lots are drawn;
On the first scroll was read Hippocoön: 655
The people shout. Upon the next was found
Young Mnestheus, late with naval honors crowned.
The third contained Eurytion's noble name,
Thy brother, Pandarus, and next in fame,
Whom Pallas urged the treaty to confound,   660
And send among the Greeks a feathered wound.
Acestes, in the bottom, last remained,
Whom not his age from youthful sports restrained.
Soon all with vigor bend their trusty bows;
And from the quiver each his arrow chose,   665
Hippocoön's was the first: with forceful sway
It flew, and, whizzing, cut the liquid way.
Fixed in the mast the feathered weapon stands:
The fearful pigeon flutters in her bands;

    661. The incident is in Book IV of the *Iliad*.

And the tree trembled; and the shouting cries   670
Of the pleased people rend the vaulted skies.
Then Mnestheus to the head his arrow drove,
With lifted eyes, and took his aim above,
But made a glancing shot, and missed the dove,
Yet missed so narrow, that he cut the cord   675
Which fastened by the foot, the flitting bird.
The captive thus released, away she flies,
And beats with clapping wings the yielding skies.
His bow already bent, Eurytion stood;
And, having first invoked his brother-god,   680
His wingèd shaft with eager haste he sped.
The fatal message reached her as she fled:
She leaves her life aloft; she strikes the ground,
And renders back the weapon in the wound.
Acestes, grudging at his lot, remains   685
Without a prize to gratify his pains.
Yet, shooting upward, sends his shaft, to show
An archer's art, and boast his twanging bow.
The feathered arrow gave a dire portent,
And latter augurs judge from this event.   690
Chafed by the speed, it fired; and, as it flew,
A train of following flames, ascending, drew:
Kindling they mount, and mark the shiny way;
Across the skies as falling meteors play,
And vanish into wind, or in a blaze decay.   695
The Trojans and Sicilians wildly stare,
And trembling, turn their wonder into prayer.
The Dardan prince put on a smiling face,
And strained Acestes with a close embrace;
Then honoring him with gifts above the rest,   700
Turned the bad omen, nor his fears confessed.
"The gods (said he) this miracle have wrought,
And ordered you the prize without the lot.
Accept this goblet, rough with figured gold,
Which Thracian Cisseus gave my sire of old: 705

672. *drove:* pulled.
683. *She leaves her life aloft: vitamque reliquit in astris.*

This pledge of ancient amity receive,
Which to my second sire I justly give."
He said, and, with the trumpet's cheerful sound,
Proclaimed him victor, and with laurel crowned.
Nor good Eurytion envied him the prize,   710
Though he transfixed the pigeon in the skies.
Who cut the line, with second gifts was graced;
The third was his whose arrow pierced the mast.

  The chief, before the games were wholly done,
Called Periphantes, tutor to his son,   715
And whispered thus: "With speed Ascanius find;
And, if his childish troop be ready joined,
On horseback let him grace his grandsire's day,
And lead his equals armed in just array." — he was there in iv .
He said; and, calling out, the cirque he clears.   720
The crowd withdrawn, an open plain appears.
And now the noble youths, of form divine,
Advance before their fathers, in a line:
The riders grace the steeds, the steeds with glory shine.

  Thus marching on in military pride,   725
Shouts of applause resound from side to side.
Their casques adorned with laurel wreaths they wear,
Each brandishing aloft a cornel spear.
Some at their backs their gilded quivers bore;
Their chains of burnished gold hung down before.   730
Three graceful troops they formed upon the green;
Three graceful leaders at their head were seen;
Twelve followed every chief, and left a space between.
The first, young Priam led—a lovely boy,
Whose grandsire was the unhappy king of Troy;   735
(His race in after-times was known to fame,
New honors adding to the Latian name)—
And well the royal boy his Thracian steed became.
White were the fetlocks of his feet before;
And on his front a snowy star he bore.   740

---

  715. *Periphantes*: Virgil calls him Epytiden, "son of Epytus." Dryden, following Ruaeus, gives him his own name from the *Iliad*, Book XVII, 323.

Then beauteous Atys, with Iülus bred,
Of equal age, the second squadron led.
The last in order, but the first in place,
First in the lovely features of his face,
Rode fair Ascanius, on a fiery steed,   745
Queen Dido's gift, and of the Tyrian breed.
Sure coursers for the rest the king ordains,
With golden bits adorned, and purple reins.

   The pleased spectators peals of shouts renew,
And all the parents in the children view;   750
Their make, their motions, and their sprightly grace,
And hopes and fears alternate in their face.

   The unfledged commanders, and their martial train,
First make the circuit of the sandy plain
Around their sires; and at the appointed sign,   755
Drawn up in beauteous order, form a line.
The second signal sounds: the troop divides
In three distinguish'd parts, with three distinguish'd guides.
Again they close, and once again disjoin:
In troop to troop opposed, and line to line.   760
They meet; they wheel; they throw their darts afar,
With harmless rage, and well-dissembled war.
Then in a round the mingled bodies run;
Flying they follow, and pursuing shun;
Broken they break; and rallying, they renew   765
In other forms the military show.
At last, in order undiscerned they join,
And march together in a friendly line.
And, as the Cretan labyrinth of old,
With wandering ways, and many a winding fold,   770
Involved the weary feet without redress,
In a round error which denied recess;
So fought the Trojan boys in warlike play,
Turned and returned, and still a different way.
Thus, dolphins in the deep each other chase   775
In circles, when they swim around the watery race.

   741. *Atys*: The mother of Augustus was Atia, daughter of M. Atius Balbus
and Julia, sister of C. Julius Caesar.
   772. *a round error*: *inremeabilis error*, "a getting lost with no way back."

This game, these carousals, Ascanius taught;
And, building Alba, to the Latins brought,
Showed what he learned: the Latin sires impart
To their succeeding sons the graceful art: 780
From these imperial Rome received the game,
Which Troy, the youths, the Trojan troop, they name.
   Thus far the sacred sports they celebrate;
But Fortune soon resumed her ancient hate;
For, while they pay the dead his annual dues,   785
Those envied rites Saturnian Juno views;
And sends the goddess of the various bow,
To try new methods of revenge below:
Supplies the winds to wing her airy way,
Where in the port secure the navy lay.   790
Swiftly fair Iris down her arch descends,
And undiscerned, her fatal voyage ends.
   She saw the gathering crowd; and, gliding thence,
The desert shore, and fleet without defense.
The Trojan matrons, on the sands alone,   795
With sighs and tears Anchises' death bemoan:
Then, turning to the sea their weeping eyes,
Their pity to themselves renews their cries.
"Alas! (said one) what oceans yet remain
For us to sail! what labors to sustain!"   800
All take the word, and, with a general groan
Implore the gods for peace, and places of their own.
The goddess, great in mischief, views their pains,
And in a woman's form her heavenly limbs restrains.
In face and shape, old Beroë she became,   805
Doryclus' wife, a venerable dame;
Once blessed with riches, and a mother's name.
Thus changed, amidst the crying crowd she ran,
Mixed with the matrons, and these words began:
"O wretched we! whom not the Grecian power   810
Nor flames destroyed, in Troy's unhappy hour!
O wretched we! reserved by cruel Fate
Beyond the ruins of the sinking state!

781. The "Trojan game" on horseback was in fact introduced at Rome by
Sulla. Caesar revived it and Augustus often had it performed.

Now, seven revolving years are wholly run,
Since this improsperous voyage we begun;   815
Since, tossed from shores to shores, from lands to lands,
Inhospitable rocks and barren sands.
Wandering in exile, through the stormy sea,
We search in vain for flying Italy.
Now cast by Fortune on this kindred land,   820
What should our rest and rising walls withstand;
Or hinder, here, to fix our banished band?
O country lost, and gods redeemed in vain,
If still in endless exile we remain!
Shall we no more the Trojan walls renew.   825
Or streams of some dissembled Simoïs view?
Haste! join with me! the unhappy fleet consume!
Cassandra bids; and I declare her doom.
In sleep I saw her; she supplied my hands
(For this I more than dreamt) with flaming brands: 830
'With these (said she) these wandering ships destroy:
These are your fatal seats, and this your Troy.'
Time calls you now; the precious hour employ;
Slack not the good presage, while heaven inspires
Our minds to dare, and gives the ready fires.   835
See! Neptune's altars minister their brands;
The God is pleased; the god supplies our hands."
    Then from the pile a flaming fir she drew,
And, tossed in air, amidst the galleys threw.
Rapt in amaze, the matrons wildly stare: 840
Then Pyrgo, reverenced for her hoary hair—
Pyrgo, the nurse of Priam's numerous race:
"No Beroë this, though she belies her face!
What terrors from her frowning front arise!
Behold a goddess in her ardent eyes!   845
What rays around her heavenly face are seen!
Mark her majestic voice, and more than mortal mien!
Beroë but now I left, whom, pined with pain,
Her age and anguish from these rites detain."
She said. The matrons, seized with new amaze,   850
Roll their malignant eyes, and on the navy gaze.

They fear, and hope, and neither part obey:
They hope the fated land, but fear the fatal way.
  The goddess, having done her task below,
Mounts up on equal wings, and bends her painted bow. 855
Struck with the sight, and seized with rage divine,
The matrons prosecute their mad design:
They shriek aloud: they snatch with impious hands
The food of altars: firs and flaming brands,
Green boughs and saplings, mingled in their haste, 860
And smoking torches, on the ships they cast.
The flame, unstopped at first, more fury gains;
And Vulcan rides at large with loosened reins:
Triumphant to the painted stern he soars,
And seizes in his way the banks and crackling oars. 865
  Eumelus was the first the news to bear,
While yet they crowd the rural theater.
Then what they hear is witnessed by their eyes:
A storm of sparkles and of flames arise.
Ascanius took the alarm, while yet he led 870
His early warriors on his prancing steed;
And, spurring on, his equals soon o'erpassed;
Nor could his frightened friends reclaim his haste.
Soon as the royal youth appeared in view,
He sent his voice before him as he flew: 875
"What madness moves you, matrons! to destroy
The last remainders of unhappy Troy?
Not hostile fleets, but your own hopes, you burn,
And on your friends your fatal fury turn.
Behold your own Ascanius!"—While he said, 880
He drew his glittering helmet from his head,
In which the youths to sportful arms he led.
By this, Aeneas and his train appear;
And now the women, seized with shame and fear,
Dispersed, to woods and caverns take their flight; 885
Abhor their actions, and avoid the light;
Their friends acknowledge, and their error find;
And shake the goddess from their altered mind.

Not so the raging fires their fury cease,
But, lurking in the seams, with seeming peace   890
Work on their way amid the smouldering tow;
Sure in destruction, but in motion slow.
The silent plague through the green timber eats,
And vomits out a tardy flame by fits.
Down to the keels, and upward to the sails,   895
The fire descends or mounts, but still prevails;
Nor buckets poured, nor strength of human hand,
Can the victorious element withstand.
    The pious hero rends his robe, and throws
To heaven his hands, and, with his hands, his vows.   900
"O Jove! (he cried) if prayers can yet have place;
If thou abhorr'st not all the Dardan race;
If any spark of pity still remain;
If gods are gods, and not invoked in vain;
Yet spare the relics of the Trojan train!   905
Yet from the flames our burning vessels free!
Or let thy fury fall alone on me:
At this devoted head thy thunder throw,
And send the willing sacrifice below."
    Scarce had he said, when southern storms arise: 910
From pole to pole the forky lightning flies:
Loud rattling shakes the mountains and the plain:
Heaven bellies downward, and descends in rain:
Whole sheets of water from the clouds are sent,
Which, hissing through the planks, the flames prevent,   915
And stop the fiery pest. Four ships alone
Burn to the waist, and for the fleet atone.
    But doubtful thoughts the hero's heart divide,
If he should still in Sicily reside,
Forgetful of his fates,—or tempt the main,   920
In hope the promised Italy to gain.
Then Nautes, old and wise—to whom alone
The will of Heaven by Pallas was foreshown;
Versed in portents, experienced, and inspired
To tell events, and what the Fates required—   925

    917. *to the waist*: i.e., from stern to waist, effectively destroyed.

Thus, while he stood to neither part inclined,
With cheerful words relieved his laboring mind:
"O goddess-born! resigned in every state,
With patience bear, with prudence push your fate.
By suffering well, our fortune we subdue;   930
Fly when she frowns, and when she calls, pursue.
Your friend Acestes is of Trojan kind;
To him disclose the secrets of your mind;
Trust in his hands your old and useless train,
Too numerous for the ships which yet remain—   935
The feeble, old, indulgent of their ease,
The dames, who dread the dangers of the seas,
With all the dastard crew, who dare not stand
The shock of battle with your foes by land.
Here you may build a common town for all,   940
And, from Ascestes' name, Acesta call."
The reasons, with his friend's experience joined,
Encouraged much, but more disturbed his mind.
    'Twas dead of night; when, to his slumbering eyes
His father's shade, descended from the skies,   945
And thus he spoke: "O, more than vital breath
Loved while I lived, and dear e'en after death!
O son, in various toils and troubles tossed!
The king of heaven employs my careful ghost
On his commands—the god who saved from fire   950
Your flaming fleet, and heard your just desire.
The wholesome counsel of your friend receive,
And here, the coward train and women, leave.
The chosen youth, and those who nobly dare,
Transport, to tempt the dangers of the war: 955
The stern Italians will their courage try:
Rough are their manners, and their minds are high.
But first to Pluto's palace you shall go,
And seek my shade among the blest below;

---

941. *Acesta*: Egesta, or Segesta. Thucydides (Book VI, 2) says Eryx and
Egesta in west Sicily were Trojan settlements.
    957. *gens dura atque aspera cultu*: "hard folk, rugged in their bringing up."

For not with impious ghosts my soul remains;   960
Nor suffers, with the damned, perpetual pains;
But breathes the living air and soft Elysian plains.
The chaste Sibylla shall your steps convey,
And blood of offered victims free the way.
There shall you know what realms the gods assign,   965
And learn the fates and fortunes of your line.
But now farewell! I vanish with the night,
And feel the blast of heaven's approaching light."
He said, and mixed with shades, and took his airy flight.
"Whither so fast? (the filial duty cried)   970
And why, ah! why the wished embrace denied?"
    He said, and rose; as holy zeal inspires,
He rakes hot embers, and renews the fires;
His country gods and Vesta then adores
With cakes and incense, and their aid implores.   975
Next, for his friends and royal host he sent,
Revealed his vision, and the god's intent,
With his own purpose. All, without delay,
The will of Jove, and his desires, obey.
They list with women, each degenerate name   980
Who dares not hazard life for future fame.
These they cashier. The brave remaining few,
Oars, banks, and cables, half-consumed, renew.
The prince designs a city with the plow:
The lots their several tenements allow.   985
This part, is named from Ilium, that, from Troy;
And the new king ascends the throne with joy;
A chosen senate from the people draws;
Appoints the judges, and ordains the laws.
Then, on the top of Eryx, they begin   990
A rising temple to the Paphian queen.
Anchises, last, is honored as a god:
A priest is added; annual gifts bestowed;
And groves are planted round his blest abode.

968. *et me saevus equis Oriens adflavit anhelis*, "the furious sun rising
breathes on me with panting horses."

991. *a rising temple*: Venus' famous temple. Tacitus wrote of it (*Annals*,
Book IV, 43) and there are recent reflections on it in *The Golden Honeycomb*,
by Vincent Cronin.

Nine days they pass in feasts, their temples crowned;   995
And fumes of incense in the fanes abound.
Then from the south arose a gentle breeze,
That curled the smoothness of the glassy seas;
The rising winds a ruffling gale afford,
And call the merry mariners aboard.   1000
    Now loud laments along the shores resound,
Of parting friends in close embraces bound.
The trembling women, the degenerate train
Who shunned the frightful dangers of the main;
E'en those desire to sail, and take their share   1005
Of the rough passage, and the promised war:
Whom good Aeneas cheers; and recommends
To their new master's care his fearful friends.
On Eryx' altars three fat calves he lays;
A lamb, new-fallen, to the stormy seas;   1010
Then slips his halsers, and his anchors weighs.
High on the deck, the godlike hero stands
With olive crowned, a charger in his hands;
Then cast the reeking entrails in the brine,
And poured the sacrifice of purple wine.   1015
Fresh gales arise: with equal strokes they vie,
And brush the buxom seas, and o'er the billows fly.
    Meantime the mother goddess, full of fears,
To Neptune thus addressed, with tender tears:
"The pride of Jove's imperious queen, the rage,   1020
The malice, which no sufferings can assuage,
Compel me to these prayers; since neither fate,
Nor time, nor pity, can remove her hate.
E'en Jove is thwarted by his haughty wife:
Still vanquished, yet she still renews the strife.   1025
As if 'twere little to consume the town
Which awed the world, and wore the imperial crown,
She prosecutes the ghost of Troy with pains,
And gnaws e'en to the bones the last remains.
Let her the causes of her hatred tell;   1030
But you can witness its effects too well.

1013. *a charger*: a *patera,* or shallow wine bowl.

You saw the storm she raised on Libyan floods,
That mixed the mounting billows with the clouds;
When, bribing Aeolus, she shook the main,
And moved rebellion in your watery reign.　　　　1035
With fury she possessed the Dardan dames,
To burn their fleet with execrable flames,
And forced Aeneas, when his ships were lost,
To leave his followers on a foreign coast.
For what remains, your godhead I implore;　　　　1040
And trust my son to your protecting power.
If neither Jove's nor Fate's decree withstand,
Secure his passage to the Latian land."
　　Then thus, the mighty ruler of the main:
"What may not Venus hope from Neptune's reign?　　1045
My kingdom claims your birth; my late defense
Of your endangered fleet may claim your confidence.
Nor less by land than sea my deeds declare,
How much your loved Aeneas is my care.
Thee, Xanthus! and thee, Simoïs! I attest—　　　　1050
Your Trojan troops when proud Achilles pressed,
And drove before him headlong on the plain;
And dashed against the walls the trembling train;
When floods were filled with bodies of the slain;
When crimson Xanthus, doubtful of his way,　　　　1055
Stood up on ridges to behold the sea
(New heaps came tumbling in, and choked his way);
When your Aeneas fought, but fought with odds
Of force unequal, and unequal gods;
I spread a cloud before the victor's sight,　　　　1060
Sustained the vanquished, and secured his flight:
E'en then secured him, when I sought with joy
The vowed destruction of ungrateful Troy.
My will's the same: fair goddess! fear no more,
Your fleet shall safely gain the Latian shore:　　　1065
Their lives are given: one destined head alone
Shall perish, and for multitudes atone."
　　Thus having armed with hopes her anxious mind,
His finny team Saturnian Neptune joined;

　　1060. The incident is in the *Iliad*, Book XX, 321.

Then adds the foamy bridle to their jaws,   1070
And to the loosened reins permits the laws.
High on the waves his azure car he guides;
Its axles thunder, and the sea subsides;
And the smooth ocean rolls her silent tides.
The tempests fly before their father's face;   1075
Trains of inferior gods his triumph grace;
And monster whales before their master play;
And choirs of Tritons crowd the watery way.
The marshaled powers in equal troops divide
To right and left: the gods his better side   1080
Inclose; and, on the worse, the Nymphs and Nereids ride.
    Now smiling hope, with sweet vicissitude,
Within the hero's mind his joys renewed.
He calls to raise the masts, the sheets display;
The cheerful crew with diligence obey: 1085
They scud before the wind, and sail in open sea.
Ahead of all, the master pilot steers;
And as he leads, the following navy veers.
    The steeds of Night had traveled half the sky:
The drowsy rowers on their benches lie;   1090
When the soft god of sleep, with easy flight
Descends, and draws behind a trail of light.
Thou, Palinurus, art his destined prey;
To thee alone he takes his fatal way.
Dire dreams to thee, and iron sleep, he bears;   1095
And, lighting on thy prow, the form of Phorbas wears.
Then thus the traitor-god began his tale:
"The winds, my friend, inspire a pleasing gale;
The ships, without thy care securely sail.
Now steal an hour of sweet repose; and I   1100
Will take the rudder, and thy room supply."
To whom, the yawning pilot, half asleep:
"Me dost thou bid to trust the treacherous deep,
The harlot-smiles of her dissembling face,
And to her faith commit the Trojan race?   1105
Shall I believe the Siren South again,
And, oft betrayed, not know the monster main!"

    1080. *better:* right.

He said: his fastened hands the rudder keep;
And, fixed on heaven, his eyes repel invading sleep.
The god was wroth, and at his temples threw   1110
A branch in Lethe dipped, and drunk with Stygian dew:
The pilot, vanquished by the power divine,
Soon closed his swimming eyes, and lay supine.
Scarce were his limbs extended at their length;
The god, insulting, with superior strength   1115
Fell heavy on him, plunged him in the sea;
And, with the stern, the rudder tore away.
Headlong he fell, and, struggling in the main,
Cried out for helping hands, but cried in vain.
The victor daemon mounts obscure in air;   1120
While the ship sails without the pilot's care.
On Neptune's faith the floating fleet relies;
But what the man forsook, the god supplies;
And, o'er the dangerous deep, secure the navy flies:
Glides by the Sirens' cliffs, a shelfy coast,   1125
Long infamous, for ships and sailors lost;
And white with bones. The impetuous ocean roars,
And rocks rebellow from the sounding shores.
The watchful hero felt the knocks, and found
The tossing vessel sailed on shoaly ground.   1130
Sure of his pilot's loss, he takes himself
The helm, and steers aloof, and shuns the shelf.
Inly he grieved, and, groaning from the breast,
Deplored his death; and thus his pain expressed:
"For faith reposed on seas, and on the flattering sky,   1135
Thy naked corpse is doom'd on shores unknown to lie."

1115. *insulting*: leaping upon [him].
1129. *fluitantem . . . sensit*: "he felt the ship yawing."

BOOK VI

THE ARGUMENT

The Sibyl foretells Aeneas the adventures he should meet with in Italy. She attends him to hell; describing to him the various scenes of that place, and conducting him to his father Anchises, who instructs him in those sublime mysteries of the soul of the world, and the transmigration; and shows him that glorious race of heroes, which was to descend from him and his posterity.

HE said, and wept; then spread his sails before
The winds, and reached at length the Cuman shore:
Their anchors dropped, his crew the vessels moor.
They turn their heads to sea, their sterns to land;
And greet with greedy joy the Italian strand.   5
Some strike from clashing flints their fiery seed;
Some gather sticks, the kindled flames to feed,
Or search for hollow trees, and fell the woods,
Or trace through valleys the discovered floods.
    Thus while their several charges they fulfill,   10
The pious prince ascends the sacred hill
Where Phoebus is adored; and seeks the shade
Which hides from sight his venerable maid
(Deep in a cave the Sibyl makes abode):
Thence full of fate returns; and of the god.   15
Through Trivia's grove they walk; and now behold,
And enter now, the temple roofed with gold.

2. *Cuman shore*: Cumae, in Campania, the earliest Greek settlement in Italy, colonized around 800 B.C.
14. *cave*: This huge grotto has been uncovered and can be visited.
16. *Trivia*: Hecate.

When Dedalus, to fly the Cretan shore,
His heavy limbs on jointed pinions bore
(The first who sailed in air), 'tis sung by Fame,   20
To the Cumaean coast at length he came;
And here alighting, built this costly frame.
Inscribed to Phoebus, here, he hung on high
The steerage of his wings, that cut the sky:
Then, o'er the lofty gate, his art embossed   25
Androgeos' death, and (offerings to his ghost)
Seven youths from Athens yearly sent, to meet
The fate appointed by revengeful Crete.
And next to these the dreadful urn was placed,
In which the destined names by lots were cast: 30
The mournful parents stand around in tears;
And rising Crete against their shore appears.
There too, in living sculpture, might be seen
The mad affection of the Cretan queen;
Then how she cheats her bellowing lover's eye: 35
The rushing leap, the doubtful progeny—
The lower part a beast, a man above—
The monument of their polluted love.
Not far from thence he graved the wondrous maze,
A thousand doors, a thousand winding ways: 40
Here dwells the monster, hid from human view;
Not to be found but by the faithful clue;
Till the kind artist, moved with pious grief,
Lent to the loving maid this last relief;
And all those erring paths described so well,   45
That Theseus conquered, and the monster fell.

18. *Dedalus*: the Cretan artisan, who made the hollow cow in which
Pasiphaë, wife of King Minos, submitted to a bull. He also devised the labyrinth
to hide the Minotaur, offspring of this miscegenation. Androgeos, son of Minos,
was killed by the Athenians, from whom Minos then exacted a yearly tribute of
seven boys and seven girls for the Minotaur to devour. The Athenian hero,
Theseus, won the love of Minos' daughter Ariadne, and on Dedalus' advice she
gave him a ball of thread to unwind behind him as he explored the labyrinth
so that after killing the Minotaur he could find his way out again. Dedalus and
his son Icarus left Crete by air on wings designed by himself, but Icarus flew too
near the sun, melting the wax that held his feathers, and fell into the sea near
Samos.

Here, hapless Icarus had found his part,
Had not the father's grief restrained his art:
He twice essayed to cast his son in gold;
Twice from his hands he dropped the forming mold.   50
   All this, with wondering eyes Aeneas viewed;
Each varying object his delight renewed.
Eager to read the rest—Achates came,
And by his side the mad divining dame,
The priestess of the god, Deïphobe her name.   55
"Time suffers not (she said), to feed your eyes
With empty pleasures: haste the sacrifice.
Seven bullocks, yet unyoked, for Phoebus choose,
And for Diana, seven unspotted ewes."
This said, the servants urge the sacred rites;   60
While to the temple she the prince invites.
A spacious cave, within its farmost part,
Was hewed and fashioned by laborious art,
Through the hill's hollow sides: before the place,
A hundred doors a hundred entries grace;   65
As many voices issue, and the sound
Of Sibyl's words as many times rebound.
Now to the mouth they come. Aloud she cries:
"This is the time! inquire your destinies!
He comes! behold the god!" Thus while she said   70
(And shivering at the sacred entry stayed),
Her color changed; her face was not the same;
And hollow groans from her deep spirit came.
Her hair stood up; convulsive rage possessed
Her trembling limbs, and heaved her laboring breast.   75
Greater than human kind she seemed to look;
And with an accent more than mortal, spoke:
Her staring eyes with sparkling fury roll,
When all the god came rushing on her soul.
Swiftly she turned, and, foaming as she spoke: 80
"Why this delay? (she cried) the powers invoke!
Thy prayers alone can open this abode;
Else vain are my demands, and dumb the god."
   She said no more. The trembling Trojans hear,
O'erspread with a damp sweat, and holy fear.   85

The prince himself, with awful dread possessed,
His vows to great Apollo thus addressed:
"Indulgent god! propitious power to Troy,
Swift to relieve, unwilling to destroy!
Directed by whose hand, the Dardan dart   90
Pierced the proud Grecian's only mortal part!
Thus far, by Fate's decrees and thy commands,
Through ambient seas and through devouring sands,
Our exiled crew has sought the Ausonian ground;
And now, at length, the flying coast is found.   95
Thus far the fate of Troy, from place to place,
With fury has pursued her wandering race.
Here cease, ye powers, and let your vengeance end,
Troy is no more, and can no more offend.
And thou, O sacred maid, inspired to see   100
The event of things in dark futurity!
Give me, what heaven has promised to my fate,
To conquer and command the Latian state;
To fix my wandering gods, and find a place
For the long exiles of the Trojan race.   105
Then shall my grateful hands a temple rear
To the twin gods, with vows and solemn prayer;
And annual rites, and festivals, and games,
Shall be performed to their auspicious names.
Nor shalt thou want thy honors in my land;   110
For there thy faithful oracles shall stand,
Preserved in shrines; and every sacred lay,
Which by thy mouth, Apollo shall convey;
All shall be treasured by a chosen train
Of holy priests, and ever shall remain.   115

91. *the proud Grecian*: Achilles, whose death from Paris' arrow was foretold by Hector in the *Iliad*, Book XXII, 359.

107. *the twin gods*: Apollo and Diana.

111. *faithful oracles*: The Roman story was that the Sibyl had first offered to sell nine "books" of her oracular leaves to Tarquin the Proud, who refused her price; she then destroyed three and offered six for the same price; again he refused; again she destroyed three, and he paid her price for the three remaining. They were kept in a stone chest in the temple of Jove on the Capitoline and consulted in times of danger. A fire in 82 B.C. destroyed them, but as the Sibyl continued to give oracles a new collection was made.

But, oh! commit not thy prophetic mind
To flitting leaves, the sport of every wind,
Lest they disperse in air our empty fate:
Write not, but, what the powers ordain, relate."
   Struggling in vain, impatient of her load,   120
And laboring underneath the ponderous god,
The more she strove to shake him from her breast,
With more, and far superior force he pressed;
Commands his entrance, and, without control,
Usurps her organs, and inspires her soul.   125
Now, with a furious blast, the hundred doors
Ope of themselves; a rushing whirlwind roars
Within the cave, and Sibyl's voice restores:
"Escaped the dangers of the watery reign,
Yet more and greater ills by land remain.   130
The coast so long desired (nor doubt the event),
Thy troops shall reach, but, having reached, repent.
Wars! horrid wars, I view!—a field of blood,
And Tiber rolling with a purple flood.
Simoïs nor Xanthus shall be wanting there: 135
A new Achilles shall in arms appear;
And he too, goddess-born. Fierce Juno's hate
Added to hostile force, shall urge thy fate.
To what strange nations shalt not thou resort;
Driven to solicit aid at every court!   140
The cause, the same which Ilium once oppressed:
A foreign mistress, and a foreign guest.
But thou, secure of soul, unbent with woes,
The more thy fortune frowns, the more oppose.
The dawnings of thy safety shall be shown,   145
From whence thou least shalt hope—a Grecian town."
   Thus, from the dark recess, the Sibyl spoke;
And the resisting air the thunder broke;
The cave rebellowed, and the temple shook.
The ambiguous god, who ruled her laboring breast,   150
In these mysterious words his mind expressed:

141-2. Paris had been a "foreign guest" of Menelaus, and Helen his "foreign
mistress." Aeneas, a foreign guest in Latium, would win King Latinus' daughter
Lavinia and fight her disappointed suitor, Turnus.

Some truth revealed, in terms involved the rest.
At length her fury fell: her foaming ceased,
And, ebbing in her soul, the god decreased.
    Then thus the chief: "No terror to my view,   155
No frightful face of danger, can be new.
Inured to suffer, and resolved to dare,
The Fates, without my power, shall be without my care.
This let me crave—since near your grove the road
To hell lies open, and the dark abode   160
Which Acheron surrounds, the innavigable flood—
Conduct me through the regions void of light,
And lead me longing to my father's sight.
For him, a thousand dangers I have sought,
And, rushing where the thickest Grecians fought,   165
Safe on my back the sacred burden brought.
He, for my sake, the raging ocean tried,
And wrath of heaven (my still auspicious guide),
And bore, beyond the strength decrepit age supplied.
Oft, since he breathed his last, in dead of night,   170
His reverend image stood before my sight;
Enjoined to seek, below, his holy shade—
Conducted there by your unerring aid.
But you, if pious minds by prayers are won,
Oblige the father, and protect the son.   175
Yours is the power; nor Proserpine in vain
Has made you priestess of her nightly reign.
If Orpheus, armed with his enchanting lyre,
The ruthless king with pity could inspire,
And from the shades below redeem his wife;   180
If Pollux, offering his alternate life,
Could free his brother, and can daily go
By turns aloft, by turns descend below;—
Why name I Theseus, or his greater friend,
Who trod the downward path, and upward could ascend?   185
Not less than theirs, from Jove my lineage came;
My mother greater, my descent the same."
    So prayed the Trojan prince, and, while he prayed,
His hand upon the holy altar laid.

    184. *his greater friend*: Hercules.

Then, thus replied the prophetess divine: 190
"O goddess-born, of great Anchises' line!
The gates of hell are open night and day;
Smooth the descent, and easy is the way:
But to return, and view the cheerful skies,
In this, the task and mighty labor lies. 195
To few, great Jupiter imparts this grace,
And those of shining worth, and heavenly race.
Betwixt those regions and our upper light,
Deep forests and impenetrable night
Possess the middle space: the infernal bounds, 200
Cocytus, with his sable waves surrounds.
But, if so dire a love your soul invades,
As twice below to view the trembling shades;
If you so hard a toil will undertake,
As twice to pass the innavigable lake; 205
Receive my counsel. In the neighboring grove
There stands a tree: the queen of Stygian Jove
Claims it her own; thick woods and gloomy night
Conceal the happy plant from human sight.
One bough it bears; but (wondrous to behold!) 210
The ductile rind and leaves of radiant gold:
This, from the vulgar branches must be torn,
And to fair Proserpine, the present borne,
Ere leave be given to tempt the nether skies.
The first thus rent, a second will arise; 215
And the same metal the same room supplies.
Look round the wood, with lifted eyes, to see
The lurking gold upon the fatal tree;
Then rend it off, as holy rites command:
The willing metal will obey thy hand, 220
Following with ease, if, favored by thy fate,
Thou art foredoomed to view the Stygian state;
If not, no labor can the tree constrain;
And strength of stubborn arms and steel, are vain.

193. *facilis descensus Averno.*
195. *hoc opus, hic labor est.*
207. *the queen of Stygian Jove:* Proserpine (Persephone), wife of Pluto (Hades).

Besides, you know not, while you here attend,   225
The unworthy fate of your unhappy friend:
Breathless he lies; and his unburied ghost,
Deprived of funeral rites, pollutes your host.
Pay first his pious dues; and, for the dead,
Two sable sheep around his hearse be led;   230
Then, living turfs upon his body lay:
This done, securely take the destined way,
To find the regions destitute of day."
    She said, and held her peace.—Aeneas went
Sad from the cave, and full of discontent,   235
Unknowing whom the sacred Sibyl meant.
Achates, the companion of his breast,
Goes grieving by his side, with equal cares oppressed.
Walking they talked, and fruitlessly divined,
What friend the priestess by those words designed.   240
    But soon they found an object to deplore:
Misenus lay extended on the shore—
Son of the god of winds:—none so renowned,
The warrior-trumpet in the field to sound,
With breathing brass to kindle fierce alarms,   245
And rouse to dare their fate in honorable arms.
He served great Hector, and was ever near,
Not with his trumpet only, but his spear.
But, by Pelides' arms when Hector fell,
He chose Aeneas; and he chose as well.   250
Swol'n with applause, and aiming still at more,
He now provokes the sea gods from the shore.
With envy, Triton heard the martial sound,
And the bold champion, for his challenge, drowned;
Then cast his mangled carcass on the strand: 255
The gazing crowd around the body stand.
All weep; but most Aeneas mourns his fate;
And hastens to perform the funeral state.
In altar-wise, a stately pile they rear;
The basis broad below, and top advanced in air.   260
An ancient wood, fit for the work designed
(The shady covert of the savage kind),

    242. *Misenus*: The name of Cape Misenum is accounted for.

The Trojans found: the sounding axe is plied:
Firs, pines, and pitch-trees, and the towering pride
Of forest ashes, feel the fatal stroke;   265
And piercing wedges cleave the stubborn oak.
Huge trunks of trees, felled from the steepy crown
Of the bare mountains, roll with ruin down.
Armed like the rest the Trojan prince appears,
And, by his pious labor, urges theirs.   270
    Thus while he wrought, involving in his mind
The ways to compass what his wish designed,
He cast his eyes upon the gloomy grove,
And then with vows implored the queen of love:
"O! may thy power, propitious still to me,   275
Conduct my steps to find the fatal tree,
In this deep forest; since the Sibyl's breath
Foretold, alas! too true, Misenus' death."
Scarce had he said, when, full before his sight,
Two doves, descending from their airy flight,   280
Secure upon the grassy plain alight.
He knew his mother's birds; and thus he prayed:
"Be you my guides, with your auspicious aid,
And lead my footsteps, till the branch be found,
Whose glittering shadow gilds the sacred ground.   285
And thou, great parent! with celestial care,
In this distress, be present to my prayer."
Thus having said, he stopped, with watchful sight
Observing still the motions of their flight,
What course they took, what happy signs they show.   290
They fed, and, fluttering, by degrees withdrew
Still farther from the place, but still in view:
Hopping and flying, thus they led him on
To the slow lake, whose baleful stench to shun,
They winged their flight aloft; then, stooping low,   295
Perched on the double tree that bears the golden bough.
Through the green leaves the glittering shadows glow;
As, on the sacred oak, the wintry misletoe,

285. Spenser, *Faerie Queen*, I, 1, 14:
                          his glistring armor made
              A little glooming light, much like a shade.

Where the proud mother views her precious brood,
And happier branches, which she never sowed.   300
Such was the glittering; such the ruddy rind,
And dancing leaves, that wantoned in the wind.
He seized the shining bough with griping hold,
And rent away with ease the lingering gold;
Then to the Sibyl's palace bore the prize.   305
    Meantime, the Trojan troops, with weeping eyes,
To dead Misenus pay his obsequies.
First, from the ground, a lofty pile they rear,
Of pitch-trees, oaks, and pines, and unctuous fir:
The fabric's front with cypress twigs they strew,   310
And stick the sides with boughs of baleful yew.
The topmost part his glittering arms adorn;
Warm waters, then, in brazen caldrons borne,
Are poured to wash his body, joint by joint;
And fragrant oils the stiffened limbs anoint.   315
With groans and cries Misenus they deplore;
Then on a bier, with purple covered o'er,
The breathless body, thus bewailed, they lay,
And fire the pile, their faces turned away:
Such reverent rites their fathers used to pay.   320
Pure oil and incense on the fire they throw,
And fat of victims, which his friends bestow.
These gifts the greedy flames to dust devour;
Then, on the living coals, red wine they pour;
And, last, the relics by themselves dispose,   325
Which in a brazen urn the priests inclose.
Old Corynaeus compassed thrice the crew,
And dipped an olive branch in holy dew,
Which thrice he sprinkled round; and thrice aloud
Invoked the dead, and then dismissed the crowd.   330
    But good Aeneas ordered on the shore
A stately tomb, whose top a trumpet bore,
A soldier's falchion, and a seaman's oar.
Thus was his friend interred; and deathless fame
Still to the lofty cape consigns his name.   335
    These rites performed, the prince, without delay,
Hastes to the nether world, his destined way.

Deep was the cave; and, downward as it went
From the wide mouth, a rocky, rough descent;
And here the access a gloomy grove defends;   340
And here the innavigable lake extends,
O'er whose unhappy waters, void of light,
No bird presumes to steer his airy flight:
Such deadly stenches from the depth arise,
And steaming sulfur, that infects the skies.   345
From hence, the Grecian bards their legends make,
And give the name Avernus, to the lake.
Four sable bullocks, in the yoke untaught,
For sacrifice the pious hero brought.
The priestess pours the wine betwixt their horns;   350
Then cuts the curling hair; that first oblation burns,
Invoking Hecate hither to repair—
A powerful name in hell and upper air,
The sacred priests, with ready knives bereave
The beasts of life, and in full bowls receive   355
The streaming blood; a lamb to Hell and Night
(The sable wool without a streak of white),
Aeneas offers; and, by Fate's decree,
A barren heifer, Proserpine, to thee!
With holocausts he Pluto's altar fills;   360
Seven brawny bulls with his own hand he kills;
Then, on the broiling entrails, oil he pours;
Which, ointed thus, the raging flame devours.
Late the nocturnal sacrifice begun,
Nor ended till the next returning sun.   365
Then earth began to bellow, trees to dance,
And howling dogs in glimmering light advance,
Ere Hecate came: "Far hence be souls profane!
(The Sibyl cried) and from the grove abstain!
Now, Trojan, take the way thy fates afford;   370
Assume thy courage, and unsheath thy sword."
She said, and passed along the gloomy space;
The prince pursued her steps with equal pace.

    346–7. This aside may not have been Virgil's but a gloss added later, deriv-
ing Avernus from Greek *a-ornos*, "birdless."

Ye realms yet unrevealed to human sight!
Ye gods who rule the regions of the night!   375
Ye gliding ghosts! permit me to relate
The mystic wonders of your silent state.
   Obscure they went through dreary shades, that led
Along the waste dominions of the dead.
Thus wander travelers in woods by night,   380
By the moon's doubtful and malignant light,
When Jove in dusky clouds involves the skies,
And the faint crescent shoots by fits before their eyes.
   Just in the gate, and in the jaws of hell,
Revengeful Cares and sullen Sorrows dwell;   385
And pale Diseases, and repining Age,
Want, Fear, and Famine's unresisted rage;
Here Toils, and Death, and Death's half-brother Sleep
(Forms terrible to view), their sentry keep;
With anxious Pleasures of a guilty mind;   390
Deep Frauds before, and open Force behind;
The Furies' iron beds; and Strife, that shakes
Her hissing tresses, and unfolds her snakes.
Full in the midst of this infernal road,
An elm displays her dusky arms abroad: 395
The god of sleep there hides his heavy head,
And empty dreams on every leaf are spread.
Of various forms unnumbered specters more,
Centaurs, and double shapes, besiege the door.
Before the passage, horrid Hydra stands,   400
And Briareus with all his hundred hands;
Gorgons, Geryon with his triple frame,
And vain Chimaera vomits empty flame.
The chief unsheathed his shining steel, prepared,
Though seized with sudden fear, to force the guard,   405
Offering his brandished weapon at their face,
Had not the Sibyl stopped his eager pace,

---

400 sqq. *Hydra*: a snake with numerous heads killed by Hercules. *Briareus*:
a giant with a hundred hands. *Gorgons*: three female monsters with snaky hair,
of whom Medusa alone was mortal. *Geryon*: a giant with three bodies killed by
Hercules. The fire-breathing *Chimaera* was reputed to have a lion's head, a goat's
body and a dragon's tail.

And told him what those empty phantoms were—
Forms without bodies, and impassive air.
 Hence to deep Acheron they take their way,   410
Whose troubled eddies, thick with ooze and clay,
Are whirled aloft, and in Cocytus lost:
There, Charon stands, who rules the dreary coast—
A sordid god: down from his hoary chin
A length of beard descends, uncombed, unclean: 415
His eyes, like hollow furnaces on fire;
A girdle foul with grease, binds his obscene attire.
He spreads his canvas; with his pole he steers;
The freights of flitting ghosts in his thin bottom bears.
He looked in years; yet, in his years were seen   420
A youthful vigor, and autumnal green.
An airy crowd came rushing where he stood,
Which filled the margin of the fatal flood:
Husbands and wives, boys and unmarried maids,
And mighty heroes' more majestic shades;   425
And youths, intombed before their fathers' eyes,
With hollow groans, and shrieks, and feeble cries.
Thick as the leaves in autumn strew the woods,
Or fowls by winter forced, forsake the floods,
And wing their hasty flight to happier lands—   430
Such, and so thick, the shivering army stands,
And press for passage, with extended hands.
 Now these, now those, the surly boatman bore:
The rest he drove to distance from the shore.
The hero, who beheld with wondering eyes,   435
The tumult mixed with shrieks, laments, and cries,
Asked of his guide, what the rude concourse meant?
Why to the shore the thronging people bent?
What forms of law among the ghosts were used?
Why some were ferried o'er, and some refused?   440
"Son of Anchises! offspring of the gods!
(The Sibyl said) you see the Stygian floods!
The sacred streams which heaven's imperial state
Attests in oaths, and fears to violate.

  432. *tendebantque manus ripae ulterioris amore:* "They stretched out their hands in longing for the farther shore." One of Virgil's great lines.

The ghosts rejected are the unhappy crew   445
Deprived of sepulchers and funeral due:
The boatman, Charon: those, the buried host,
He ferries over to the farther coast;
Nor dares his transport vessel cross the waves
With such whose bones are not composed in graves.   450
A hundred years they wander on the shore;
At length, their penance done, are wafted o'er."
     The Trojan chief his forward pace repressed,
Revolving anxious thoughts within his breast.
He saw his friends, who, whelmed beneath the waves,   455
Their funeral honors claimed, and asked their quiet graves.
The lost Leucaspis in the crowd he knew,
And the brave leader of the Lycian crew,
Whom, on the Tyrrhene seas, the tempests met;
The sailors mastered, and the ship o'erset.   460
Amidst the spirits, Palinurus pressed,
Yet fresh from life, a new-admitted guest.
Who, while he steering viewed the stars, and bore
His course from Afric to the Latian shore,
Fell headlong down. The Trojan fixed his view,   465
And scarcely through the gloom the sullen shadow knew.
Then thus the prince: "What envious power, O friend!
Brought your loved life to this disastrous end?
For Phoebus, ever true in all he said,
Has in your fate alone, my faith betrayed.   470
The god foretold you should not die before
You reached, secure from seas, the Italian shore.
Is this the unerring power?" The ghost replied:
"Nor Phoebus flattered, nor his answers lied;
Nor envious gods have sent me to the deep;   475
But, while the stars and course of heaven I keep,
My wearied eyes were seized with fatal sleep.
I fell; and with my weight the helm, constrained,
Was drawn along, which yet my gripe retained.
Now by the winds and raging waves I swear,   480
Your safety, more than mine, was then my care;
Lest, of the guide bereft, the rudder lost,
Your ship should run against the rocky coast.

Three blustering nights, borne by the southern blast,
I floated, and discovered land at last: 485
High on a mounting wave my head I bore,
Forcing my strength, and gathering to the shore:
Panting, but past the danger, now I seized
The craggy cliffs, and my tired members eased.
While, cumbered with my dropping clothes I lay,   490
The cruel nation, covetous of prey,
Stained with my blood the unhospitable coast;
And now, by winds and waves, my lifeless limbs are tossed;
Which, O! avert, by yon ethereal light,
Which I have lost for this eternal night.   495
Or, if by dearer ties you may be won,
By your dead sire, and by your living son,
Redeem from this reproach my wandering ghost.
Or with your navy seek the Velin coast,
And in a peaceful grave my corpse compose;   500
Or, if a nearer way your mother shows
(Without whose aid, you durst not undertake
This frightful passage o'er the Stygian lake),
Lend to this wretch your hand, and waft him o'er
To the sweet banks of yon forbidden shore."   505
Scarce had he said; the prophetess began:
"What hopes delude thee, miserable man?
Thinkest thou thus unintombed to cross the floods,
To view the Furies and infernal gods,
And visit without leave, the dark abodes?   510
Attend the term of long revolving years;
Fate, and the dooming gods, are deaf to tears.
This comfort of thy dire misfortune take—
The wrath of heaven, inflicted for thy sake,
With vengeance shall pursue the inhuman coast,   515
Till they propitiate thy offended ghost;
And raise a tomb, with vows and solemn prayer;
And Palinurus' name the place shall bear."
This calmed his cares—soothed with his future fame,
And pleased to hear his propagated name.   520

499. *Velin coast*: near Velia, in Lucania.
518. *the place*: Point Palinurus.

Now nearer to the Stygian lake they draw:
Whom from the shore the surly boatman saw;
Observed this passage through the shady wood,
And marked their near approaches to the flood:
Then thus he called aloud, inflamed with wrath: 525
"Mortal, whate'er, who this forbidden path
In arms presum'st to tread! I charge thee, stand,
And tell thy name, and business in the land!
Know, this the realm of night—the Stygian shore:
My boat conveys no living bodies o'er: 530
Nor was I pleased great Theseus once to bear
(Who forced a passage with his pointed spear),
Nor strong Alcides—men of mighty fame;
And from the immortal gods their lineage came.
In fetters, one, the barking porter tied,   535
And took him trembling from his sovereign's side:
Two, sought by force to seize his beauteous bride."
To whom the Sibyl thus: "Compose thy mind:
Nor frauds are here contrived, nor force designed.
Still may the dog the wandering troops constrain   540
Of airy ghosts, and vex the guilty train;
And with her grisly lord his lovely queen remain.
The Trojan chief, whose lineage is from Jove,
Much famed for arms, and more for filial love,
Is sent to seek his sire in your Elysian grove.   545
If neither piety, nor heaven's command,
Can gain his passage to thy Stygian strand,
This fatal present shall prevail at least"—
Then showed the shining bough, concealed within her vest.
No more was needful; for the gloomy god   550
Stood mute with awe, to see the golden rod;
Admired the destined offering to his queen—
A venerable gift, so rarely seen.
His fury thus appeased, he puts to land:
The ghosts forsake their seats at his command: 555
He clears the deck, receives the mighty freight;
The leaky vessel groans beneath the weight.

535. *barking porter*: Cerberus, captured by Hercules. Theseus and Pirithoüs tried to abduct Proserpine.

Slowly she sails, and scarcely stems the tides;
The pressing water pours within her sides.
His passengers at length are wafted o'er,   560
Exposed, in muddy weeds upon the miry shore.
  No sooner landed, in his den they found
The triple porter of the Stygian sound,
Grim Cerberus; who soon began to rear
His crested snakes, and armed his bristling hair.   565
The prudent Sibyl had before prepared
A sop, in honey steeped, to charm the guard;
Which, mixed with powerful drugs, she cast before
His greedy grinning jaws, just oped to roar.
With three enormous mouths he gapes, and straight,   570
With hunger pressed, devours the pleasing bait.
Long draughts of sleep his monstrous limbs enslave;
He reels, and falling, fills the spacious cave.
The keeper charmed, the chief without delay
Passed on, and took the irremeable way.   575
Before the gates, the cries of babes new-born,
Whom Fate had from their tender mothers torn,
Assault his ears: then, those whom form of laws
Condemned to die, when traitors judged their cause.
Nor want they lots, nor judges to review   580
The wrongful sentence, and award a new.
Minos, the strict inquisitor, appears;
And lives and crimes, with his assessors, hears.
Round, in his urn, the blended balls he rolls,
Absolves the just, and dooms the guilty souls.   585
The next, in place and punishment, are they
Who prodigally threw their souls away:
Fools, who, repining at their wretched state,
And loathing anxious life, suborned their fate.
With late repentance, now they would retrieve   590
The bodies they forsook, and wish to live;
Their pains and poverty desire to bear,
To view the light of heaven, and breathe the vital air:

584. *blended balls he rolls*: As usual in antiquity, choice or precedence was
determined by lots shaken in some open receptacle until one jumped out.

But Fate forbids; the Stygian floods oppose,
And, with nine circling streams, the captive souls inclose.   595
  Not far from thence, the Mournful Fields appear,
So called from lovers that inhabit there.
The souls whom that unhappy flame invades,
In secret solitude and myrtle shades
Make endless moans, and, pining with desire,   600
Lament too late their unextinguished fire.
Here Procris, Eriphyle here he found
Baring her breast, yet bleeding with the wound
Made by her son. He saw Pasiphaë there,
With Phaedra's ghost; a foul incestuous pair.   605
There Laodamia, with Evadne, moves:
Unhappy both, but loyal in their loves:
Caeneus, a woman once, and once a man,
But ending in the sex she first began.
Not far from these Phoenician Dido stood,   610
Fresh from her wound, her bosom bathed in blood;
Whom when the Trojan hero hardly knew,
Obscure in shades, and with a doubtful view
(Doubtful as he who sees, through dusky night,
Or thinks he sees, the moon's uncertain light),   615
With tears he first approached the sullen shade;
And as his love inspired him, thus he said:
"Unhappy queen! then is the common breath
Of rumor true, in your reported death,
And I, alas! the cause?—By Heaven, I vow,   620
And all the powers that rule the realms below,
Unwilling I forsook your friendly state,
Commanded by the gods, and forced by Fate!

602 sqq. From jealousy *Procris* spied on her husband's hunting, and he killed
her, quite by accident. *Eriphyle*, bribed by a necklace, persuaded her husband to
join the fatal expedition of the Seven Against Thebes; she was killed by her son,
Alcmaeon. *Phaedra*, spurned by her stepson Hippolytus, brought about his death
as well as her own. *Laodamia's* husband Protesilaus was the first Greek killed at
Troy; the gods allowed him to return to her for three hours, after which she
took her own life. *Evadne* threw herself on the funeral pyre of her husband
Capaneus, one of the Seven Against Thebes. Caeneus owed her change of sex
to Neptune (Poseidon).

Those gods, that Fate, whose unresisted might
Have sent me to these regions void of light,   625
Through the vast empire of eternal night!
Nor dared I to presume, that, pressed with grief,
My flight should urge you to this dire relief.
Stay, stay your steps, and listen to my vows!
'Tis the last interview that Fate allows!"   630
In vain he thus attempts her mind to move
With tears and prayers, and late repenting love.
Disdainfully she looked; then turning round,
She fixed her eyes unmoved upon the ground;
And, what he says and swears, regards no more   635
Than the deaf rocks, when the loud billows roar:
But whirled away, to shun his hateful sight,
Hid in the forest, and the shades of night:
Then sought Sichaeus through the shady grove,
Who answered all her cares, and equaled all her love.   640
    Some pious tears the pitying hero paid,
And followed with his eyes the flitting shade;
Then took the forward way, by Fate ordained,
And, with his guide, the farther fields attained,
Where, severed from the rest, the warrior souls remained.   645
Tydeus he met, with Meleager's race,
The pride of armies, and the soldiers' grace;
And pale Adrastus with his ghastly face.
Of Trojan chiefs he viewed a numerous train,
All much lamented, all in battle slain: 650
Glaucus and Medon, high above the rest,
Antenor's sons and Ceres' sacred priest,
And proud Idaeus, Priam's charioteer,
Who shakes his empty reins, and aims his airy spear.
The gladsome ghosts, in circling troops, attend,   655
And with unwearied eyes behold their friend;
Delight to hover near, and long to know
What business brought him to the realms below.

646. *Tydeus*: one of the Seven Against Thebes and Diomedes' father.
Meleager's race: Parthenopaeus, another of the Seven, son of Meleager and
Atalanta.
    648. *Adrastus*: king of Argos, leader of the Seven.

But Argive chiefs, and Agamemnon's train,
When his refulgent arms flashed through the shady plain,   660
Fled from his well-known face with wonted fear;
As when his thundering sword and pointed spear
Drove headlong to their ships, and gleaned the routed rear.
They raised a feeble cry, with trembling notes,
But the weak voice deceived their gasping throats.   665
Here Priam's son, Deïphobus, he found,
Whose face and limbs were one continued wound;
Dishonest, with lopped arms, the youth appears,
Spoiled of his nose, and shortened of his ear.
He scarcely knew him, striving to disown   670
His blotted form, and blushing to be known;
And therefore first began: "O Teucer's race!
Who durst thy faultless figure thus deface?
What heart could wish, what hand inflict this dire disgrace?
'Twas famed, that in our last and fatal night,   675
Your single prowess long sustained the fight;
Till tired, not forced, a glorious fate you chose,
And fell upon a heap of slaughtered foes.
But, in remembrance of so brave a deed,
A tomb and funeral honors I decreed;   680
Thrice called your manës on the Trojan plains:
The place your armor and your name retains.
Your body too I sought, and, had I found,
Designed for burial in your native ground."
    The ghost replied: "Your piety has paid   685
All needful rites to rest my wandering shade;
But cruel Fate, and my more cruel wife,
To Grecian swords betrayed my sleeping life.
These are the monuments of Helen's love:
The shame I bear below, the marks I bore above.   690
You know in what deluding joys, we passed
The night that was by heaven decreed our last.
For, when the fatal horse, descending down
Pregnant with arms o'erwhelmed the unhappy town,

666. Deïphobus: he married Helen after the death of Paris.
668. dishonest: inglorious. From truncas inhonesto vulnere nares, "his nose
shorn off by a shameful wound."

She feigned nocturnal orgies; left my bed;   695
And, mixed with Trojan dames, the dances led;
Then, waving high her torch, the signal made,
Which roused the Grecians from their ambuscade.
With watching overworn, with cares oppressed,
Unhappy I had laid me down to rest;   700
And heavy sleep my weary limbs possessed.
Meantime my worthy wife our arms mislaid,
And, from beneath my head, my sword conveyed;
The door unlatched, and, with repeated calls
Invites her former lord within my walls.   705
Thus, in her crime her confidence she placed,
And with new treasons would redeem the past.
What need I more? Into the room they ran,
And meanly murdered a defenseless man.
Ulysses, basely born, first led the way.—   710
Avenging powers! with justice if I pray,
That fortune be their own another day!
But answer you; and in your turn relate
What brought you, living, to the Stygian state:
Driven by the winds and errors of the sea,   715
Or did you heaven's superior doom obey?
Or tell what other chance conducts your way,
To view with mortal eyes, our dark retreats,
Tumults and torments of the infernal seats."
     While thus, in talk the flying hours they pass,   720
The sun had finished more than half his race;
And they, perhaps, in words and tears had spent
The little time of stay which heaven had lent:
But thus the Sibyl chides their long delay:
"Night rushes down, and headlong drives the day: 725
'Tis here, in different paths, the way divides;
The right to Pluto's golden palace guides;
The left to that unhappy region tends,
Which to the depth of Tartarus descends:
The seat of night profound, and punished fiends."   730

    695. *orgies*: revels.
    715. *errors*: wanderings.

Then thus Deïphobus: "O sacred maid!
Forbear to chide; and be your will obeyed.
Lo! to the secret shadows I retire,
To pay my penance till my years expire.
Proceed, auspicious prince, with glory crowned,   735
And born to better fates than I have found."
He said; and, while he said, his steps he turned
To secret shadows, and in silence mourned.
   The hero, looking on the left, espied
A lofty tower, and strong on every side   740
With treble walls, which Phlegethon surrounds,
Whose fiery flood the burning empire bounds;
And, pressed betwixt the rocks, the bellowing noise resounds.
Wide is the fronting gate, and raised on high
With adamantine columns, threats the sky.   745
Vain is the force of man, and heaven's as vain,
To crush the pillars which the pile sustain.
Sublime on these, a tower of steel is reared;
And dire Tisiphonë there keeps the ward,
Girt in her sanguine gown, by night and day   750
Observant of the souls that pass the downward way.
From hence are heard the groans of ghosts, the pains
Of sounding lashes, and of dragging chains.
The Trojan stood astonished at their cries;
And asked his guide, from whence those yells arise,   755
And what the crimes, and what the tortures were,
And loud laments that rent the liquid air?
   She thus replied: "The chaste and holy race
Are all forbidden this polluted place.
But Hecate, when she gave to rule the woods,   760
Then led me trembling through these dire abodes,
And taught the tortures of the avenging gods.
These are the realms of unrelenting Fate;
And awful Rhadamanthus rules the state:

----

734. *To pay my penance*: *explebo numerum*, etc., "I will fill up again the
number [of shades]." Dryden found this obscure and wrote a long confusing note
about it. His rendering, he said, accorded with "the common interpretation."
Ruaeus, in fact, offered him the Platonic sense that he adopted: *Discedam:
impleturus numerum annorum purgationis, quae fit his in tenebris.*
   749. *Tisiphonë*: one of the Furies; the others were Allecto and Megaera.

He hears and judges each committed crime; 765
Inquires into the manner, place, and time.
The conscious wretch must all his acts reveal
(Loth to confess, unable to conceal),
From the first moment of his vital breath,
To his last hour of unrepenting death. 770
Straight o'er the guilty ghost, the Fury shakes
The sounding whip, and brandishes her snakes,
And the pale sinner, with her sisters, takes."
    Then, of itself, unfolds the eternal door;
With dreadful sounds the brazen hinges roar, 775
You see, before the gate, what stalking ghost
Commands the guard, what sentries keep the post.
More formidable Hydra stands within,
Whose jaws with iron teeth severely grin.
The gaping gulf low to the center lies, 780
And twice as deep, as earth is distant from the skies.
The rivals of the gods, the Titan race,
Here singed with lightning, roll within the unfathomed space.
Here lie the Aloëan twins (I saw them both):
Enormous bodies of gigantic growth, 785
Who dared in fight the Thunderer to defy,
Affect his heaven, and force him from the sky.
Salmoneus, suffering cruel pains, I found,
For emulating Jove, the rattling sound
Of mimic thunder, and the glittering blaze 790
Of pointed lightnings, and their forky rays.
Through Elis, and the Grecian towns, he flew,
The audacious wretch four fiery coursers drew:
He waved a torch aloft, and, madly vain,
Sought servile worship from a servile train. 795
Ambitious fool! with horny hoofs to pass
O'er hollow arches of resounding brass;
To rival thunder in its rapid course,
And imitate inimitable force!
But he, the king of heaven, obscure on high, 800
Bared his red arm, and launching from the sky

784. *Aloëan twins*: Otus and Ephialtes, sons of Aloeus.
788. *Salmoneus*: a son of Aeolus, father of Tyro.
801. *his red arm*: not from Virgil but Horace, *Carmina*, Book I, 2, *rubente dextera*.

His writhen bolt, not shaking empty smoke,
Down to the deep abyss the flaming felon struck.
   There Tityus was to see, who took his birth
From heaven, his nursing from the foodful earth.   805
Here his gigantic limbs, with large embrace,
Infold nine acres of infernal space.
A ravenous vulture, in his opened side,
Her crooked beak and cruel talons tried;
Still for the growing liver digged his breast: 810
The growing liver still supplied the feast;
Still are his entrails fruitful to their pains:
The immortal hunger lasts, the immortal food remains.
   Ixion and Pirithoüs I could name,
And more Thessalian chiefs of mighty fame.   815
High o'er their heads a moldering rock is placed,
That promises a fall, and shakes at every blast.
They lie below, on golden beds displayed;
And genial feasts with regal pomp are made.
The queen of Furies by their sides is set,   820
And snatches from their mouths the untasted meat;
Which if they touch, her hissing snakes she rears,
Tossing her torch, and thundering in their ears.
   Then they, who brothers' better claim disown,
Expel their parents, and usurp the throne;   825
Defraud their clients, and, to lucre sold,
Sit brooding on unprofitable gold—
Who dare not give, and e'en refuse to lend,
To their poor kindred, or a wanting friend.
Vast is the throng of these; nor less the train   830
Of lustful youths, for foul adultery slain:
Hosts of deserters, who their honor sold,
And basely broke their faith for bribes of gold.
All these within the dungeon's depth remain,
Despairing pardon, and expecting pain.   835

---

   804. *Tityus*: a giant who attacked Latona (Leto) and was killed by her children, Apollo and Diana.
   814. *Ixion*: a treacherous murderer, father of the Centaurs.

Ask not what pains; nor further seek to know
Their process, or the forms of law below.
Some roll a mighty stone; some, laid along
And bound with burning wires, on spokes of wheels are hung.
Unhappy Theseus doomed for ever, there   840
Is fixed by Fate, on his eternal chair;
And wretched Phlegyas warns the world with cries
(Could warning make the world more just or wise):
"Learn righteousness, and dread the avenging deities."
To tyrants others have their country sold,   845
Imposing foreign lords for foreign gold:
Some have old laws repealed, new statutes made;
Not as the people pleased, but as they paid.
With incest some their daughters' bed profaned:
All dared the worst of ills, and, what they dared, attained.   850
Had I a hundred mouths, a hundred tongues,
And throats of brass, inspired with iron lungs,
I could not half those horrid crimes repeat,
Nor half the punishments those crimes have met.
    But let us haste our voyage to pursue: 855
The walls of Pluto's palace are in view;
The gate, and iron arch above it, stands,
On anvils labored by the Cyclops' hands.
Before our farther way the Fates allow,
Here must we fix on high the golden bough."   860
She said: and through the gloomy shades they passed,
And chose the middle path.—Arrived at last,
The prince, with living water sprinkled o'er
His limbs and body; then approached the door,
Possessed the porch, and on the front above   865
He fixed the fatal bough, required by Pluto's love.
    These holy rites performed, they took their way,
Where long extended plains of pleasure lay.

---

840 sqq. Theseus, with Pirithoüs, punished for their attempt on Proserpine.
A man of action, he suffers a sedentary fate, *sedet aeternumque sedebit*. Phlegyas
had set fire to Apollo's temple at Delphi.

858. Hesiod had named these Cyclops and said they forged thunderbolts for
Jove.

The verdant fields with those of heaven may vie,
With ether vested, and a purple sky—   870
The blissful seats of happy souls below:
Stars of their own, and their own suns, they know.
Their airy limbs in sports they exercise,
And, on the green, contend the wrestler's prize.
Some, in heroic verse, divinely sing;   875
Others in artful measures lead the ring.
The Thracian bard, surrounded by the rest,
There stands conspicuous in his flowing vest.
His flying fingers, and harmonious quill,
Strike seven distinguished notes, and seven at once they fill.   880
Here found they Teucer's old heroic race,
Born better times and happier years to grace.
Assaracus and Ilus here enjoy
Perpetual fame, with him who founded Troy.
The chief beheld their chariots from afar,   885
Their shining arms, and coursers trained to war.
Their lances fixed in earth, their steeds around,
Free from their harness, graze the flowery ground.
The love of horses which they had, alive,
And care of chariots, after death survive.   890
Some cheerful souls were feasting on the plain;
Some did the song, and some the choir, maintain,
Beneath a laurel shade, where mighty Po
Mounts up to woods above, and hides his head below.
Here patriots live, who, for their country's good,   895
In fighting fields, were prodigal of blood:
Priests of unblemished lives here make abode,
And poets worthy their inspiring god;
And searching wits, of more mechanic parts,
Who graced their age with new invented arts;   900

872. *suns*: Dr. Johnson thought the plural curious. Virgil has *solemque suum*, "their own sun."

877. *The Thracian bard*: Orpheus.

883. *Assaracus and Ilus*: Trojan forbears, with Dardanus, "him who founded Troy."

893–4. The source of the Po, which as a young stream flows for a short way underground.

Those who, to worth their bounty did extend,
And those who knew that bounty to commend.
The heads of these with holy fillets bound,
And all their temples were with garlands crowned.
   To these the Sibyl thus her speech addressed,   905
And first to him surrounded by the rest
(Towering his height, and ample was his breast):
"Say, happy souls! divine Musaeus! say
Where lives Anchises, and where lies our way
To find the hero, for whose only sake   910
We sought the dark abodes, and crossed the bitter lake?"
To this the sacred poet thus replied:
"In no fixed place the happy souls reside:
In groves we live, and lie on mossy beds,
By crystal streams, that murmur through the meads,   915
But pass yon easy hill, and thence descend;
The path conducts you to your journey's end."
This said, he led them up the mountain's brow,
And shows them all the shining fields below:
They wind the hill, and through the blissful meadows go.   920
But old Anchises, in a flowery vale,
Reviewed his mustered race, and took the tale—
Those happy spirits, which, ordained by Fate,
For future being and new bodies wait:
With studious thought observed the illustrious throng,   925
In nature's order, as they passed along:
Their names, their fates, their conduct, and their care,
In peaceful senates, and successful war.
He, when Aeneas on the plain appears,
Meets him with open arms, and falling tears: 930
"Welcome (he said), the gods' undoubted race!
O long expected, to my dear embrace!
Once more 'tis given me to behold your face!
The love and pious duty which you pay,
Have passed the perils of so hard a way.   935

   901. *Those who*: patrons. Virgil's meaning is simpler: *quique sui memores alios fecere merendo,* "and those who by their merit made others remember them."
   908. *Musaeus*: a poet, forerunner of Homer.

'Tis true, computing times, I now believed
The happy day approached, nor are my hopes deceived.
What length of lands, what oceans have you passed,
What storms sustained, and on what shores been cast!
How have I feared your fate! but feared it most,   940
When love assailed you on the Libyan coast."
To this, the filial duty thus replies:
"Your sacred ghost, before my sleeping eyes
Appeared, and often urged this painful enterprise.
After long tossing on the Tyrrhene sea,   945
My navy rides at anchor in the bay.
But reach your hand, oh parent shade! nor shun
The dear embraces of your longing son!"
He said; and falling tears his face bedew;
Then thrice, around his neck, his arms he threw;   950
And thrice the flitting shadow slipped away,
Like winds, or empty dreams, that fly the day.
    Now, in a secret vale, the Trojan sees
A separate grove, through which a gentle breeze
Plays with a passing breath, and whispers through the trees;   955
And, just before the confines of the wood,
The gliding Lethe leads her silent flood.
About the boughs an airy nation flew,
Thick as the humming bees, that hunt the golden dew
In summer's heat; on tops of lilies feed,   960
And creep within their bells, to suck the balmy seed:
The wingèd army roams the field around;
The rivers and the rocks remurmur to the sound.
Aeneas wondering stood, then asked the cause
Which to the stream the crowding people draws.   965
Then thus the sire: "The souls that throng the flood,
Are those to whom, by Fate, are other bodies owed;
In Lethe's lake they long oblivion taste,
Of future life secure, forgetful of the past.
Long has my soul desired this time and place,   970
To set before your sight your glorious race;
That this presaging joy may fire your mind,
To seek the shores by destiny designed."

"O father! can it be, that souls sublime
Return, to visit our terrestrial clime; 975
And that the generous mind, released by death,
Can covet lazy limbs, and mortal breath?"
Anchises, then, in order, thus begun
To clear those wonders to his godlike son:
"Know, first, that heaven and earth's compacted frame, 980
And flowing waters, and the starry flame,
And both the radiant lights, one common soul
Inspires and feeds, and animates the whole.
This active mind, infused through all the space,
Unites and mingles with the mighty mass. 985
Hence men and beasts the breath of life obtain,
And birds of air, and monsters of the main.
The ethereal vigor is in all the same;
And every soul is filled with equal flame:
As much as earthly limbs, and gross allay 990
Of mortal members, subject to decay,
Blunt not the beams of heaven and edge of day.
From this coarse mixture of terrestrial parts,
Desire and fear by turns possess their hearts,
And grief, and joy! nor can the groveling mind, 995
In the dark dungeon of the limbs confined,
Assert the native skies, or own its heavenly kind:
Nor death itself can wholly wash their stains;
But long-contracted filth e'en in the soul remains.
The relics of inveterate vice they wear; 1000
And spots of sin obscene in every face appear.
For this are various penances enjoined;
And some are hung to bleach upon the wind;
Some plunged in waters, others purged in fires,
Till all the dregs are drained, and all the rust expires. 1005
All have their manës, and those manës bear:
The few, so cleansed, to these abodes repair,
And breathe, in ample fields, the soft Elysian air.

977. *lazy: tarda,* "sluggish."
982. *one common soul: anima mundi.*
1006. *quisque suos patimur Manes:* "we endure each one his own ghosts
(or ghost)," an ambiguous and awesome line, in context or out.

Then are they happy, when by length of time
The scurf is worn away, of each committed crime;   1010
No speck is left of their habitual stains;
But the pure ether of the soul remains.
But, when a thousand rolling years are past
(So long their punishments and penance last),
Whole droves of minds are by the driving god   1015
Compelled to drink the deep Lethaean flood;
In large forgetful drafts to steep the cares
Of their past labors, and their irksome years;
That, unremembering of its former pain,
The soul may suffer mortal flesh again."   1020
    Thus having said, the father-spirit leads
The priestess and his son through swarms of shades,
And takes a rising ground, from thence to see
The long procession of his progeny.
"Survey (pursued the sire) this airy throng,   1025
As, offered to the view, they pass along.
These are the Italian names, which Fate will join
With ours, and graft upon the Trojan line.
Observe, the youth who first appears in sight,
And holds the nearest station to the light,   1030
Already seems to snuff the vital air,
And leans just forward on a shining spear:
Silvius is he, thy last-begotten race,
But first in order sent, to fill thy place—
An Alban name, but mixed with Dardan blood;   1035
Born in the covert of a shady wood.
Him fair Lavinia, thy surviving wife,
Shall breed in groves, to lead a solitary life.
In Alba he shall fix his royal seat,
And, born a king, a race of kings beget;   1040
Then Procas, honor of the Trojan name,
Capys, and Numitor, of endless fame.
A second Silvius after these appears
(Silvius Aeneas, for thy name he bears);

1033. *Silvius*: here called *tua postuma proles*, i.e., last begotten of Aeneas'
children by Lavinia. By other accounts he was Aeneas' grandson, son of Ascanius,
and Ascanius was the first king of Alba Longa. There were to be fifteen kings in
all, according to Roman mythology.

For arms and justice equally renowned; 1045
Who, late restored, in Alba shall be crowned.
How great they look! how vigorously they wield
Their weighty lances, and sustain the shield!
But they, who crowned with oaken wreaths appear,
Shall Gabian walls and strong Fidenae rear; 1050
Nomentum, Bola, with Pometia, found;
And raise Collatian towers on rocky ground.
All these shall then be towns of mighty fame,
Though now they lie obscure, and lands without a name.
   See Romulus the great! born to restore 1055
The crown that once his injured grandsire wore.
This prince, a priestess of our blood shall bear;
And like his sire in arms he shall appear.
Two rising crests his royal head adorn:
Born from a god, himself to godhead born; 1060
His sire already signs him for the skies,
And marks his seat amidst the deities.
Auspicious chief! thy race, in times to come,
Shall spread the conquests of imperial Rome—
Rome, whose ascending towers shall heaven invade, 1065
Involving earth and ocean in her shade;
High as the mother of the gods in place,
And proud, like her, of an immortal race.
Then, when in pomp she makes the Phrygian round,
With golden turrets on her temples crowned: 1070
A hundred gods her sweeping train supply,
Her offspring all; and all command the sky.
   Now fix your sight, and stand intent, to see
Your Roman race, and Julian progeny!
There mighty Caesar waits his vital hour, 1075
Impatient for the world, and grasps his promised power.
But next behold the youth of form divine—
Caesar himself exalted in his line—

1050 sqq. *Gabian walls, Fidenae, Nomentum, Bola, Pometia, Colatia*: old
Latin towns near Rome.
   1056. *grandsire*: Numitor, father of Rhea Silvia, who bore Romulus and
Remus to the god Mars.
   1067. *mother of the gods*: Cybele, *Magna Mater*, who wore a diadem of
towers.

Augustus, promised oft, and long foretold,
Sent to the realm that Saturn ruled of old;   1080
Born to restore a better age of gold.
Afric and India shall his power obey;
He shall extend his propagated sway
Beyond the solar year; without the starry way,
Where Atlas turns the rolling heavens around,   1085
And his broad shoulders with their lights are crowned.
At his foreseen approach, already quake
The Caspian kingdoms and Maeotian lake.
Their seers behold the tempest from afar;
And threatening oracles denounce the war.   1090
Nile hears him knocking at his seven-fold gates,
And seeks his hidden spring, and fears his nephew's fates.
Nor Hercules more lands or labors knew,
Not though the brazen-footed hind he slew,
Freed Erymanthus from the foaming boar,   1095
And dipped his arrows in Lernaean gore;
Nor Bacchus, turning from his Indian war,
By tigers drawn triumphant in his car,
From Nysa's top descending on the plains,
With curling vines around his purple reins.   1100
And doubt we, yet through dangers to pursue
The paths of honor, and a crown in view?
   But what's the man who from afar appears,
His head with olive crowned, his hand a censer bears?
His hoary beard and holy vestments bring   1105
His lost idea back: I know the Roman king.
He shall to peaceful Rome new laws ordain,
Called from his mean abode, a scepter to sustain.
Him, Tullus next in dignity succeeds;
An active prince, and prone to martial deeds.   1110

   1084. That is, South and North of the region that lies under the Zodiacal
belt in the heavens, corresponding to the annual path of the sun.
   1088. *Maeotian lake*: the Sea of Azov.
   1099. *Nysa's top*: Bacchus was brought up by nymphs on Nysa, a mountain
vaguely located in India whence he extended his conquests.
   1106. *His lost idea*: his identity as the lawgiver, Numa Pompilius.
   1109 sqq. Tullus Hostilius, the third king of Rome. Ancus Martius, the
fourth. Tarquinius, the fifth, an Etruscan. Servius Tullius, the sixth. L. Tarquinius

He shall his troops for fighting fields prepare,
Disused to toils, and triumphs of the war.
By dint of sword his crown he shall increase,
And scour his armor from the rust of peace.
Whom Ancus follows, with a fawning air,   1115
But vain within, and proudly popular.
  Next view the Tarquin kings, the avenging sword
Of Brutus, justly drawn, and Rome restored.
He first renews the rods and axe severe,
And gives the consuls royal robes to wear.   1120
His sons, who seek the tyrant to sustain,
And long for arbitrary lords again,
With ignominy scourged in open sight,
He dooms to death deserved, asserting public right.
Unhappy man! to break the pious laws   1125
Of nature, pleading in his children's cause!
Howe'er the doubtful fact is understood,
'Tis love of honor, and his country's good:
The consul, not the father, sheds the blood.
Behold Torquatus the same tract pursue;   1130
And, next, the two devoted Decii view:
The Drusian line, Camillus loaded home
With standards well redeemed, and foreign foes o'ercome.
  The pair you see in equal armor shine,
Now, friends below, in close embraces join;   1135
But, when they leave the shady realms of night,
And, clothed in bodies, breathe your upper light,
With mortal hate each other shall pursue:
What wars, what wounds, what slaughter, shall ensue!

Superbus, the seventh and last, banished in an uprising led by Brutus, who established the consulate and republic (510 B.C.). The bundle of rods (*fasces*) and
axes was a symbol of kingly, later of consular, authority.

  1130–31. *Torquatus*: when consul in 340 B.C. put his son to death for dis-
obeying orders in war. The *Decii*, father and son, were plebeian consuls, each
"devoted" to his own death in battle.

  1132. *Drusian line*: Drusus was a consul who defeated Hasdrubal on the
Metaurus in 207 B.C. To the "Drusian line" belonged Livia Drusilla, wife of
Augustus. *Camillus*: recovered Rome from the Gauls, who had captured it in
390 B.C.

  1134. *The pair*: Julius Caesar and Pompey, who married Caesar's daughter
Julia. With his eastern friends he was defeated by Caesar at Pharsalia in 48 B.C.

From Alpine heights the father first descends;   1140
His daughter's husband in the plain attends:
His daughter's husband arms his eastern friends.
Embrace again, my sons! be foes no more;
Nor stain your country with her children's gore!
And thou, the first, lay down thy lawless claim,   1145
Thou, of my blood, who bear'st the Julian name!
Another comes, who shall in triumph ride,
And to the Capitol his chariot guide,
From conquered Corinth, rich with Grecian spoils.
And yet another, famed for warlike toils,   1150
On Argos shall impose the Roman laws,
And on the Greeks, revenge the Trojan cause;
Shall drag in chains their Achillean race;
Shall vindicate his ancestors' disgrace,
And Pallas, for her violated place.   1155
Great Cato there, for gravity renowned;
And conquering Cossus goes with laurels crowned.
Who can omit the Gracchi? who declare
The Scipios' worth, those thunderbolts of war,
The double bane of Carthage! Who can see,   1160
Without esteem for virtuous poverty,
Severe Fabricius; or can cease to admire
The plowman consul in his coarse attire?

1145. *lawless claim*: the suspected aspiration to kingship for which he was assassinated. This is Dryden's addition.

1149. Mummius destroyed Corinth in 146 B.C. L. Aemilius Paullus crushed Perseus, the last king of Macedonia, at Pydna in 168 B.C.

1156 sqq. M. Porcius *Cato*, "the Censor," said to have ended every speech he made in the Roman Senate by saying, "Carthage must be destroyed." *Cossus*, consul in 428 B.C., killed the king of Veii in battle. Tiberius Sempronius *Gracchus* was twice consul, in 215 and 212 B.C., in the Second Punic War. A later Gracchus of the same name and his brother Caius were tribunes of the people and the most famous reformers in Roman history. Publius Cornelius *Scipio* Africanus Major defeated Hannibal at Zama in 202 B.C.; his adopted son, P. C. Sc. Af. Minor, destroyed Carthage in 146 B.C. His grandson, M. Porcius Cato, "of Utica," appears in Book VIII, 890.

1162. *Fabricius*: a consul in 282 and 278 B.C. who fought Pyrrhus.

1163. *The plowman consul*: Serranus, consul in 257 B.C. Two types of old Roman rectitude and simplicity.

Tired as I am, my praise the Fabii claim;
And thou, great hero, greatest of thy name,   1165
Ordained in war to save the sinking state,
And, by delays, to put a stop to fate!
  Let others better mold the running mass
Of metals, and inform the breathing brass,
And soften into flesh a marble face;   1170
Plead better at the bar; describe the skies,
And when the stars descend, and when they rise.
But, Rome! 'tis thine alone, with awful sway,
To rule mankind, and make the world obey:
Disposing peace and war thy own majestic way.   1175
To tame the proud, the fettered slave to free,
These are imperial arts, and worthy thee."
  He paused—and, while with wondering eyes they viewed
The passing spirits, thus his speech renewed:
"See great Marcellus! how, untired in toils,   1180
He moves with manly grace, how rich with regal spoils!
He, when his country (threatened with alarms)
Requires his courage and his conquering arms,
Shall more than once the Punic bands affright;
Shall kill the Gaulish king in single fight;   1185
Then to the Capitol in triumph move;
And the third spoils shall grace Feretrian Jove."
  Aeneas here beheld, of form divine,
A godlike youth in glittering armor shine;

1165. *And thou*: Quintus Fabius Maximus, Cunctator, "the delayer," who took command after the Roman disaster at Lake Trasimene, 217 B.C., and wore Hannibal down without risking a pitched battle.

1168–75. A famous passage distinguishing the Roman from the Greek achievement. Dryden has done well by it, but either of the two possible readings, *pacisque imponere morem*, "to impose the custom of peace," or *pacique imponere morem*, "to impose custom upon peace," is faintly rendered by "Disposing peace."

1180. *great Marcellus*: M. Claudius Marcellus in 222 B.C., in his first consulship (he was five times consul) killed the king of the Insubrian Gauls in battle. Thereby he won the highest honors of a Roman commander, the *spolia opima*, achieved only by Romulus, Cossus, and himself. Virgil says he hung up the captured arms to "Quirinus" (Romulus), but Dryden follows other authorities in making it Feretrian Jove (Jupiter Feretrius), the god in his aspect as patron of striking power.

1189. *godlike youth*: Augustus' son and presumptive heir, Marcellus, who died in his twentieth year in 23 B.C.

With great Marcellus keeping equal pace;   1190
But gloomy were his eyes, dejected was his face.
He saw, and, wondering, asked his airy guide,
What, and of whence, was he who pressed the hero's side?
"His son, or one of his illustrious name?
How like the former, and almost the same!   1195
Observe the crowds that compass him around:
All gaze and all admire, and raise a shouting sound:
But hovering mists around his brows are spread;
And night, with sable shades, involves his head."
"Seek not to know (the ghost replied with tears)   1200
The sorrows of thy sons in future years.
This youth, the blissful vision of a day,
Shall just be shown on earth, and snatched away.
The gods, too high had raised the Roman state:
Were but their gifts as permanent as great!   1205
What groans of men shall fill the Martian field!
How fierce a blaze his flaming pile shall yield!
What funeral pomp shall floating Tiber see,
When, rising from his bed, he views the sad solemnity!
No youth shall equal hopes of glory give;   1210
No youth afford so great a cause to grieve.
The Trojan honor, and the Roman boast;
Admired when living, and adored when lost!
Mirror of ancient faith in early youth!
Undaunted worth, inviolable truth!   1215
No foe, unpunished, in the fighting field
Shall dare thee, foot to foot, with sword and shield;
Much less in arms oppose thy matchless force,
When thy sharp spurs shall urge thy foaming horse.
Ah! couldst thou break through Fate's severe decree,   1220
A new Marcellus shall arise in thee!

1206. *Martian field*: the Campus Martius, where Augustus had built a
mausoleum for his family.

1220-21. *heu, miserande puer, si qua fata aspera rumpas! tu Marcellus eris*:
"Alas, poor boy, if only somehow you might break through cruel destiny! You
will be Marcellus." The first line was taken as conditional, not as a despairing
exclamation, by the editor of Dryden's text. In order to make sense of the second
line Dryden had to take Marcellus to mean a "new," that is, a second, mature
hero of that name, like the one praised in 1180 sqq. The story is that the boy's
mother fainted at these lines when Virgil read them for the first time aloud.

Full canisters of fragrant lilies bring,
Mixed with the purple roses of the spring:
Let me with funeral flowers his body strow;
This gift which parents to their children owe,   1225
This unavailing gift, at least, I may bestow!"
    Thus having said, he led the hero round
The confines of the blest Elysian ground;
Which when Anchises to his son had shown,
And fired his mind to mount the promised throne,   1230
He tells the future wars, ordained by Fate;
The strength and customs of the Latian state;
The prince and people; and fore-arms his care
With rules, to push his fortune, or to bear.
    Two gates the silent house of Sleep adorn;   1235
Of polished ivory this, that of transparent horn.
True visions through transparent horn arise;
Through polished ivory pass deluding lies.
Of various things discoursing as he passed,
Anchises hither bends his steps at last;   1240
Then, through the gate of ivory, he dismissed
His valiant offspring, and divining guest.
Straight to the ships Aeneas took his way,
Embarked his men, and skimmed along the sea;
Still coasting, till he gained Caieta's bay.   1245
At length on oozy ground his galleys moor:
Their heads are turned to sea, their sterns to shore.

    1222. *manibus date lilia plenis*: "give handsfull of lilies." More lilies could
certainly be brought in canisters (baskets).
    1237 sqq. Here are the gates of dream described by Penelope in the *Odyssey*,
Book XIX, 562. Why true dreams should issue through horn gates is a question
Dryden solved by making the horn "transparent." Why Anchises ushered Aeneas
through the ivory gates is a puzzle. In logic it might suggest that Aeneas was a
false dream, or more vaguely that the vision of the underworld was a fiction.

꒒꒒꒒꒒

BOOK VII

THE ARGUMENT

King Latinus entertains Aeneas, and promises him his only daughter
Lavinia, the heiress of his crown. Turnus, being in love with her, favored
by her mother, and stirred up by Juno and Alecto, breaks the treaty which
was made, and engages in his quarrel Mezentius, Camilla, Messapus, and
many other of the neighboring princes; whose forces, and the names of
their commanders, are particularly related.

AND thou, O matron of immortal fame!
Here dying, to the shore hast left thy name:
Caieta still the place is called from thee,
The nurse of great Aeneas' infancy.
Here rest thy bones in rich Hesperia's plains: 5
Thy name ('tis all a ghost can have) remains.
    Now, when the prince her funeral rites had paid,
He plowed the Tyrrhene seas with sails displayed.
From land a gentle breeze arose by night;
Serenely shone the stars; the moon was bright,   10
And the sea trembled with her silver light.
Now near the shelves of Circe's shores they run
(Circe the rich, the daughter of the sun):
A dangerous coast!—The goddess wastes her days
In joyous songs; the rocks resound her lays.   15

3. *Caieta*: Gaeta.
6. *'tis all a ghost can have*: Virgil wrote *si qua est ea gloria*, "if that is any
glory [for you]," and Dryden translates by answering: it is, at any rate, all, etc.
12. *Circe's shores*: now a promontory, Monte Circello. Circe was an en-
chantress with a drug that changed men outwardly to animals, especially swine;
she appears in Books X and XII of the *Odyssey*.

In spinning, or the loom, she spends the night;
And cedar brands supply her father's light.
From hence were heard, rebellowing to the main,
The roars of lions that refuse the chain;
The grunts of bristled boars, and groans of bears,   20
And herds of howling wolves that stun the sailors' ears.
These from their caverns, at the close of night,
Fill the sad isle with horror and affright.
Darkling they mourn their fate, whom Circe's power
(That watched the moon, and planetary hour),   25
With words and wicked herbs, from human kind
Had altered, and in brutal shapes confined.
Which monsters, lest the Trojans' pious host
Should bear, or touch upon the enchanted coast,
Propitious Neptune steered their course by night,   30
With rising gales, that sped their happy flight.
Supplied with these, they skim the sounding shore,
And hear the swelling surges vainly roar.
Now, when the rosy morn began to rise,
And waved her saffron streamer through the skies;   35
When Thetis blushed in purple, not her own,
And from her face the breathing winds were blown,
A sudden silence sate upon the sea,
And sweeping oars, with struggling, urge their way.

The Trojan, from the main, beheld a wood,   40
Which thick with shades, and a brown horror, stood:
Betwixt the trees the Tiber took his course,
With whirlpools dimpled; and with downward force
That drove the sand along, he took his way,
And rolled his yellow billows to the sea.   45
About him, and above, and round the wood,
The birds that haunt the borders of his flood,
That bathed within, or basked upon his side,
To tuneful songs their narrow throats applied.

26. The practice of witchcraft is implied in this and the preceding line,
though Virgil said only *potentibus herbis*, "with potent herbs."
36. *Thetis*: the sea.
41. *a brown horror*: a dark bristling.

The captain gives command; the joyful train   50
Glide through the gloomy shade, and leave the main.
    Now, Erato! thy poet's mind inspire,
And fill his soul with thy celestial fire.
Relate what Latium was; her ancient kings:
Declare the past and present state of things;   55
When first the Trojan fleet Ausonia sought,
And how the rivals loved, and how they fought.
These are my theme; and how the war began,
And how concluded by the godlike man;
For I shall sing of battles, blood, and rage,   60
Which princes and their people did engage;
And haughty souls, that, moved with mutual hate,
In fighting fields pursued and found their fate;
That roused the Tyrrhene realm with loud alarms,
And peaceful Italy involved in arms.   65
A larger scene of action is displayed;
And, rising hence, a greater work is weighed.
    Latinus, old and mild, had long possessed
The Latian scepter, and his people blessed:
His father Faunus: a Laurentian dame   70
His mother; fair Marica was her name.
But Faunus came from Picus: Picus drew
His birth from Saturn, if records be true.
Thus king Latinus, in the third degree,
Had Saturn author of his family.   75
But this old peaceful prince, as heaven decreed,
Was blessed with no male issue to succeed:
His sons in blooming youth were snatched by fate;
One only daughter heired the royal state.
Fired with her love, and with ambition led,   80
The neighboring princes court her nuptial bed.
Among the crowd, but far above the rest,
Young Turnus to the beauteous maid addressed.
Turnus, for high descent and graceful mien
Was first, and favored by the Latian queen: 85
With him she strove to join Lavinia's hand;
But dire portents the purposed match withstand.

    52. *Erato*: the muse of love poetry, here simply The Muse.

Deep in the palace, of long growth there stood
A laurel's trunk, a venerable wood;
Where rites divine were paid; whose holy hair   90
Was kept and cut with superstitious care.
This plant, Latinus, when his town he walled
Then found, and from the tree Laurentum called;
And last, in honor of his new abode,
He vowed the laurel to the laurel's god.   95
It happened once (a boding prodigy!)
A swarm of bees, that cut the liquid sky
(Unknown from whence they took their airy flight),
Upon the topmost branch in clouds alight;
There, with their clasping feet, together clung,   100
And a long cluster from the laurel hung.
An ancient augur prophesied from hence:
"Behold! on Latian shores a foreign prince;
From the same parts of heaven his navy stands,
To the same parts on earth: his army lands;   105
The town he conquers, and the tower commands."
    Yet more; when fair Lavinia fed the fire
Before the gods, and stood beside her sire,
(Strange to relate!) the flames, involved in smoke
Of incense, from the sacred altar broke,   110
Caught her disheveled hair, and rich attire;
Her crown and jewels crackled in the fire:
From thence the fuming trail began to spread,
And lambent glories danced about her head.
This new portent the seer with wonder views,   115
Then pausing, thus his prophecy renews:
"The nymph who scatters flaming fires around,
Shall shine with honor, shall herself be crowned;
But, caused by her irrevocable fate,
War shall the country waste, and change the state."   120
    Latinus, frightened with this dire ostent,
For counsel to his father Faunus went;

90. *hair*: foliage.
95. *the laurel's god*: Apollo.
121. *ostent*: sign.

And sought the shades renowned for prophecy,
Which near Albunea's sulfurous fountain lie.
To those, the Latian and the Sabine land   125
Fly when distressed; and thence relief demand.
The priest on skins of offerings takes his ease,
And nightly visions in his slumber sees;
A swarm of thin aërial shapes appears,
And, fluttering round his temples, deafs his ears. 130
These he consults, the future fates to know,
From powers above, and from the fiends below.
Here, for the god's advice, Latinus flies,
Offering a hundred sheep for sacrifice:
Their woolly fleeces, as the rites required,   135
He laid beneath him, and to rest retired.
No sooner were his eyes in slumber bound,
When, from above, a more than mortal sound
Invades his ears; and thus the vision spoke:
"Seek not, my seed, in Latian bands to yoke   140
Our fair Lavinia, nor the gods provoke.
A foreign son upon the shore descends,
Whose martial fame from pole to pole extends.
His race, in arms and arts of peace renowned,
Not Latium shall contain, nor Europe bound: 145
'Tis theirs, whate'er the sun surveys around."
These answers, in the silent night received,
The king himself divulged, the land believed:
The fame through all the neighboring nations flew,
When now the Trojan navy was in view.   150
    Beneath a shady tree, the hero spread
His table on the turf, with cakes of bread;
And, with his chiefs, on forest fruits he fed.
They sat; and (not without the god's command),
Their homely fare dispatched; the hungry band   155
Invade their trenchers next, and soon devour—
To mend the scanty meal—their cakes of flour.
Ascanius this observed, and, smiling, said:
"See! we devour the plates on which we fed."

159. As Celaeno prophesied in Book III, 336.

The speech had omen, that the Trojan race   160
Should find repose; and this the time and place.
   Aeneas took the word, and thus replies
(Confessing fate with wonder in his eyes):
"All hail, O earth! all hail, my household gods!
Behold the destined place of your abodes!   165
For thus Anchises prophesied of old,
And this our fatal place of rest foretold:
'When, on a foreign shore, instead of meat,
By famine forced, your trenchers you shall eat,
Then ease your weary Trojans will attend,   170
And the long labors of your voyage end.
Remember on that happy coast to build;
And with a trench inclose the fruitful field.'
This was that famine, this the fatal place;
Which ends the wandering of our exiled race.   175
Then, on tomorrow's dawn, your care employ
To search the land, and where the cities lie,
And what the men; but give this day to joy.
Now pour to Jove; and after Jove is blest,
Call great Anchises to the genial feast: 180
Crown high the goblets with a cheerful draught,
Enjoy the present hour; adjourn the future thought."
   Thus having said, the hero bound his brows
With leafy branches, then performed his vows:
Adoring first the genius of the place;   185
Then Earth, the mother of the heavenly race;
The nymphs, and native godheads yet unknown;
And Night, and all the stars that gild her sable throne.
And ancient Cybel, and Idaean Jove;
And last his sire below, and mother-queen above.   190
   Then heaven's high monarch thundered thrice aloud;
And thrice he shook aloft a golden cloud.
Soon through the joyful camp a rumor flew,
The time was come their city to renew:
Then every brow with cheerful green is crowned;   195
The feasts are doubled, and the bowls go round.

   166. *Anchises*: An unhappy confusion of Anchises with a harpy. The *Aeneid* was unrevised.

When next the rosy morn disclosed the day,
The scouts to several parts divide their way,
To learn the natives' names, their towns explore,
The coasts, and trendings of the crooked shore: 200
Here Tiber flows, and here Numicus stands;
Here warlike Latins hold the happy lands.
    The pious chief, who sought by peaceful ways
To found his empire, and his town to raise,
A hundred youths from all his train selects,   205
And to the Latian court their course directs
(The spacious palace where their prince resides),
And all their heads with wreaths of olive hides.
They go, commissioned to require a peace;
And carry presents, to procure access.   210
Thus while they speed their pace, the prince designs
The new-elected seat, and draws the lines:
The Trojans round the place a rampire cast,
And palisades about the trenches placed.
    Meantime, the train, proceeding on their way,   215
From far the town and lofty towers, survey;
At length approach the walls. Without the gate,
They see the boys and Latian youth debate
The martial prizes on the dusty plain:
Some drive the cars, and some the coursers rein;   220
Some bend the stubborn bow for victory;
And some with darts their active sinews try.
A posting messenger, dispatched from hence,
Of this fair troop, advised their aged prince
That foreign men of mighty stature came;   225
Uncouth their habit, and unknown their name.
    The king ordains their entrance, and ascends
His regal seat, surrounded by his friends.
The palace, built by Picus, vast and proud,
Supported by a hundred pillars stood,   230
And round encompassed with a rising wood.
The pile o'erlooked the town, and drew the sight,
Surprised at once with reverence and delight.

201. *Numicus*: the Numicius River in Latium.

There, kings received the marks of sovereign power:
In state the monarchs marched; the lictors bore   235
Their awful axes, and the rods, before.
Here the tribunal stood, the house of prayer;
And here the sacred senators repair;
All at large tables, in long order set,
A ram their offering, and a ram their meat.   240
Above the portal, carved in cedar wood,
Placed in their ranks, their godlike grandsires stood:
Old Saturn, with his crooked scythe, on high;
And Italus, that led the colony;
And ancient Janus, with his double face,   245
And bunch of keys, the porter of the place.
There stood Sabinus, planter of the vines;
On a short pruning hook his head reclines,
And studiously surveys his generous wines:
Then warlike kings, who for their country fought,   250
And honorable wounds from battle brought.
Around the posts, hung helmets, darts, and spears,
And captive chariots, axes, shields, and bars,
And broken beaks of ships, the trophies of their wars.
Above the rest, as chief of all the band,   255
Was Picus placed, a buckler in his hand,
His other waved a long divining wand.
Girt in his Gabine gown the hero sat,
Yet could not with his art avoid his fate;
For Circe long had loved the youth in vain,   260
Till love, refused, converted to disdain:
Then, mixing powerful herbs, with magic art;
She changed his form, who could not change his heart:
Constrained him in a bird, and made him fly,
With particolored plumes, a chattering pie.   265
   In this high temple, on a chair of state,
The seat of audience, old Latinus sat;
Then gave admission to the Trojan train;
And thus with pleasing accents he began:

236. *axes . . . rods*: the Roman *fasces*.
258. *Gabine gown*: Dryden supplied this alliterative equivalent (from Gabii,
an old Latin town) for the *trabea*, a striped toga.

"Tell me, ye Trojans—for that name you own;   270
Nor is your course upon our coasts unknown—
Say what you seek, and whither were you bound;
Were you by stress of weather cast aground?
(Such dangers of the sea are often seen,
And oft befall to miserable men),   275
Or come your shipping in our ports to lay,
Spent and disabled in so long a way?
Say what you want, the Latians you shall find
Not forced to goodness, but by will inclined;
For, since the time of Saturn's holy reign,   280
His hospitable customs we retain.
I call to mind (but time the tale has worn)
The Aurunci told that Dardanus, though born
On Latian plains, yet sought the Phrygian shore,
And Samothracia, Samos called, before.   285
From Tuscan Corythum he claimed his birth;
But after, when exempt from mortal earth,
From thence ascended to his kindred skies,
A god, and, as a god, augments their sacrifice."

    He said.—Ilioneus made this reply: 290
"O king, of Faunus' royal family!
Nor wintry winds to Latium forced our way,
Nor did the stars our wandering course betray.
Willing we sought your shores; and, hither bound,
The port, so long desired, at length we found;   295
From our sweet homes and ancient realms expelled—
Great as the greatest that the sun beheld.
The god began our line, who rules above;
And, as our race, our king descends from Jove:
And hither are we come, by his command,   300
To crave admission in your happy land.
How dire a tempest, from Mycenae poured,
Our plains, our temples, and our town, devoured;
What was the waste of war, what fierce alarms
Shook Asia's crown with European arms;   305

    283. *The Aurunci*: *Auruncos*, Ausonians, Italians.
    285. *Samos*: in Thrace, is distinguished as "Samothrace" from Samos in Asia
Minor.
    286. *Corythum*: Cortona.

E'en such have heard, if any such there be,
Whose earth is bounded by the frozen sea;
And such as, born beneath the burning sky
And sultry sun, betwixt the tropics lie.
From that dire deluge, through the watery waste 310
(Such length of years, such various perils, passed),
At last escaped, to Latium we repair,
To beg what you without your want may spare—
The common water, and the common air;
Sheds which ourselves will build, and mean abodes, 315
Fit to receive and serve our banished gods.
Nor our admission shall your realm disgrace,
Nor length of time our gratitude efface;
Besides what endless honor you shall gain,
To save and shelter Troy's unhappy train. 320
Now, by my sovereign, and his fate, I swear
(Renowned for faith in peace, for force in war),
Oft our alliance other lands desired,
And, what we seek of you, of us required.
Despise not then, that in our hands we bear 325
These holy boughs, and sue with words of prayer.
Fate and the gods, by their supreme command,
Have doomed our ships to seek the Latian land.
To these abodes our fleet Apollo sends;
Here Dardanus was born, and hither tends; 330
Where Tuscan Tiber rolls with rapid force,
And where Numicus opes his holy source.
Besides, our prince presents with his request,
Some small remains of what his sire possessed:
This golden charger, snatched from burning Troy, 335
Anchises did in sacrifice employ:
This royal robe and this tiara wore
Old Priam, and this golden scepter bore
In full assemblies, and in solemn games:
These purple vests were weaved by Dardan dames." 340
Thus while he spoke, Latinus rolled around
His eyes, and fixed awhile upon the ground:
Intent he seemed, and anxious in his breast;
Not by the scepter moved, or kingly vest,

But pondering future things of wondrous weight—   345
Succession, empire, and his daughter's fate.
On these he mused within his thoughtful mind;
And then revolved what Faunus had divined.
This was the foreign prince, by fate decreed
To share his scepter, and Lavinia's bed;   350
This was the race that sure portents foreshow
To sway the world, and land and sea subdue.
At length he raised his cheerful head, and spoke:
"The powers (said he), the powers we both invoke,
To you, and yours, and mine, propitious be,   355
And firm our purpose with their augury!
Have what you ask: your presents I receive:
Land, where and when you please, with ample leave:
Partake and use my kingdom as your own:
All shall be yours, while I command the crown.   360
And, if my wished alliance please your king,
Tell him he should not send the peace, but bring:
Then let him not a friend's embraces fear;
The peace is made when I behold him here.
Besides this answer, tell my royal guest   365
I add to his commands my own request:
Only one daughter heirs my crown and state,
Whom not our oracles, nor heaven, nor fate,
Nor frequent prodigies, permit to join
With any native of the Ausonian line.   370
A foreign son-in-law shall come from far
(Such is our doom), a chief renowned in war,
Whose race shall bear aloft the Latian name,
And through the conquered world diffuse our fame.
Himself to be the man the fates require,   375
I firmly judge, and what I judge, desire."
He said; and then on each bestowed a steed.
Three hundred horses, in high stables fed,
Stood ready, shining all, and smoothly dressed:
Of these, he chose the fairest and the best   380
To mount the Trojan troop. At his command,
The steeds caparisoned with purple stand,

With golden trappings, glorious to behold,
And champ betwixt their teeth the foaming gold.
Then to his absent guest the king decreed   385
A pair of coursers born of heavenly breed;
Who from their nostrils breathed ethereal fire;
Whom Circe stole from her celestial sire,
By substituting mares produced on earth,
Whose wombs conceived a more than mortal birth.   390
These draw the chariot which Latinus sends,
And the rich present to the prince commends.
Sublime on stately steeds the Trojans borne,
To their expecting lord with peace return.

But jealous Juno, from Pachynus' height,   395
As she from Argos took her airy flight,
Beheld, with envious eyes this hateful sight.
She saw the Trojan and his joyful train
Descend upon the shore; desert the main;
Design a town; and, with unhoped success,   400
The ambassadors return with promised peace.
Then, pierced with pain, she shook her haughty head,
Sighed from her inward soul, and thus she said:
"O hated offspring of my Phrygian foes!
O fates of Troy, which Juno's fates oppose!   405
Could they not fall unpitied on the plain?
But, slain, revive, and, taken, 'scape again!
When execrable Troy in ashes lay,
Through fires and swords and seas they forced their way!
Then vanquished Juno must in vain contend;   410
Her rage disarmed, her empire at an end!
Breathless and tired, is all my fury spent?
Or does my glutted spleen at length relent?
As if 'twere little from their town to chase,
I through the seas pursued their exiled race;   415
Engaged the heavens, opposed the stormy main;
But billows roared and tempests raged in vain.
What have my Scyllas and my Syrtes done,
When these they overpass, and those they shun?

389. *substituting mares*: i.e., by putting a divine stallion to earthly mares.

On Tiber's shores they land, secure of fate,   420
Triumphant o'er the storms and Juno's hate!
Mars could in mutual blood the Centaurs bathe;
And Jove himself gave way to Cynthia's wrath,
Who sent the tusky boar to Calydon;
(What great offense had either people done?)   425
But I, the consort of the Thunderer,
Have waged a long and unsuccessful war;
With various arts and arms in vain have toiled;
And by a mortal man at length am foiled!
If native power prevail not, shall I doubt   430
To seek for needful succor from without?
If Jove and heaven my just desires deny,
Hell shall the power of heaven and Jove supply!
Grant that the Fates have firmed, by their decree,
The Trojan race to reign in Italy: 435
At least I can defer the nuptial day,
And, with protracted wars, the peace delay:
With blood the dear alliance shall be bought,
And both the people near destruction brought.
So shall the son-in-law and father join,   440
With ruin, war, and waste of either line.
O fatal maid! thy marriage is endowed
With Phrygian, Latian, and Rutulian blood.
Bellona leads thee to thy lover's hand:
Another queen brings forth another brand,   445
To burn with foreign fires another land:
A second Paris, differing but in name,
Shall fire his country with a second flame."
     Thus having said, she sinks beneath the ground
With furious haste, and shoots the Stygian sound,   450

     422. *Mars*: said to have stirred up the famous battle between the Lapiths and
the Centaurs.
     424. *tusky boar*: Diana (Cynthia) sent the boar to punish Calydon for King
Oineus' failure to do her honor.
     432–3. *flectere si nequeo superos, Acheronta movebo*: "if I cannot sway the
gods above, I shall arouse [those of] Acheron."
     444. *Bellona*: goddess of war.
     445. *queen . . . brand*: Before the birth of Paris, Queen Hecuba dreamed she
was pregnant with a torch.
     450. *shoots*: as in shooting rapids.

To rouse Alecto from the infernal seat
Of her dire sisters, and their dark retreat.
This Fury, fit for her intent, she chose;
One who delights in wars, and human woes.
E'en Pluto hates his own misshapen race;   455
Her sister Furies fly her hideous face;
So frightful are the forms the monster takes,
So fierce the hissings of her speckled snakes.
Her, Juno finds, and thus inflames her spite:
"O virgin daughter of eternal Night!   460
Give me this once thy labor, to sustain
My right, and execute my just disdain.
Let not the Trojans with a feigned pretense
Of proffered peace, delude the Latian prince:
Expel from Italy that odious name,   465
And let not Juno suffer in her fame.
'Tis thine to ruin realms, o'erturn a state,
Betwixt the dearest friends to raise debate,
And kindle kindred blood to mutual hate.
Thy hand o'er towns the funeral torch displays,   470
And forms a thousand ills ten thousand ways.
Now, shake from out thy fruitful breast, the seeds
Of envy, discord, and of cruel deeds:
Confound the peace established, and prepare
Their souls to hatred, and their hands to war."   475
     Smeared as she was with black Gorgonean blood,
The Fury sprang above the Stygian flood;
And on her wicker wings, sublime, through night,
She to the Latian palace took her flight;
There sought the queen's apartment, stood before   480
The peaceful threshold, and besieged the door.
Restless Amata lay, her swelling breast
Fired with disdain for Turnus dispossessed,
And the new nuptials of the Trojan guest.
From her black bloody locks, the Fury shakes   485
Her darling plague, the favorite of her snakes.
With her full force she threw the poisonous dart,
And fixed it deep within Amata's heart;

478. *wicker*: pliant.

That, thus envenomed, she might kindle rage,
And sacrifice to strife her house and husband's age.   490
Unseen, unfelt, the fiery serpent skims
Betwixt her linen and her naked limbs;
His baneful breath inspiring as he glides:
Now like a chain around her neck he rides;
Now like a fillet to her head repairs,   495
And with his circling volumes folds her hairs.
At first the silent venom slid with ease,
And seized her cooler senses by degrees;
Then, ere the infected mass was fired too far,
In plaintive accents she began the war,   500
And thus bespoke her husband: "Shall (she said)
A wandering prince enjoy Lavinia's bed?
If nature plead not in a parent's heart,
Pity my tears, and pity her desert.
I know, my dearest lord, the time will come,   505
You would, in vain, reverse your cruel doom:
The faithless pirate soon will set to sea,
And bear the royal virgin far away!
A guest like him (a Trojan guest) before,
In show of friendship sought the Spartan shore,   510
And ravished Helen from her husband bore.
Think on a king's inviolable word;
And think on Turnus, her once plighted lord.
To this false foreigner you give your throne,
And wrong a friend, a kinsman, and a son.   515
Resume your ancient care; and, if the god
Your sire, and you, resolve on foreign blood,
Know all are foreign, in a larger sense,
Not born your subjects, or derived from hence.
Then, if the line of Turnus you retrace,   520
He springs from Inachus of Argive race."
But, when she saw her reasons idly spent,
And could not move him from his fixed intent,
She flew to rage; for now the snake possessed
Her vital parts, and poisoned all her breast.   525

493. *inspiring*: breathing into her.

She raves, she runs with a distracted pace,
And fills with horrid howls the public place.
And, as young striplings whip the top for sport,
On the smooth pavement of an empty court;
The wooden engine flies and whirls about,   530
Admired with clamors of the beardless rout:
They lash aloud; each other they provoke,
And lend their little souls at every stroke:
Thus fares the queen; and thus her fury blows
Amidst the crowd, and kindles as she goes.   535
   Not yet content, she strains her malice more,
And adds new ills to those contrived before:
She flies the town, and, mixing with the throng
Of madding matrons, bears the bride along;
Wandering through woods and wilds, and devious ways,   540
And with these arts the Trojan match delays.
She feigned the rites of Bacchus, cried aloud,
And to the buxom god the virgin vowed.
"Evoe! O Bacchus!" thus began the song;
And "Evoe!" answered all the female throng.   545
"O virgin worthy thee alone!" she cried;
"O worthy thee alone!" the crew replied.
"For thee she feeds her hair, she leads thy dance,
And with thy winding ivy wreathes her lance."
Like fury seized the rest: the progress known,   550
All seek the mountains, and forsake the town;
All, clad in skins of beasts, the javelin bear,
Give to the wanton winds their flowing hair;
And shrieks and shoutings rend the suffering air.
The queen herself, inspired with rage divine,   555
Shook high above her head a flaming pine;
Then rolled her haggard eyes around the throng,
And sung in Turnus' name the nuptial song:
"Io! ye Latian dames, if any here
Hold your unhappy queen, Amata, dear;   560
If there be here (she said), who dare maintain
My right, nor think the name of mother vain;

   539. *the bride*: her daughter, Lavinia.

Unbind your fillets, loose your flowing hair,
And orgies and nocturnal rites prepare."
   Amata's breast the Fury thus invades,   565
And fires with rage, amid the sylvan shades.
Then, when she found her venom spread so far,
The royal house embroiled in civil war,
Raised on her dusky wings, she cleaves the skies,
And seeks the palace where young Turnus lies.   570
His town (as fame reports) was built of old
By Danaë, pregnant with almighty gold;
Who fled her father's rage, and, with a train
Of following Argives, through the stormy main
Driven by the southern blasts, was fated here to reign.   575
   'Twas Ardua once; now Ardea's name it bears;
Once a fair city, now consumed with years.
Here, in his lofty palace, Turnus lay,
Betwixt the confines of the night and day,
Secure in sleep.—The Fury laid aside   580
Her looks and limbs, and with new methods tried
The foulness of the infernal form to hide.
Propped on a staff, she takes a trembling mien;
Her face is furrowed, and her front obscene;
Deep-dinted wrinkles on her cheek she draws;   585
Sunk are her eyes, and toothless are her jaws;
Her hoary hair with holy fillets bound;
Her temples with an olive wreath are crowned.
Old Chalybë, who kept the secret fane
Of Juno, now she seemed, and thus began   590
(Appearing in a dream) to rouse the careless man:
"Shall Turnus then such endless toil sustain
In fighting fields, and conquer towns in vain?
Win, for a Trojan head to wear the prize,
Usurp thy crown, enjoy thy victories?   595
The bride and scepter, which thy blood has bought,
The king transfers; and foreign heirs are sought!

   572. *Danaë*: upon whom Zeus, in love, descended as a shower of gold.
   584. *front obscene: frontem obscenam*, "ugly forehead." Dryden uses "obscene" elsewhere in the sense "ill-omened," as of birds in Book III, 341; IV, 674
and XII, 1250.

Go now, deluded man, and seek again
New toils, new dangers, on the dusty plain!
Repel the Tuscan foes, their city seize: 600
Protect the Latians in luxurious ease!
This dream all-powerful Juno sends: I bear
Her mighty mandates, and her words you hear.
Haste! arm your Ardeans; issue to the plain;
With faith to friend, assault the Trojan train: 605
Their thoughtless chiefs, their painted ships that lie
In Tiber's mouth, with fire and sword destroy.
The Latian king, unless he shall submit,
Own his old promise, and his new forget—
Let him in arms the power of Turnus prove;   610
And learn to fear whom he disdains to love.
For such is heaven's command." The youthful prince
With scorn replied, and made this bold defense:
"You tell me, mother, what I knew before,
The Phrygian fleet is landed on the shore.   615
I neither fear nor will provoke the war;
My fate is Juno's most peculiar care.
But time has made you dote, and vainly tell
Of arms imagined in your lonely cell.
Go! be the temple and the gods your care: 620
Permit to men the thought of peace and war."
    These haughty words Alecto's rage provoke,
And frightened Turnus trembled as she spoke.
Her eyes grow stiffened, and with sulfur burn;
Her hideous looks and hellish form return;   625
Her curling snakes with hissings fill the place,
And open all the furies of her face:
Then, darting fire from her malignant eyes,
She cast him backward as he strove to rise,
And lingering sought to frame some new replies.   630
High on her head she rears two twisted snakes;
Her chains she rattles, and her whip she shakes;
And churning bloody foam, thus loudly speaks:
"Behold whom time has made to dote and tell
Of arms imagined in her lonely cell!   635

Behold the Fates' infernal minister!
War, death, destruction, in my hand I bear."
　Thus having said, her smoldering torch, impressed
With her full force, she plunged into his breast.
Aghast he waked; and starting from his bed,　　　　　640
Cold sweat, in clammy drops, his limbs o'erspread.
"Arms! arms! (he cries): my sword and shield prepare!"
He breathes defiance, blood, and mortal war.
So, when with crackling flames a caldron fries,
The bubbling waters from the bottom rise;　　　　　645
Above the brims they force their fiery way;
Black vapors climb aloft, and cloud the day.
　The peace polluted thus, a chosen band
He first commissions to the Latian land,
In threatening embassy; then raised the rest　　　　650
To meet in arms the intruding Trojan guest;
To force the foes from the Lavinian shore,
And Italy's endangered peace restore.
Himself alone an equal match he boasts,
To fight the Phrygian and Ausonian hosts.　　　　　655
The gods invoked, the Rutuli prepare
Their arms, and warm each other to the war.
His beauty these, and those his blooming age,
The rest, his house and his own fame engage.
　While Turnus urges thus his enterprise,　　　　　660
The Stygian Fury to the Trojans flies;
New frauds invents, and takes a steepy stand,
Which overlooks the vale with wide command;
Where fair Ascanius and his youthful train,
With horns and hounds a hunting match ordain,　　　665
And pitch their toils around the shady plain.
The Fury fires the pack; they snuff, they vent,
And feed their hungry nostrils with the scent.
'Twas of a well-grown stag, whose antlers rise
High o'er his front, his beams invade the skies.　　　670
From this light cause, the infernal maid prepares
The country churls to mischief, hate, and wars.

The stately beast the two Tyrrhidae bred,
Snatched from his dam, and the tame youngling fed.
Their father, Tyrrheus, did his fodder bring—   675
Tyrrheus chief ranger to the Latian king:
Their sister Silvia, cherished with her care
The little wanton, and did wreaths prepare
To hang his budding horns; with ribbons tied
His tender neck, and combed his silken hide,   680
And bathed his body. Patient of command
In time he grew, and, growing used to hand,
He waited at his master's board for food;
Then sought his savage kindred in the wood,
Where grazing all the day; at night he came   685
To his known lodgings, and his country dame.
This household beast, that used the woodland grounds,
Was viewed at first by the young hero's hounds,
As down the stream he swam, to seek retreat
In the cool waters, and to quench his heat.   690
Ascanius, young and eager of his game,
Soon bent his bow, uncertain in his aim;
But the dire fiend the fatal arrow guides,
Which pierced his bowels through his panting sides.
The bleeding creature issues from the floods,   695
Possessed with fear, and seeks his known abodes,
His old familiar hearth, and household gods.
He falls; he fills the house with heavy groans;
Implores their pity, and his pain bemoans.
Young Silvia beats her breast, and cries aloud   700
For succor from the clownish neighborhood.
The churls assemble; for the fiend who lay
In the close woody covert, urged their way.
One with a brand yet burning from the flame;
Armed with a knotty club another came: 705
Whate'er they catch or find, without their care,
Their fury makes an instrument of war.

673. *Tyrrhidae*: sons of Tyrrheus.
701. *clownish*: rustic.

Tyrrheus, the foster father of the beast,
Then clenched a hatchet in his horny fist,
But held his hand from the descending stroke,   710
And left his wedge within the cloven oak,
To whet their courage, and their rage provoke.
  And now the goddess, exercised in ill,
Who watched an hour to work her impious will,
Ascends the roof, and to her crooked horn,   715
Such as was then by Latian shepherds borne,
Adds all her breath. The rocks and woods around,
And mountains, tremble at the infernal sound.
The sacred lake of Trivia from afar;
The Veline fountains, and sulfureous Nar,   720
Shake at the baleful blast, the signal of the war.
Young mothers wildly stare, with fear possessed,
And strain their helpless infants to their breast.
  The clowns, a boisterous, rude, ungoverned crew,
With furious haste to the loud summons flew.   725
The powers of Troy, then issuing on the plain,
With fresh recruits their youthful chief sustain:
Nor theirs a raw and unexperienced train,
But a firm body of embattled men.
At first, while fortune favored neither side,   730
The fight with clubs and burning brands was tried;
But now, both parties reinforced, the fields
Are bright with flaming swords and brazen shields.
A shining harvest either host displays,
And shoots against the sun with equal rays.   735
  Thus, when a black-browed gust begins to rise,
White foam at first on the curled ocean fries;
Then roars the main, the billows mount the skies;
Till, by the fury of the storm full blown,
The muddy bottom o'er the clouds is thrown.   740

---

719. Lake of Trivia: the Lake of Nemi in the Alban Hills near Aricia and the grove of Diana whose cult Sir James Frazer studied in *The Golden Bough*.

733. *horrescit strictis seges ensibus, aeraque fulgent*: a notable Virgilian sound-and-sight effect: "bristled a crop of unscabbarded swords and the bronze flashed."

First Almon falls, old Tyrrheus' eldest care,
Pierced with an arrow from the distant war;
Fixed in his throat the flying weapon stood,
And stopped his breath, and drank his vital blood.
Huge heaps of slain around the body rise;   745
Among the rest, the rich Galesus lies—
A good old man, while peace he preached in vain,
Amidst the madness of the unruly train:
Five herds, five bleating flocks, his pastures filled;
His lands a hundred yoke of oxen tilled.   750
Thus, while in equal scales their fortune stood,
The Fury bathed them in each other's blood;
Then, having fixed the fight, exulting flies,
And bears fulfilled her promise to the skies.
    To Juno thus she speaks: "Behold! 'tis done,   755
The blood already drawn, the war begun;
The discord is complete; nor can they cease
The dire debate, nor you command the peace.
Now, since the Latian and the Trojan brood
Have tasted vengeance, and the sweets of blood;   760
Speak, and my power shall add this office more:
The neighboring nations of the Ausonian shore
Shall hear the dreadful rumor from afar,
Of armed invasion, and embrace the war."
Then Juno thus: "The grateful work is done,   765
The seeds of discord sowed, the war begun:
Frauds, fears, and fury, have possessed the state,
And fixed the causes of a lasting hate.
A bloody Hymen shall the alliance join
Betwixt the Trojan and the Ausonian line: 770
But thou with speed to night and hell repair;
For not the gods, nor angry Jove, will bear
Thy lawless wandering walks in upper air.
Leave what remains to me." Saturnia said:
The sullen fiend her sounding wings displayed,   775
Unwilling left the light, and sought the nether shade.

    769. Hymen: the god of weddings.

In midst of Italy, well known to fame,
There lies a lake (Amsanctus is the name),
Below the lofty mounts: on either side
Thick forests the forbidden entrance hide.   780
Full in the center of the sacred wood
An arm arises of the Stygian flood,
Which, breaking from beneath with bellowing sound,
Whirls the black waves and rattling stones around.
Here Pluto pants for breath from out his cell;   785
And opens wide the grinning jaws of hell.
To this infernal lake the Fury flies;
Here hides her hated head, and frees the laboring skies.
    Saturnian Juno, now, with double care,
Attends the fatal process of the war.   790
The clowns, returned from battle, bear the slain;
Implore the gods, and to their king complain.
The corpse of Almon, and the rest, are shown:
Shrieks, clamors, murmurs, fill the frighted town.
Ambitious Turnus in the press appears,   795
And, aggravating crimes, augments their fears;
Proclaims his private injuries aloud—
A solemn promise made, and disavowed;
A foreign son is sought, and a mixed mongrel brood.
Then they, whose mothers, frantic with their fear,   800
In woods and wilds the flags of Bacchus bear,
And lead his dances with disheveled hair,
Increase the clamor, and the war demand
(Such was Amata's interest in the land),
Against the public sanctions of the peace,   805
Against all omens of their ill success.
    With fates averse, the rout in arms resort
To force their monarch, and insult the court.
But, like a rock unmoved, a rock that braves
The raging tempest and the rising waves,   810
Propped on himself he stands: his solid sides
Wash off the seaweeds, and the sounding tides—

778. *Amsanctus*: now Lago d'Ansante.
    785. *hic . . . saevi spiracula Ditis*: "here are breathing vents of furious Dis,"
i.e., natural gas outlets.

So stood the pious prince unmoved; and long
Sustained the madness of the noisy throng.
But, when he found that Juno's power prevailed,   815
And all the methods of cool counsel failed,
He calls the gods to witness their offense;
Disclaims the war, asserts his innocence.
"Hurried by fate (he cries), and borne before
A furious wind, we leave the faithful shore!   820
O more than madmen! you yourselves shall bear
The guilt of blood and sacrilegious war:
Thou, Turnus, shall atone it by thy fate,
And pray to Heaven for peace, but pray too late.
For me, my stormy voyage at an end,   825
I to the port of death securely tend.
The funeral pomp which to your kings you pay,
Is all I want, and all you take away."
He said no more, but, in his walls confined,
Shut out the woes which he too well divined;   830
Nor with the rising storm would vainly strive,
But left the helm, and let the vessel drive.

    A solemn custom was observed of old,
Which Latium held, and now the Romans hold;
Their standard when in fighting fields they rear   835
Against the fierce Hyrcanians, or declare
The Scythian, Indian, or Arabian war;
Or from the boasting Parthians would regain
Their eagles, lost in Carrae's bloody plain.
Two gates of steel (the name of Mars they bear,   840
And still are worshipped with religious fear)
Before his temple stand: the dire abode,
And the feared issues of the furious god,
Are fenced with brazen bolts; without the gates,
The wary guardian Janus doubly waits.   845

    825–8. These four lines render *nam mihi parta quies, omnisque in limine*
portus/ funere felici spolior, "for me rest is at hand, and just at the harbor's
entrance I am deprived of a happy death."

    836 sqq. *Hyrcanians*: a people south of the Caspian Sea. *Scythians*: a general
term for all nomads north and east of the Black Sea. *Parthians*: a tribe south and
east of the Caspian Sea. Crassus was defeated and killed by the Parthians at
Carrae in 53 B.C. and lost the "eagles," or standards, of his legions. Augustus
recovered them.

Then, when the sacred senate votes the wars,
The Roman consul their decree declares,
And in his robes the sounding gates unbars.
The youth in military shouts arise,
And the loud trumpets break the yielding skies.   850
These rites, of old by sovereign princes used,
Were the king's office: but the king refused,
Deaf to their cries; nor would the gates unbar
Of sacred peace, or loose the imprisoned war;
But hid his head, and, safe from loud alarms,   855
Abhorred the wicked ministry of arms.
Then, heaven's imperious queen shot down from high;
At her approach the brazen hinges fly;
The gates are forced, and every falling bar;
And like a tempest, issues out the war.   860
    The peaceful cities of the Ausonian shore,
Lulled in their ease, and undisturbed before,
Are all on fire; and some, with studious care,
Their restive steeds in sandy plains prepare;
Some their soft limbs in painful marches try;   865
And war is all their wish, and arms the general cry.
Part scour their rusty shields with seam; and part
New-grind the blunted axe, and point the dart;
With joy they view the waving ensigns fly,
And hear the trumpet's clangor pierce the sky.   870
Five cities forge their arms—the Atinian powers,
Antemnae, Tibur with her lofty towers,
Ardea the proud, the Crustumerian town:
All these of old were places of renown.
Some hammer helmets for the fighting field;   875
Some twine young sallows to support the shield;
The corselet some, and some the cuishes mold,
With silver plated, and with ductile gold.
The rustic honors of the scythe and share,
Give place to swords and plumes, the pride of war.   880
Old falchions are new-tempered in the fires:
The sounding trumpet every soul inspires.

867. *seam*: grease.
877. *cuishes*: cuisses, greaves.

The word is given; with eager speed they lace
The shining headpiece, and the shield embrace.
The neighing steeds are to the chariots tied;   885
The trusty weapon sits on every side.
  And now the mighty labor is begun:
Ye muses, open all your Helicon!
Sing you the chiefs that swayed the Ausonian land,
Their arms, and armies under their command;   890
What warriors in our ancient clime were bred;
What soldiers followed, and what heroes led.
For well you know, and can record alone,
What fame to future times conveys but darkly down.
  Mezentius first appeared upon the plain: 895
Scorn sat upon his brows, and sour disdain,
Defying earth and heaven. Etruria lost,
He brings to Turnus' aid his baffled host.
The charming Lausus, full of youthful fire,
Rode in the rank, and next his sullen sire;   900
To Turnus only second in the grace
Of manly mien, and features of the face.
A skillful horseman, and a huntsman bred;
With fates averse, a thousand men he led:
His sire unworthy of so brave a son;   905
Himself well worthy of a happier throne.
  Next Aventinus drives his chariot round
The Latian plains, with palms and laurels crowned;
Proud of his steeds, he smokes along the field;
His father's hydra fills his ample shield;   910
A hundred serpents hiss about the brims;
The son of Hercules he justly seems,
By his broad shoulders and gigantic limbs—
Of heavenly, part, and part, of earthly blood,
A mortal woman mixing with a god.   915
For strong Alcides, after he had slain
The triple Geryon, drove from conquered Spain

---

897. *Etruria lost*: Mezentius had been exiled from Etruria, for what good
cause will be told in Book VIII.
916. *Alcides*: Hercules; the story appears in Book VIII.

His captive herds; and, thence in triumph led,
On Tuscan Tiber's flowery banks they fed.
Then, on mount Aventine, the son of Jove   920
The priestess Rhea found, and forced to love.

For arms, his men long piles and javelins bore,
And poles with pointed steel their foes in battle gore.
Like Hercules himself, his son appears
In savage pomp; a lion's hide he wears;   925
About his shoulders hangs the shaggy skin;
The teeth and gaping jaws severely grin.
Thus, like the god his father, homely dressed,
He strides into the hall, a horrid guest.

   Then two twin brothers from fair Tibur came   930
(Which from their brother Tiburs took the name),
Fierce Coras and Catillus, void of fear:
Armed Argive horse they led, and in the front appear.
Like cloud-born Centaurs, from the mountain's height
With rapid course descending to the fight   935
They rush along; the rattling woods give way;
The branches bend before their sweepy sway.

   Nor was Praeneste's founder wanting there,
Whom fame reports the son of Mulciber:
Found in the fire, and fostered in the plains,   940
A shepherd and a king at once he reigns;
And leads to Turnus' aid his country swains.
His own Praeneste sends a chosen band,
With those who plow Saturnia's Gabine land;
Besides the succor which cold Anien yields,   945
The rocks of Hernicus, and dewy fields,
Anagnia fat, and father Amasene—
A numerous rout, but all of naked men:
Nor arms they wear, nor swords and bucklers wield,
Nor drive the chariot through the dusty field;   950

   921. Here Hercules, with an earlier priestess Rhea, plays the part of Mars
with a later Rhea Silvia, mother of Romulus and Remus.
   929. *strides: subibat,* "he used to enter."
   934–7. *cloud-born Centaurs:* Virgil has a strong image of two centaurs plunging down a wooded mountainside. Dryden's final alliteration is so silly it sounds
like parody.
   939. *Mulciber:* Vulcan (Hephaestus).

But whirl from leathern slings huge balls of lead;
And spoils of yellow wolves adorn their head:
The left foot naked, when they march to fight;
But in a bull's raw hide they sheath the right.

   Messapus next (great Neptune was his sire),   955
Secure of steel, and fated from the fire,
In pomp appears; and with his ardor warms
A heartless train, unexercised in arms:
The just Faliscans he to battle brings;
And those who live where lake Ciminius springs;   960
And where Feronia's grove and temple stands,
Who till Fescennian or Flavinian lands:
All these in order march, and marching, sing
The warlike actions of their sea-born king:
Like a long team of snowy swans on high,   965
Which clap their wings, and cleave the liquid sky,
When, homeward from their watery pastures borne,
They sing, and Asia's lakes their notes return.
Not one who heard their music from afar,
Would think these troops an army trained to war,   970
But flocks of fowl, that, when the tempests roar,
With their hoarse gabbling seek the silent shore.

   Then Clausus came, who led a numerous band
Of troops embodied from the Sabine land;
And, in himself alone, an army brought.   975
'Twas he the noble Claudian race begot—
The Claudian race, ordained, in times to come,
To share the greatness of imperial Rome.
He led the Cures forth of old renown,
Mutuscans from their olive-bearing town,   980
And all the Eretian powers; besides a band
That followed from Velinum's dewy land;
And Amiternian troops, of mighty fame,
And mountaineers, that from Severus came,
And from the craggy cliffs of Tetrica;   985
And those where yellow Tiber takes his way,
And where Himella's wanton waters play.

   979. *Cures*: Sabines.

Casperia sends her arms, with those that lie
By Fabaris, and fruitful Foruli:
The warlike aids of Horta next appear;   990
And the cold Nursians come to close the rear,
Mixed with the natives born of Latine blood;
Whom Allia washes with her fatal flood.
Not thicker billows beat the Libyan main,
When pale Orion sets in wintry rain;   995
Nor thicker harvests on rich Hermus rise,
Or Lycian fields, when Phoebus burns the skies,
Than stand these troops: their bucklers ring around:
Their trampling turns the turf, and shakes the solid ground.
    High in his chariot then Halesus came,   1000
A foe by birth to Troy's unhappy name:
From Agamemnon born: to Turnus' aid,
A thousand men the youthful hero led,
Who till the Massic soil, for wine renowned;
And fierce Auruncans from their hilly ground;   1005
And those who live by Sidicinian shores;
And where with shoaly fords Vulturnus roars;
Cales' and Osca's old inhabitants;
And rough Saticulans, inured to wants.
Light demi-lances from afar they throw,   1010
Fastened with leathern thongs, to gall the foe:
Short crooked swords in closer fight they wear;
And on their warding arm light bucklers bear.
    Nor, Oebalus, shalt thou be left unsung;
From nymph Sebethis and old Telon sprung,   1015
Who then in Teleboan Capri reigned;
But that short isle the ambitious youth disdained,
And o'er Campania stretched his ample sway,
Where swelling Sarnus seeks the Tyrrhene sea—
O'er Batulum, and where Abella sees   1020
From her high towers, the harvest of her trees.

991. *cold*: Nursia (Norcia) is in the high and snowy Apennines.
1004 sqq. *Massic soil, Auruncans, Sidicinian shores, the Vulturnus, Cales,
Saticula*: all in Campania. The Oscan language survived to Roman times.
1015. *Sebethis*: a stream that flows into the Bay of Naples. The place names
that follow are all Campanian.

And these (as was the Teuton use of old)
Wield brazen swords, and brazen bucklers hold;
Sling weighty stones when from afar they fight—
Their casques are cork, a covering thick and light.   1025
  Next these in rank, the warlike Ufens went,
And led the mountain troops that Nursia sent.
The rude Aequiculae his rule obeyed;
Hunting their sport, and plundering was their trade.
In arms they plowed, to battle still prepared;   1030
Their soil was barren, and their hearts were hard.
  Umbro the priest the proud Marrubians led,
By king Archippus sent to Turnus' aid;
And peaceful olives crowned his hoary head.
His wand and holy words, the viper's rage   1035
And venomed wounds of serpents, could assuage.
He, when he pleased with powerful juice to steep
Their temples, shut their eyes in pleasing sleep.
But vain were Marsian herbs, and magic art,
To cure the wound given by the Dardan dart.   1040
Yet his untimely fate, the Angitian woods
In sighs remurmured to the Fucine floods.
  The son of famed Hippolytus was there,
Famed as his sire, and, as his mother, fair;
Whom in Egerian groves Aricia bore,   1045
And nursed his youth along the marshy shore,
Where great Diana's peaceful altars flame,
In fruitful fields; and Virbius was his name.
Hippolytus, as old records have said,
Was by his stepdame sought to share her bed;   1050

1022. *Teuton use*: Virgil gave these warriors slings like those of German tribes in his day.

1032. *Marrubians*: the Marsi, a mountain tribe near Lake Fucinus.

1041. *Angitian*: Angitia was a snake goddess of the Marrubians.

1043 sqq. A Roman sequel to the Greek story of Hippolytus, son of Theseus and the Amazon Hippolyta. His "stepdame" Phaedra loved him, he spurned her, and she killed herself, giving Theseus to understand that the boy had seduced her. Invoked by Theseus, Neptune contrived to get Hippolytus thrown from his chariot and dragged to death by his horses. Diana is here said to have restored him to life with the aid of Asclepius (Aesculapius), "founder of the godlike art" of healing, destroyed in his turn by Jove. Egeria was a Roman goddess who had a sacred spring near the Porta Capena as well as a sacred grove near Aricia.

But, when no female arts his mind could move,
She turned to furious hate her impious love.
Torn by wild horses on the sandy shore,
Another's crimes the unhappy hunter bore,
Glutting his father's eyes with guiltless gore.   1055
But chaste Diana, who his death deplored,
With Aesculapian herbs his life restored:
When Jove, who saw from high, with just disdain,
The dead inspired with vital breath again,
Struck to the center, with his flaming dart,   1060
The unhappy founder of the godlike art.
But Trivia kept in secret shades alone
Her care, Hippolytus, to fate unknown;
And called him Virbius in the Egerian grove
Where then he lived obscure, but safe from Jove.   1065
For this, from Trivia's temple and her wood,
Are coursers driven who shed their master's blood—
Affrighted by the monsters of the flood.
His son, the second Virbius, yet retained
His father's art; and warrior steeds he reined.   1070
    Amid the troops, and like the leading god,
High o'er the rest in arms, the graceful Turnus rode;
A triple pile of plumes his crest adorned,
On which with belching flames Chimaera burned:
The more the kindled combat rises higher,   1075
The more with fury burns the blazing fire.
Fair Iö graced his shield; but Iö now
With horns exalted stands, and seems to low—
A noble charge! Her keeper by her side,
To watch her, walks, his hundred eyes applied;   1080
And on the brims her sire, the watery god,
Rolled from his silver urn his crystal flood.
    A cloud of foot succeeds, and fills the fields
With swords, and pointed spears, and clattering shields;

1077. *Fair Iö*: had been changed by jealous Juno into a cow, guarded by the
giant Argos with a hundred eyes. Iö's father, King Inachus of Argos, is identified
by Virgil with a river of that name.

Of Argive, and of old Sicanian bands, 1085
And those who plow the rich Rutulian lands;
Auruncan youth, and those Sacrana yields;
And the proud Labicans, with painted shields;
And those who near Numician streams reside;
And those whom Tiber's holy forests hide, 1090
Or Circe's hills from the main land divide;
Where Ufens glides along the lowly lands,
Or the black water of Pomptina stands.

    Last, from the Volscians fair Camilla came,
And led her warlike troops—a warrior dame; 1095
Unbred to spinning, in the loom unskilled;
She chose the nobler Pallas of the field.
Mixed with the first, the fierce virago fought;
Sustained the toils of arms, the danger sought;
Outstripped the winds in speed upon the plain, 1100
Flew o'er the field, nor hurt the bearded grain:
She swept the seas, and, as she skimmed along,
Her flying feet unbathed on billows hung.
Men, boys, and women, stupid with surprise,
Where'er she passes, fixed their wondering eyes: 1105
Longing they look, and gaping at the sight,
Devour her o'er and o'er with vast delight.
Her purple habit sits with such a grace
On her smooth shoulders, and so suits her face;
Her head with ringlets of her hair is crowned; 1110
And in a golden caul the curls are bound.
She shakes her myrtle javelin; and, behind,
Her Lycian quiver dances in the wind.

    1085. *Sicanian*: Sicilian.
    1097. *Pallas*: Minerva (Pallas Athena) in her role as a warrior-goddess, not as a patroness of housewifely arts.
    1101–3. Dryden states flatly what in Virgil is expressive hyperbole: *volaret . . . laesisset . . . ferret iter . . . nec tingueret.* Her speed was so great it seemed "she might fly," etc. and "would not have hurt," etc.
    1111. *caul*: snood, though the Latin word here is *fibula*, brooch.

⌐⌐⌐⌐

BOOK VIII

THE ARGUMENT

The war being now begun, both the generals make all possible prepara-
tions. Turnus sends to Diomedes. Aeneas goes in person to beg succors
from Evander and the Tuscans. Evander receives him kindly, furnishes
him with men, and sends his son Pallas with him. Vulcan, at the request
of Venus, makes arms for her son Aeneas, and draws on his shield the
most memorable actions of his posterity.

WHEN Turnus had assembled all his powers,
His standard planted on Laurentum's towers,
When now the sprightly trumpet, from afar,
Had given the signal of approaching war,
Had roused the neighing steeds to scour the fields,   5
While the fierce riders clattered on their shields,
Trembling with rage, the Latian youth prepare
To join the allies, and headlong rush to war.
Fierce Ufens, and Messapus, led the crowd,
With bold Mezentius, who blasphemed aloud.   10
These through the country took their wasteful course,
The fields to forage, and to gather force.
Then Venulus to Diomede they send,
To beg his aid, Ausonia to defend,
Declare the common danger, and inform   15
The Grecian leader of the growing storm:

13. *Diomede*: King of Argos and Tiryns. After the war at Troy he is supposed to have settled in Apulia, founding Brundisium, Beneventum, and other
towns.

246

"Aeneas, landed on the Latian coast,
With banished gods, and with a baffled host,
Yet now aspired to conquest of the state.
And claimed a title from the gods and fate; 20
What numerous nations in his quarrel came
And how they spread his formidable name.
What he designed, what mischiefs might arise
If fortune favored his first enterprise,
Was left for him to weigh, whose equal fears 25
And common interest was involved in theirs."

    While Turnus and the allies thus urge the war,
The Trojan, floating in a flood of care,
Beholds the tempest which his foes prepare.
This way, and that, he turns his anxious mind; 30
Thinks, and rejects the counsels he designed;
Explores himself in vain in every part,
And gives no rest to his distracted heart.
So, when the sun by day, or moon by night,
Strike on the polished brass their trembling light, 35
The glittering species here and there divide,
And cast their dubious beams from side to side;
Now on the walls, now on the pavement play,
And to the ceiling flash the glaring day.

    Twas night; and weary nature lulled asleep 40
The birds of air, and fishes of the deep,
And beasts, and mortal men. The Trojan chief
Was laid on Tiber's banks, oppressed with grief,
And found in silent slumber, late relief.
Then, through the shadows of the poplar wood, 45
Arose the father of the Roman flood;
An azure robe was o'er his body spread,
A wreath of shady reeds adorned his head:

    25. Dryden alters the sense; . . . *manifestius ipsi/ quam Turno regi aut regi apparere Latino*: "it would be plainer to him [as an old foe of the Trojans] than to King Turnus or King Latinus."
    30. This and the three following lines translate the identical Latin rendered by a couplet in Book IV, 411–12.
    36. *species*: reflections. In the Latin these are from water trembling in a basin, a clearer simile for the worried play of thought.

Thus, manifest to sight, the god appeared,
And with these pleasing words his sorrow cheered: 50
"Undoubted offspring of ethereal race,
O long expected in this promised place!
Who, through the foes, hast borne thy banished gods,
Restored them to their hearths, and old abodes;
This is thy happy home, the clime where fate   55
Ordains thee to restore the Trojan state.
Fear not! The war shall end in lasting peace,
And all the rage of haughty Juno cease.
And that this nightly vision may not seem
The effect of fancy, or an idle dream,   60
A sow beneath an oak shall lie along,
All white herself, and white her thirty young.
When thirty rolling years have run their race,
Thy son Ascanius, on this empty space,
Shall build a royal town, of lasting fame,   65
Which from this omen shall receive the name.
Time shall approve the truth.—For what remains,
And how with sure success to crown thy pains,
With patience next attend. A banished band,
Driven with Evander from the Arcadian land,   70
Have planted here, and placed on high their walls:
Their town the founder, Pallanteum calls,
Derived from Pallas, his great grandsire's name:
But the fierce Latians old possession claim,
With war infesting the new colony: 75
These make thy friends, and on their aid rely.
To thy free passage I submit my streams.
Wake, son of Venus, from thy pleasing dreams!
And when the setting stars are lost in day,
To Juno's power thy just devotion pay;   80
With sacrifice the wrathful queen appease:
Her pride at length shall fall, her fury cease.

61. A repetition of the prophecy of Helenus, Book III, 500 sqq.
70. *Arcadian land*: Arcadia is in the north central Peloponnesus. Virgil here
provides a Greek history for the Palatine hill, site of Augustus' palace.

When thou return'st victorious from the war,
Perform thy vows to me with grateful care.
The god am I, whose yellow water flows   85
Around these fields, and fattens as it goes:
Tiber my name—among the rolling floods
Renowned on earth, esteemed among the gods.
This is my certain seat. In times to come,
My waves shall wash the walls of mighty Rome!"   90
　　He said; and plunged below. While yet he spoke,
His dream Aeneas and his sleep forsook.
He rose, and looking up, beheld the skies
With purple blushing, and the day arise.
Then water in his hollow palm he took   95
From Tiber's flood, and thus the powers bespoke:
"Laurentian nymphs, by whom the streams are fed,
And father Tiber, in thy sacred bed
Receive Aeneas, and from danger keep!
Whatever fount, whatever holy deep,   100
Conceals thy watery stores—where'er they rise,
And, bubbling from below, salute the skies—
Thou, king of horned floods, whose plenteous urn
Suffices fatness to the fruitful corn,
For this, thy kind compassion of our woes,   105
Shalt share my morning song, and evening vows.
But, oh! be present to thy people's aid,
And firm the gracious promise thou hast made."
　　Thus having said, two galleys from his stores
With care he chooses, mans, and fits with oars.   110
Now on the shore the fatal swine is found—
Wondrous to tell!—She lay along the ground:
Her well-fed offspring at her udders hung;
She white herself, and white her thirty young.
Aeneas takes the mother and her brood,   115
And all on Juno's altar are bestowed.
The following night, and the succeeding day,
Propitious Tiber smoothed his watery way;

103. *horned*: rivers were often represented as bulls.

He rolled his river back, and poised he stood,
A gentle swelling, and a peaceful flood.   120
The Trojans mount their ships; they put from shore,
Borne on the waves, and scarcely dip an oar.
Shouts from the land give omen to their course;
And the pitched vessels glide with easy force.
The woods and waters wonder at the gleam   125
Of shields, and painted ships that stem the stream.
One summer's night and one whole day they pass
Betwixt the greenwood shades, and cut the liquid glass.
The fiery sun had finished half his race,
Looked back and doubted in the middle space,   130
When they from far beheld the rising towers,
The tops of sheds, and shepherds' lowly bowers,
Thin as they stood, which then of homely clay,
Now rise in marble, from the Roman sway.
These cots (Evander's kingdom, mean and poor)   135
The Trojan saw, and turned his ships to shore.
    'Twas on a solemn day: the Arcadian states,
The king and prince, without the city gates,
Then paid their offerings in a sacred grove
To Hercules, the warrior son of Jove.   140
Thick clouds of rolling smoke involve the skies;
And fat of entrails on his altar fries.
    But when they saw the ships that stemmed the flood,
And glittered through the covert of the wood,
They rose with fear, and left the unfinished feast,   145
Till dauntless Pallas reassured the rest
To pay the rites. Himself without delay
A javelin seized, and singly took his way;
Then gained a rising ground, and called from far:
"Resolve me, strangers, whence and what you are;   150
Your business here; and bring you peace or war?"

---

130. This fancy is all Dryden's.
141–2. *tepidusque cruor fumabat ad aras*: "hot blood smoked at the altars,"
i.e., fresh-spilt blood of victims fumed in cooler air. On the other hand, entrails
and fat were usually distinguished in burnt sacrifice, the smoke of fat being
regarded as more gratifying to the gods.

High on the stern Aeneas took his stand,
And held a branch of olive in his hand,
While thus he spoke: "The Phrygians' arms you see;
Expelled from Troy, provoked in Italy 155
By Latian foes, with war unjustly made—
At first affianced, and at last betrayed.
This message bear: The Trojans and their chief
Bring holy peace, and beg the king's relief."
Struck with so great a name, and all on fire, 160
The youth replies: "Whatever you require,
Your fame exacts. Upon our shores descend
A welcome guest, and, what you wish, a friend."
He said, and downward hasting to the strand,
Embraced the stranger-prince, and joined his hand. 165
Conducted to the grove, Aeneas broke
The silence first, and thus the king bespoke:
"Best of the Greeks! to whom, by Fate's command,
I bear these peaceful branches in my hand:
Undaunted I approach you, though I know 170
Your birth is Grecian, and your land my foe:
From Atreus though your ancient lineage came,
And both the brother-kings your kindred claim;
Yet, my self-conscious worth, your high renown,
Your virtue, through the neighboring nations blown; 175
Our fathers' mingled blood, Apollo's voice,
Have led me hither; less by need than choice.
Our father Dardanus, as fame has sung
And Greeks acknowledge, from Electra sprung:
Electra from the loins of Atlas came— 180
Atlas, whose head sustains the starry frame.
Your sire is Mercury, whom long before
On cold Cyllene's top fair Maia bore.
Maia the fair, on fame if we rely,
Was Atlas' daughter, who sustains the sky. 185
Thus from one common source our streams divide;
Ours is the Trojan, yours the Arcadian side.
Raised by these hopes, I sent no news before,
Nor asked your leave, nor did your faith implore;

But come without a pledge, my own ambassador.   190
The same Rutulians, who with arms pursue
The Trojan race, are equal foes to you.
Our host expelled, what further force can stay
The victor troops from universal sway?
Then will they stretch their power athwart the land,   195
And either sea from side to side command.
Receive our offered faith, and give us thine;
Ours is a generous and experienced line:
We want not hearts nor bodies for the war;
In council cautious, and in fields we dare."   200
He said; and, while he spoke, with piercing eyes
Evander viewed the man with vast surprise—
Pleased with his action, ravished with his face;
Then answered briefly with a royal grace:
"O valiant leader of the Trojan line,   205
In whom the features of thy father shine!
How I recall Anchises! how I see
His motions, mien, and all my friend, in thee!
Long though it be, 'tis fresh within my mind,
When Priam to his sister's court designed   210
A welcome visit, with a friendly stay;
And through the Arcadian kingdom took his way.
Then, past a boy, the callow down began
To shade my chin, and call me first a man.
I saw the shining train with vast delight;   215
And Priam's goodly person pleased my sight;
But great Anchises, far above the rest,
With awful wonder fired my youthful breast.
I longed to join in friendship's holy bands
Our mutual hearts, and plight our mutual hands.   220
I first accosted him: I sued, I sought,
And with a loving force, to Pheneus brought.
He gave me, when at length constrained to go,
A Lycian quiver and a Gnossian bow;

210. *Priam . . . court*: Priam's sister Hesione married Telamon, king of
Salamis.
222. *Pheneus*: a town in Arcadia.

A vest embroidered, glorious to behold, 225
And two rich bridles, with their bits of gold,
Which my son's coursers in obedience hold.
The league you ask, I offer as your right;
And, when tomorrow's sun reveals the light,
With swift supplies you shall be sent away. 230
Now celebrate, with us, this solemn day,
Whose holy rites admit no long delay.
Honor our annual feast; and take your seat
With friendly welcome, at a homely treat."
    Thus having said, the bowls (removed for fear) 235
The youths replaced, and soon restored the cheer.
On sods of turf he set the soldiers round:
A maple throne, raised higher from the ground,
Received the Trojan chief; and, o'er the bed
A lion's shaggy hide, for ornament, they spread. 240
The loaves were served in canisters; the wine
In bowls; the priest renewed the rites divine:
Broiled entrails are their food, and beef's continued chine.
But, when the rage of hunger was repressed,
Thus spoke Evander to his royal guest: 245
    "These rites, these altars, and this feast, O king!
From no vain fears or superstition spring;
Or blind devotion, or from blinder chance,
Or heady zeal, or brutal ignorance:
But, saved from danger, with a grateful sense, 250
The labors of a god we recompense.
See, from afar, yon rock that mates the sky;
About whose feet such heaps of rubbish lie;
Such indigested ruin; bleak and bare,
How desert now it stands, exposed in air! 255
'Twas once a robber's den, enclosed around
With living stone, and deep beneath the ground.
The monster Cacus, more than half a beast,
This hold, impervious to the sun, possessed.

243. *continued*: long.
254. *indigested*: scattered.

The pavement ever foul with human gore; 260
Heads, and their mangled members, hung the door.
Vulcan this plague begot; and, like his sire,
Black clouds he belched, and flakes of livid fire.
Time, long expected, eased us of our load,
And brought the needful presence of a god. 265
The avenging force of Hercules, from Spain
Arrived in triumph; from Geryon slain:—
Thrice lived the giant, and thrice lived in vain.
His prize, the lowing herds, Alcides drove
Near Tiber's banks, to graze the shady grove. 270
Allured with hope of plunder, and intent
By force to rob, by fraud to circumvent,
The brutal Cacus, as by chance they strayed,
Four oxen thence, and four fair kine, conveyed.
And, lest the printed footsteps might be seen, 275
He dragged them backwards to his rocky den.
The tracks averse a lying notice gave,
And led the searcher backward from the cave.
Meantime the herdsman hero shifts his place,
To find fresh pasture, and untrodden grass. 280
The beasts, who missed their mates, filled all around
With bellowings; and the rocks restored the sound.
One heifer, who had heard her love complain,
Roared from the cave, and made the project vain.
Alcides found the fraud; with rage he shook, 285
And tossed about his head his knotted oak.
Swift as the winds, or Scythian arrows' flight,
He clomb with eager haste, the aërial height.
Then first we saw the monster mend his pace:
Fear in his eyes, and paleness in his face, 290
Confessed the god's approach. Trembling he springs,
As terror had increased his feet with wings;
Nor stayed for stairs; but down the depth he threw
His body: on his back the door he drew;
(The door, a rib of living rock; with pains 295
His father hewed it out, and bound with iron chains:)
He broke the heavy links; the mountain closed,
And bars and levers to his foe opposed.

The wretch had hardly made his dungeon fast;
The fierce avenger came with bounding haste;   300
Surveyed the mouth of the forbidden hold;
And here and there his raging eyes he rolled.
He gnashed his teeth; and thrice he compassed round
With wingèd speed the circuit of the ground.
Thrice at the cavern's mouth he pulled in vain;   305
And, panting, thrice desisted from his pain.
   A pointed flinty rock, all bare and black,
Grew gibbous from behind the mountain's back:
Owls, ravens, all ill omens of the night,
Here built their nests, and hither winged their flight.   310
The leaning head hung threatening o'er the flood,
And nodded to the left. The hero stood
Averse, with planted feet, and from the right
Tugged at the solid stone with all his might.
Thus heaved, the fixed foundations of the rock   315
Gave way: heaven echoed at the rattling shock.
Tumbling, it choked the flood: on either side
The banks leap backward, and the streams divide:
The sky shrunk upward with unusual dread;
And trembling Tiber dived beneath his bed.   320
The court of Cacus stands revealed to sight;
The cavern glares with new-admitted light.
So the pent vapors, with a rumbling sound,
Heave from below, and rend the hollow ground.
A sounding flaw succeeds; and, from on high,   325
The gods with hate behold the nether sky:
The ghosts repine at violated night,
And curse the invading sun, and sicken at the sight.
The graceless monster, caught in open day,
Enclosed, and in despair to fly away,   330
Howls horrible from underneath, and fills
His hollow palace with unmanly yells.
The hero stands above, and from afar
Plies him with darts, and stones, and distant war.

308. *gibbous*: humped. In fact it rose out of the roof of the cave.
320. *refluitque exterritus amnis*: Dryden makes it a comic line.

He, from his nostrils and huge mouth, expires   335
Black clouds of smoke, amidst his father's fires;
Gathering, with each repeated blast, the night,
To make uncertain aim, and erring sight.
The wrathful god then plunges from above,
And, where in thickest waves the sparkles drove,   340
There lights; and wades through fumes; and gropes his way,
Half singed, half stifled, till he grasps his prey.
The monster, spewing fruitless flames, he found;
He squeezed his throat; he writhed his neck around,
And in a knot his crippled members bound;   345
Then, from their sockets tore his burning eyes:
Rolled on a heap the breathless robber lies.
The doors, unbarred, received the rushing day;
And thorough lights disclose the ravished prey.
The bulls, redeemed, breathe open air again.   350
Next, by the feet, they drag him from his den.
The wondering neighborhood, with glad surprise,
Beheld his shagged breast, his giant size,
His mouth that flames no more, and his extinguished eyes.

   From that auspicious day, with rites divine,   355
We worship at the hero's holy shrine.
Potitius first ordained these annual vows:
As priests, were added the Pinarian house,
Who raised this altar in the sacred shade,
Where honors, ever due, for ever shall be paid.   360
For these deserts, and this high virtue shown,
Ye warlike youths, your heads with garlands crown:
Fill high the goblets with a sparkling flood;
And with deep drafts invoke our common god."
This said, a double wreath Evander twined;   365
And poplars black and white his temples bind:
Then brims his ample bowl. With like design
The rest invoke the gods, with sprinkled wine.
   Meantime the sun descended from the skies,
And the bright evening star began to rise.   370

---

   360. Between the Palatine and the river in Virgil's day stood the *ara maxima*,
"the biggest altar," before a temple to Hercules Victor, whose rites were performed by priests called the Pinarii.

And now the priests, Potitius at their head,
In skins of beasts involved, the long procession led;
Held high the flaming tapers in their hands,
As custom had prescribed their holy bands;
Then with a second course the tables load, 375
And with full chargers offer to the god.
The Salii sing, and 'cense his altars round
With Saban smoke, their heads with poplar bound—
One choir of old, another of the young,
To dance, and bear the burden of the song. 380
The lay records the labors, and the praise,
And all the immortal acts of Hercules.
First, how the mighty babe, when swathed in bands,
The serpents strangled with his infant hands;
Then, as in years and matchless force he grew, 385
The Oechalian walls, and Trojan, overthrew.
Besides, a thousand hazards they relate,
Procured by Juno's and Eurystheus' hate.
"Thy hands, unconquered hero, could subdue
The cloud-born Centaurs, and the monster-crew: 390
Nor thy resistless arm the bull withstood,
Nor he, the roaring terror of the wood:
The triple porter of the Stygian seat,
With lolling tongue, lay fawning at thy feet;
And, seized with fear, forgot his mangled meat. 395
The infernal waters trembled at thy sight;
Thee, god! no face of danger could affright;
No huge Typhöeus, nor the unnumbered snake,
Increased with hissing heads, in Lerna's lake.
Hail, Jove's undoubted son! an added grace 400
To heaven and the great author of thy race!
Receive the grateful offerings which we pay,
And smile propitious on thy solemn day!"

377. *The Salii*: called "leaping" priests (from *salire*) in line 879. So far as anyone knows these were priests of Mars, not Hercules; this may be another instance in which god and demigod were fused or confused, as in Book VII, 921. There is no "censing" in Virgil, who refers to the altars as *incensa*, "afire."

386. *Oechalian walls*: Eurytus, king of Oechalia, refused Hercules his daughter Iolë, so Hercules stormed the town. He "overthrew" the walls of Troy when King Laomedon cheated him.

In numbers thus they sung: above the rest,
The den and death of Cacus crown the feast.   405
The woods to hollow vales convey the sound;
The vales to hills; and hills the notes rebound.
    The rites performed, the cheerful train retire.
Betwixt young Pallas and his aged sire,
The Trojan passed, the city to survey;   410
And pleasing talk beguiled the tedious way.
The stranger cast around his curious eyes,
New objects viewing still with new surprise;
With greedy joy inquires of various things,
And acts and monuments of ancient kings.   415
Then thus the founder of the Roman towers:
"These woods were first the seat of sylvan powers,
Of nymphs and fauns, and savage men who took
Their birth from trunks of trees and stubborn oak.
Nor laws they knew, nor manners, nor the care   420
Of laboring oxen, nor the shining share,
Nor arts of gain, nor what they gained to spare.
Their exercise the chase: the running flood
Supplied their thirst; the trees supplied their food.
Then Saturn came, who fled the power of Jove,   425
Robbed of his realms, and banished from above.
The men dispersed on hills, to towns he brought;
And laws ordained, and civil customs taught;
And Latium called the land where safe he lay
From his unduteous son, and his usurping sway.   430
With his mild empire, peace and plenty came;
And hence the golden times derived their name.
A more degenerate and discolored age
Succeeded this, with avarice and rage.
The Ausonians then, and bold Sicanians, came;   435
And Saturn's empire often changed the name.
Then kings (gigantic Tibris, and the rest)
With arbitrary sway the land oppressed:

    425. *Saturn*: a Latin god of sowing, identified with the Greek Cronus (Kronos), father of Jove.
    429. *Latiumque vocari/ maluit, his quoniam latuisset tutus in oris*: a fair example of ancient etymology, fairly rendered.

For Tiber's flood was Albula before,
Till, from the tyrant's fate, his name it bore.   440
I last arrived, driven from my native home
By fortune's power, and fate's resistless doom.
Long tossed on seas, I sought this happy land,
Warned by my mother-nymph, and called by heaven's command."
   Thus, walking on, he spoke, and showed the gate,   445
Since called Carmental by the Roman state;
Where stood an altar, sacred to the name
Of old Carmenta; the prophetic dame
Who to her son foretold the Aenean race,
Sublime in fame, and Rome's imperial place.   450
Then shows the forests, which, in after-times,
Fierce Romulus, for perpetrated crimes,
A sacred refuge made:—with this, the shrine
Where Pan below the rock had rites divine.
Then tells of Argus' death, his murdered guest,   455
Whose grave and tomb his innocence attest.
Thence, to the steep Tarpeian rock he leads—
Now roofed with gold, then thatched with homely reeds.
A reverent fear (such superstition reigns
Among the rude) e'en then possessed the swains: 460
Some god, they knew (what god, they could not tell)
Did there amidst the sacred horror dwell.
The Arcadians thought him Jove; and said they saw
The mighty Thunderer with majestic awe;
Who shook his shield, and dealt his bolts around,   465
And scattered tempests on the teeming ground.
Then saw two heaps of ruins (once they stood
Two stately towns, on either side the flood),

---

453 sqq. The Lupercal was a cave on the north side of the Palatine, sacred
to Lupercus, a wolf god or protector against wolves (*lupi*). Virgil has him called
Pan Lycaeus, "after the Arcadian mode," as though this name came from the
Greek for wolf (*lykos*). The obscure story of Argus is given here to explain the
name of the Argiletum, a district of Rome between the Quirinal and the Forum.
Criminals were hurled to death from the Tarpeian rock on the southwest side of
the Capitoline, where the temple of Jove was "roofed with gold." By Virgil's
account, the two towns on either side of the Tiber were Saturn's (apparently on
the Capitoline where Jove succeeded him) and Janus's (on the Janiculum), and
only one "the founder's name retains."

Saturnia's and Janiculum's remains;
And either place the founder's name retains.   470
  Discoursing thus together, they resort
Where poor Evander kept his country court.
They viewed the ground of Rome's litigious hall:
(Once oxen lowed, where now the lawyers bawl),
Then, stooping, through the narrow gate they pressed,   475
When thus the king bespoke his Trojan guest:
"Mean as it is, this palace, and this door,
Received Alcides, then a conqueror.
Dare to be poor: accept our homely food,
Which feasted him; and emulate a god."   480
Then underneath a lowly roof he led
The weary prince, and laid him on a bed;
The stuffing leaves with hides of bears o'erspread.
  Now night had shed her silver dews around,
And with her sable wings embraced the ground,   485
When love's fair goddess, anxious for her son
(New tumults rising, and new wars begun),
Couched with her husband in his golden bed,
With these alluring words invokes his aid—
And, that her pleasing speech his mind may move,   490
Inspires each accent with the charms of love:
"While cruel fate conspired with Grecian powers,
To level with the ground the Trojan towers,
I asked not aid the unhappy to restore;
Nor did the succor of thy skill implore;   495
Nor urged the labors of my lord in vain,
A sinking empire longer to sustain:
Though much I owed to Priam's house, and more
The danger of Aeneas did deplore.
But now by Jove's command, and fate's decree,   500
His race is doomed to reign in Italy;

473–4. The Forum.
479–80. *aude, hospes, contemnere opes et te quoque dignum/ finge deo*:
Dryden evidently gave up without a struggle to render the quality of this, which
he greatly admired.
488. *her husband*: Vulcan.

With humble suit I beg thy needful art,
O still propitious power, that rul'st my heart!
A mother kneels a suppliant for her son.
By Thetis and Aurora thou wert won   505
To forge impenetrable shields, and grace
With fated arms a less illustrious race.
Behold, what haughty nations are combined
Against the relics of the Phrygian kind!
With fire and sword my people to destroy,   510
And conquer Venus twice, in conquering Troy."
    She said; and straight, her arms of snowy hue
About her unresolving husband threw.
Her soft embraces soon infuse desire;
His bones and marrow sudden warmth inspire;   515
And all the godhead feels the wonted fire.
Not half so swift the rattling thunder flies,
Or forky lightnings flash along the skies.
The goddess, proud of her successful wiles,
And conscious of her form, in secret smiles.   520
Then thus the power, obnoxious to her charms,
Panting, and half dissolving in her arms:
"Why seek you reasons for a cause so just;
Or your own beauties or my love distrust?
Long since, had you required my helpful hand,   525
The artificer, and art, you might command,
To labor arms for Troy: nor Jove, nor Fate,
Confined their empire to so short a date.
And, if you now desire new wars to wage,
My skill I promise, and my pains engage: 530
Whatever melting metals can conspire,
Or breathing bellows, or the forming fire,
Is freely yours: your anxious fears remove,
And think no task is difficult to love."
Trembling he spoke; and, eager of her charms,   535
He snatched the willing goddess to his arms;

505. *Thetis . . . won*: Thetis won him to forge arms for her son, Achilles,
Aurora for her son, Memnon.
    521. *obnoxious*: subject.

Till, in her lap infused, he lay possessed
Of full desire, and sunk to pleasing rest.
  Now when the night her middle race had rode,
And his first slumber had refreshed the god—   540
The time when early housewives leave the bed;
When living embers on the hearth they spread:
Supply the lamp, and call the maids to rise;
With yawning mouths, and with half-opened eyes,
They ply the distaff by the winking light,   545
And to their daily labor add the night:
Thus frugally they earn their children's bread,
And uncorrupted keep their nuptial bed:
Not less concerned, nor at a later hour,
Rose from his downy couch the forging Power.   550
  Sacred to Vulcan's name, an isle there lay,
Betwixt Sicilia's coasts and Lipare,
Raised high on smoking rocks; and, deep below,
In hollow caves the fires of Aetna glow.
The Cyclops here their heavy hammers deal: 555
Loud strokes, and hissing of tormented steel,
Are heard around: the boiling waters roar;
And smoky flames through fuming tunnels soar.
Hither the father of the fire, by night,
Through the brown air precipitates his flight.   560
On their eternal anvils here he found
The brethren beating, and the blows go round;
A load of pointless thunder now there lies
Before their hands, to ripen for the skies:
These darts, for angry Jove, they daily cast—   565
Consumed on mortals with prodigious waste.
Three rays of writhen rain, of fire three more;
Of wingèd southern winds and cloudy store
As many parts, the dreadful mixture frame;
And fears are added, and avenging flame.   570
Inferior ministers, for Mars, repair
His broken axle-trees, and blunted war;

   551. *Vulcan's name*: One of the volcanic Aeolian islands north of Sicily is called Volcano.

And send him forth again with furbished arms,
To wake the lazy war, with trumpet's loud alarms.
The rest refresh the scaly snakes that fold   575
The shield of Pallas, and renew their gold:
Full on the crest the Gorgon's head they place,
With eyes that roll in death, and with distorted face.
   "My sons! (said Vulcan), set your tasks aside;
Your strength and master-skill must now be tried.   580
Arms for a hero forge—arms that require
Your force, your speed, and all your forming fire."
He said. They set their former work aside,
And their new toils with eager haste divide.
A flood of molten silver, brass, and gold,   585
And deadly steel, in the large furnace rolled:
Of this, their artful hands a shield prepare,
Alone sufficient to sustain the war.
Seven orbs within a spacious round they close.
One stirs the fire, and one the bellows blows.   590
The hissing steel is in the smithy drowned;
The grot with beaten anvils groans around.
By turns, their arms advance in equal time;
By turns, their hands descend, and hammers chime.
They turn the glowing mass with crooked tongs;   595
The fiery work proceeds with rustic songs.
   While, at the Lemnian god's command they urge
Their labors thus, and ply the Aeolian forge,
The cheerful morn salutes Evander's eyes;
And songs of chirping birds invite to rise.   600
He leaves his lowly bed: his buskins meet
Above his ankles; sandals sheath his feet:
He sets his trusty sword upon his side,
And o'er his shoulder throws a panther's hide.
Two menial dogs before their master pressed.   605
Thus clad, and guarded thus, he seeks his kingly guest.
Mindful of promised aid, he mends his pace,
But meets Aeneas in the middle space.
Young Pallas did his father's steps attend;
And true Achates waited on his friend.   610

They join their hands: a secret seat they choose;
The Arcadian first their former talk renews:
  "Undaunted prince! I never can believe
The Trojan empire lost, while you survive.
Command the assistance of a faithful friend: 615
But feeble are the succors I can send.
Our narrow kingdom here the Tiber bounds:
That other side the Latian state surrounds,
Insults our walls, and wastes our fruitful grounds.
But mighty nations I prepare, to join   620
Their arms with yours, and aid your just design.
You come, as by your better genius sent;
And Fortune seems to favor your intent.
Not far from hence there stands a hilly town,
Of ancient building, and of high renown,   625
Torn from the Tuscans by the Lydian race,
Who gave the name of Caere to the place—
Once Agyllina called. It flourished long,
In pride of wealth and warlike people strong;
Till cursed Mezentius, in a fatal hour   630
Assumed the crown, with arbitrary power.
What words can paint those execrable times,
The subjects' sufferings, and the tyrant's crimes?
That blood, those murders, O ye gods! replace
On his own head, and on his impious race!   635
The living and the dead, at his command
Were coupled face to face, and hand to hand;
Till, choked with stench, in loathed embraces tied,
The lingering wretches pined away and died.
Thus plunged in ills, and meditating more—   640
The people's patience, tried, no longer bore
The raging monster; but with arms beset
His house, and vengeance and destruction threat.
They fire his palace: while the flame ascends,
They force his guards and execute his friends.   645

626–27. Herodotus in Book I of his *History* tells of a Lydian migration to Etruria. Caere, one of the twelve towns of the Tuscan league, is now Cervetri.

He cleaves the crowd, and, favored by the night,
To Turnus' friendly court directs his flight.
By just revenge the Tuscans set on fire,
With arms, their king to punishment require:
Their numerous troops, now mustered on the strand, 650
My counsel shall submit to your command.
Their navy swarms upon the coasts; they cry
To hoist their anchors; but the gods deny.
An ancient augur, skilled in future fate,
With these foreboding words restrains their hate: 655
'Ye brave in arms, ye Lydian blood, the flower
Of Tuscan youth, and choice of all their power,
Whom just revenge against Mezentius arms,
To seek your tyrant's death by lawful arms!
Know this: no native of our land may lead 660
This powerful people: seek a foreign head.'
Awed with these words, in camps they still abide;
And wait with longing looks their promised guide.
Tarchon, the Tuscan chief, to me has sent
Their crown, and every regal ornament: 665
The people join their own with his desire;
And all, my conduct as their king, require.
But the chill blood that creeps within my veins,
And age, and listless limbs unfit for pains;
And a soul conscious of its own decay, 670
Have forced me to refuse imperial sway.
My Pallas were more fit to mount the throne
And should; but he's a Sabine mother's son,
And half a native: but, in you combine
A manly vigor, and a foreign line. 675
Where Fate and smiling Fortune show the way,
Pursue the ready path to sovereign sway.
The staff of my declining days, my son,
Shall make your good or ill success his own;
In fighting fields, from you shall learn to dare, 680
And serve the hard apprenticeship of war;
Your matchless courage and your conduct view;
And early shall begin t' admire and copy you.

Besides, two hundred horse he shall command—
Though few, a warlike and well-chosen band.   685
These in my name are listed; and my son
As many more has added in his own."
    Scarce had he said; Achates and his guest,
With downcast eyes, their silent grief expressed;
Who, short of succors, and in deep despair,   690
Shook at the dismal prospect of the war.
But his bright mother, from a breaking cloud,
To cheer her issue, thundered thrice aloud:
Thrice forky lightning flashed along the sky;
And Tyrrhene trumpets thrice were heard on high.   695
Then, gazing up, repeated peals they hear;
And, in a heaven serene, refulgent arms appear:
Reddening the skies, and glittering all around,
The tempered metals clash, and yield a silver sound.
The rest stood trembling: struck with awe divine: 700
Aeneas only, conscious to the sign,
Presaged the event, and joyful viewed, above,
The accomplished promise of the queen of love.
Then to the Arcadian king: "This prodigy
(Dismiss your fear) belongs alone to me.   705
Heaven calls me to the war: the expected sign
Is given of promised aid, and arms divine.
My goddess-mother, whose indulgent care
Foresaw the dangers of the growing war,
This omen gave; when bright Vulcanian arms,   710
Fated from force of steel by Stygian charms,
Suspended, shone on high: she then foreshowed
Approaching fights, and fields to float in blood.
Turnus shall dearly pay for faith forsworn:
And corpse, and swords, and shields on Tiber borne,   715
Shall choke his flood: now sound the loud alarms;
And, Latian troops, prepare your perjured arms!"
    He said, and, rising from his homely throne,
The solemn rites of Hercules begun;
And on his altars waked the sleeping fires;   720
Then cheerful to his household gods retires:

There offers chosen sheep. The Arcadian king
And Trojan youth the same oblations bring.
Next, of his men and ships he makes review;
Draws out the best and ablest of the crew.   725
Down with the falling stream the refuse run,
To raise with joyful news his drooping son.
Steeds are prepared to mount the Trojan band,
Who wait their leader to the Tyrrhene land.
A sprightly courser, fairer than the rest,   730
The king himself presents his royal guest.
A lion's hide his back and limbs infold,
Precious with studded work, and paws of gold.
Fame through the little city spreads aloud
The intended march: amid the fearful crowd,   735
The matrons beat their breasts, dissolve in tears,
And double their devotion in their fears.
The war at hand appears with more affright,
And rises every moment to the sight.
Then old Evander, with a close embrace,   740
Strained his departing friend; and tears o'erflow his face.
"Would heaven (said he) my strength and youth recall,
Such as I was beneath Praeneste's wall—
Then when I made the foremost foes retire,
And set whole heaps of conquered shields on fire;   745
When Herilus in single fight I slew,
Whom with three lives Feronia did endue;
And thrice I sent him to the Stygian shore,
Till the last ebbing soul returned no more—
Such if I stood renewed; not these alarms   750
Nor death, should rend me from my Pallas' arms;
Nor proud Mezentius thus, unpunished, boast
His rapes and murders on the Tuscan coast.
Ye gods! and mighty Jove! in pity bring
Relief, and hear a father and a king!   755
If fate and you reserve these eyes, to see
My son returned with peace and victory;

726. *refuse*: remainder.
747. *Feronia*: a goddess identified with Juno by the Virgilian commentator, Servius.

If the loved boy shall bless his father's sight;
If we shall meet again with more delight;
Then draw my life in length; let me sustain,   760
In hopes of his embrace, the worst of pain.
But, if your hard decrees—which, O! I dread—
Have doomed to death his undeserving head;
This, O! this very moment let me die,
While hopes and fears in equal balance lie;   765
While, yet possessed of all his youthful charms,
I strain him close within these aged arms:
Before that fatal news my soul shall wound!"
He said; and swooning, sunk upon the ground.
His servants bore him off, and softly laid   770
His languished limbs upon his homely bed.
    The horsemen march; the gates are opened wide;
Aeneas at their head, Achates by his side.
Next these the Trojan leaders rode along:
Last, follows in the rear the Arcadian throng.   775
Young Pallas shone conspicuous o'er the rest:
Gilded his arms, embroidered was his vest.
So, from the seas, exerts his radiant head
The star by whom the lights of heaven are led;
Shakes from his rosy locks the pearly dews;   780
Dispels the darkness, and the day renews.
The trembling wives, the walls and turrets crowd,
And follow with their eyes the dusty cloud,
Which winds disperse by fits, and show from far
The blaze of arms, and shields, and shining war.   785
The troops, drawn up in beautiful array,
O'er heathy plains pursue the ready way.
Repeated peals of shouts are heard around;
The neighing coursers answer to the sound;
And shake with horny hoofs the solid ground.   790

    778. *exerts*: lifts out. Homer had likened Achilles to the morning star.
    790. *quadrupedante putrem sonitu quatit ungula campum*: Virgil's line has
been urged on generations as an example of onomatopeia, a word hereby invited
to vanish from the language. After two slow lines this one breaks into a dactyllic
gallop.

A greenwood shade, long for religion known,
Stands by the streams that wash the Tuscan town;
Encompassed round with gloomy hills above,
Which add a holy horror to the grove.
The first inhabitants, of Grecian blood,   795
That sacred forest to Silvanus vowed
(The guardian of their flocks and fields), and pay
Their due devotions on his annual day.
Not far from hence, along the river side
In tents secure, the Tuscan troops abide,   800
By Tarchon led. Now, from a rising ground,
Aeneas cast his wondering eyes around,
And all the Tyrrhene army had in sight,
Stretched on the spacious plain from left to right.
Thither his warlike train the Trojan led,   805
Refreshed his men, and wearied horses fed.
    Meantime the mother-goddess, crowned with charms,
Breaks through the clouds, and brings the fated arms.
Within a winding vale she finds her son,
On the cool river's banks retired, alone.   810
She shows her heavenly form without disguise,
And gives herself to his desiring eyes.
"Behold! (she said) performed in every part,
My promise made, and Vulcan's labored art.
Now seek, secure, the Latian enemy;   815
And haughty Turnus to the field defy."
She said: and, having first her son embraced,
The radiant arms beneath an oak she placed.
Proud of the gift, he rolled his greedy sight
Around the work, and gazed with vast delight.   820
He lifts, he turns, he poises, and admires
The crested helm, that vomits radiant fires:
His hands the fatal sword and corslet hold—
One keen with tempered steel, one stiff with gold—
Both ample, flaming both, and beamy bright: 825
So shines a cloud, when edged with adverse light.
He shakes the pointed spear; and longs to try
The plaited cuishes on his manly thigh;

But most admires the shield's mysterious mold,
And Roman triumphs rising on the gold: 830
For there, embossed, the heavenly smith had wrought
(Not in the rolls of future fate untaught)
The wars in order; and the race divine
Of warriors issuing from the Julian line.
The cave of Mars was dressed with mossy greens: 835
There, by the wolf, were laid the martial twins.
Intrepid on her swelling dugs they hung:
The foster dam lolled out her fawning tongue:
They sucked secure, while, bending back her head,
She licked their tender limbs, and formed them as they fed.   840
Not far from thence new Rome appears; with games
Projected for the rape of Sabine dames.
The pit resounds with shrieks; a war succeeds,
For breach of public faith, and unexampled deeds.
Here, for revenge the Sabine troops contend;   845
The Romans there, with arms the prey defend:
Wearied with tedious war, at length they cease;
And both the kings and kingdoms plight the peace.
The friendly chiefs before Jove's altar stand,
Both armed, with each a charger in his hand: 850
A fatted sow for sacrifice is led,
With imprecations on the perjured head.
Near this, the traitor Metius, stretched between
Four fiery steeds, is dragged along the green,
By Tullus' doom: the brambles drink his blood;   855
And his torn limbs are left, the vulture's food.
   There, Porsena to Rome, proud Tarquin brings;
And would by force restore the banished kings:
One tyrant for his fellow-tyrant fights:
The Roman youth assert their native rights.   860

842. The story was that Romulus provided his men with wives by arranging
a mass abduction of Sabine women.
853. *Metius*: Mettus Fuffetius, whose punishment for betraying Tullus
Hostilius was to be torn apart by two four-horse chariots.
857. *Porsena*: Lars Porsena of Clusium, chief of the Etruscans, marched on
republican Rome to restore the *Tarquin* line to kingship.

Before the town the Tuscan army lies.
To win by famine, or by fraud surprise.
Their king, half threatening, half disdaining, stood,
While Cocles broke the bridge, and stemmed the flood.
The captive maids there tempt the raging tide;   865
'Scaped from their chains, with Cloelia for their guide.
  High on a rock, heroic Manlius stood
To guard the temple, and the temple's god.
Then Rome was poor; and there you might behold
The palace thatched with straw, now roofed with gold.   870
The silver goose before the shining gate
There flew, and by her cackle saved the state.
She told the Gaul's approach: the approaching Gauls,
Obscure in night, ascend and seize the walls.
The gold dissembled well their yellow hair;   875
And golden chains on their white necks they wear.
Gold are their vests; long Alpine spears they wield;
And their left arm sustains a length of shield.
Hard by, the leaping Salian priests advance;
And naked through the streets the mad Luperci dance,   880
In caps of wool: the targets drop from heaven.
Here modest matrons, in soft litters driven,
To pay their vows in solemn pomp appear;
And odorous gums in their chaste hands they bear.
  Far hence removed, the Stygian seats are seen;   885
Pains of the damned; and punished Cataline
Hung on a rock—the traitor; and, around,
The Furies hissing from the nether ground.

864. *Cocles*: Horatius Cocles, who held off an attack on the Tiber bridge until it could be broken, then swam the river.

866. *Cloelia*: a Roman girl held hostage by Porsena, who escaped and swam the Tiber.

871. *silver goose*: One of the sacred geese on the Capitoline warned of a night raid by Gauls in 390 B.C.

881–2. In the reign of Numa a shield dropped from heaven. He had eleven others made exactly like it, so that if it were lost no one could be sure. All twelve were kept in the temple of Mars and carried in procession by the Salii once a year.

884. The origin of this line is in neither Virgil nor Ruaeus.

886. *Cataline*: the conspirator, subject of Cicero's well-known orations in 63 B.C.

Apart from these, the happy souls he draws;
And Cato's holy ghost dispensing laws.   890
   Betwixt the quarters, flows a golden sea;
But foaming surges there in silver play.
The dancing dolphins with their tails divide
The glittering waves, and cut the precious tide.
Amid the main, two mighty fleets engage: 895
Their brazen beaks opposed with equal rage.
Actium surveys the well disputed prize:
Leucate's watery plain with foamy billows fries.
Young Caesar, on the stern in armor bright,
Here leads the Romans and their gods to fight: 900
His beamy temples shoot their flames afar;
And o'er his head is hung the Julian star.
Agrippa seconds him, with prosperous gales,
And, with propitious gods, his foes assails.
A naval crown, that binds his manly brows,   905
The happy fortune of the fight foreshows.
   Ranged on the line opposed, Antonius brings
Barbarian aids, and troops of eastern kings,
The Arabians near, and Bactrians from afar,
Of tongues discordant, and a mingled war: 910
And, rich in gaudy robes, amidst the strife,
His ill fate follows him—the Egyptian wife.
Moving they fight: with oars and forky prows
The froth is gathered and the water glows.
It seems as if the Cyclades again   915
Were rooted up, and justled in the main;

890. *secretosque pios, his dantem iura Catonem*: M. Porcius Cato, "of Utica"
because he committed suicide there in 46 B.C. rather than submit to Caesar,
whom he had opposed on republican principles. His integrity, celebrated here by
no republican, won him the esteem of Dante, who not only placed him in the
Christian purgatory but made him guardian of its shore.
   897. *Actium*: a naval battle (31 B.C.) in the Adriatic off the coast of
Acarnania. Octavius Caesar defeated Marcus Antonius and the Egyptian queen
Cleopatra and became the ruler of the Roman world.
   898. *Leucate*: a promontory nearby, south of the island of Leucas.
   902. *the Julian star*: Venus, because the goddess was the grandmother of
Iulus.
   903. *Agrippa*: M. Vipsanius Agrippa, the general, was Octavius' right hand.
   915. *the Cyclades*: a line of Greek islands in the southern Aegean.

Or floating mountains floating mountains meet;
Such is the fierce encounter of the fleet.
Fire-balls are thrown, and pointed javelins fly;
The fields of Neptune take a purple dye. 920
The queen herself, amidst the loud alarms,
With cymbal tossed, her fainting soldiers warms—
Fool as she was! who had not yet divined
Her cruel fate; nor saw the snakes behind.
Her country gods, the monsters of the sky, 925
Great Neptune, Pallas, and love's queen, defy.
The dog Anubis barks, but barks in vain,
Nor longer dares oppose the ethereal train.
Mars, in the middle of the shining shield
Is graved, and strides along the liquid field. 930
The Dirae souse from heaven with swift descent;
And Discord, dyed in blood, with garments rent,
Divides the press: her steps Bellona treads,
And shakes her iron rod above their heads.
   This seen, Apollo, from his Actian height 935
Pours down his arrows; at whose wingèd flight
The trembling Indians and Egyptians yield,
And soft Sabaeans quit the watery field.
The fatal mistress hoists her silken sails,
And shrinking from the fight, invokes the gales. 940
Aghast she looks, and heaves her breast for breath,
Panting, and pale with fear of future death.
The god had figured her, as driven along
By winds and waves, and scudding through the throng.
Just opposite, sad Nilus opens wide 945
His arms and ample bosom to the tide,
And spreads his mantle o'er the winding coast;
In which he wraps his queen and hides the flying host.
   The victor to the gods his thanks expressed;
And Rome triumphant with his presence blessed. 950
Three hundred temples in the town he placed;
With spoils and altars every temple graced.

931. *The Dirae*: Furies.

Three shining nights, and three succeeding days,
The fields resound with shouts, the streets with praise,
The domes with songs, the theaters with plays.   955
All altars flame: before each altar lies,
Drenched in his gore, the destined sacrifice.
Great Caesar sits sublime upon his throne,
Before Apollo's porch of Parian stone;
Accepts the presents vowed for victory;   960
And hangs the monumental crowns on high.
Vast crowds of vanquished nations march along,
Various in arms, in habit, and in tongue.
Here, Mulciber assigns the proper place
For Carians, and the ungirt Numidian race;   965
Then ranks the Thracians in the second row,
With Scythians, expert in the dart and bow.
And here the tamed Euphrates humbly glides;
And there the Rhine submits her swelling tides;
And proud Araxes, whom no bridge could bind.   970
The Danes' unconquered offspring march behind;
And Morini, the last of human kind.
    These figures, on the shield divinely wrought,
By Vulcan labored, and by Venus brought,
With joy and wonder fill the hero's thought.   975
Unknown the names, he yet admires the grace;
And bears aloft the fame and fortune of his race.

   971. *Danes*: for Dahae, a Scythian tribe.
   972. *Morini*: a tribe in Gaul.

BOOK IX

THE ARGUMENT

THE ARGUMENT

Turnus takes advantage of Aeneas' absence, fires some of his ships (which are transformed into sea-nymphs), and assaults his camp. The Trojans, reduced to the last extremities, send Nisus and Euryalus to recall Aeneas; which furnishes the poet with that admirable episode of their friendship, generosity, and the conclusion of their adventures.

WHILE these affairs in distant places passed,
The various Iris Juno sends with haste
To find bold Turnus; who, with anxious thought,
The secret shade of his great grandsire sought.
Retired alone she found the daring man,   5
And oped her rosy lips, and thus began:
"What none of all the gods could grant thy vows—
That, Turnus, this auspicious day bestows.
Aeneas, gone to seek the Arcadian prince,
Has left the Trojan camp without defense;   10
And, short of succors there, employs his pains
In parts remote, to raise the Tuscan swains.
Now snatch an hour that favors thy designs;
Unite thy forces, and attack their lines."
This said, on equal wings she poised her weight,   15
And formed a radiant rainbow in her flight.
    The Daunian hero lifts his hands and eyes,
And thus invokes the goddess as she flies:
"Iris, the grace of heaven! what power divine
Has sent thee down, through dusky clouds to shine?   20

17. *Daunian*: from his ancestor, Daunus.

275

See, they divide: immortal day appears,
And glittering planets dancing in their spheres!
With joy these happy omens I obey,
And follow, to the war the god that leads the way."
    Thus having said, as by the brook he stood,   25
He scooped the water from the crystal flood;
Then with his hands the drops to heaven he throws,
And loads the powers above with offered vows.
    Now march the bold confederates through the plain,
Well horsed, well clad, a rich and shining train.   30
Messapus leads the van; and, in the rear,
The sons of Tyrrheus in bright arms appear.
In the main battle, with his flaming crest,
The mighty Turnus towers above the rest.
Silent they move, majestically slow,   35
Like ebbing Nile, or Ganges in his flow.
The Trojans view the dusty cloud from far,
And the dark menace of the distant war.
Caïcus from the rampire saw it rise,
Black'ning the fields, and thick'ning through the skies: 40
Then to his fellows thus aloud he calls:
"What rolling clouds, my friends, approach the walls?
Arm! arm! and man the works! prepare your spears,
And pointed darts! the Latian host appears."
    Thus warned, they shut their gates; with shouts ascend   45
The bulwarks, and, secure, their foes attend:
For their wise general, with foreseeing care,
Had charged them not to tempt the doubtful war,
Nor, though provoked, in open fields advance,
But close within their lines attend their chance.   50
Unwilling, yet they keep the strict command,
And sourly wait in arms the hostile band.
The fiery Turnus flew before the rest:
A piebald steed of Thracian strain he pressed;
His helm of massy gold; and crimson was his crest.   55
With twenty horse to second his designs,
An unexpected foe, he faced the lines.
"Is there (he said), in arms who bravely dare
His leader's honor and his danger share?"

Then spurring on, his brandished dart he threw   60
In sign of war: applauding shouts ensue.
   Amazed to find a dastard race that run
Behind the rampires, and the battle shun,
He rides around the camp, with rolling eyes,
And stops at every post, and every passage tries.   65
So roams the nightly wolf about the fold:
Wet with descending showers, and stiff with cold,
He howls for hunger, and he grins for pain
(His gnashing teeth are exercised in vain);
And, impotent of anger, finds no way   70
In his distended paws to grasp the prey.
The mothers listen; but the bleating lambs
Securely swig the dug beneath the dams.
Thus ranges eager Turnus o'er the plain,
Sharp with desire, and furious with disdain;   75
Surveys each passage with a piercing sight,
To force his foes in equal field to fight.
Thus while he gazes round, at length he spies,
Where, fenced with strong redoubts, their navy lies
Close underneath the walls: the washing tide   80
Secures from all approach this weaker side.
He takes the wished occasion, fills his hand
With ready fires, and shakes a flaming brand.
Urged by his presence, every soul is warmed,
And every hand with kindled fires is armed;   85
From the fired pines the scattering sparkles fly;
Fat vapors, mixed with flames, involve the sky.
What power, O Muses! could avert the flame,
Which threatened, in the fleet, the Trojan name?
Tell: for the fact, through length of time obscure,   90
Is hard to faith; yet shall the fame endure.
   'Tis said, that when the chief prepared his flight,
And felled his timber from mount Ida's height,
The grandame goddess then approached her son,

---

94. *grandame goddess*: Cybele, the Great Mother, worshipped on Mount
Berecynthus in Phrygia. She is identified here with Rhea, the wife of Saturn
(Kronos) and mother of Jove.

And with a mother's majesty begun: 95
"Grant me (she said) the sole request I bring,
Since conquered heaven has owned you for its king.
On Ida's brows, for ages past, there stood,
With firs and maples filled, a shady wood;
And on the summit rose a sacred grove,   100
Where I was worshipped with religious love.
These woods, that holy grove, my long delight,
I gave the Trojan prince, to speed his flight.
Now, filled with fear, on their behalf I come;
Let neither winds o'erset, nor waves entomb,   105
The floating forests of the sacred pine;
But let it be their safety to be mine."
Then thus replied her awful son, who rolls
The radiant stars, and heaven and earth controls:
"How dare you, mother, endless date demand   110
For vessels molded by a mortal hand?
What then is fate? Shall bold Aeneas ride,
Of safety certain, on the uncertain tide?
Yet, what I can, I grant: when, wafted o'er,
The chief is landed on the Latian shore,   115
Whatever ships escape the raging storms,
At my command shall change their fading forms
To nymphs divine, and plow the watery way,
Like Doto and the daughters of the sea."
    To seal his sacred vow, by Styx he swore,   120
The lake of liquid pitch, the dreary shore,
And Phlegethon's innavigable flood,
And the black regions of his brother-god.
He said; and shook the skies with his imperial nod.
    And now at length the numbered hours were come, 125
Prefixed by fate's irrevocable doom,
When the great mother of the gods was free
To save her ships, and finish Jove's decree.
First, from the quarter of the morn, there sprung
A light that signed the heavens, and shot along;   130
Then from a cloud, fringed round with golden fires,
Were timbrels heard, and Berecynthian choirs;

And, last, a voice with more than mortal sounds,
Both hosts, in arms opposed, with equal horror wounds:
"O Trojan race! your needless aid forbear; 135
And know, my ships are my peculiar care.
With greater ease, the bold Rutulian may
With hissing brands attempt to burn the sea,
Than singe my sacred pines. But you, my charge,
Loosed from your crooked anchors, launch at large, 140
Exalted each a nymph: forsake the sand,
And swim the seas, at Cybele's command."
No sooner had the goddess ceased to speak,
When, lo! the obedient ships their halsers break;
And strange to tell, like dolphins, in the main 145
They plunge their prows, and dive, and spring again:
As many beauteous maids the billows sweep,
As rode before tall vessels on the deep.
The foes, surprised with wonder, stood aghast;
Messapus curbed his fiery courser's haste; 150
Old Tiber roared, and, raising up his head,
Called back his waters to their oozy bed.
Turnus alone, undaunted, bore the shock,
And with these words his trembling troops bespoke:
"These monsters for the Trojans' fate are meant, 155
And are by Jove for black presages sent.
He takes the cowards' last relief away;
For fly they cannot, and, constrained to stay,
Must yield unfought, a base inglorious prey.
The liquid half of all the globe is lost; 160
Heaven shuts the seas, and we secure the coast.
Theirs is no more than that small spot of ground,
Which myriads of our martial men surround.
Their fates I fear not, or vain oracles.
'Twas given to Venus, they should cross the seas, 165
And land secure upon the Latian plains:
Their promised hour is passed, and mine remains.
'Tis in the fate of Turnus, to destroy
With sword and fire, the faithless race of Troy.

Shall such affronts as these, alone, inflame   170
The Grecian brothers, and the Grecian name?
My cause and theirs is one; a fatal strife,
And final ruin, for a ravished wife.
Was't not enough, that, punished for the crime,
They fell—but will they fall a second time?   175
One would have thought they paid enough before,
To curse the costly sex, and durst offend no more.
Can they securely trust their feeble wall,
A slight partition, a thin interval
Betwixt their fate and them; when Troy, though built   180
By hands divine, yet perished by their guilt?
Lend me for once, my friends, your valiant hands,
To force from out their lines these dastard bands.
Less than a thousand ships will end this war;
Nor Vulcan needs his fated arms prepare.   185
Let all the Tuscans, all the Arcadians, join;
Nor these, nor those, shall frustrate my design.
Let them not fear the treasons of the night,
The robbed Palladium, the pretended flight:
Our onset shall be made in open light.   190
No wooden engine shall their town betray:
Fires they shall have around, but fires by day.
No Grecian babes before their camp appear,
Whom Hector's arms detained to the tenth tardy year.
Now, since the sun is rolling to the west,   195
Give we the silent night to needful rest:
Refresh your bodies, and your arms prepare:
The morn shall end the small remains of war."
    The post of honor to Messapus falls,
To keep the nightly guard, to watch the walls,   200
To pitch the fires at distances around,
And close the Trojans in their scanty ground.
Twice seven Rutulian captains ready stand;
And twice seven hundred horse these chiefs command.
All clad in shining arms the works invest,   205
Each with a radiant helm, and waving crest.

    193. *babes*: *pube Pelasga*, "Pelasgian youth."

Stretched at their length, they press the grassy ground;
They laugh; they sing (the jolly bowls go round);
With lights and cheerful fires renew the day;
And pass the wakeful night in feasts and play. 210
    The Trojans, from above, their foes beheld,
And with armed legions all the rampires filled.
Seized with affright, their gates they first explore;
Join works to works with bridges, tower to tower:
Thus all things needful for defense abound: 215
Mnestheus and brave Serestus walk the round,
Commissioned by their absent prince to share
The common danger, and divide the care.
The soldiers draw their lots, and, as they fall,
By turns relieve each other on the wall. 220
    Nigh where the foes their utmost guards advance,
To watch the gate was warlike Nisus' chance.
His father Hyrtacus, of noble blood;
His mother was a huntress of the wood,
And sent him to the wars. Well could he bear 225
His lance in fight, and dart the flying spear;
But better skilled unerring shafts to send.
Beside him stood Euryalus, his friend—
Euryalus, than whom, the Trojan host
No fairer face, or sweeter air, could boast: 230
Scarce had the down to shade his cheeks begun.
One was their care, and their delight was one:
One common hazard in the war they shared;
And now were both by choice upon the guard.
    Then Nisus thus: "Or do the gods inspire 235
This warmth, or make we gods of our desire?
A generous ardor boils within my breast,
Eager of action, enemy to rest:
This urges me to fight, and fires my mind
To leave a memorable name behind. 240
Thou seest the foe secure: how faintly shine
Their scattered fires: the most, in sleep supine
Along the ground, an easy conquest lie:
The wakeful few the fuming flagon ply:

All hushed around. Now hear what I revolve—   245
A thought unripe—and scarcely yet resolve.
Our absent prince both camp and council mourn;
By message both would hasten his return:
If they confer what I demand, on thee
(For fame is recompense enough for me),   250
Methinks, beneath yon hill, I have espied
A way that safely will my passage guide."
Euryalus stood listening while he spoke;
With love of praise and noble envy struck;
Then to his ardent friend exposed his mind: 255
"All this, alone, and leaving me behind!
Am I unworthy, Nisus, to be joined?
Think'st thou I can my share of glory yield,
Or send thee, unassisted, to the field?
Not so my father taught my childhood arms—   260
Born in a siege, and bred among alarms.
Nor is my youth unworthy of my friend,
Nor of the heaven-born hero I attend.
The thing called life with ease I can disclaim,
And think it over-sold to purchase fame."   265
   Then Nisus thus: "Alas! thy tender years
Would minister new matter to my fears.
So may the gods who view this friendly strife,
Restore me to thy loved embrace with life,
Condemned to pay my vows (as sure I trust),   270
This thy request is cruel and unjust.
But if some chance—as many chances are,
And doubtful hazards, in the deeds of war—
If one should reach my head, there let it fall,
And spare thy life: I would not perish all.   275
Thy blooming youth deserves a longer date:
Live thou to mourn thy love's unhappy fate,
To bear my mangled body from the foe,
Or buy it back, and funeral rites bestow.
Or, if hard fortune shall those dues deny,   280
Thou canst at least an empty tomb supply.

O! let not me the widow's tears renew;
Nor let a mother's curse my name pursue—
Thy pious parent, who, for love of thee,
Forsook the coasts of friendly Sicily;   285
Her age committing to the seas and wind,
When every weary matron stayed behind."
To this, Euryalus: "You plead in vain,
And but protract the cause you cannot gain.
No more delays! but haste!" With that, he wakes   290
The nodding watch: each to his office takes.

   The guard relieved, the generous couple went
To find the council at the royal tent.
All creatures else forgot their daily care,
And sleep, the common gift of nature, share;   295
Except the Trojan peers, who wakeful sat
In nightly council for the endangered state.
They vote a message to their absent chief,
Show their distress, and beg a swift relief.
Amid the camp a silent seat they chose,   300
Remote from clamor, and secure from foes.
On their left arms their ample shields they bear,
Their right reclined upon the bending spear.

   Now Nisus and his friend approach the guard,
And beg admission, eager to be heard—   305
The affair important, not to be deferred.
Ascanius bids them be conducted in,
Ordering the more experienced to begin.
Then Nisus thus: "Ye fathers, lend your ears;
Nor judge our bold attempt beyond our years.   310
The foe, securely drenched in sleep and wine,
Neglect their watch; the fires but thinly shine;
And where the smoke in cloudy vapors flies,
Covering the plain, and curling to the skies,
Betwixt two paths which at the gate divide,   315
Close by the sea, a passage we have spied,
Which will our way to great Aeneas guide.

Expect each hour to see him safe again,
Loaded with spoils of foes in battle slain.
Snatch we the lucky minute while we may;   320
Nor can we be mistaken in the way;
For, hunting in the vales, we both have seen
The rising turrets, and the stream between;
And know the winding course, with every ford."
He ceased; and old Aletes took the word: 325
"Our country gods, in whom our trust we place,
Will yet from ruin save the Trojan race,
While we behold such dauntless worth appear
In dawning youth, and souls so void of fear."
Then into tears of joy the father broke: 330
Each in his longing arms by turns he took;
Panted and paused; and thus again he spoke:
"Ye brave young men, what equal gifts can we,
In recompense of such desert, decree?
The greatest, sure, and best you can receive,   335
The gods and your own conscious worth will give.
The rest our grateful general will bestow,
And young Ascanius, till his manhood, owe."
"And I, whose welfare in my father lies,
(Ascanius adds) by the great deities,   340
By my dear country, by my household gods,
By hoary Vesta's rites and dark abodes,
Adjure you both (on you my fortune stands:
That and my faith I plight into your hands):
Make me but happy in his safe return,   345
Whose wanted presence I can only mourn;
Your common gift shall two large goblets be
Of silver, wrought with curious imagery,
And high embossed, which, when old Priam reigned,
My conquering sire at sacked Arisba gained;   350
And, more, two tripods cast in antique mold,
With two great talents of the finest gold;
Beside a costly bowl, engraved with art,
Which Dido gave, when first she gave her heart.

But, if in conquered Italy we reign,   355
When spoils by lot the victor shall obtain—
Thou saw'st the courser by proud Turnus pressed,
That, Nisus! and his arms, and nodding crest,
And shield, from chance exempt, shall be thy share;
Twelve laboring slaves, twelve handmaids young and fair,   360
All clad in rich attire, and trained with care;
And, last, a Latian field with fruitful plains,
And a large portion of the king's domains.
But thou, whose years are more to mine allied,
No fate my vowed affection shall divide   365
From thee, heroic youth! Be wholly mine:
Take full possession: all my soul is thine.
One faith, one fame, one fate, shall both attend:
My life's companion, and my bosom friend—
My peace shall be committed to thy care;   370
And, to thy conduct, my concerns in war."
　　Then thus the young Euryalus replied:
"Whatever fortune, good or bad, betide,
The same shall be my age, as now my youth;
No time shall find me wanting to my truth,   375
This only from your goodness let me gain
(And, this ungranted, all rewards are vain):
Of Priam's royal race my mother came—
And sure the best that ever bore the name—
Whom neither Troy nor Sicily could hold   380
From me departing, but, o'erspent and old,
My fate she followed. Ignorant of this
(Whatever) danger, neither parting kiss
Nor pious blessing taken, her I leave,
And in this only act of all my life deceive.   385
By this right hand, and conscious night, I swear,
My soul so sad a farewell could not bear.
Be you her comfort; fill my vacant place
(Permit me to presume so great a grace);
Support her age, forsaken and distressed.   390
That hope alone will fortify my breast

Against the worst of fortunes and of fears."
He said. The moved assistants melt in tears.
Then thus Ascanius, wonderstruck to see
That image of his filial piety: 395
"So great beginnings, in so green an age,
Exact the faith which I again engage.
Thy mother all the dues shall justly claim,
Creüsa had, and only want the name.
Whate'er event thy bold attempt shall have,   400
'Tis merit to have borne a son so brave.
Now by my head, a sacred oath, I swear
(My father used it), what, returning here
Crowned with success, I for thyself prepare;
That, if thou fail, shall thy loved mother share."   405
    He said, and, weeping while he spoke the word,
From his broad belt he drew a shining sword,
Magnificent with gold. Lycaon made,
And in an ivory scabbard sheathed the blade.
This was his gift. Great Mnestheus gave his friend   410
A lion's hide, his body to defend;
And good Aletes furnished him, beside,
With his own trusty helm, of temper tried.
    Thus armed they went. The noble Trojans wait
Their issuing forth, and follow to the gate   415
With prayers and vows. Above the rest appears
Ascanius, manly far beyond his years,
And messages committed to their care,
Which all in winds were lost, and flitting air.
The trenches first they passed; then took their way   420
Where their proud foes in pitched pavilions lay:
To many fatal, ere themselves were slain.
They found the careless host dispersed upon the plain,
Who, gorged, and drunk with wine, supinely snore.
Unharnessed chariots stand along the shore: 425
Amidst the wheels and reins, the goblet by,
A medley of debauch and war, they lie.
Observing Nisus showed his friend the sight:
"Behold a conquest gained without a fight.

Occasion offers; and I stand prepared: 430
There lies our way: be thou upon the guard,
And look around, while I securely go,
And hew a passage through the sleeping foe."
Softly he spoke; then, striding took his way,
With his drawn sword, where haughty Rhamnes lay;   435
His head raised high on tapestry beneath,
And heaving from his breast, he drew his breath—
A king and prophet, by king Turnus loved;
But fate by prescience cannot be removed.
Him and his sleeping slaves he slew; then spies   440
Where Remus, with his rich retinue, lies.
His armor-bearer first, and next he kills
His charioteer, intrenched betwixt the wheels
And his loved horses: last invades their lord;
Full on his neck he drives the fatal sword;   445
The gasping head flies off; a purple flood
Flows from the trunk, that welters in the blood,
Which, by the spurning heels dispersed around,
The bed besprinkles, and bedews the ground.
Lamus the bold and Lamyrus the strong,   450
He slew, and then Sarranus fair and young.
From dice and wine the youth retired to rest,
And puffed the fumy god from out his breast:
E'en then he dreamt of drink and lucky play—
More lucky, had it lasted till the day.   455
    The famished lion thus, with hunger bold,
O'erleaps the fences of the nightly fold,
And tears the peaceful flocks: with silent awe
Trembling they lie, and pant beneath his paw.
Nor with less rage Euryalus employs   460
The wrathful sword, or fewer foes destroys:
But on the ignoble crowd his fury flew:
He Fadus, Hebesus, and Rhoetus, slew.
Oppressed with heavy sleep the former fall,
But Rhoetus wakeful, and observing all: 465
Behind a spacious jar he slinked for fear:
The fatal iron found and reached him there;

For, as he rose, it pierced his naked side,
And, reeking, thence returned in crimson dyed.
The wound pours out a stream of wine and blood;   470
The purple soul comes floating in the flood.
   Now, where Messapus quartered, they arrive.
The fires were fainting there, and just alive;
The warrior-horses, tied in order, fed:
Nisus observed the discipline, and said: 475
"Our eager thirst of blood may both betray:
And see, the scattered streaks of dawning day,
Foe to nocturnal thefts! No more, my friend:
Here let our glutted execution end.
A lane through slaughtered bodies we have made."   480
The bold Euryalus, though loth, obeyed.
Of arms, and arras, and of plate, they find
A precious load; but these they leave behind.
Yet, fond of gaudy spoils, the boy would stay
To make the rich caparison his prey,   485
Which on the steed of conquered Rhamnes lay.
Nor did his eyes less longingly behold
The girdle-belt, with nails of burnished gold.
This present Caedicus the rich bestowed
On Remulus, when friendship first they vowed,   490
And, absent, joined in hospitable ties;
He, dying, to his heir bequeathed the prize;
Till, by the conquering Ardean troops oppressed,
He fell; and they the glorious gift possessed.
These glittering spoils (now made the victor's gain)   495
He to his body suits, but suits in vain.
Messapus' helm he finds among the rest,
And laces on, and wears the waving crest.
Proud of their conquest, prouder of their prey,
They leave the camp, and take the ready way.   500
   But far they had not passed, before they spied
Three hundred horse, with Volscens for their guide.

---

471. *The purple soul*: Dryden rises superior to the law of contradiction. H`
has already translated *purpureum* as a modifier of the sword, "in crimson dyed·`
Then it cannot be *purpuream* and modify *animam*, "soul."

The queen a legion to king Turnus sent;
But the swift horse the slower foot prevent,
And now, advancing, sought the leader's tent.   505
They saw the pair; for, through the doubtful shade,
His shining helm Euryalus betrayed,
On which the moon with full reflection played.
" 'Tis not for nought (cried Volscens from the crowd),
These men go there (then raised his voice aloud):   510
Stand! stand! why thus in arms? and whither bent
From whence, to whom, and on what errand sent?"
Silent they scud away, and haste their flight
To neighboring woods, and trust themselves to night.
The speedy horse all passages belay,   515
And spur their smoking steeds to cross their way,
And watch each entrance of the winding wood.
Black was the forest: thick with beech it stood,
Horrid with fern, and intricate with thorn:
Few paths of human feet, or tracks of beasts, were worn.   520
The darkness of the shades, his heavy prey,
And fear, misled the younger from his way.
But Nisus hit the turns with happier haste,
And thoughtless of his friend, the forest passed,
And Alban plains (from Alba's name so called)   525
Where king Latinus then his oxen stalled;
Till, turning at the length, he stood his ground,
And missed his friend, and cast his eyes around.
"Ah wretch! (he cried) where have I left behind
The unhappy youth? where shall I hope to find?   530
Or what way take?" Again he ventures back,
And treads the mazes of his former track.
He winds the wood, and, listening, hears the noise
Of trampling coursers, and the riders' voice.
The sound approached; and suddenly he viewed   535
The foes inclosing, and his friend pursued,

503. *The queen*: Amata, wife of Latinus.
515. *belay*: bar. In sailing, a running line is stopped and held by being
belayed around a cleat or belaying pin.
521. *prey*: Messapus' helmet.

Forelaid and taken, while he strove in vain
The shelter of the friendly shades to gain.
What should he next attempt? what arms employ,
What fruitless force, to free the captive boy?   540
Or desperate should he rush and lose his life,
With odds oppressed, in such unequal strife?
Resolved at length, his pointed spear he shook;
And, casting on the moon a mournful look:
"Guardian of groves, and goddess of the night!   545
Fair queen! (he said) direct my dart aright.
If e'er my pious father, for my sake,
Did grateful off'rings on thy altars make,
Or I increased them with my sylvan toils,
And hung thy holy roofs with savage spoils,   550
Give me to scatter these." Then from his ear
He poised, and aimed, and launched the trembling spear.
The deadly weapon, hissing from the grove,
Impetuous on the back of Sulmo drove;
Pierced his thin armor, drank his vital blood,   555
And in his body left the broken wood.
He staggers round; his eyeballs roll in death;
And with short sobs he gasps away his breath.
All stand amazed:—a second javelin flies
With equal strength, and quivers through the skies.   560
This through thy temples, Tagus, forced the way,
And in the brain-pan warmly buried lay.
Fierce Volscens foams with rage, and gazing round,
Descried not him who gave the deadly wound,
Nor knew to fix revenge: "But thou (he cries),   565
Shalt pay for both," and at the prisoner flies
With his drawn sword. Then, struck with deep despair,
That cruel sight the lover could not bear;
But from his covert rushed in open view.
And sent his voice before him as he flew: 570
"Me! me! (he cried) turn all your swords alone
On me—the fact confessed, the fault my own.
He neither could nor durst, the guiltless youth—
Ye moon and stars, bear witness to the truth!

His only crime (if friendship can offend) 575
Is too much love to his unhappy friend."
Too late he speaks: the sword, which fury guides,
Driven with full force, had pierced his tender sides.
Down fell the beauteous youth: the yawning wound
Gushed out a purple stream, and stained the ground. 580
His snowy neck reclines upon his breast,
Like a fair flower by the keen share oppressed—
Like a white poppy sinking on the plain,
Whose heavy head is overcharged with rain.

Despair, and rage, and vengeance justly vowed, 585
Drove Nisus headlong on the hostile crowd.
Volscens he seeks; on him alone he bends:
Borne back and bored by his surrounding friends,
Onward he pressed, and kept him still in sight,
Then whirled aloft his sword with all his might: 590
The unerring steel descended while he spoke,
Pierced his wide mouth, and through his weazon broke.
Dying, he slew; and staggering on the plain,
With swimming eyes he sought his lover slain;
Then quiet on his bleeding bosom fell, 595
Content, in death, to be revenged so well.

O happy friends! for, if my verse can give
Immortal life, your fame shall ever live,
Fixed as the Capitol's foundation lies,
And spread, where'er the Roman eagle flies! 600

The conquering party first divide the prey,
Then their slain leader to the camp convey.
With wonder, as they went, the troops were filled,
To see such numbers whom so few had killed.
Sarranus, Rhamnes, and the rest, they found: 605
Vast crowds the dying and the dead surround;
And the yet reeking blood overflows the ground.
All knew the helmet which Messapus lost,
But mourned a purchase that so dear had cost.

588. *bored*: warded off, for *proturbant*.
592. *weazon*: gullet.

Now rose the ruddy morn from Tithon's bed,   610
And with the dawn of day the skies o'erspread;
Nor long the sun his daily course withheld,
But added colors to the world revealed;
When, early, Turnus, wakening with the light,
All clad in armor, calls his troops to fight.   615
His martial men with fierce harangues he fired,
And his own ardor in their souls inspired.
This done—to give new terror to his foes,
The heads of Nisus and his friend he shows,
Raised high on pointed spears—a ghastly sight!   620
Loud peals of shouts ensue, and barbarous delight.

Meantime the Trojans run where danger calls;
They line their trenches, and they man their walls.
In front extended to the left they stood:
Safe was the right, surrounded by the flood.   625
But, casting from their towers a frightful view,
They saw the faces, which too well they knew,
Though then disguised in death, and smeared all o'er
With filth obscene, and dropping putrid gore.

Soon, hasty fame through the sad city bears   630
The mournful message to the mother's ears.
An icy cold benumbs her limbs; she shakes;
Her cheeks the blood, her hand the web, forsakes.
She runs the rampires round, amidst the war,
Nor fears the flying darts: she rends her hair,   635
And fills with loud laments the liquid air.
"Thus, then, my loved Euryalus appears!
Thus looks the prop of my declining years!
Was't on this face my famished eyes I fed?
Ah! how unlike the living is the dead!   640
And couldst thou leave me, cruel, thus alone!
Not one kind kiss from a departing son!
No look, no last adieu, before he went,
In an ill-boding hour to slaughter sent!
Cold on the ground, and pressing foreign clay,   645
To Latian dogs and fowls he lies a prey!

610. *Tithon's*: Tithonus'.

Nor was I near to close his dying eyes,
To wash his wounds, to weep his obsequies,
To call about his corpse his crying friends,
Or spread the mantle (made for other ends)   650
On his dear body, which I wove with care,
Nor did my daily pains or nightly labor spare.
Where shall I find his corpse? what earth sustains
His trunk dismembered, and his cold remains?
For this, alas! I left my needful ease,   655
Exposed my life to winds, and winter seas!
If any pity touch Rutulian hearts,
Here empty all your quivers, all your darts:
Or, if they fail, thou, Jove, conclude my woe,
And send me thunderstruck to shades below!"   660
    Her shrieks and clamors pierce the Trojans' ears,
Unman their courage, and augment their fears:
Nor young Ascanius could the sight sustain,
Nor old Ilioneus his tears restrain,
But Actor and Idaeus jointly sent,   665
To bear the madding mother to her tent.
    And now the trumpets terribly, from far,
With rattling clangor, rouse the sleepy war.
The soldiers' shouts succeed the brazen sounds;
And heaven, from pole to pole, the noise rebounds. 670
The Volscians bear their shields upon their head,
And, rushing forward, form a moving shed.
These fill the ditch; those pull the bulwarks down;
Some raise the ladders; others scale the town.
But, where void spaces on the walls appear,   675
Or thin defense, they pour their forces there.
With poles and missive weapons, from afar,
The Trojans keep aloof the rising war.
Taught, by their ten years' siege, defensive fight,
They roll down ribs of rocks, an unresisted weight, 680

667–8. *at tuba terribilem sonitum procul aere canoro/ increpuit*: elegantly echoing a better line by Ennius: *at tuba terribili sonitu taratantara dixit*.

671. *Volscians*: Latins. Roman legionaries approaching an enemy wall formed the "tortoise" with shields overlapping overhead.

To break the penthouse with the ponderous blow,
Which yet the patient Volscians undergo—
But could not bear the unequal combat long;
For, where the Trojans find the thickest throng,
The ruin falls: their shattered shields give way, 685
And their crushed heads become an easy prey.
They shrink for fear, abated of their rage,
Nor longer dare in a blind fight engage—
Contented now to gall them from below
With darts and slings, and with the distant bow. 690
    Elsewhere Mezentius, terrible to view,
A blazing pine within the trenches threw.
But brave Messapus, Neptune's warlike son,
Broke down the palisades, the trenches won,
And loud for ladders calls, to scale the town. 695
    Calliope, begin! Ye sacred Nine,
Inspire your poet in his high design,
To sing what slaughter manly Turnus made,
What souls he sent below the Stygian shade,
What fame the soldiers with their captain share, 700
And the vast circuit of the fatal war:
For you, in singing martial facts, excel;
You best remember, and alone can tell.
    There stood a tower, amazing to the sight,
Built up of beams, and of stupendous height: 705
Art, and the nature of the place, conspired
To furnish all the strength that war required.
To level this, the bold Italians join:
The wary Trojans obviate their design;
With weighty stones o'erwhelm their troops below, 710
Shoot through the loopholes, and sharp javelins throw.
Turnus, the chief, tossed from his thundering hand,
Against the wooden walls, a flaming brand:
It stuck, the fiery plague; the winds were high;
The planks were seasoned, and the timber dry. 715
Contagion caught the posts; it spread along,
Scorched, and to distance drove, the scattered throng.

681. *penthouse*: the "shed" of shields.
696. *Calliope*: the muse of epic poetry.

The Trojans fled; the fire pursued amain,
Still gathering fast upon the trembling train;
Till, crowding to the corners of the wall,   720
Down, the defense and the defenders fall.
The mighty flaw makes heaven itself resound:
The dead and dying Trojans strew the ground.
The tower, that followed on the falling crew,
Whelmed o'er their heads, and buried whom it slew: 725
Some stuck upon the darts themselves had sent;
All the same equal ruin underwent.
    Young Lycus and Helenor only 'scape;
Saved—how, they know not—from the steepy leap.
Helenor, elder of the two; by birth,   730
On one side royal, one a son of earth,
Whom, to the Lydian king, Licymnia bare,
And sent her boasted bastard to the war
(A privilege which none but freemen share).
Slight were his arms, a sword and silver shield;   735
No marks of honor charged its empty field.
Light as he fell, so light the youth arose,
And, rising, found himself amidst his foes;
Nor flight was left, nor hopes to force his way.
Emboldened by despair, he stood at bay;   740
And, like a stag, whom all the troop surrounds
Of eager huntsmen and invading hounds—
Resolved on death, he dissipates his fears,
And bounds aloft against the pointed spears:
So dares the youth, secure of death; and throws   745
His dying body on his thickest foes.
    But Lycus, swifter of his feet by far,
Runs, doubles, winds, and turns, amidst the war;
Springs to the walls, and leaves his foes behind,
And snatches at the beam he first can find;   750
Looks up, and leaps aloft at all the stretch,
In hopes the helping hand of some kind friend to reach.
But Turnus followed hard his hunted prey—
His spear had almost reached him in the way,
Short of his reins, and scarce a span behind: 755
"Fool (said the chief) though fleeter than the wind,

Could'st thou presume to 'scape when I pursue?"
He said, and downward by the feet he drew
The trembling dastard: at the tug he falls:
Vast ruins come along, rent from the smoking walls.   760
Thus on some silver swan, or timorous hare,
Jove's bird comes sousing down from upper air;
Her crooked talons truss the fearful prey;
Then out of sight she soars, and wings her way.
So seizes the grim wolf the tender lamb,   765
In vain lamented by the bleating dam.
    Then rushing onward with a barbarous cry,
The troops of Turnus to the combat fly.
The ditch with faggots filled, the daring foe
Tossed firebrands to the steepy turrets throw.   770
    Ilioneus, as bold Lucetius came
To force the gate, and feed the kindling flame,
Rolled down the fragment of a rock so right,
It crushed him double underneath the weight.
Two more, young Liger and Asylas slew: 775
To bend the bow young Liger better knew;
Asylas best the pointed javelin threw.
Brave Caeneus laid Ortygius on the plain;
The victor Caeneus was by Turnus slain.
By the same hand, Clonius and Itys fall,   780
Sagar, and Idas standing on the wall.
From Capys' arms his fate Privernus found:
Hurt by Temilla first—but slight the wound—
His shield thrown by, to mitigate the smart,
He clapped his hand upon the wounded part: 785
The second shaft came swift and unespied,
And pierced his hand, and nailed it to his side,
Transfixed his breathing lungs, and beating heart:
The soul came hissing out, and hissed against the dart.
    The son of Arcens shone amid the rest,   790
In glittering armor and a purple vest:

---

786. sqq. *ergo alis adlapsa sagitta/ et laevo infixa est lateri manus, abditaque
intus/ spiramenta animae letali vulnere rupit.* This ingenious death is ingeniously
and closely rendered, since even the hiss of a punctured lung is implied by the
Latin.

Fair was his face, his eyes inspiring love—
Bred by his father in the Martian grove,
Where the fat altars of Palicus flame,
And sent in arms to purchase early fame.   795
Him when he spied from far, the Tuscan king
Laid by the lance, and took him to the sling;
Thrice whirled the thong around his head, and threw;
The heated lead half melted as it flew:
It pierced his hollow temples and his brain;   800
The youth came tumbling down, and spurned the plain.
    Then young Ascanius, who, before this day,
Was wont in woods to shoot the savage prey,
First bent in martial strife the twanging bow,
And exercised against a human foe—   805
With this bereft Numanus of his life,
Who Turnus' younger sister took to wife.
Proud of his realm, and of his royal bride,
Vaunting before his troops, and lengthened with a stride,
In these insulting terms the Trojans he defied: 810
"Twice-conquered cowards! now your shame is shown—
Cooped up a second time within your town!
Who dare not issue forth in open field,
But hold your walls before you for a shield.
Thus threat you war? thus our alliance force?   815
What gods, what madness, hither steered your course?
You shall not find the sons of Atreus here,
Nor need the frauds of sly Ulysses fear,
Strong from the cradle, of a sturdy brood,
We bear our new-born infants to the flood;   820
There bathed amid the stream, our boys we hold,
With winter hardened, and inured to cold.
They wake before the day to range the wood.
Kill ere they eat, nor taste unconquered food.
No sports, but what belong to war, they know—   825
To break the stubborn colt, to bend the bow.
Our youth, of labor patient, earn their bread;
Hardly they work, with frugal diet fed.

794. *Palicus*: a Sicilian deity.

From plows and harrows sent to seek renown,
They fight in fields, and storm the shaken town.   830
No part of life from toils of war is free,
No change in age, or difference in degree.
We plow and till in arms: our oxen feel,
Instead of goads, the spur and pointed steel:
The inverted lance makes furrows in the plain.   835
E'en time, that changes all, yet changes us in vain—
The body, not the mind—nor can control
The immortal vigor, or abate the soul.
Our helms defend the young, disguise the gray;
We live by plunder, and delight in prey.   840
Your vests embroidered with rich purple shine;
In sloth you glory, and in dances join.
Your vests have sweeping sleeves: with female pride,
Your turbans underneath your chins are tied.
Go, Phrygians, to your Dindymus again!   845
Go, less than women, in the shapes of men!
Go! mixed with eunuchs in the mother's rites
(Where with unequal sound the flute invites),
Sing, dance, and howl, by turns, in Ida's shade:
Resign the war to men, who know the martial trade."   850
    This foul reproach Ascanius could not hear
With patience, or a vowed revenge forbear.
At the full stretch of both his hands, he drew
And almost joined, the horns of the tough yew.
But, first, before the throne of Jove he stood,   855
And thus with lifted hands invoked the god:
"My first attempt, great Jupiter, succeed!
An annual offering in thy grove shall bleed,

845. *Dindymus*: a mountain in Phrygia, like Berecynthus sacred to Cybele.
    853-4. Dryden noted: "The first of these lines is all of monosyllables; and
both verses are very rough: but of choice; for it had been easy for me to have
smoothed them. But either my ear deceives me, or they express the thing which
I intended in their sound: for the stress of a bow which is drawn to the full
extent, is expressed in the harshness of the first verse, clogged not only with
monosyllables, but with consonants; and these words, 'the tough yew,' which
conclude the second line, seem as forceful as they are unharmonious. Homer and
Virgil are both frequent in their adapting sounds to the thing they signify. . . ."

A snow-white steer, before thy altar led,
Who, like his mother, bears aloft his head,   860
Butts with his threatening brows, and bellowing stands,
And dares the fight, and spurns the yellow sands."

   Jove bowed the heavens, and lent a gracious ear,
And thundered on the left, amidst the clear.
Sounded at once the bow; and swiftly flies   865
The feathered death, and hisses through the skies.
The steel through both his temples forced the way:
Extended on the ground, Numanus lay.
"Go now, vain boaster! and true valor scorn!
The Phrygians, twice subdued, yet make this third return."   870
Ascanius said no more. The Trojans shake
The heavens with shouting, and new vigor take.

   Apollo then bestrode a golden cloud,
To view the feats of arms, and fighting crowd;
And thus the beardless victor he bespoke aloud: 875
"Advance, illustrious youth! increase in fame,
And wide from east to west extend thy name—
Offspring of gods thyself; and Rome shall owe
To thee a race of demigods below.
This is the way to heaven: the powers divine   880
From this beginning date the Julian line.
To thee, to them, and their victorious heirs,
The conquered war is due, and the vast world is theirs.
Troy is too narrow for thy name." He said,
And plunging downward shot his radiant head;   885
Dispelled the breathing air, that broke his flight:
Shorn of his beams, a man to mortal sight:
Old Butes' form he took, Anchises' squire,
Now left, to rule Ascanius, by his sire:
His wrinkled visage, and his hoary hairs,   890
His mien, his habit, and his arms, he wears,
And thus salutes the boy, too forward for his years:
"Suffice it thee, thy father's worthy son,
The warlike prize thou hast already won.
The god of archers gives thy youth a part   895
Of his own praise, nor envies equal art.

Now tempt the war no more." He said, and flew
Obscure in air, and vanished from their view.
The Trojans, by his arms, their patron know,
And hear the twanging of his heavenly bow. 900
  Then duteous force they use, and Phoebus' name,
To keep from fight the youth too fond of fame.
Undaunted, they themselves no danger shun:
From wall to wall the shouts and clamors run:
They bend their bows; they whirl their slings around: 905
Heaps of spent arrows fall, and strew the ground;
And helms, and shields, and rattling arms, resound.
The combat thickens, like the storm that flies
From westward, when the showery Kids arise;
Or pattering hail comes pouring on the main, 910
When Jupiter descends in hardened rain;
Or bellowing clouds burst with a stormy sound,
And with an armèd winter strew the ground.
  Pandarus and Bitias, thunderbolts of war,
Whom Hiera to bold Alcanor bare 915
On Ida's top (two youths of height and size
Like firs that on their mother-mountain rise):
Presuming on their force, the gates unbar,
And of their own accord invite the war,
With fates averse, against their king's command. 920
Armed, on the right and on the left they stand,
And flank the passage: shining steel they wear,
And waving crests above their heads appear.
Thus two tall oaks, that Padus' banks adorn,
Lift up to heaven their leafy heads unshorn, 925
And overpressed with nature's heavy load,
Dance to the whistling winds, and at each other nod.
  In flows a tide of Latians, when they see
The gate set open and the passage free:
Bold Quercens, with rash Tmarus, rushing on, 930
Aquicolus, that in bright armor shone,

  909. *Kids*: the Haedi, a double star that rose in October.
  924. *Padus*: Po.

And Haemon first: but soon repulsed they fly,
Or in the well-defended pass they die.
These with success are fired, and those with rage;
And each on equal terms at length engage.   935
Drawn from their lines, and issuing from the plain,
The Trojans hand to hand the fight maintain.

   Fierce Turnus in another quarter fought,
When suddenly the unhoped-for news was brought,
The foes had left the fastness of their place,   940
Prevailed in fight, and had his men in chase.
He quits the attack, and, to prevent their fate,
Runs, where the giant brothers guard the gate.
The first he met, Antiphates the brave
(But base-begotten on a Theban slave—   945
Sarpedon's son), he slew: the deadly dart
Found passage through his breast, and pierced his heart.
Fixed in the wound the Italian cornel stood,
Warmed in his lungs, and in his vital blood.
Aphidnus next, and Erymanthus dies,   950
And Meropes, and the gigantic size
Of Bitias, threatening with his ardent eyes.
Not by the feeble dart he fell oppressed
(A dart were lost within that roomy breast),
But from a knotted lance, large, heavy, strong.   955
Which roared like thunder as it whirled along:
Not two bull hides the impetuous force withhold,
Nor coat of double mail, with scales of gold.
Down sunk the monster bulk, and pressed the ground
(His arms and clattering shield on the vast body sound).   960
Not with less ruin than the Baian mole,
Raised on the seas, the surges to control—
At once comes tumbling down the rocky wall;
Prone to the deep, the stones disjointed fall
Of the vast pile; the scattered ocean flies,   965
Black sands, discolored froth, and mingled mud, arise:

961. *Baian*: on the Bay of Baia near Naples and Cumae.

The frighted billows roll, and seek the shores:
Then trembles Prochyta, then Ischia roars:
Typhöeus, thrown beneath by Jove's command,
Astonished at the flaw that shakes the land,   970
Soon shifts his weary side, and scarce awake,
With wonder feels the weight press lighter on his back.

   The warrior-god the Latian troops inspired,
New strung their sinews, and their courage fired,
But chills the Trojan hearts with cold affright: 975
Then black despair precipitates their flight.

   When Pandarus beheld his brother killed,
The town with fear and wild confusion filled,
He turns the hinges of the heavy gate
With both his hands, and adds his shoulders to the weight;   980
Some happier friends within the walls inclosed;
The rest shut out, to certain death exposed:
Fool as he was, and frantic in his care,
To admit young Turnus, and include the war!
He thrust amid the crowd, securely bold,   985
Like a fierce tiger pent amid the fold.
Too late his blazing buckler they descry,
And sparkling fires that shot from either eye,
His mighty members, and his ample breast,
His rattling armor, and his crimson crest.   990

   Far from that hated face the Trojans fly,
All but the fool who sought his destiny.
Mad Pandarus steps forth, with vengeance vowed
For Bitias' death, and threatens thus aloud:
"These are not Ardea's walls, nor this the town   995
Amata proffers with Lavinia's crown:
'Tis hostile earth you tread. Of hope bereft,
No means of safe return by flight are left."
To whom, with count'nance calm, and soul sedate,
Thus Turnus: "Then begin, and try thy fate: 1000

   968. *Prochyta* . . . *Ischia*: islands off the Bay of Naples.
   969 sqq. Typhöeus' restiveness, "not in the Latin" here, was suggested by
Enceladus in Book III, 759–60.

My message to the ghost of Priam bear;
Tell him a new Achilles sent thee there."
  A lance of tough ground-ash the Trojan threw,
Rough in the rind, and knotted as it grew:
With his full force he whirled it first around,   1005
But the soft yielding air received the wound:
Imperial Juno turned the course before,
And fixed the wandering weapon in the door.
  "But hope not thou (said Turnus), when I strike,
To shun thy fate: our force is not alike,   1010
Nor thy steel tempered by the Lemnian god."
Then rising, on his utmost stretch he stood,
And aimed from high: the full descending blow
Cleaves the broad front and beardless cheeks in two,
Down sinks the giant with a thundering sound: 1015
His ponderous limbs oppress the trembling ground;
Blood, brains, and foam, gush from the gaping wound.
Scalp, face, and shoulders, the keen steel divides;
And the shared visage hangs on equal sides.
  The Trojans fly from their approaching fate: 1020
And, had the victor then secured the gate,
And to his troops without, unclosed the bars,
One lucky day had ended all his wars.
But boiling youth, and blind desire of blood,
Push on his fury, to pursue the crowd.   1025
Hamstringed behind, unhappy Gyges died;
Then Phalaris is added to his side.
The pointed javelins from the dead he drew,
And their friend's arms against their fellows threw.
Strong Halys stands in vain; weak Phegeus flies;   1030
Saturnia, still at hand, new force and fire supplies.
Then Halius, Prytanis, Alcander fall—
Engaged against the foes who scaled the wall:
But, whom they feared without, they found within.
At last, though late, by Lynceus he was seen.   1035
He calls new succors, and assaults the prince:
But weak his force, and vain is their defense.

Turned to the right, his sword the hero drew,
And at one blow the bold aggressor slew—
He joints the neck, and, with a stroke so strong, 1040
The helm flies off, and bears the head along.
Next him, the huntsman Amycus he killed,
In darts envenomed, and in poison, skilled.
Then Clytius fell beneath his fatal spear,
And Cretheus, whom the Muses held so dear: 1045
He fought with courage, and he sung the fight:
Arms were his business, verses his delight.

The Trojan chiefs behold, with rage and grief,
Their slaughtered friends, and hasten their relief.
Bold Mnestheus rallies first the broken train, 1050
Whom brave Serestus and his troop sustain.
To save the living, and revenge the dead,
Against one warrior's arms all Troy they led.
"O, void of sense and courage! (Mnestheus cried)
Where can you hope your coward heads to hide? 1055
Ah! where beyond these rampires can you run?
One man, and in your camp inclosed, you shun!
Shall then a single sword such slaughter boast,
And pass unpunished from a numerous host?
Forsaking honor, and renouncing fame, 1060
Your gods, your country, and your king, you shame!"
This just reproach their virtue does excite:
They stand, they join, they thicken to the fight.

Now Turnus doubts, and yet disdains to yield,
But with slow paces measures back the field, 1065
And inches to the walls, where Tiber's tide,
Washing the camp, defends the weaker side.
The more he loses, they advance the more,
And tread in every step he trod before.
They shout; they bear him back; and, whom by might 1070
They cannot conquer, they oppress with weight.

As, compassed with a wood of spears around,
The lordly lion still maintains his ground;
Grins horrible, retires, and turns again;
Threats his distended paws, and shakes his mane; 1075

He loses while in vain he presses on,
Nor will his courage let him dare to run:
So Turnus fares, and unresolved of flight,
Moves tardy back, and just recedes from fight.
Yet twice, enraged, the combat he renews,   1080
Twice breaks, and twice his broken foes pursues.
But now they swarm, and with fresh troops supplied
Come rolling on, and rush from every side:
Nor Juno, who sustained his arms before,
Dares with new strength suffice the exhausted store;   1085
For Jove, with sour commands, sent Iris down,
To force the invader from the frighted town.
  With labor spent, no longer can he wield
The heavy falchion, or sustain the shield;
O'erwhelmed with darts, which from afar they fling;   1090
The weapons round his hollow temples ring:
His golden helm gives way, with stony blows
Battered, and flat, and beaten to his brows.
His crest is rashed away; his ample shield
Is falsified, and round with javelins filled.   1095
  The foe, now faint, the Trojans overwhelm;
And Mnestheus lays hard load upon his helm.
Sick sweat succeeds; he drops at every pore;
With driving dust his cheeks are pasted o'er;
Shorter and shorter every gasp he takes;   1100
And vain efforts and hurtless blows he makes.
Armed as he was, at length he leaped from high,
Plunged in the flood, and made the waters fly.
The yellow god the welcome burden bore,
And wiped the sweat, and washed away the gore;   1105
Then gently wafts him to the farther coast,
And sends him safe to cheer his anxious host.

  1094. *rashed*: slashed.
  1095. *falsified*: belied as a shield.

𝄞𝄞𝄞

BOOK X

THE ARGUMENT

Jupiter, calling a council of the gods, forbids them to engage in either
party. At Aeneas' return there is a bloody battle; Turnus killing Pallas;
Aeneas, Lausus and Mezentius. Mezentius is described as an atheist;
Lausus as a pious and virtuous youth. The different actions and death of
these two are the subject of a noble episode.

THE gates of heaven unfold: Jove summons all
The gods to council in the common hall.
Sublimely seated, he surveys from far
The fields, the camp, the fortune of the war,
And all the inferior world. From first to last,   5
The sovereign senate in degrees are placed.
  Then thus the almighty sire began: "Ye gods,
Natives or denizens of blest abodes!
From whence these murmurs, and this change of mind,
This backward fate from what was first designed?   10
Why this protracted war, when my commands
Pronounced a peace, and gave the Latian lands?
What fear or hope on either part divides
Our heavens, and arms our powers on different sides?
A lawful time of war at length will come   15
(Nor need your haste anticipate the doom),
When Carthage shall contend the world with Rome;
Shall force the rigid rocks and Alpine chains,
And, like a flood, come pouring on the plains.
Then is your time for faction and debate,   20
For partial favor, and permitted hate.

Let now your immature dissension cease;
Sit quiet, and compose your souls to peace."
      Thus Jupiter in few unfolds the charge;
But lovely Venus thus replies at large: 25
"O power immense! eternal energy!
(For to what else protection can we fly?)
Seest thou the proud Rutulians, how they dare
In fields, unpunished, and insult my care?
How lofty Turnus vaunts amidst his train,   30
In shining arms triumphant on the plain?
E'en in their lines and trenches they contend;
And scarce their walls the Trojan troops defend.
The town is filled with slaughter, and o'erfloats,
With a red deluge, their increasing moats.   35
Aeneas, ignorant, and far from thence,
Has left a camp exposed, without defense.
This endless outrage shall they still sustain?
Shall Troy renewed be forced and fired again?
A second siege my banished issue fears;   40
And a new Diomede in arms appears.
One more audacious mortal will be found;
And I, thy daughter, wait another wound.
Yet if, with fates averse, without thy leave,
The Latian lands my progeny receive,   45
Bear they the pains of violated law,
And thy protection from their aid withdraw.
But, if the gods their sure success foretell—
If those of heaven consent with those of hell,
To promise Italy; who dare debate   50
The power of Jove, or fix another fate?
What should I tell of tempests on the main,
Of Aeolus usurping Neptune's reign?
Of Iris sent, with Bacchanalian heat
T' inspire the matrons and destroy the fleet?   55
Now Juno to the Stygian sky descends,
Solicits hell for aid, and arms the fiends.
That new example wanted yet above—
An act that well became the wife of Jove!

Alecto, raised by her, with rage inflames   60
The peaceful bosoms of the Latian dames.
Imperial sway no more exalts my mind;
Such hopes I had indeed, while heaven was kind,
Now let my happier foes possess my place,
Whom Jove prefers before the Trojan race;   65
And conquer they, whom you with conquest grace.
Since you can spare from all your wide command,
No spot of earth, no hospitable land,
Which may my wandering fugitives receive
(Since haughty Juno will not give you leave);   70
Then, father (if I still may use that name),
By ruined Troy, yet smoking from the flame,
I beg you, let Ascanius, by my care,
Be freed from danger, and dismissed the war:
Inglorious let him live, without a crown: 75
The father may be cast on coasts unknown,
Struggling with fate; but let me save the son.
Mine is Cythera, mine the Cyprian towers:
In those recesses, and those sacred bowers,
Obscurely let him rest; his right resign   80
To promised empire, and his Julian line.
Then Carthage may the Ausonian towns destroy,
Nor fear the race of a rejected boy.
What profits it my son, to 'scape the fire,
Armed with his gods, and loaded with his sire;   85
To pass the perils of the seas and wind;
Evade the Greeks, and leave the war behind;
To reach the Italian shores; if, after all,
Our second Pergamus is doomed to fall?
Much better had he curbed his high desires,   90
And hovered o'er his ill-extinguished fires.
To Simoïs' banks the fugitives restore,
And give them back to war, and all the woes before."
   Deep indignation swelled Saturnia's heart:
"And must I own (she said) my secret smart—   95
What with more decence were in silence kept.
And, but for this unjust reproach, had slept?

Did god or man your favorite son advise,
With war unhoped the Latians to surprise?
By fate, you boast, and by the gods' decree,   100
He left his native land for Italy!
Confess the truth; by mad Cassandra, more
Than heaven, inspired, he sought a foreign shore.
Did I persuade to trust his second Troy
To the raw conduct of a beardless boy,   105
With walls unfinished, which himself forsakes,
And through the waves a wandering voyage takes?
When have I urged him meanly to demand
The Tuscan aid, and arm a quiet land?
Did I or Iris give this mad advice?   110
Or made the fool himself the fatal choice?
You think it hard, the Latians should destroy
With swords your Trojans, and with fires your Troy!
Hard and unjust indeed, for men to draw
Their native air, nor take a foreign law!   115
That Turnus is permitted still to live,
To whom his birth a god and goddess give!
But yet 'tis just and lawful for your line
To drive their fields, and force with fraud to join;
Realms, not your own, among your clans divide,   120
And from the bridegroom tear the promised bride;
Petition, while you public arms prepare;
Pretend a peace, and yet provoke a war!
'Twas given to you, your darling son to shroud
To draw the dastard from the fighting crowd,   125
And, for a man, obtend an empty cloud.
From flaming fleets you turned the fire away,
And changed the ships to daughters of the sea.
But 'tis my crime—the queen of heaven offends,
If she presume to save her suffering friends!   130
Your son, not knowing what his foes decree,
You say, is absent: absent let him be.

124. In the *Iliad*, Book V, 315, Venus protected Aeneas with her cloak.
126. *obtend*: direct from the Latin, *proque viro nebulam et ventos obtendere
inanes*, "to spread a cloud before the man, and empty winds." In fact Apollo did
so after Venus was wounded, *Iliad*, Book V, 344.

Yours is Cythera, yours the Cyprian towers,
The soft recesses, and the sacred bowers.
Why do you then these needless arms prepare,   135
And thus provoke a people prone to war?
Did I with fire the Trojan town deface,
Or hinder from return your exiled race?
Was I the cause of mischief, or the man
Whose lawless lust the fatal war began?   140
Think on whose faith the adulterous youth relied;
Who promised, who procured, the Spartan bride?
When all the united states of Greece combined,
To purge the world of the perfidious kind,
Then was your time to fear the Trojan fate:—   145
Your quarrels and complaints are now too late."
    Thus Juno. Murmurs rise with mixed applause,
Just as they favor or dislike the cause.
So winds, when yet unfledged in woods they lie,
In whispers first their tender voices try,   150
Then issue on the main with bellowing rage,
And storms to trembling mariners presage.
    Then thus to both replied the imperial god,
Who shakes heaven's axles with his awful nod.
(When he begins, the silent senate stand,   155
With reverence listening to the dread command:
The clouds dispel; the winds their breath restrain;
And the hushed waves lie flatted on the main.)
"Celestials! your attentive ears incline!
Since (said the god) the Trojans must not join   160
In wished alliance with the Latian line—
Since endless jarrings, and immortal hate,
Tend but to discompose our happy state—
The war henceforward be resigned to fate:
Each to his proper fortune stand or fall;   165
Equal and unconcerned I look on all.
Rutulians, Trojans, are the same to me;
And both shall draw the lots their fates decree.
Let these assault, if Fortune be their friend;
And, if she favors those, let those defend: 170

The fates will find their way." The Thunderer said;
And shook the sacred honors of his head,
Attesting Styx, the inviolable flood,
And the black regions of his brother-god.
Trembled the poles of heaven; and earth confessed the nod.   175
This end the sessions had: the senate rise,
And to his palace wait their sovereign through the skies.

   Meantime, intent upon their siege, the foes
Within their walls the Trojan host inclose:
They wound, they kill, they watch at every gate;   180
Renew the fires, and urge their happy fate.

   The Aeneans wish in vain their wanted chief,
Hopeless of flight, more hopeless of relief.
Thin on the towers they stand; and e'en those few,
A feeble, fainting, and dejected crew.   185
Yet in the face of danger some there stood:
The two bold brothers of Sarpedon's blood,
Asius, Acmon: both the Assaraci;
Young Haemon, and, though young, resolved to die.
With these were Clarus and Thymoetes joined;   190
Thymbris and Castor, both of Lycian kind.
From Acmon's hands a rolling stone there came,
So large, it half deserved a mountain's name!
Strong-sinewed was the youth, and big of bone:
His brother Mnestheus could not more have done,   195
Or the great father of the intrepid son.
Some firebrands throw, some flights of arrows send;
And some with darts, and some with stones, defend.
Amid the press appears the beauteous boy,
The care of Venus, and the hope of Troy.   200
His lovely face unarmed, his head was bare;
In ringlets o'er his shoulders hung his hair.
His forehead circled with a diadem;
Distinguished from the crowd, he shines a gem,
Enchased in gold, or polished ivory set,   205
Amidst the meaner foil of sable jet.

   Nor Ismarus was wanting to the war,
Directing ointed arrows from afar,

And death with poison armed—in Lydia born,
Where plenteous harvests the fat fields adorn;   210
Where proud Pactolus floats the fruitful lands,
And leaves a rich manure of golden sands.
There Capys, author of the Capuan name,
And there was Mnestheus too, increased in fame,
Since Turnus from the camp he cast with shame.   215
    Thus mortal war was waged on either side.
Meantime the hero cuts the nightly tide;
For, anxious, from Evander when he went,
He sought the Tyrrhene camp, and Tarchon's tent;
Exposed the cause of coming to the chief;   220
His name and country told, and asked relief;
Proposed the terms; his own small strength declared:
What vengeance proud Mezentius had prepared;
What Turnus, bold and violent, designed;
Then showed the slippery state of human kind,   225
And fickle fortune; warned him to beware,
And to his wholesome counsel added prayer.
Tarchon, without delay, the treaty signs,
And to the Trojan troops the Tuscan joins.
    They soon set sail; nor now the Fates withstand;   230
Their forces trusted with a foreign hand.
Aeneas leads; upon his stern appear
Two lions carved, which rising Ida bear—
Ida, to wandering Trojans ever dear.
Under their grateful shade Aeneas sat,   235
Revolving war's events, and various fate.
His left young Pallas kept, fixed to his side,
And oft of winds inquired, and of the tide;
Oft of the stars, and of their watery way;
And what he suffered both by land and sea.   240
    Now, sacred sisters, open all your spring!
The Tuscan leaders, and their army, sing,
Which followed great Aeneas to the war:
Their arms, their numbers, and their names, declare.

    211. *floats*: floods.

A thousand youths brave Massicus obey,   245
Borne in the Tiger through the foaming sea;
From Clusium brought, and Cosa, by his care:
For arms, light quivers, bows and shafts, they bear.
Fierce Abas next: his men bright armor wore:
His stern Apollo's golden statue bore.   250
Six hundred, Populonia sent along,
All skilled in martial exercise, and strong.
Three hundred more, for battle, Ilva joins,
An isle renowned for steel, and unexhausted mines.
Asylas on his prow the third appears,   255
Who heaven interprets, and the wandering stars;
From offered entrails, prodigies expounds,
And peals of thunder, with presaging sounds.
A thousand spears in warlike order stand,
Sent by the Pisans under his command.   260
Fair Astur follows in the watery field,
Proud of his managed horse and painted shield.
Gravisca, noisome from the neighboring fen,
And his own Caere, sent three hundred men,
With those which Minio's fields, and Pyrgi gave;   265
All bred in arms, unanimous and brave.
   Thou, muse, the name of Cinyras renew,
And brave Cupavo followed but by few;
Whose helm confessed the lineage of the man,
And bore, with wings displayed, a silver swan.   270
Love was the fault of his famed ancestry,
Whose forms and fortunes in his ensign fly.
For Cycnus loved unhappy Phaëthon,
And sung his loss in poplar groves, alone,
Beneath the sister-shades, to soothe his grief.   275
Heaven heard his song, and hastened his relief,
And changed to snowy plumes his hoary hair,
And winged his flight, to chant aloft in air.

251. *Populonia*: a town on the Etrurian coast near Piombino.
253. *Ilva*: Elba.
263 sqq. *Gravisca, Caere, Minio, Pyrgi*: towns in Etruria.
273. *Cycnus*: Swan.

His son Cupavo brushed the briny flood;
Upon his stern a brawny Centaur stood,   280
Who heaved a rock, and, threatening still to throw,
With lifted hands alarmed the seas below:
They seemed to fear the formidable sight,
And rolled their billows on, to speed his flight.

Ocnus was next, who led his native train   285
Of hardy warriors through the watery plain—
The son of Manto, by the Tuscan stream,
From whence the Mantuan town derives the name—
An ancient city, but of mixed descent;
Three several tribes compose the government;   290
Four towns are under each; but all obey
The Mantuan laws, and own the Tuscan sway.

Hate to Mezentius armed five hundred more,
Whom Mincius from his sire Benacus bore—
Mincius, with wreaths of reeds his forehead covered o'er.   295
These grave Aulestes leads: a hundred sweep
With stretching oars at once the glassy deep.
Him, and his martial train, the Triton bears;
High on his poop the sea-green god appears:
Frowning he seems his crooked shell to sound,   300
And at the blast the billows dance around.
A hairy man above the waist he shows;
A porpoise-tail beneath his belly grows;
And ends a fish: his breast the waves divides,
And froth and foam augment the murmuring tides.   305

Full thirty ships transport the chosen train,
For Troy's relief, and scour the briny main.

Now was the world forsaken by the sun,
And Phoebe half her nightly race had run.
The careful chief, who never closed his eyes,   310
Himself the rudder holds, the sails supplies.
A choir of Nereids meet him on the flood,
Once his own galleys, hewn from Ida's wood;
But now, as many nymphs, the sea they sweep,
As rode, before, tall vessels on the deep.   315

---

287. *Manto*: a goddess associated with Mantova, Virgil's home town.
294. *Mincius*: The river Mincius flows out of Lake Garda (Benacus).

They know him from afar; and in a ring
Inclose the ship that bore the Trojan king.
Cymodoce, whose voice excelled the rest,
Above the waves advanced her snowy breast;
Her right hand stops the stern; her left divides   320
The curling ocean, and corrects the tides.
She spoke for all the choir; and thus began
With pleasing words to warn the unknowing man:
"Sleeps our loved lord? O goddess-born! awake!
Spread every sail, pursue your watery track,   325
And haste your course. Your navy once were we,
From Ida's height descending to the sea;
Till Turnus—as at anchor fixed we stood,
Presumed to violate our holy wood.
Then, loosed from shore, we fled his fires profane   330
(Unwillingly we broke our master's chain),
And since have sought you through the Tuscan main.
The mighty Mother changed our forms to these,
And gave us life immortal in the seas.
But young Ascanius, in his camp distressed,   335
By your insulting foes is hardly pressed.
The Arcadian horsemen, and Etrurian host,
Advance in order on the Latian coast:
To cut their way the Daunian chief designs,
Before their troops can reach the Trojan lines.   340
Thou, when the rosy morn restores the light,
First arm thy soldiers for the ensuing fight;
Thyself the fated sword of Vulcan wield,
And bear aloft the impenetrable shield.
Tomorrow's sun, unless my skill be vain,   345
Shall see huge heaps of foes in battle slain."
Parting, she spoke; and with immortal force
Pushed on the vessel in her watery course;
For well she knew the way. Impelled behind,
The ship flew forward, and outstript the wind.   350
The rest make up. Unknowing of the cause,
The chief admires their speed, and happy omens draws.
      Then thus he prayed, and fixed on heaven his eyes:
"Hear thou, great Mother of the deities,

With turrets crowned! (on Ida's holy hill,   355
Fierce tigers, reined and curbed, obey thy will.)
Firm thy own omens; lead us on to fight;
And let thy Phrygians conquer in thy right."
    He said no more. And now renewing day
Had chased the shadows of the night away.   360
He charged the soldiers, with preventing care,
Their flags to follow, and their arms prepare;
Warned of the ensuing fight, and bade them hope the war.
    Now, from his lofty poop, he viewed below
His camp encompassed, and the inclosing foe.   365
His blazing shield, embraced, he held on high;
The camp receive the sign, and with loud shouts reply.
Hope arms their courage: from their towers they throw
Their darts with double force, and drive the foe.
Thus, at the signal given, the cranes arise   370
Before the stormy south, and blacken all the skies.
    King Turnus wondered at the fight renewed,
Till, looking back, the Trojan fleet he viewed,
The seas with swelling canvas covered o'er,
And the swift ships descending on the shore.   375
The Latians saw from far, with dazzled eyes,
The radiant crest that seemed in flames to rise,
And dart diffusive fires around the field,
And the keen glittering of the golden shield.
    Thus threatening comets, when by night they rise,   380
Shoot sanguine streams, and sadden all the skies:
So Sirius, flashing forth sinister lights,
Pale human kind with plagues and with dry famine frights.
Yet Turnus, with undaunted mind, is bent
To man the shores, and hinder their descent,   385
And thus awakes the courage of his friends:
"What you so long have wished, kind Fortune sends—
In ardent arms to meet the invading foe:
You find, and find him at advantage now.
Yours is the day: you need but only dare;   390
Your swords will make you masters of the war.
Your sires, your sons, your houses, and your lands,
And dearest wives, are all within your hands:

Be mindful of the race from whence you came,
And emulate in arms your fathers' fame.   395
Now take the time, while staggering yet they stand
With feet unfirm, and prepossess the strand:
Fortune befriends the bold." No more he said,
But balanced, whom to leave, and whom to lead;
Then these elects, the landing to prevent;   400
And those he leaves, to keep the city pent.
  Meantime the Trojan sends his troops ashore:
Some are by boats exposed, by bridges more.
With laboring oars they bear along the strand,
Where the tide languishes, and leap a-land.   405
Tarchon observes the coast with careful eyes,
And, where no ford he finds, no water fries,
Nor billows with unequal murmurs roar,
But smoothly slide along, and swell the shore,
That course he steered, and thus he gave command: 410
"Here ply your oars, and at all hazard land:
Force on the vessel, that her keel may wound
This hated soil, and furrow hostile ground.
Let me securely land—I ask no more;
Then sink my ships, or shatter on the shore."   415
  This fiery speech inflames his fearful friends:
They tug at every oar, and every stretcher bends;
They run their ships aground; the vessels knock
(Thus forced ashore), and tremble with the shock.
Tarchon's alone was lost, and stranded stood;   420
Stuck on a bank, and beaten by the flood,
She breaks her back; the loosened sides give way,
And plunge the Tuscan soldiers in the sea.
Their broken oars and floating planks withstand
Their passage, while they labor to the land;   425
And ebbing tides bear back upon the uncertain sand.
  Now Turnus leads his troops without delay,
Advancing to the margin of the sea.
The trumpets sound: Aeneas first assailed
The clowns new-raised and raw, and soon prevailed.   430

---

397. *prepossess*: do not yet possess.
417. *stretcher*: a brace for the feet of oarsmen.

Great Theron fell, an omen of the fight—
Great Theron, large of limbs, of giant height.
He first in open fields defied the prince:
But armor scaled with gold was no defense
Against the fated sword, which opened wide   435
His plated shield, and pierced his naked side.
   Next Lichas fell, who, not like others born,
Was from his wretched mother ripped and torn;
Sacred, O Phoebus! from his birth to thee;
For his beginning life from biting steel was free.   440
Not far from him was Gyas laid along,
Of monstrous bulk; with Cisseus fierce and strong:
Vain bulk and strength! for, when the chief assailed,
Nor valor nor Herculean arms availed,
Nor their famed father, wont in war to go   445
With great Alcides, while he toiled below.
The noisy Pharos next received his death:
Aeneas writhed his dart, and stopped his bawling breath.
Then wretched Cydon had received his doom,
Who courted Clytius in his beardless bloom,   450
And sought with lust obscene polluted joys—
The Trojan sword had cured his love of boys,
Had not his seven bold brethren stopped the course
Of the fierce champion, with united force.
Seven darts were thrown at once; and some rebound   455
From his bright shield, some on his helmet sound:
The rest had reached him; but his mother's care
Prevented those, and turned aside in air.
   The prince then called Achates, to supply
The spears, that knew the way to victory: 460
"Those fatal weapons, which, inured to blood,
In Grecian bodies under Ilium stood:
Not one of those my hand shall toss in vain
Against our foes, on this contended plain."

   440. *biting steel*: i.e., unharmed by the surgeon's knife.
   445. *their famed father*: Melampus, a Greek seer whose story is told in Book
XV of the *Odyssey*.
   451. *polluted joys*: The tone is all Dryden's. Virgil's emotive words on this
pederast are *infelix . . . miserande*, "unfortunate . . . pitiable."

He said; then seized a mighty spear, and threw;   465
Which, winged with fate, through Maeon's buckler flew,
Pierced all the brazen plates, and reached his heart:
He staggered with intolerable smart.
Alcanor saw; and reached, but reached in vain,
His helping hand, his brother to sustain.   470
A second spear, which kept the former course,
From the same hand, and sent with equal force,
His right arm pierced, and holding on, bereft
His use of both, and pinioned down his left.
Then Numitor from his dead brother drew   475
The ill-omened spear, and at the Trojan threw:
Preventing fate directs the lance awry,
Which, glancing, only marked Achates' thigh.
    In pride of youth the Sabine Clausus came,
And, from afar, at Dryops took his aim.   480
The spear flew hissing through the middle space,
And pierced his throat, directed at his face:
It stopped at once the passage of his wind,
And the free soul to flitting air resigned:
His forehead was the first that struck the ground;   485
Life-blood and life rushed mingled through the wound.
He slew three brothers of the Borean race,
And three, whom Ismarus, their native place,
Had sent to war, but all the sons of Thrace.
Halesus, next, the bold Aurunci leads: 490
The son of Neptune to his aid succeeds,
Conspicuous on his horse. On either hand,
These fight to keep, and those to win, the land.
With mutual blood the Ausonian soil is dyed,
While on its borders each their claim decide.   495
    As wintry winds, contending in the sky,
With equal force of lungs their titles try:
They rage, they roar; the doubtful rack of heaven
Stands without motion, and the tide undriven:
Each bent to conquer, neither side to yield,   500
They long suspend the fortune of the field.

    488. *Ismarus*: in Thrace, a coastal town sacked by Odysseus in Book IX of
the *Odyssey*.

Both armies thus perform what courage can;
Foot set to foot, and mingled, man to man.
   But, in another part, the Arcadian horse
With ill success engage the Latian force: 505
For, where the impetuous torrent, rushing down,
Huge craggy stones and rooted trees had thrown,
They left their coursers, and, unused to fight
On foot, were scattered in a shameful flight.
Pallas, who, with disdain and grief, had viewed   510
His foes pursuing and his friends pursued,
Used threatenings mixed with prayers, his last resource,
With these to move their minds, with those to fire their force.
"Which way, companions, whither would you run?
By you yourselves, and mighty battles won,   515
By my great sire, by his established name,
And early promise of my future fame;
By my youth, emulous of equal right
To share his honors—shun ignoble flight!
Trust not your feet: your hands must hew your way   520
Through yon black body, and that thick array:
'Tis through that forward path that we must come;
There lies our way, and that our passage home.
Nor powers above, nor destinies below,
Oppress our arms: with equal strength we go,   525
With mortal hands to meet a mortal foe.
See on what foot we stand! a scanty shore—
The sea behind, our enemies before:
No passage left, unless we swim the main;
Or, forcing these, the Trojan trenches gain."   530
This said, he strode with eager haste along,
And bore amidst the thickest of the throng.
Lagus, the first he met, with fate to foe,
Had heaved a stone of mighty weight, to throw:
Stooping, the spear descended on his chine,   535
Just where the bone distinguished either loin;
It stuck so fast, so deeply buried lay,
That scarce the victor forced the steel away.
   Hisbo came on; but, while he moved too slow
To wished revenge, the prince prevents his blow; 540

For, warding his at once, at once he pressed,
And plunged the fatal weapon in his breast.
Then lewd Anchemolus he laid in dust,
Who stained his stepdame's bed with impious lust.
And, after him, the Daunian twins were slain,   545
Laris and Thymbrus, on the Latian plain;
So wondrous like in feature, shape, and size,
As caused an error in their parents' eyes—
Grateful mistake! but soon the sword decides
The nice distinction, and their fate divides: 550
For Thymbrus' head was lopped; and Laris' hand,
Dismembered, sought its owner on the strand:
The trembling fingers yet the falchion strain,
And threaten still the extended stroke in vain.
    Now, to renew the charge, the Arcadians came: 555
Sight of such acts, and sense of honest shame,
And grief, with anger mixed, their minds inflame.
Then, with a casual blow was Rhoeteus slain,
Who chanced, as Pallas threw, to cross the plain:
The flying spear was after Ilus sent;   560
But Rhoeteus happened on a death unmeant:
From Teuthras and from Tyres while he fled,
The lance, athwart his body, laid him dead:
Rolled from his chariot with a mortal wound,
And intercepted fate, he spurned the ground.   565
    As when, in summer, welcome winds arise,
The watchful shepherd to the forest flies,
And fires the midmost plants; contagion spreads,
And catching flames infect the neighboring heads;
Around the forest flies the furious blast,   570
And all the leafy nation sinks at last;
And Vulcan rides in triumph o'er the waste;
The pastor, pleased with his dire victory,
Beholds the satiate flames in sheets ascend the sky:
So Pallas' troops their scattered strength unite,   575
And, pouring on their foes, their prince delight.
    Halesus came, fierce with desire of blood;
But first collected in his arms he stood:

    567 sqq. A drastic expedient for making pasture land.

Advancing then, he plied the spear so well,
Ladon, Demodocus, and Pheres, fell.   580
Around his head he tossed his glittering brand,
And from Strymonius hewed his better hand,
Held up to guard his throat; then hurled a stone
At Thoas' ample front, and pierced the bone:
It struck beneath the space of either eye;   585
And blood, and mingled brains, together fly.
Deep skilled in future fates, Halesus' sire
Did with the youth to lonely groves retire;
But, when the father's mortal race was run,
Dire destiny laid hold upon the son,   590
And hauled him to the war, to find, beneath
The Evandrian spear, a memorable death.
Pallas the encounter seeks, but, ere he throws,
To Tuscan Tiber thus addressed his vows:
"O sacred stream! direct my flying dart,   595
And give to pass the proud Halesus' heart:
His arms and spoils thy holy oak shall bear."
Pleased with the bribe, the god received his prayer:
For, while his shield protects a friend distressed,
The dart came driving on, and pierced his breast.   600
    But Lausus, no small portion of the war,
Permits not panic fear to reign too far,
Caused by the death of so renowned a knight;
But by his own example cheers the fight.
Fierce Abas first he slew—Abas, the stay   605
Of Trojan hopes, and hindrance of the day.
The Phrygian troops escaped the Greeks in vain:
They, and their mixed allies, now load the plain.
    To the rude shock of war both armies came;
Their leaders equal, and their strength the same.   610
The rear so pressed the front, they could not wield
Their angry weapons, to dispute the field.
Here Pallas urges on, and Lausus there:
Of equal youth and beauty both appear,
But both by fate forbid to breathe their native air.   615

605. *the stay*: *pugnae nodumque moramque*, "the knot and snag of battle."

Their congress in the field great Jove withstands—
Both doomed to fall, but fall by greater hands.
　　Meantime Juturna warns the Daunian chief
Of Lausus' danger, urging swift relief.
With his driven chariot he divides the crowd,　　　　　　620
And, making to his friends, thus calls aloud:
"Let none presume his needless aid to join:
Retire, and clear the field; the fight is mine:
To this right hand is Pallas only due:
Oh! were his father here, my just revenge to view!"　　625
From the forbidden space his men retired.
Pallas their awe, and his stern words, admired;
Surveyed him o'er and o'er with wondering sight,
Struck with his haughty mien and towering height.
Then to the king: "Your empty vaunts forbear:　　　　630
Success I hope and fate I cannot fear.
Alive, or dead, I shall deserve a name:
Jove is impartial, and to both the same."
He said, and to the void advanced his pace:
Pale horror sat on each Arcadian face.　　　　　　　　635
Then Turnus, from his chariot leaping light,
Addressed himself on foot to single fight.
And, as a lion—when he spies from far
A bull that seems to meditate the war,
Bending his neck, and spurning back the sand—　　　640
Runs roaring downward from his hilly stand:
Imagine eager Turnus not more slow
To rush from high on his unequal foe.
　　Young Pallas, when he saw the chief advance
Within due distance of his flying lance,　　　　　　　645
Prepares to charge him first—resolved to try
If Fortune would his want of force supply;
And thus to heaven and Hercules addressed:
"Alcides, once on earth Evander's guest!
His son adjures thee by those holy rights,　　　　　　650
That hospitable board, those genial nights;

---

633. *sorti pater aequus utrique est*: Dryden objected to Ruaeus' interpretation
of *pater* as "my father" and insisted it must refer to Father Jove.

Assist my great attempt to gain this prize,
And let proud Turnus view, with dying eyes,
His ravished spoils." 'Twas heard, the vain request;
Alcides mourned, and stifled sighs within his breast.   655
Then Jove, to soothe his sorrow, thus began:
"Short bounds of life are set to mortal man:
'Tis virtue's work alone to stretch the narrow span.
So many sons of gods, in bloody fight
Around the walls of Troy, have lost the light: 660
My own Sarpedon fell beneath his foe;
Nor I, his mighty sire, could ward the blow.
E'en Turnus shortly shall resign his breath,
And stands already on the verge of death."
This said, the god permits the fatal fight,   665
But from the Latian fields averts his sight.
   Now with full force his spear young Pallas threw;
And, having thrown, his shining falchion drew.
The steel just grazed along the shoulder-joint,
And marked it slightly with the glancing point.   670
Fierce Turnus first to nearer distance drew,
And poised his pointed spear, before he threw:
Then, as the wingèd weapon whizzed along,
"See now (said he), whose arm is better strung."
The spear kept on the fatal course unstayed   675
By plates of iron, which o'er the shield were laid:
Through folded brass, and tough bull-hides, it passed,
His corselet pierced, and reached his heart at last.
In vain the youth tugs at the broken wood;
The soul comes issuing with the vital blood: 680
He falls; his arms upon his body sound;
And with his bloody teeth he bites the ground.
   Turnus bestrode the corpse: "Arcadians, hear
(Said he), my message to your master bear:
Such as the sire deserved, the son I send;   685
It costs him dear to be the Phrygian's friend.
The lifeless body, tell him, I bestow
Unasked, to rest his wandering ghost below."

657. *stat sua cuique dies; breve et inreparabile tempus/ omnibus est vitae* . . .

He said, and trampled down, with all the force
Of his left foot, and spurned the wretched corpse;   690
Then snatched the shining belt, with gold inlaid—
The belt Eurytion's artful hands had made,
Where fifty fatal brides, expressed to sight,
All, in the compass of one mournful night,
Deprived their bridegrooms of returning light.   695
   In an ill hour insulting Turnus tore
Those golden spoils, and in a worse he wore.
O mortals! blind in fate, who never know
To bear high fortune, or endure the low!
The time shall come, when Turnus, but in vain,   700
Shall wish untouched the trophies of the slain
Shall wish the fatal belt were far away,
And curse the dire remembrance of the day.
   The sad Arcadians, from the unhappy field,
Bear back the breathless body on a shield.   705
O grace and grief of war! at once restored,
With praises, to thy sire, at once deplored.
One day first sent thee to the fighting-field,
Beheld whole heaps of foes in battle killed;
One day beheld thee dead, and borne upon thy shield.   710
This dismal news, not from uncertain fame,
But sad spectators, to the hero came:
His friends upon the brink of ruin stand,
Unless relieved by his victorious hand.
He whirls his sword around, without delay,   715
And hews through adverse foes an ample way,
To find fierce Turnus, of his conquest proud.
Evander, Pallas, all that friendship owed
To large deserts, are present to his eyes—
His plighted hand, and hospitable ties.   720
   Four sons of Sulmo, four whom Ufens bred,
He took in fight, and living victims led,

693. *fifty fatal brides*: The fifty daughters of Danaus were required by their father to kill their husbands, the fifty sons of Aegyptus, on the wedding night. This myth is the subject of Aeschylus' *Suppliants*.

721–24. So did Achilles (*Iliad*, XXIII) provide living victims for Patroclus' pyre.

To please the ghost of Pallas, and expire,
In sacrifice, before his funeral fire.
At Magus next he threw: he stooped below   725
The flying spear, and shunned the promised blow,
Then, creeping, clasped the hero's knees, and prayed:
"By young Iulus, by thy father's shade,
O! spare my life, and send me back to see
My longing sire, and tender progeny,   730
A lofty house I have, and wealth untold,
In silver ingots, and in bars of gold:
All these, and sums besides, which see no day,
The ransom of this one poor life shall pay.
If I survive, will Troy the less prevail?   735
A single soul's too light to turn the scale."
He said. The hero sternly thus replied:
"Thy bars and ingots, and the sums beside,
Leave for thy children's lot. Thy Turnus broke
All rules of war by one relentless stroke,   740
When Pallas fell: so deems, nor deems alone,
My father's shadow, but my living son."
Thus having said, of kind remorse bereft,
He seized his helm, and dragged him with his left;
Then with his right hand, while his neck he wreathed, 745
Up to the hilts his shining falchion sheathed.
   Apollo's priest, Haemonides, was near;
His holy fillets on his front appear;
Glittering in arms, he shone amidst the crowd,
Much of his god, more of his purple, proud.   750
Him the fierce Trojan followed through the field:
The holy coward fell; and, forced to yield,
The prince stood o'er the priest, and, at one blow,
Sent him an offering to the shades below.
His arms Serestus on his shoulders bears,   755
Designed a trophy to the god of wars.
   Vulcanian Caeculus renews the fight,
And Umbro born upon the mountain's height.

   750. The anticlericalism is exclusively Dryden's; so, for that matter, is the
line.

The champion cheers his troops t' encounter those,
And seeks revenge himself on other foes.   760
At Anxur's shield he drove; and, at the blow,
Both shield and arm to ground together go.
Anxur had boasted much of magic charms,
And thought he wore impenetrable arms,
So made by muttered spells; and, from the spheres,   765
Had life secured, in vain, for length of years.
Then Tarquitus the field in triumph trod;
A nymph his mother, and his sire a god.
Exulting in bright arms, he braves the prince:
With his protended lance he makes defense;   770
Bears back his feeble foe; then, pressing on,
Arrests his better hand, and drags him down;
Stands o'er the prostrate wretch, and (as he lay,
Vain tales inventing, and prepared to pray)
Mows off his head: the trunk a moment stood,   775
Then sunk, and rolled along the sand in blood.
　　The vengeful victor thus upbraids the slain:
"Lie there, proud man, unpitied on the plain:
Lie there, inglorious, and without a tomb,
Far from thy mother and thy native home;   780
Exposed to savage beasts, and birds of prey,
Or thrown for food to monsters of the sea."
　　On Lucas and Antaeus next he ran,
Two chiefs of Turnus, and who led his van.
They fled for fear; with these, he chased along   785
Camers the yellow-locked, and Numa strong;
Both great in arms, and both were fair and young.
Camers was son to Volscens lately slain,
In wealth surpassing all the Latian train,
And in Amyclae fixed his silent easy reign.   790
　　And, as Aegaeon, when with heaven he strove,
Stood opposite in arms to mighty Jove;

　　790. *Amyclae*: in Latium, a "silent" town because after many false alarms of
invasion its citizens were forbidden to report "the arrival of an enemy." Naturally
they lost their town—and their silence.

Moved all his hundred hands, provoked the war,
Defied the forky lightning from afar;
At fifty mouths his flaming breath expires,   795
And flash for flash returns, and fires for fires;
In his right hand as many swords he wields,
And takes the thunder on as many shields:
With strength like this, the Trojan hero stood;
And soon the fields with falling corpse were strewed,   800
When once his falchion found the taste of blood.
    With fury scarce to be conceived, he flew
Against Niphaeus, whom four coursers drew.
They, when they see the fiery chief advance,
And pushing at their chests his pointed lance,   805
Wheeled with so swift a motion, mad with fear,
They threw their master headlong from the chair.
They stare, they start, nor stop their course, before
They bear the bounding chariot to the shore.
    Now Lucagus and Liger scour the plains,   810
With two white steeds; but Liger holds the reins,
And Lucagus the lofty seat maintains—
Bold brethren both. The former waved in air
His flaming sword: Aeneas couched his spear,
Unused to threats, and more unused to fear.   815
Then Liger thus: "Thy confidence is vain
To 'scape from hence, as from the Trojan plain;
Nor these the steeds which Diomede bestrode,
Nor this the chariot where Achilles rode:
Nor Venus' veil is here, nor Neptune's shield;   820
Thy fatal hour is come; and this the field."
Thus Liger vainly vaunts: the Trojan peer
Returned his answer with his flying spear.
As Lucagus, to lash his horses, bends,
Prone to the wheels, and his left foot protends,   825
Prepared for fight: the fatal dart arrives,
And through the border of his buckler drives;
Passed through, and pierced his groin. The deadly wound,
Cast from his chariot, rolled him on the ground;

Whom thus the chief upbraids with scornful spite: 830
"Blame not the slowness of your steeds in flight:
Vain shadows did not force their swift retreat;
But you yourself forsake your empty seat."
He said, and seized at once the loosened rein;
For Liger lay already on the plain   835
By the same shock; then, stretching out his hands,
The recreant thus his wretched life demands:
"Now, by thyself, O more than mortal man!
By her and him from whom thy breath began,
Who formed thee thus divine, I beg thee, spare   840
This forfeit life, and hear thy suppliant's prayer."
Thus much he spoke, and more he would have said;
But the stern hero turned aside his head,
And cut him short: "I hear another man:
You talked not thus before the fight began.   845
Now take your turn; and, as a brother should,
Attend your brother to the Stygian flood."
Then through his breast his fatal sword he sent;
And the soul issued at the gaping vent.
As storms the skies, and torrents tear the ground,   850
Thus raged the prince, and scattered deaths around.
  At length, Ascanius and the Trojan train
Broke from the camp, so long besieged in vain.
Meantime the king of gods and mortal man
Held conference with his queen, and thus began: 855
"My sister-goddess, and well-pleasing wife,
Still think you Venus' aid supports the strife—
Sustains her Trojans—or themselves, alone,
With inborn valor force their fortune on?
How fierce in fight, with courage undecayed!   860
Judge if such warriors want immortal aid."
To whom the goddess with the charming eyes,
Soft in her tone, submissively replies:
"Why, O my sovereign lord, whose frown I fear,
And cannot, unconcerned, your anger bear—   865
Why urge you thus my grief? when, if I still
(As once I was) were mistress of your will,

From your almighty power your pleasing wife
Might gain the grace of lengthening Turnus' life,
Securely snatch him from the fatal fight,   870
And give him to his aged father's sight.
Now let him perish, since you hold it good,
And glut the Trojans with his pious blood!
Yet, from our lineage he derives his name,
And, in the fourth degree, from god Pilumnus came;   875
Yet he devoutly pays you rites divine,
And offers daily incense at your shrine."

　　Then shortly thus the sovereign god replied:
"Since in my power and goodness you confide,
If, for a little space, a lengthened span,   880
You beg reprieve for this expiring man,
I grant you leave to take your Turnus hence
From instant fate, and can so far dispense.
But, if some secret meaning lies beneath,
To save the short-lived youth from destined death;   885
Or, if a further thought you entertain,
To change the fates; you feed your hopes in vain."

　　To whom the goddess thus, with weeping eyes:
"And what if that request your tongue denies,
Your heart should grant—and not a short reprieve.   890
But length of certain life, to Turnus give?
Now speedy death attends the guiltless youth,
If my presaging soul divines with truth;
Which, O! I wish might err, through causeless fears,
And you (for you have power) prolong his years!"   895

　　Thus having said, involved in clouds, she flies,
And drives a storm before her through the skies.
Swift she descends, alighting on the plain,
Where the fierce foes a dubious fight maintain.
Of air condensed, a specter soon she made;   900
And, what Aeneas was, such seemed the shade.
Adorned with Dardan arms, the phantom bore
His head aloft; a plumy crest he wore:

　　875. *Pilumnus*: That is, Pilumnus was his great-grandfather. Picumnus, a
woodpecker god (*picus*), and Pilumnus, a pestle god (*pilus*), were brother deities
of the Latins.

This hand appeared a shining sword to wield,
And that sustained an imitated shield.   905
With manly mien he stalked along the ground,
Nor wanted voice belied, nor vaunting sound.
(Thus haunting ghosts appear to waking sight,
Or dreadful visions in our dreams by night.)
The specter seems the Daunian chief to dare,   910
And flourishes his empty sword in air.
At this, advancing, Turnus hurled his spear:
The phantom wheeled, and seemed to fly for fear.
Deluded Turnus thought the Trojan fled,
And with vain hopes his haughty fancy fed.   915
"Whither, O coward? (thus he calls aloud,
Nor found he spoke to wind, and chased a cloud),
Why thus forsake your bride! Receive from me
The fated land you sought so long by sea."
He said, and, brandishing at once his blade,   920
With eager pace pursued the flying shade.
By chance a ship was fastened to the shore,
Which from old Clusium king Osinius bore:
The plank was ready laid for safe ascent;
For shelter there the trembling shadow bent,   925
And skipped and skulked, and under hatches went.
Exulting Turnus, with regardless haste,
Ascends the plank, and to the galley passed.
Scarce had he reached the prow; Saturnia's hand
The halsers cut, and shoots the ship from land.   930
With wind in poop, the vessel plows the sea,
And measures back with speed her former way.
Meantime Aeneas seeks his absent foe,
And sends his slaughtered troops to shades below.
   The guileful phantom now forsook the shroud,   935
And flew sublime, and vanished in a cloud.
Too late young Turnus the delusion found,
Far on the sea, still making from the ground.
Then, thankless for a life redeemed by shame,
With sense of honor stung, and forfeit fame,   940
Fearful besides of what in fight had passed,
His hands and haggard eyes to heaven he cast:

"O Jove! (he cried) for what offense have I
Deserved to bear this endless infamy?
Whence am I forced, and whither am I borne?   945
How, and with what reproach, shall I return?
Shall ever I behold the Latian plain,
Or see Laurentum's lofty towers again?
What will they say of their deserting chief?
The war was mine: I fly from their relief!   950
I led to slaughter, and in slaughter leave;
And e'en from hence their dying groans receive.
Here, over-matched in fight, in heaps they lie;
There, scattered o'er the fields, ignobly fly.
Gape wide, O earth, and draw me down alive!   955
Or, oh! ye pitying winds, a wretch relieve!
On sands or shelves the splitting vessel drive;
Or set me shipwrecked on some desert shore,
Where no Rutulian eyes may see me more—
Unknown to friends, or foes, or conscious fame,   960
Lest she should follow, and my flight proclaim."
    Thus Turnus raved, and various fates revolved:
The choice was doubtful, but the death resolved.
And now the sword, and now the sea, took place—
That to revenge, and this to purge disgrace.   965
Sometimes he thought to swim the stormy main,
By stretch of arms the distant shore to gain.
Thrice he the sword essayed, and thrice the flood;
But Juno, moved with pity, both withstood,
And thrice repressed his rage; strong gales supplied   970
And pushed the vessel o'er the swelling tide.
At length she lands him on his native shores,
And to his father's longing arms restores.
    Meantime, by Jove's impulse, Mezentius armed,
Succeeding Turnus, with his ardor warmed   975
His fainting friends, reproached their shameful flight,
Repelled the victors, and renewed the fight.
Against their king the Tuscan troops conspire;
Such is their hate, and such their fierce desire

Of wished revenge—on him, and him alone,   980
All hands employed, and all their darts are thrown.
He, like a solid rock by seas inclosed,
To raging winds and roaring waves opposed,
From his proud summit looking down, disdains
Their empty menace, and unmoved remains.   985
   Beneath his feet fell haughty Hebrus dead,
Then Latagus, and Palmus as he fled.
At Latagus a weighty stone he flung:
His face was flatted, and his helmet rung.
But Palmus from behind receives his wound: 990
Hamstringed he falls, and grovels on the ground:
His crest and armor, from his body torn,
Thy shoulders, Lausus, and thy head, adorn.
Evas and Mimas, both of Troy, he slew.
Mimas his birth from fair Theano drew—   995
Born on that fatal night, when, big with fire,
The queen produced young Paris to his sire.
But Paris in the Phrygian fields was slain,
Unthinking Mimas on the Latian plain.
   And, as a savage boar, on mountains bred,   1000
With forest mast and fattening marshes fed,
When once he sees himself in toils inclosed,
By huntsmen and their eager hounds opposed,
He whets his tusks, and turns, and dares the war:
The invaders dart their javelins from afar: 1005
All keep aloof, and safely shout around;
But none presumes to give a nearer wound:
He frets and froths, erects his bristled hide,
And shakes a grove of lances from his side:
Not otherwise the troops, with hate inspired,   1010
And just revenge against the tyrant fired,
Their darts with clamor at a distance drive,
And only keep the languished war alive.
   From Corythus came Acron to the fight,
Who left his spouse betrothed, and unconsummate night.   1015
Mezentius sees him through the squadron ride.
Proud of the purple favors of his bride.

Then, as a hungry lion, who beholds
A gamesome goat, who frisks about the folds,
Or beamy stag, that grazes on the plain—   1020
He runs, he roars, he shakes his rising mane;
He grins, and opens wide his greedy jaws:
The prey lies panting underneath his paws:
He fills his famished maw; his mouth runs o'er
With unchewed morsels, while he churns the gore: 1025
So proud Mezentius rushes on his foes,
And first unhappy Acron overthrows:
Stretched at his length, he spurns the swarthy ground;
The lance, besmeared with blood, lies broken in the wound.
Then with disdain the haughty victor viewed   1030
Orodes flying, nor the wretch pursued,
Nor thought the dastard's back deserved a wound,
But, running, gained the advantage of the ground:
Then turning short, he met him face to face,
To give his victory the better grace.   1035
Orodes falls, in equal fight oppressed:
Mezentius fixed his foot upon his breast,
And rested lance; and thus aloud he cries:
"Lo! here the champion of my rebels lies!"
The fields around with "Iö Paean!" ring;   1040
And peals of shouts applaud the conquering king.
At this the vanquished, with his dying breath,
Thus faintly spoke, and prophesied in death:
"Nor thou, proud man, unpunished shalt remain;
Like death attends thee on this fatal plain."   1045
Then, sourly smiling, thus the king replied:
"For what belongs to me, let Jove provide;
But die thou first, whatever chance ensue."
He said, and from the wound the weapon drew.
A hovering mist came swimming o'er his sight,   1050
And sealed his eyes in everlasting night.
   By Caedicus, Alcathöus was slain:
Sacrator laid Hydaspes on the plain:
Orses the strong to greater strength must yield;
He, with Parthenius, were by Rapo killed.   1055

Then brave Messapus Ericetes slew,
Who from Lycaon's blood his lineage drew;
But from his headstrong horse his fate he found,
Who threw his master, as he made a bound:
The chief, alighting, stuck him to the ground;   1060
Then Clonius, hand to hand, on foot assails:
The Trojan sinks, and Neptune's son prevails.
　　Agis the Lycian, stepping forth with pride,
To single fight the boldest foe defied;
Whom Tuscan Valerus by force o'ercame,   1065
And not belied his mighty father's fame.
Salius to death the great Authronius sent:
But the same fate the victor underwent,
Slain by Nealces' hand, well skilled to throw
The flying dart, and draw the far-deceiving bow.   1070
　　Thus equal deaths are dealt with equal chance:
By turns they quit their ground, by turns advance,
Victors and vanquished in the various field,
Nor wholly overcome, nor wholly yield.
The gods from heaven survey the fatal strife,   1075
And mourn the miseries of human life.
Above the rest, two goddesses appear
Concerned for each: here Venus, Juno there.
Amidst the crowd, infernal Atè shakes
Her scourge aloft, and crest of hissing snakes.   1080
　　Once more the proud Mezentius, with disdain,
Brandished his spear, and rushed into the plain,
Where towering in the midmost ranks he stood,
Like tall Orion stalking o'er the flood;
(When with his brawny breast he cuts the waves,   1085
His shoulders scarce the topmost billow laves),
Or like a mountain-ash, whose roots are spread,
Deep fixed in earth—in clouds he hides his head.
　　The Trojan prince beheld him from afar,
And dauntless undertook the doubtful war.   1090
Collected in his strength, and like a rock
Poised on his base, Mezentius stood the shock.

　　1079. Atè: Tisiphone, a Fury.

He stood, and, measuring first with careful eyes
The space his spear could reach, aloud he cries:
"My strong right hand, and sword, assist my stroke!   1095
(Those only gods Mezentius will invoke),
His armor from the Trojan pirate torn,
By my triumphant Lausus shall be worn."
He said; and with his utmost force he threw
The massy spear, which, hissing as it flew,   1100
Reached the celestial shield: that stopped the course;
But, glancing thence, the yet unbroken force
Took a new bent obliquely, and, betwixt
The side and bowels, famed Antores fixed.
Antores had from Argos traveled far,   1105
Alcides' friend, and brother of the war;
Till, tired with toils, fair Italy he chose,
And in Evander's palace sought repose.
Now falling by another's wound, his eyes
He casts to heaven, on Argos thinks, and dies.   1110
    The pious Trojan then his javelin sent:
The shield gave way: through triple plates it went
Of solid brass, of linen triply rolled,
And three bull hides which round the buckler rolled.
All these it passed, resistless in the course,   1115
Transpierced his thigh, and spent its dying force.
The gaping wound gushed out a crimson flood.
The Trojan, glad with sight of hostile blood,
His falchion drew, to closer fight addressed,
And with new force his fainting foe oppressed.   1120
    His father's peril Lausus viewed with grief;
He sighed, he wept, he ran to his relief.
And here, heroic youth, 'tis here I must
To thy immortal memory be just,
And sing an act so noble and so new,   1125
Posterity will scarce believe 'tis true.
Pained with his wound, and useless for the fight,
The father sought to save himself by flight:
Encumbered, slow he dragged the spear along,
Which pierced his thigh, and in his buckler hung.   1130

The pious youth, resolved on death, below
The lifted sword, springs forth to face the foe;
Protects his parent, and prevents the blow.
Shouts of applause ran ringing through the field,
To see the son the vanquished father shield.   1135
All, fired with generous indignation, strive,
And, with a storm of darts, to distance drive
The Trojan chief, who, held at bay from far,
On his Vulcanian orb sustained the war.
　　As, when thick hail comes rattling in the wind,   1140
The plowman, passenger, and laboring hind,
For shelter to the neighboring covert fly,
Or housed, or safe in hollow caverns, lie;
But that o'erblown, when heaven above them smiles,
Return to travail, and renew their toils: 1145
Aeneas thus, o'erwhelmed on every side,
The storm of darts, undaunted, did abide;
And thus to Lausus, loud, with friendly threatening cried:
"Why wilt thou rush to certain death, and rage
In rash attempts, beyond thy tender age,   1150
Betrayed by pious love?"—Nor, thus forborne,
The youth desists, but with insulting scorn
Provokes the lingering prince, whose patience, tired,
Gave place; and all his breast with fury fired.
For now the Fates prepared their sharpened shears;   1155
And lifted high the flaming sword appears,
Which, full descending with a frightful sway,
Through shield and corselet forced the impetuous way,
And buried deep in his fair bosom lay.
The purple streams through the thin armor strove,   1160
And drenched the embroidered coat his mother wove;
And life at length forsook his heaving heart,
Loth from so sweet a mansion to depart.
　　But when, with blood and paleness all o'erspread,
The pious prince beheld young Lausus dead,   1165
He grieved; he wept (the sight an image brought
Of his own filial love—a sadly pleasing thought),

　　1141. *passenger*: traveler.

Then stretched his hand to hold him up, and said:
"Poor hapless youth! what praises can be paid
To love so great, to such transcendent store   1170
Of early worth, and sure presage of more?
Accept whate'er Aeneas can afford:
Untouched thy arms, untaken be thy sword;
And all that pleased thee living, still remain
Inviolate, and sacred to the slain.   1175
Thy body on thy parents I bestow,
To rest thy soul, at least, if shadows know,
Or have a sense of human things below.
There to thy fellow-ghosts with glory tell,
'Twas by the great Aeneas' hand I fell."   1180
With this, his distant friends he beckons near,
Provokes their duty, and prevents their fear:
Himself assists to lift him from the ground,
With clotted locks, and blood that welled from out the wound.
    Meantime, his father (now no father) stood,   1185
And washed his wounds, by Tiber's yellow flood:
Oppressed with anguish, panting, and o'erspent,
His fainting limbs against an oak he leant.
A bough his brazen helmet did sustain;
His heavier arms lay scattered on the plain: 1190
A chosen train of youth around him stand;
His drooping head was rested on his hand;
His grisly beard his pensive bosom sought;
And all on Lausus ran his restless thought.
Careful, concerned his danger to prevent,   1195
He much inquired, and many a message sent
To warn him from the field—alas! in vain!
Behold! his mournful followers bear him slain:
O'er his broad shield still gushed the yawning wound,
And drew a bloody trail along the ground.   1200
Far off he heard their cries, far off divined
The dire event with a foreboding mind.
With dust he sprinkled first his hoary head;
Then both his lifted hands to heaven he spread;
Last, the dear corpse embracing, thus he said: 1205

"What joys, alas! could this frail being give,
That I have been so covetous to live?
To see my son, and such a son, resign
His life a ransom for preserving mine?
And am I then preserved, and art thou lost?   1210
How much too dear has that redemption cost!
'Tis now my bitter banishment I feel:
This is a wound too deep for time to heal.
My guilt thy growing virtues did defame:
My blackness blotted thy unblemished name.   1215
Chased from a throne, abandoned, and exiled
For foul misdeeds, were punishments too mild.
I owed my people these, and, from their hate,
With less resentment could have borne my fate.
And yet I live, and yet sustain the sight   1220
Of hated men, and of more hated light—
But will not long." With that he raised from ground
His fainting limbs that staggered with his wound;
Yet, with a mind resolved, and unappalled
With pains or perils, for his courser called—   1225
Well-mouthed, well-managed, whom himself did dress
With daily care, and mounted with success—
His aid in arms, his ornament in peace.
   Soothing his courage with a gentle stroke,
The steed seemed sensible, while thus he spoke: 1230
"O Rhoebus! we have lived too long for me—
If life and long were terms that could agree.
This day thou either shalt bring back the head
And bloody trophies of the Trojan dead—
This day thou either shalt revenge my woe,   1235
For murdered Lausus, on his cruel foe;
Or, if inexorable Fate deny
Our conquest, with thy conquered master die:
For, after such a lord, I rest secure,
Thou wilt no foreign reins, or Trojan load, endure."   1240
He said; and straight the officious courser kneels,
To take his wonted weight. His hands he fills

1231–2. *diu, res si qua diu mortalibus ulla est,/ viximus.*

With pointed javelins; on his head he laced
His glittering helm, which terribly was graced
With waving horse-hair, nodding from afar;   1245
Then spurred his thundering steed amidst the war.
Love, anguish, wrath, and grief, to madness wrought,
Despair, and secret shame, and conscious thought
Of inborn worth, his laboring soul oppressed,
Rolled in his eyes, and raged within his breast.   1250
Then loud he called Aeneas thrice by name:
The loud repeated voice to glad Aeneas came.
"Great Jove (he said), and the far-shooting god,
Inspire thy mind to make thy challenge good!"
He spoke no more, but hastened, void of fear,   1255
And threatened with his long protended spear.
   To whom Mezentius thus: "Thy vaunts are vain.
My Lausus lies extended on the plain:
He's lost! thy conquest is already won;
The wretched sire is murdered in the son.   1260
Nor fate I fear, but all the gods defy.
Forbear thy threats: my business is to die;
But first receive this parting legacy."
He said; and straight a whirling dart he sent;
Another after, and another, went.   1265
Round in a spacious ring he rides the field,
And vainly plies the impenetrable shield.
Thrice rode he round; and thrice Aeneas wheeled,
Turned as he turned: the golden orb withstood
The strokes, and bore about an iron wood.   1270
Impatient of delay, and weary grown,
Still to defend, and to defend alone,
To wrench the darts which in his buckler light,
Urged and o'erlabored in unequal fight—
At length resolved, he throws, with all his force,   1275
Full at the temples of the warrior-horse.
Just where the stroke was aimed, the unerring spear
Made way, and stood transfixed through either ear.

1270. *an iron wood*: a thicket of stuck darts.

Seized with unwonted pain, surprised with fright,
The wounded steed curvets, and raised upright,   1280
Light on his feet before; his hoofs behind
Spring up in air aloft, and lash the wind.
Down comes the rider headlong from his height;
His horse came after with unwieldy weight,
And, floundering forward, pitching on his head,   1285
His lord's encumbered shoulder overlaid.
    From either host, the mingled shouts and cries
Of Trojans and Rutulians rend the skies:
Aeneas, hastening, waved his fatal sword
High o'er his head, with this reproachful word: 1290
"Now! where are now thy vaunts, the fierce disdain
Of proud Mezentius, and the lofty strain?"
    Struggling, and wildly staring on the skies
With scarce recovered sight, he thus replies:
"Why these insulting words, this waste of breath,   1295
To souls undaunted, and secure of death?
'Tis no dishonor for the brave to die!
Nor came I here with hopes of victory;
Nor ask I life, nor fought with that design:
As I had used my fortune, use thou thine.   1300
My dying son contracted no such band;
The gift is hateful from his murderer's hand.
For this, this only favor, let me sue;
If pity can to conquered foes be due,
Refuse it not; but let my body have   1305
The last retreat of human-kind, a grave.
Too well I know the insulting people's hate:
Protect me from their vengeance after fate:
This refuge for my poor remains provide;
And lay my much-loved Lausus by my side."   1310
He said, and to the sword his throat applied:
The crimson stream distained his arms around,
And the disdainful soul came rushing through the wound.

1312–13. *undantique animam diffundit in arma cruore*: "in a wave of blood
he poured out his life upon his armor." Dryden repeated his couplet at the end
of the poem, Book XII, 1377, where it is still more loosely related to the Latin.

BOOK XI

THE ARGUMENT

Aeneas erects a trophy of the spoils of Mezentius, grants a truce for bury-
ing the dead, and sends home the body of Pallas with great solemnity.
Latinus calls a council, to propose offers of peace to Aeneas; which occasions great animosity betwixt Turnus and Drances. In the meantime there
is a sharp engagement of the horse, wherein Camilla signalizes herself, is
killed, and the Latin troops are entirely defeated.

SCARCE had the rosy morning raised her head
Above the waves, and left her watery bed:
The pious chief, whom double cares attend
For his unburied soldiers and his friend,
Yet first to heaven performed a victor's vows: 5
He bared an ancient oak of all her boughs;
Then on a rising ground the trunk he placed,
Which with the spoils of his dead foe he graced.
The coat of arms by proud Mezentius worn,
Now on a naked snag in triumph borne,   10
Was hung on high, and glittered from afar,
A trophy sacred to the god of war.
Above his arms, fixed on the leafless wood,
Appeared his plumy crest, besmeared with blood.
His brazen buckler on the left was seen: 15
Truncheons of shivered lances hung between;
And on the right was placed his corselet, bored;
And to the neck was tied his unavailing sword.

10. *snag:* one of the lopped boughs of the oak.

A crowd of chiefs inclose the godlike man,
Who thus, conspicuous in the midst, began: 20
"Our toils, my friends, are crowned with sure success:
The greater part performed, achieve the less.
Now follow cheerful to the trembling town:
Press but an entrance, and presume it won.
Fear is no more: for fierce Mezentius lies,   25
As the first fruits of war, a sacrifice.
Turnus shall fall extended on the plain,
And, in this omen, is already slain.
Prepared in arms, pursue your happy chance;
That none unwarned may plead his ignorance,   30
And I, at heaven's appointed hour, may find
Your warlike ensigns waving in the wind.
Meantime the rites and funeral pomps prepare,
Due to your dead companions of the war—
The last respect the living can bestow,   35
To shield their shadows from contempt below.
That conquered earth be theirs, for which they fought,
And which for us with their own blood they bought.
But first the corpse of our unhappy friend,
To the sad city of Evander send,   40
Who, not inglorious, in his age's bloom
Was hurried hence by too severe a doom."
    Thus, weeping while he spoke, he took his way,
Where, new in death, lamented Pallas lay.
Acoetes watched the corpse; whose youth deserved   45
The father's trust; and now the son he served
With equal faith, but less auspicious care.
The attendants of the slain his sorrow share.
A troop of Trojans mixed with these appear,
And mourning matrons with disheveled hair.   50
Soon as the prince appears, they raise a cry;
All beat their breasts, and echoes rend the sky.
They rear his drooping forehead from the ground:
But, when Aeneas viewed the grisly wound
Which Pallas in his manly bosom bore,   55
And the fair flesh distained with purple gore,

First, melting into tears, the pious man
Deplored so sad a sight, then thus began:
"Unhappy youth! when Fortune gave the rest
Of my full wishes, she refused the best!   60
She came; but brought not thee along, to bless
My longing eyes, and share in my success:
She grudged thy safe return, the triumphs due
To prosperous valor, in the public view.
Not thus I promised, when thy father lent   65
Thy needless succor with a sad consent;
Embraced me, parting for the Etrurian land,
And sent me to possess a large command.
He warned, and from his own experience told,
Our foes were warlike, disciplined, and bold.   70
And now, perhaps, in hopes of thy return,
Rich odors on his loaded altars burn,
While we, with vain officious pomp, prepare
To send him back his portion of the war,
A bloody breathless body, which can owe   75
No farther debt, but to the powers below.
The wretched father, ere his race is run,
Shall view the funeral honors of his son!
These are my triumphs of the Latian war,
Fruits of my plighted faith and boasted care!   80
And yet, unhappy sire, thou shalt not see
A son, whose death disgraced his ancestry:
Thou shalt not blush, old man, however grieved:
Thy Pallas no dishonest wound received.
He died no death to make thee wish, too late,   85
Thou hadst not lived to see his shameful fate.
But what a champion has the Ausonian coast,
And what a friend hast thou, Ascanius, lost!"
    Thus having mourned, he gave the word around,
To raise the breathless body from the ground;   90
And chose a thousand horse, the flower of all
His warlike troops, to wait the funeral,
To bear him back, and share Evander's grief—
A well becoming, but a weak relief.

94. *well becoming*: appropriate.

Of oaken twigs they twist an easy bier,   95
Then on their shoulders the sad burden rear.
The body on this rural hearse is borne:
Strewed leaves and funeral greens the bier adorn.
All pale he lies, and looks a lovely flower,
New cropt by virgin hands, to dress the bower: 100
Unfaded yet, but yet, unfed below,
No more to mother earth or the green stem shall owe.
Then two fair vests, of wondrous work and cost,
Of purple woven, and with gold embossed,
For ornament the Trojan hero brought,   105
Which with her hands Sidonian Dido wrought.
One vest arrayed the corpse; and one they spread
O'er his closed eyes, and wrapped around his head,
That, when the yellow hair in flame should fall,
The catching fire might burn the golden caul.   110
Besides, the spoils of foes in battle slain,
When he descended on the Latian plain—
Arms, trappings, horses, by the hearse are led
In long array—the achievements of the dead.
Then, pinioned with their hands behind, appear   115
The unhappy captives, marching in the rear,
Appointed offerings in the victor's name,
To sprinkle with their blood the funeral flame.
Inferior trophies by the chiefs are borne:
Gauntlets and helms their loaded hands adorn;   120
And fair inscriptions fixed, and titles read
Of Latian leaders conquered by the dead.
    Acoetes on his pupil's corpse attends,
With feeble steps, supported by his friends;
Pausing at every pace, in sorrow drowned,   125
Betwixt their arms he sinks upon the ground;
Where groveling while he lies in deep despair,
He beats his breast, and rends his hoary hair.
The champion's chariot next is seen to roll,
Besmeared with hostile blood, and honorably foul.   130
To close the pomp, Aethon, the steed of state,
Is led, the funerals of his lord to wait.

    103. *vests*: robes.

Stripped of his trappings, with a sullen pace
He walks; and the big tears run rolling down his face.
The lance of Pallas, and the crimson crest,   135
Are borne behind: the victor seized the rest.
The march begins: the trumpets hoarsely sound:
The pikes and lances trail along the ground.
Thus while the Trojan and Arcadian horse
To Palantean towers direct their course,   140
In long procession ranked; the pious chief
Stopped in the rear, and gave a vent to grief.
"The public care (he said) which war attends,
Diverts our present woes, at least suspends.
Peace with the manës of great Pallas dwell!   145
Hail, holy relics! and a last farewell!"
He said no more, but, inly though he mourned,
Restrained his tears, and to the camp returned.
 Now suppliants, from Laurentum sent, demand
A truce, with olive-branches in their hand;   150
Obtest his clemency, and from the plain
Beg leave to draw the bodies of their slain.
They plead, that none those common rites deny
To conquered foes, that in fair battle die.
All cause of hate was ended in their death;   155
Nor could he war with bodies void of breath.
A king, they hoped, would hear a king's request,
Whose son he once was called, and once his guest.
 Their suit, which was too just to be denied,
The hero grants, and further thus replied: 160
"O Latian princes! how severe a fate
In causeless quarrels has involved your state,
And armed against an unoffending man,
Who sought your friendship ere the war began!
You beg a truce, which I would gladly give,   165
Not only for the slain, but those who live.
I came not hither but by heaven's command,
And sent by fate to share the Latian land.
Nor wage I wars unjust: your king denied

  151. *Obtest*: invoke.

My proffered friendship and my promised bride: 170
Left me for Turnus. Turnus then should try
His cause in arms, to conquer or to die.
My right and his are in dispute: the slain
Fell without fault, our quarrel to maintain.
In equal arms let us alone contend;   175
And let him vanquish, whom his fates befriend.
This is the way (so tell him) to possess
The royal virgin, and restore the peace.
Bear this my message back—with ample leave
That your slain friends may funeral rites receive."   180
    Thus having said—the ambassadors, amazed,
Stood mute awhile, and on each other gazed.
Drances, their chief, who harbored in his breast
Long hate to Turnus, as his foe professed,
Broke silence first, and to the godlike man,   185
With graceful action bowing, thus began:
    "Auspicious prince, in arms a mighty name,
But yet whose actions far transcend your fame!
Would I your justice or your force express,
Thought can but equal; and all words are less.   190
Your answer we shall thankfully relate,
And favors granted to the Latian state.
If wished success our labors shall attend,
Think peace concluded, and the king your friend;
Let Turnus leave the realm to your command;   195
And seek alliance in some other land:
Build you the city which your fates assign;
We shall be proud in the great work to join."
Thus Drances; and his words so well persuade
The rest empowered, that soon a truce is made.   200
Twelve days the term allowed; and, during those,
Latians and Trojans, now no longer foes,
Mixed in the woods, for funeral piles prepare
To fell the timber, and forget the war.
Loud axes through the groaning groves resound: 205
Oak, mountain-ash, and poplar, spread the ground;
Firs fall from high; and some the trunks receive
In laden wains; with wedges some they cleave.

And now the fatal news by Fame is blown
Through the short circuit of the Arcadian town,   210
Of Pallas slain—by Fame, which just before
His triumph on distended pinions bore.
Rushing from out the gate, the people stand,
Each with a funeral flambeau in his hand.
Wildly they stare, distracted with amaze: 215
The fields are lightened with a fiery blaze,
That casts a sullen splendor on their friends—
The marching troop which their dead prince attends.
Both parties meet: they raise a doleful cry:
The matrons from the walls with shrieks reply;   220
And their mixed mourning rends the vaulted sky.
The town is filled with tumult and with tears,
Till the loud clamors reach Evander's ears:
Forgetful of his state, he runs along,
With a disordered pace, and cleaves the throng;   225
Falls on the corpse; and groaning there he lies,
With silent grief, that speaks but at his eyes.
Short sighs and sobs succeed; till sorrow breaks
A passage, and at once he weeps and speaks:
"O Pallas! thou hast failed thy plighted word!   230
To fight with caution, not to tempt the sword,
I warned thee, but in vain; for well I knew
What perils youthful ardor would pursue—
That boiling blood would carry thee too far,
Young as thou wert in dangers, raw to war!   235
O curst essay of arms! disastrous doom!
Prelude of bloody fields, and fights to come!
Hard elements of inauspicious war!
Vain vows to heaven, and unavailing care!
Thrice happy thou, dear partner of my bed!   240
Whose holy soul the stroke of Fortune fled—
Prescious of ills, and leaving me behind,
To drink the dregs of life by fate assigned.
Beyond the goal of nature I have gone:
My Pallas late set out, but reached too soon.   245

238. *inauspicious*: an epithet supplied by Dryden for war in general. Evander
did not call the wars to come inauspicious, nor were they, for Rome.

If, for my league against the Ausonian state,
Amidst their weapons I had found my fate
(Deserved from them), then I had been returned
A breathless victor, and my son had mourned.
Yet will I not my Trojan friend upbraid, 250
Nor grudge the alliance I so gladly made.
'Twas not his fault, my Pallas fell so young,
But my own crime for having lived too long.
Yet, since the gods had destined him to die,
At least, he led the way to victory: 255
First for his friends he won the fatal shore,
And sent whole herds of slaughtered foes before—
A death too great, too glorious to deplore.
Nor will I add new honors to thy grave,
Content with those the Trojan hero gave— 260
That funeral pomp thy Phrygian friends designed,
In which the Tuscan chiefs and army joined.
Great spoils and trophies, gained by thee, they bear:
Then let thy own achievements be thy share.
E'en thou, O Turnus, hadst a trophy stood, 265
Whose mighty trunk had better graced the wood,
If Pallas had arrived, with equal length
Of years, to match thy bulk with equal strength.
But why, unhappy man! dost thou detain
These troops, to view the tears thou shedd'st in vain? 270
Go, friends! this message to your lord relate:
Tell him, that, if I bear my bitter fate,
And, after Pallas' death, live lingering on,
'Tis to behold his vengeance for my son.
I stay for Turnus, whose devoted head 275
Is owing to the living and the dead.

My son and I expect it from his hand;
'Tis all that he can give, or we demand.
Joy is no more: but I would gladly go,
To greet my Pallas with such news below." 280
    The morn had now dispelled the shades of night,
Restoring toils, when she restored the light.
The Trojan king, and Tuscan chief, command
To raise the piles along the winding strand.

Their friends convey the dead to funeral fires;   285
Black smoldering smoke from the green wood expires;
The light of heaven is choked, and the new day retires.
Then thrice around the kindled piles they go
(For ancient custom had ordained it so):
Thrice horse and foot about the fires are led;   290
And thrice with loud laments they hail the dead.
Tears, trickling down their breasts, bedew the ground;
And drums and trumpets mix their mournful sound.
Amid the blaze, their pious brethren throw
The spoils, in battle taken from the foe—   295
Helms, bits embossed, and swords of shining steel;
One casts a target, one a chariot wheel;
Some to their fellows their own arms restore—
The falchions which in luckless fight they bore,
Their bucklers pierced, their darts bestowed in vain,   300
And shivered lances gathered from the plain.
Whole herds of offered bulls, about the fire,
And bristled boars, and woolly sheep, expire.
Around the piles a careful troop attends,
To watch the wasting flames, and weep their burning friends—   305
Lingering along the shore, till dewy night
New decks the face of heaven with starry light.
    The conquered Latians, with like pious care,
Piles without number for their dead prepare.
Part, in the places where they fell, are laid;   310
And part are to the neighboring fields conveyed.
The corpse of kings, and captains of renown,
Borne off in state, are buried in the town;
The rest, unhonored, and without a name,
Are cast a common heap to feed the flame.   315
Trojans and Latians vie with like desires
To make the field of battle shine with fires;
And the promiscuous blaze to heaven aspires.
    Now had the morning thrice renewed the light,
And thrice dispelled the shadows of the night,   320
When those who round the wasted fires remain,
Perform the last sad office to the slain.

    293. *drums*: of Dryden's time, not Virgil's.

They rake the yet warm ashes from below;
These, and the bones unburned, in earth bestow:
These relics with their country rites they grace,   325
And raise a mount of turf to mark the place.
   But, in the palace of the king, appears
A scene more solemn, and a pomp of tears.
Maids, matrons, widows, mix their common moans:
Orphans their sires, and sires lament their sons.   330
All in that universal sorrow share,
And curse the cause of this unhappy war—
A broken league, a bride unjustly sought,
A crown usurped, which with their blood is bought.
These are the crimes, with which they load the name   335
Of Turnus, and on him alone exclaim:
"Let him, who lords it o'er the Ausonian land,
Engage the Trojan hero hand to hand:
His is the gain; our lot is but to serve:
'Tis just, the sway he seeks, he should deserve."   340
This Drances aggravates; and adds, with spite,
"His foe expects, and dares him to the fight."
Nor Turnus wants a party, to support
His cause and credit in the Latian court.
His former acts secure his present fame;   345
And the queen shades him with her mighty name.
   While thus their factious minds with fury burn,
The legates from the Aetolian prince return:
Sad news they bring, that, after all the cost
And care employed, their embassy is lost;   350
That Diomede refused his aid in war,
Unmoved with presents, and as deaf to prayer.
Some new alliance must elsewhere be sought,
Or peace with Troy on hard conditions bought.
   Latinus, sunk in sorrow, finds too late   355
A foreign son is pointed out by fate;
And, till Aeneas shall Lavinia wed,
The wrath of heaven is hovering o'er his head.
The gods, he saw, espoused the juster side,
When late their titles in the field were tried: 360
Witness the fresh laments, and funeral tears undried.

Thus full of anxious thought, he summons all
The Latian senate to the council hall.
The princes come, commanded by their head,
And crowd the paths that to the palace lead.   365
Supreme in power, and reverenced for his years,
He takes the throne, and in the midst appears.
Majestically sad, he sits in state,
And bids his envoys their success relate.

When Venulus began, the murmuring sound   370
Was hushed, and sacred silence reigned around.
"We have (said he) performed your high command,
And passed with peril a long tract of land:
We reached the place desired; with wonder filled,
The Grecian tents and rising towers beheld.   375
Great Diomede has compassed round with walls
The city, which Argyripa he calls,
From his own Argos named. We touched, with joy,
The royal hand that razed unhappy Troy.
When introduced, our presents first we bring,   380
Then crave an instant audience from the king.
His leave obtained, our native soil we name,
And tell the important cause for which we came.
Attentively he heard us, while we spoke;
Then, with soft accents, and a pleasing look,   385
Made this return: 'Ausonian race, of old
Renowned for peace, and for an age of gold,
What madness has your altered minds possessed,
To change for war hereditary rest,
Solicit arms unknown, and tempt the sword—   390
A needless ill, your ancestors abhorred?
We—for myself I speak, and all the name
Of Grecians, who to Troy's destruction came
(Omitting those who were in battle slain,
Or borne by rolling Simoïs to the main)—   395
Not one but suffered, and too dearly bought
The prize of honor which in arms he sought.
Some doomed to death, and some in exile driven,
Outcasts, abandoned by the care of Heaven—

377. *Argyripa*: Arpi.

So worn, so wretched, so despised a crew,   400
As e'en old Priam might with pity view.
Witness the vessels by Minerva tossed
In storms—the vengeful Capharean coast—
The Euboean rocks—the prince, whose brother led
Our armies to revenge his injured bed,   405
In Egypt lost. Ulysses, with his men,
Have seen Charybdis, and the Cyclop's den.
Why should I name Idomeneus, in vain
Restored to scepters, and expelled again?
Or young Achilles, by his rival slain?   410
E'en he, the king of men, the foremost name
Of all the Greeks, and most renowned by fame,
The proud revenger of another's wife,
Yet by his own adulteress lost his life—
Fell at his threshold: and the spoils of Troy   415
The foul polluters of his bed enjoy.
The gods have envied me the sweets of life,
My much-loved country, and my more loved wife:
Banished from both, I mourn; while in the sky,
Transformed to birds, my lost companions fly;   420
Hovering about the coasts they make their moan,
And cuff the cliffs with pinions not their own.
What squalid specters, in the dead of night,
Break my short sleep, and skim before my sight!
I might have promised to myself those harms,   425
Mad as I was, when I, with mortal arms,
Presumed against immortal powers to move,
And violate with wounds the queen of love.
Such arms this hand shall never more employ.
No hate remains with me to ruined Troy,   430

---

403 sqq. Certain Greeks homeward bound from Troy were wrecked on the
promontory of Capharius in Eubaea. The storm drove Menelaus to Egypt where
he was "lost" for seven years. King Idomeneus of Crete vowed that if the sea
spared him he would sacrifice the first creature he met on going ashore; he met
his son, and his people exiled him for carrying out his vow. The "King of men"
in line 411 is of course Agamemnon.

417 sqq. For wounding Venus in battle at Troy Diomedes suffered the misfortunes he refers to: an unfaithful wife, exile from Argos, and haunting by birds
and specters.

I war not with its dust; nor am I glad
To think of past events, or good or bad.
Your presents I return; whate'er you bring
To buy my friendship, send the Trojan king.
We met in fight: I know him, to my cost: 435
With what a whirling force his lance he tossed!
Heavens! what a spring was in his arm, to throw!
How high he held his shield, and rose at every blow!
Had Troy produced two more his match in might,
They would have changed the fortune of the fight: 440
The invasion of the Greeks had been returned,
Our empire wasted, and our cities burned.
The long defense the Trojan people made,
The war protracted, and the siege delayed,
Were due to Hector's and this hero's hand: 445
Both brave alike, and equal in command;
Aeneas, not inferior in the field,
In pious reverence to the gods, excelled.
Make peace, ye Latians, and avoid with care
The impending dangers of a fatal war.'   450
He said no more; but with this cold excuse,
Refused the alliance, and advised a truce."
    Thus Venulus concluded his report.
A jarring murmur filled the factious court:
As, when a torrent rolls with rapid force,   455
And dashes o'er the stones that stop the course,
The flood, constrained within a scanty space,
Roars horrible along the uneasy race;
White foam in gathering eddies floats around;
The rocky shores rebellow to the sound.   460
    The murmur ceased: then from his lofty throne
The king invoked the gods, and thus begun:
"I wish, ye Latians, what ye now debate
Had been resolved before it was too late.
Much better had it been for you and me,   465
Unforced by this our last necessity,

---

438. *rose at every blow*: *quantus/ in clipeum adsurgat*, "how he towered up against his shield!"

To have been earlier wise, than now to call
A council, when the foe surrounds the wall.
O citizens! we wage unequal war,
With men, not only Heaven's peculiar care,   470
But Heaven's own race—unconquered in the field,
Or, conquered, yet unknowing how to yield.
What hopes you had in Diomede, lay down;
Our hopes must center on ourselves alone.
Yet those how feeble, and, indeed, how vain,   475
You see too well; nor need my words explain—
Vanquished without resource—laid flat by fate—
Factions within, a foe without the gate!
Not but I grant that all performed their parts
With manly force, and with undaunted hearts: 480
With our united strength the war we waged;
With equal numbers, equal arms, engaged:
You see the event.—Now hear what I propose,
To save our friends, and satisfy our foes.

 A tract of land the Latians have possessed   485
Along the Tiber, stretching to the west,
Which now Rutulians and Auruncans till;
And their mixed cattle graze the fruitful hill.
Those mountains filled with firs, that lower land,
If you consent, the Trojans shall command,   490
Called into part of what is ours; and there,
On terms agreed, the common country share.
There let them build and settle, if they please;
Unless they choose once more to cross the seas,
In search of seats remote from Italy,   495
And from unwelcome inmates set us free.
Then twice ten galleys let us build with speed,
Or twice as many more, if more they need.
Materials are at hand: a well-grown wood
Runs equal with the margin of the flood: 500
Let them the number and the form assign:
The care and cost of all the stores be mine.
To treat the peace, a hundred senators
Shall be commissioned hence with ample powers,

With olive crowned: the presents they shall bear, 505
A purple robe, a royal ivory chair,
And all the marks of sway that Latian monarchs wear,
And sums of gold. Among yourselves debate
This great affair, and save the sinking state."
 Then Drances took the word, who grudged long since, 510
The rising glories of the Daunian prince.
Factious and rich, bold at the council board,
But cautious in the field, he shunned the sword—
A close caballer, and tongue-valiant lord.
Noble his mother was, and near the throne: 515
But, what his father's parentage, unknown.
He rose, and took the advantage of the times,
To load young Turnus with invidious crimes.
"Such truths, O king (said he), your words contain,
As strike the sense, and all replies are vain; 520
Nor are your loyal subjects now to seek
What common needs require, but fear to speak.
Let him give leave of speech, that haughty man,
Whose pride this inauspicious war began;
For whose ambition (let me dare to say, 525
Fear set apart, though death is in my way),
The plains of Latium run with blood around;
So many valiant heroes bite the ground;
Dejected grief in every face appears;
A town in mourning, and a land in tears; 530
While he, the undoubted author of our harms,
The man who menaces the gods with arms,
Yet, after all his boasts, forsook the fight,
And sought his safety in ignoble flight.
Now, best of kings, since you propose to send 535
Such bounteous presents to your Trojan friend;
Add yet a greater at our joint request,
One which he values more than all the rest:
Give him the fair Lavinia for his bride:
With that alliance let the league be tied, 540
And for the bleeding land a lasting peace provide.
Let insolence no longer awe the throne;
But, with a father's right, bestow your own.

For this maligner of the general good,
If still we fear his force, he must be wooed: 545
His haughty godhead we with prayers implore,
Your scepter to release, and your just rites restore.
O cursed cause of all our ills! must we
Wage wars unjust, and fall in fight, for thee?
What right hast thou to rule the Latian state,   550
And send us out to meet our certain fate?
'Tis a destructive war: from Turnus' hand
Our peace and public safety we demand.
Let the fair bride to the brave chief remain:
If not, the peace, without the pledge, is vain.   555
Turnus, I know you think me not your friend,
Nor will I much with your belief contend:
I beg your greatness not to give the law
In other realms, but, beaten, to withdraw.
Pity your own, or pity our estate;   560
Nor twist our fortunes with your sinking fate.
Your interest is, the war should never cease;
But we have felt enough, to wish the peace—
A land exhausted to the last remains,
Depopulated towns, and driven plains.   565
Yet, if desire of fame, and thirst of power,
A beauteous princess, with a crown in dower,
So fire your mind, in arms assert your right,
And meet your foe, who dares you to the fight.
Mankind, it seems, is made for you alone!   570
We, but the slaves who mount you to the throne—
A base ignoble crowd, without a name,
Unwept, unworthy of the funeral flame,
By duty bound to forfeit each his life,
That Turnus may possess a royal wife!   575
Permit not, mighty man, so mean a crew
Should share such triumphs, and detain from you
The post of honor, your undoubted due.
Rather alone your matchless force employ,
To merit what alone you must enjoy."   580
   These words, so full of malice mixed with art,
Inflamed with rage the youthful hero's heart.

Then groaning from the bottom of his breast,
He heaved for wind, and thus his wrath expressed:
"You, Drances, never want a stream of words,   585
Then, when the public need requires our swords.
First in the council hall to steer the state,
And ever foremost in a tongue-debate,
While our strong walls secure us from the foe,
Ere yet with blood our ditches overflow: 590
But let the potent orator declaim,
And with the brand of coward blot my name;
Free leave is given him, when his fatal hand
Has covered with more corpse the sanguine strand,
And high as mine his towering trophies stand.   595
If any doubt remains who dares the most,
Let us decide it at the Trojans' cost,
And issue both abreast, where honor calls—
(Foes are not far to seek without the walls),
Unless his noisy tongue can only fight,   600
And feet were given him but to speed his flight.
I beaten from the field! I forced away!
Who, but so known a dastard, dares to say?
Had he but e'en beheld the fight, his eyes
Had witnessed for me what his tongue denies—   605
What heaps of Trojans by this hand were slain,
And how the bloody Tiber swelled the main.
All saw, but he, the Arcadian troops retire
In scattered squadrons, and their prince expire.
The giant brothers, in their camp, have found   610
I was not forced with ease to quit my ground.
Not such the Trojans tried me, when, inclosed,
I singly their united arms opposed—
First forced an entrance through their thick array,
Then, glutted with their slaughter, freed my way.   615
'Tis a destructive war! So let it be,
But to the Phrygian pirate, and to thee!
Meantime proceed to fill the people's ears
With false reports, their minds with panic fears:
Extol the strength of a twice-conquered race;   620
Our foes encourage, and our friends debase.

Believe thy fables, and the Trojan town
Triumphant stands; the Grecians are o'erthrown;
Suppliant at Hector's feet Achilles lies;
And Diomede from fierce Aeneas flies!   625
Say, rapid Aufidus with awful dread
Runs backward from the sea, and hides his head,
When the great Trojan on his bank appears;
For that's as true as thy dissembled fears
Of my revenge: dismiss that vanity: 630
Thou, Drances, art below a death from me.
Let that vile soul in that vile body rest,
The lodging is well worthy of the guest.
Now, royal father, to the present state
Of our affairs, and of this high debate—   635
If in your arms thus early you diffide,
And think your fortune is already tried;
If one defeat has brought us down so low,
As never more in fields to meet the foe;
Then I conclude for peace: 'tis time to treat,   640
And lie like vassals at the victor's feet.
But, oh! if any ancient blood remains,
One drop of all our father's, in our veins,
That man would I prefer before the rest,
Who dared his death with an undaunted breast;   645
Who comely fell by no dishonest wound,
To shun that sight, and, dying, gnawed the ground.
But, if we still have fresh recruits in store,
If our confederates can afford us more;
If the contended field we bravely fought,   650
And not a bloodless victory was bought;
Their losses equalled ours; and, for their slain,
With equal fires they filled the shining plain;
Why thus, unforced, should we so tamely yield,
And, ere the trumpet sounds, resign the field?   655
Good unexpected, evils unforeseen,
Appear by turns, as Fortune shifts the scene.
Some, raised aloft, come tumbling down amain;
Then fall so hard, they bound and rise again.

626. *Aufidus*: the river Ofanto in Apulia.

If Diomede refuse his aid to lend,   660
The great Messapus yet remains our friend:
Tolumnius, who foretells events, is ours;
The Italian chiefs, and princes, join their powers;
Nor least in number, nor in name the last,
Your own brave subjects have our cause embraced.   665
Above the rest, the Volscian Amazon
Contains an army in herself alone,
And heads a squadron, terrible to sight,
With glittering shields, in brazen armor bright.
Yet, if the foe a single fight demand,   670
And I alone the public peace withstand;
If you consent, he shall not be refused,
Nor find a hand to victory unused.
This new Achilles, let him take the field,
With fated armor, and Vulcanian shield!   675
For you, my royal father, and my fame,
I, Turnus, not the least of all my name,
Devote my soul. He calls me hand to hand;
And I alone will answer his demand.
Drances shall rest secure, and neither share   680
The danger, nor divide the prize, of war."
    While they debate, nor these nor those will yield,
Aeneas draws his forces to the field,
And moves his camp. The scouts with flying speed
Return, and through the frighted city spread   685
The unpleasing news: "The Trojans are described,
In battle marching by the riverside,
And bending to the town." They take the alarm:
Some tremble; some are bold; all in confusion arm.
The impetuous youth press forward to the field;   690
They clash the sword, and clatter on the shield:
The fearful matrons raise a screaming cry;
Old feeble men with fainter groans reply;
A jarring sound results, and mingles in the sky,
Like that of swans remurmuring to the floods,   695
Or birds of differing kinds in hollow woods.

    666. *Volscian Amazon*: Camilla.

Turnus the occasion takes, and cries aloud:
"Talk on, ye quaint haranguers of the crowd;
Declaim in praise of peace, when danger calls,
And the fierce foes in arms approach the walls."   700
He said, and, turning short with speedy pace,
Casts back a scornful glance, and quits the place.
"Thou, Volusus, the Volscian troops command
To mount; and lead thyself our Ardean band.
Messapus, and Catillus, post your force   705
Along the fields, to charge the Trojan horse.
Some guard the passes; others man the wall;
Drawn up in arms, the rest attend my call."
   They swarm from every quarter of the town,
And with disordered haste the rampires crown.   710
Good old Latinus, when he saw, too late,
The gathering storm just breaking on the state,
Dismissed the council till a fitter time,
And owned his easy temper as his crime,
Who, forced against his reason, had complied   715
To break the treaty for the promised bride.
   Some help to sink new trenches; others aid
To ram the stones, or raise the palisade.
Hoarse trumpets sound the alarm: around the walls
Runs a distracted crew, whom their last labor calls.   720
A sad procession in the streets is seen,
Of matrons, that attend the mother queen:
High in her chair she sits, and, at her side,
With downcast eyes, appears the fatal bride.
They mount the cliff, where Pallas' temple stands;   725
Prayers in their mouths, and presents in their hands.
With censers first they fume the sacred shrine,
Then in this common supplication join:
"O patroness of arms! unspotted maid!
Propitious hear, and lend thy Latins aid!   730
Break short the pirate's lance; pronounce his fate,
And lay the Phrygian low before the gate."

   718. *to ram the stones: saxa . . . subvectant,* "bring up stones" as missiles,
but not for cannon.

Now Turnus arms for fight. His back and breast
Well tempered steel and scaly brass invest:
The cuishes, which his brawny thighs infold,   735
Are mingled metal damasked o'er with gold.
His faithful falchion sits upon his side;
Nor casque, nor crest, his manly features hide
But, bare to view, amid surrounding friends,
With godlike grace, he from the tower descends.   740
Exulting in his strength, he seems to dare
His absent rival, and to promise war.

Freed from his keepers, thus, with broken reins,
The wanton courser prances o'er the plains,
Or in the pride of youth o'erleaps the mounds,   745
And snuffs the females in forbidden grounds;
Or seeks his watering in the well-known flood,
To quench his thirst, and cool his fiery blood:
He swims luxuriant in the liquid plain,
And o'er his shoulder flows his waving mane: 750
He neighs, he snorts, he bears his head on high;
Before his ample chest the frothy waters fly.

Soon as the prince appears without the gate,
The Volscians, and their virgin leader, wait
His last commands. Then, with a graceful mien,   755
Lights from her lofty steed the warrior-queen:
Her squadron imitates, and each descends;
Whose common suit Camilla thus commends:
"If sense of honor, if a soul secure
Of inborn worth, that can all tests endure,   760
Can promise aught, or on itself rely,
Greatly to dare to conquer or to die;
Then, I alone, sustained by these, will meet
The Tyrrhene troops, and promise their defeat.
Ours be the danger, ours the sole renown: 765
You, general, stay behind, and guard the town."
Turnus awhile stood mute with glad surprise,
And on the fierce virago fixed his eyes,
Then thus returned: "O grace of Italy!
With what becoming thanks can I reply?   770

Not only words lie laboring in my breast,
But thought itself is by thy praise oppressed.
Yet rob me not of all; but let me join
My toils, my hazard, and my fame, with thine.
The Trojan, not in stratagem unskilled,   775
Sends his light horse before to scour the field:
Himself, through steep ascents and thorny brakes,
A larger compass to the city takes.
This news my scouts confirm: and I prepare
To foil his cunning, and his force to dare;   780
With chosen foot his passage to forelay,
And place an ambush in the winding way.
Thou, with thy Volscians, face the Tuscan horse:
The brave Messapus shall my troops inforce
With those of Tibur, and the Latian band,   785
Subjected all to thy supreme command."
　　This said, he warns Messapus to the war,
Then every chief exhorts with equal care.
All thus encouraged, his own troop he joins,
And hastes to prosecute his deep designs.   790
　　Inclosed with hills, a winding valley lies,
By nature formed for fraud, and fitted for surprise.
A narrow track, by human steps untrode,
Leads, through perplexing thorns, to this obscure abode.
High o'er the vale a steepy mountain stands,   795
Whence the surveying sight the nether ground commands.
The top is level—an offensive seat
Of war; and from the war a safe retreat:
For, on the right and left, is room to press
The foes at hand, or from afar distress;   800
To drive them headlong downward; and to pour,
On their descending backs, a stony shower.
Thither young Turnus took the well-known way,
Possessed the pass, and in blind ambush lay.
　　Meantime, Latonian Phoebe, from the skies,   805
Beheld the approaching war with hateful eyes.

805. *Latonian*: daughter of Latona.

And called the light-foot Opis to her aid,
Her most beloved and ever-trusty maid;
Then with a sigh began: "Camilla goes
To meet her death amidst her fatal foes—   810
The nymph I loved of all my mortal train,
Invested with Diana's arms, in vain.
Nor is my kindness for the virgin new:
'Twas born with her; and with her years it grew.
Her father Metabus, when forced away   815
From old Privernum for tyrannic sway,
Snatched up, and saved from his prevailing foes,
This tender babe, companion of his woes.
Casmilla was her mother; but he drowned
One hissing letter in a softer sound,   820
And called Camilla. Through the woods he flies;
Wrapped in his robe the royal infant lies.
His foes in sight, he mends his weary pace;
With shouts and clamors they pursue the chase.
The banks of Amasene at length he gains;   825
The raging flood his farther flight restrains,
Raised o'er the borders with unusual rains.
Prepared to plunge into the stream, he fears,
Not for himself, but for the charge he bears.
Anxious, he stops awhile, and thinks in haste,   830
Then, desperate in distress, resolves at last.
A knotty lance of well boiled oak he bore;
The middle part with cork he covered o'er:
He closed the child within the hollow space;
With twigs of bending osier bound the case,   835
Then poised the spear, heavy with human weight,
And thus invoked my favor for the freight:
'Accept, great goddess of the woods (he said),
Sent by her sire, this dedicated maid!
Through air she flies a suppliant to thy shrine;   840
And the first weapons that she knows, are thine.'
He said; and with full force the spear he threw:
Above the sounding waves Camilla flew.

819–20. *drowned One hissing letter: mutata parte*, "one syllable changed."

Then, pressed by foes, he stemmed the stormy tide,
And gained, by stress of arms, the farther side.   845
His fastened spear he pulled from out the ground,
And, victor of his vows, his infant nymph unbound:
Nor, after that, in towns which walls inclose,
Would trust his hunted life amidst his foes;
But, rough, in open air he chose to lie;   850
Earth was his couch, his covering was the sky.
On hills unshorn, or in a desert den,
He shunned the dire society of men.
A shepherd's solitary life he led;
His daughter with the milk of mares he fed.   855
The dugs of bears, and every savage beast,
He drew, and through her lips the liquor pressed.
The little Amazon could scarcely go—
He loads her with a quiver and a bow;
And, that she might her staggering steps command,   860
He with a slender javelin fills her hand.
Her flowing hair no golden fillet bound:
Nor swept her trailing robe the dusty ground.
Instead of these, a tiger's hide o'erspread
Her back and shoulders, fastened to her head.   865
The flying dart she first attempts to fling,
And round her tender temples tossed the sling;
Then, as her strength with years increased, began
To pierce aloft in air the soaring swan,
And from the clouds to fetch the heron and the crane.   870
The Tuscan matrons with each other vied,
To bless their rival sons with such a bride:
But she disdains their love, to share with me
The sylvan shades, and vowed virginity.
And, oh! I wish, contented with my cares   875
Of savage spoils, she had not sought the wars:
Then had she been of my celestial train,
And shunned the fate that dooms her to be slain.
But since, opposing heaven's decree, she goes
To find her death among forbidden foes,   880
Haste with these arms, and take thy steepy flight,
Where, with the gods adverse, the Latins fight.

This bow to thee, this quiver, I bequeath,
This chosen arrow, to revenge her death:
By whate'er hand Camilla shall be slain,   885
Or of the Trojan or Italian train,
Let him not pass unpunished from the plain.
Then, in a hollow cloud, myself will aid
To bear the breathless body of my maid:
Unspoiled shall be her arms, and unprofaned   890
Her holy limbs with any human hand,
And in a marble tomb laid in her native land."
    She said. The faithful nymph descends from high
With rapid flight, and cuts the sounding sky:
Black clouds and stormy winds around her body fly.   895
    By this, the Trojan and the Tuscan horse,
Drawn up in squadrons, with united force
Approach the walls: the sprightly coursers bound,
Press forward on their bits, and shift their ground.
Shields, arms, and spears, flash horribly from far;   900
And the fields glitter with a waving war.
Opposed to these, come on with furious force
Messapus, Coras, and the Latian horse;
These in the body placed, on either hand
Sustained and closed by fair Camilla's band.   905
Advancing in a line, they couch their spears;
And less and less the middle space appears.
Thick smoke obscures the field; and scarce are seen
The neighing coursers, and the shouting men.
In distance of their darts they stop their course;   910
Then man to man they rush, and horse to horse.
The face of heaven their flying javelins hide,
And deaths unseen are dealt on either side.
Tyrrhenus, and Aconteus void of fear,
By mettled coursers borne in full career,   915
Meet first opposed; and, with a mighty shock,
Their horses' heads against each other knock.
Far from his steed is fierce Aconteus cast,
As with an engine's force, or lightning's blast:
He rolls along in blood, and breathes his last.   920

The Latian squadrons take a sudden fright,
And sling their shields behind, to save their backs in flight.
Spurring at speed, to their own walls they drew:
Close in the rear the Tuscan troops pursue,
And urge their flight: Asylas leads the chase; 925
Till, seized with shame, they wheel about, and face,
Receive their foes, and raise a threatening cry.
The Tuscans take their turn to fear and fly.
  So swelling surges, with a thundering roar,
Driven on each other's backs, insult the shore, 930
Bound o'er the rocks, encroach upon the land,
And far upon the beach eject the sand;
Then backward, with a swing, they take their way,
Repulsed from upper ground, and seek their mother sea;
With equal hurry quit the invaded shore, 935
And swallow back the sand and stones they spewed before.
Twice were the Tuscans masters of the field,
Twice by the Latins, in their turn, repelled.
Ashamed at length, to the third charge they ran—
Both hosts resolved, and mingled man to man. 940
Now dying groans are heard; the fields are strewed
With falling bodies, and are drunk with blood.
Arms, horses, men, on heaps together lie;
Confused the fight, and more confused the cry.
  Orsilochus, who durst not press too near 945
Strong Remulus, at distance drove his spear,
And stuck the steel beneath his horse's ear.
The fiery steed, impatient of the wound,
Curvets, and, springing upward with a bound,
His helpless lord cast backward on the ground. 950
Catillus pierced Iölas first; then drew
His reeking lance, and at Herminius threw,
The mighty champion of the Tuscan crew.
His neck and throat unarmed, his head was bare,
But shaded with a length of yellow hair: 955
Secure, he fought, exposed on every part,
A spacious mark for swords, and for the flying dart.

Across the shoulders came the feathered wound;
Transfixed, he fell, and doubled to the ground.
   The sands with streaming blood are sanguine dyed,   960
And death, with honor, sought on either side.
   Resistless, through the war Camilla rode,
In danger unappalled, and pleased with blood.
One side was bare for her exerted breast;
One shoulder with her painted quiver pressed.   965
Now from afar her fatal javelins play;
Now with her axe's edge, she hews her way:
Diana's arms upon her shoulder sound;
And when, too closely pressed, she quits the ground,
From her bent bow she sends a backward wound.   970
Her maids, in martial pomp, on either side,
Larina, Tulla, fierce Tarpeia, ride—
Italians all—in peace their queen's delight;
In war, the bold companions of the fight.
   So marched the Thracian Amazons of old,   975
When Thermoden with bloody billows rolled:
Such troops as these in shining arms were seen,
When Theseus met in fight their maiden queen:
Such to the field Penthesilea led,
From the fierce virgin when the Grecians fled;   980
With such returned triumphant from the war.
Her maids with cries attend the lofty car;
They clash with manly force their moony shields;
With female shouts resound the Phrygian fields.
   Who foremost, and who last, heroic maid,   985
On the cold earth were by thy courage laid?
Thy spear, of mountain-ash, Eunaeus first,
With fury driven, from side to side transpierced:
A purple stream came spouting from the wound;
Bathed in his blood he lies, and bites the ground.   990
Liris and Pegasus at once she slew:
The former, as the slackened reins he drew,
Of his faint steed—the latter, as he stretched
His arm to prop his friend—the javelin reached.

   964. *unum exserta latus pugnae*: "on one side bare-breasted for the fight."
Same effect as in Book I, 692.

By the same weapon, sent from the same hand, 995
Both fall together, and both spurn the sand.
Amastrus next is added to the slain:
The rest in rout she follows o'er the plain:
Tereus, Harpalycus, Demophoön,
And Chromis, at full speed her fury shun. 1000
Of all her deadly darts, not one she lost;
Each was attended with a Trojan ghost.
   Young Ornytus bestrode a hunter steed,
Swift for the chase, and of Apulian breed.
Him, from afar, she spied in arms unknown: 1005
O'er his broad back an ox's hide was thrown;
His helm a wolf, whose gaping jaws were spread
A covering for his cheeks, and grinned around his head.
He clenched within his hand an iron prong,
And towered above the rest, conspicuous in the throng. 1010
Him soon she singled from the flying train,
And slew with ease; then thus insults the slain:
"Vain hunter! didst thou think through woods to chase
The savage herd, a vile and trembling race?
Here cease thy vaunts, and own my victory: 1015
A woman warrior was too strong for thee.
Yet, if the ghosts demand the conqueror's name,
Confessing great Camilla, save thy shame."
   Then Butès and Orsilochus she slew,
The bulkiest bodies of the Trojan crew— 1020
But Butès breast to breast: the spear descends
Above the gorget, where his helmet ends,
And o'er the shield which his left side defends.
Orsilochus, and she, their coursers ply:
He seems to follow, and she seems to fly. 1025
But in a narrower ring she makes the race;
And then he flies, and she pursues the chase.
Gathering at length on her deluded foe,
She swings her axe, and rises to the blow;
Full on the helm behind, with such a sway 1030
The weapon falls, the riven steel gives way:

    1026. *a narrower ring*: a maneuver much later employed for dogfighting in
pursuit planes.

He groans, he roars, he sues in vain for grace:
Brains, mingled with his blood, besmear his face.
Astonished Aunus just arrives by chance,
To see his fall, nor farther dares advance;   1035
But, fixing on the horrid maid his eye,
He stares, and shakes, and finds it vain to fly;
Yet, like a true Ligurian, born to cheat,
(At least while Fortune favored his deceit),
Cries out aloud: "What courage have you shown,   1040
Who trust your courser's strength, and not your own?
Forego the 'vantage of your horse, alight,
And then on equal terms begin the fight:
It shall be seen, weak woman, what you can,
When foot to foot, you combat with a man."   1045
He said. She glows with anger and disdain,
Dismounts with speed to dare him on the plain,
And leaves her horse at large among her train;
With her drawn sword defies him to the field,
And, marching, lifts aloft her maiden shield.   1050
The youth, who thought his cunning did succeed,
Reins round his horse, and urges all his speed:
Adds the remembrance of the spur, and hides
The goring rowels in his bleeding sides.
"Vain fool, and coward! (said the lofty maid),   1055
Caught in the train which thou thyself hast laid!
On others practice thy Ligurian arts:
Thin stratagems, and tricks of little hearts,
Are lost on me; nor shalt thou safe retire,
With vaunting lies, to thy fallacious sire."   1060
    At this, so fast her flying feet she sped,
That soon she strained beyond his horse's head:
Then turning short, at once she seized the rein,
And laid the boaster groveling on the plain.
Not with more ease the falcon, from above,   1065
Trusses, in middle air, the trembling dove,

1038. *Ligurian*: Liguria lies northwest of Tuscany. Its coast is now the
Italian Riviera.

Then plumes the prey, in her strong pounces bound:
The feathers, foul with blood, come tumbling to the ground.
   Now mighty Jove, from his superior height,
With his broad eye surveys the unequal fight.   1070
He fires the breast of Tarchon with disdain,
And sends him to redeem the abandoned plain.
Between the broken ranks the Tuscan rides,
And these encourages, and those he chides;
Recalls each leader, by his name, from flight;   1075
Renews their ardor, and restores the fight.
"What panic fear has seized your souls? O shame,
O brand perpetual of the Etrurian name!
Cowards incurable! a woman's hand
Drives, breaks, and scatters, your ignoble band!   1080
Now cast away the sword, and quit the shield!
What use of weapons which you dare not wield?
Not thus you fly your female foes by night,
Nor shun the feast, when the full bowls invite;
When to fat offerings the glad augur calls,   1085
And the shrill horn-pipe sounds to bacchanals.
These are your studied cares, your lewd delight—
Swift to debauch, but slow to manly fight."
Thus having said, he spurs amidst the foes,
Not managing the life he meant to lose.   1090
The first he found he seized, with headlong haste,
In his strong gripe, and clasped around the waist:
'Twas Venulus, whom from his horse he tore,
And (laid athwart his own) in triumph bore.
Loud shouts ensue; the Latins turn their eyes,   1095
And view the unusual sight with vast surprise.
The fiery Tarchon, flying o'er the plains,
Pressed in his arms the ponderous prey sustains,
Then, with his shortened spear, explores around
His jointed arms, to fix a deadly wound.   1100
Nor less the captive struggles for his life:
He writhes his body to prolong the strife,
And, fencing for his naked throat, exerts
His utmost vigor, and the point averts.

So stoops the yellow eagle from on high,   1105
And bears a speckled serpent through the sky,
Fastening his crooked talons on the prey:
The prisoner hisses through the liquid way;
Resists the royal hawk; and, though oppressed,
She fights in volumes, and erects her crest: 1110
Turned to her foe, she stiffens every scale,
And shoots her forky tongue, and whisks her threatening tail.
Against the victor, all defense is weak:
The imperial bird still plies her with his beak;
He tears her bowels, and her breast he gores,   1115
Then claps his pinions, and securely soars.
    Thus, through the midst of circling enemies,
Strong Tarchon snatched and bore away his prize.
The Tyrrhene troops, that shrunk before, now press
The Latins, and presume the like success.   1120
    Then Arruns, doomed to death, his arts essayed
To murder, unespied, the Volscian maid:
This way and that his winding course he bends,
And wheresoe'er she turns, her steps attends.
When she retires victorious from the chase,   1125
He wheels about with care, and shifts his place:
When, rushing on, she seeks her foes in fight,
He keeps aloof, but keeps her still in sight;
He threats, and trembles, trying every way,
Unseen to kill, and safely to betray.   1130
    Chloreus, the priest of Cybele, from far,
Glittering in Phrygian arms amidst the war,
Was by the virgin viewed. The steed he pressed
Was proud with trappings; and his brawny chest
With scales of gilded brass was covered o'er: 1135
A robe of Tyrian dye the rider wore.
With deadly wounds he galled the distant foe;
Gnossian his shafts, and Lycian was his bow:
A golden helm his front and head surrounds;
A gilded quiver from his shoulder sounds.   1140

    1110. *volumes*: coils.

Gold, weaved with linen, on his thighs he wore,
With flowers of needlework distinguished o'er,
With golden buckles bound, and gathered up before.
Him the fierce maid beheld with ardent eyes,
Fond and ambitious of so rich a prize,   1145
Or that the temple might his trophies hold,
Or else to shine herself in Trojan gold.
Blind in her haste, she chases him alone,
And seeks his life, regardless of her own.
This lucky moment the sly traitor chose;   1150
Then, starting from his ambush, up he rose,
And threw, but first to heaven addressed his vows
"O patron of Soracte's high abodes!
Phoebus, the ruling power among the gods!
Whom first we serve; whole woods of unctuous pine   1155
Are felled for thee, and to thy glory shine;
By thee protected, with our naked soles,
Through flames unsinged we march, and tread the kindled coals.
Give me, propitious power, to wash away
The stains of this dishonorable day: 1160
Nor spoils, nor triumph, from the fact I claim,
But with my future actions trust my fame.
Let me, by stealth, this female plague o'ercome,
And from the field return inglorious home."

    Apollo heard, and, granting half his prayer,   1165
Shuffled in winds the rest, and tossed in empty air.
He gives the death desired: his safe return
By southern tempests to the seas is borne.

    Now, when the javelin whizzed along the skies,
Both armies on Camilla turned their eyes,   1170
Directed by the sound. Of either host,
The unhappy virgin, though concerned the most,
Was only deaf; so greedy was she bent
On golden spoils, and on her prey intent;

    1153. *Soracte's high abodes*: Mount Soracte in Latium, site of an ancient cult
of the god Soranus, later identified with Apollo. Pliny in his *Natural History*
(Book VII, 2, 19) speaks of the worshippers walking unharmed over live embers.

Till in her pap the wingèd weapon stood   1175
Infixed, and deeply drunk the purple blood.
Her sad attendants hasten to sustain
Their dying lady drooping on the plain.
Far from their sight the trembling Arruns flies,
With beating heart, and fear confused with joys;   1180
Nor dares he farther to pursue his blow,
Or e'en to bear the sight of his expiring foe.
    As, when the wolf has torn a bullock's hide
At unawares, or ranched a shepherd's side,
Conscious of his audacious deed, he flies,   1185
And claps his quivering tail between his thighs:
So, speeding once, the wretch no more attends,
But, spurring forward, herds among his friends.
She wrenched the javelin with her dying hands,
But wedged within her breast the weapon stands;   1190
The wood she draws, the steely point remains:
She staggers in her seat with agonizing pains
(A gathering mist o'erclouds her cheerful eyes;
And from her cheeks the rosy color flies):
Then turns to her, whom, of her female train   1195
She trusted most, and thus she speaks with pain:
"Acca, 'tis past! he swims before my sight,
Inexorable Death; and claims his right.
Bear my last words to Turnus: fly with speed,
And bid him timely to my charge succeed,   1200
Repel the Trojans, and the town relieve:
Farewell! and in this kiss my parting breath receive."
She said, and, sliding, sunk upon the plain:
Dying, her opened hand forsakes the rein:
Short, and more short, she pants: by slow degrees   1205
Her mind the passage from her body frees.
She drops her sword; she nods her plumy crest,
Her drooping head declining on her breast;
In the last sigh her struggling soul expires,
And, murmuring with disdain, to Stygian sounds retires. 1210

1184. *ranched:* probably a nasal dialect form of "rashed," or "slashed,"
"lacerated."

A shout, that struck the golden stars ensued;
Despair and rage, and languished fight renewed.
The Trojan troops and Tuscans, in a line,
Advance to charge; the mixed Arcadians join.
    But Cynthia's maid, high seated, from afar   1215
Surveys the field, and fortune of the war,
Unmoved awhile, till, prostrate on the plain,
Weltering in blood, she sees Camilla slain,
And, round her corpse, of friends and foes a fighting train.
Then, from the bottom of her breast, she drew   1220
A mournful sigh, and these sad words ensue:
"Too dear a fine, ah, much lamented maid!
For warring with the Trojans thou hast paid:
Nor aught availed, in this unhappy strife,
Diana's sacred arms, to have thy life.   1225
Yet unrevenged thy goddess will not leave
Her votary's death, nor with vain sorrow grieve.
Branded the wretch, and be his name abhorred;
But, after ages shall thy praise record.
The inglorious coward soon shall press the plain: 1230
Thus vows thy queen, and thus the Fates ordain."
    High o'er the field, there stood a hilly mound—
Sacred the place, and spread with oaks around—
Where, in a marble tomb, Dercennus lay,
A king that once in Latium bore the sway.   1235
The beauteous Opis thither bent her flight,
To mark the traitor Arruns from the height.
Him in refulgent arms she soon espied,
Swoln with success; and loudly thus she cried.
"Thy backward steps, vain boaster, are too late;   1240
Turn, like a man, at length, and meet thy fate.
Charged with my message, to Camilla go,
And say I sent thee to the shades below—
An honor undeserved from Cynthia's bow."
    She said, and from her quiver chose with speed   1245
The wingèd shaft, predestined for the deed;
Then to the stubborn yew her strength applied,
Till the far distant horns approached on either side.

The bowstring touched her breast, so strong she drew;
Whizzing in air the fatal arrow flew.   1250
At once the twanging bow and sounding dart
The traitor heard, and felt the point within his heart.
Him, beating with his heels in pangs of death,
His flying friends to foreign fields bequeath.
The conquering damsel, with expanded wings,   1255
The welcome message to her mistress brings.
   Their leader lost, the Volscians quit the field;
And, unsustained, the chiefs of Turnus yield.
The frighted soldiers, when their captains fly,
More on their speed than on their strength rely.   1260
Confused in flight, they bear each other down,
And spur their horses headlong to the town.
Driven by their foes, and to their fears resigned,
Not once they turn, but take their wounds behind.
These drop the shield, and those the lance forego,   1265
Or on their shoulders bear the slackened bow.
The hoofs of horses, with a rattling sound,
Beat short and thick, and shake the rotten ground.
Black clouds of dust come rolling in the sky,
And o'er the darkened walls and rampires fly.   1270
The trembling matrons, from their lofty stands,
Rend heaven with female shrieks, and wring their hands.
All pressing on, pursuers and pursued,
Are crushed in crowds, a mingled multitude.
Some happy few escape: the throng too late   1275
Rush on for entrance, till they choke the gate.
E'en in the sight of home, the wretched sire
Looks on, and sees his helpless son expire.
Then, in a fright, the folding gates they close,
But leave their friends excluded with their foes.   1280
The vanquished cry; the victors loudly shout:
'Tis terror all within, and slaughter all without.

   1267–8. *quadrupedumque putrem cursu quatit ungula campum*: a variation
on the line translated in Book VIII, 790. Here Dryden apparently thought he
might do something with it, and did.
   1268. *rotten*: crumbling, friable.

Blind in their fear, they bounce against the wall,
Or, to the moats pursued, precipitate their fall.
    The Latian virgins, valiant with despair,   1285
Armed on the towers, the common danger share:
So much of zeal their country's cause inspired;
So much Camilla's great example fired.
Poles, sharpened in the flames, from high they throw,
With imitated darts to gall the foe.   1290
Their lives for godlike freedom they bequeath,
And crowd each other to be first in death.
Meantime to Turnus, ambushed in the shade,
With heavy tidings came the unhappy maid:
"The Volscians overthrown—Camilla killed—   1295
The foes entirely masters of the field,
Like a resistless flood, come rolling on:
The cry goes off the plain, and thickens to the town."
    Inflamed with rage (for so the Furies fire
The Daunian's breast, and so the Fates require),   1300
He leaves the hilly pass, the woods in vain
Possessed, and downward issues on the plain.
Scarce was he gone, when to the straits, now freed
From secret foes, the Trojan troops succeed.
Through the black forest and the ferny brake,   1305
Unknowingly secure, their way they take;
From the rough mountains to the plain descend,
And there, in order drawn, their line extend.
Both armies now in open fields are seen;
Not far the distance of the space between.   1310
Both to the city bend. Aeneas sees,
Through smoking fields, his hastening enemies;
And Turnus views the Trojans in array,
And hears the approaching horses proudly neigh.
Soon had their hosts in bloody battle joined;   1315
But westward to the sea the sun declined.
Intrenched before the town, both armies lie,
While night with sable wings involves the sky.

♫♫♫

BOOK XII

THE ARGUMENT

Turnus challenges Aeneas to a single combat: articles are agreed on, but
broken by the Rutuli, who wound Aeneas. He is miraculously cured by
Venus, forces Turnus to a duel, and concludes the poem with his death.

WHEN Turnus saw the Latins leave the field,
Their armies broken, and their courage quelled,
Himself become the mark of public spite,
His honor questioned for the promised fight—
The more he was with vulgar hate oppressed,   5
The more his fury boiled within his breast:
He roused his vigor for the last debate,
And raised his haughty soul, to meet his fate.
　As, when the swains the Libyan lion chase,
He makes a sour retreat, nor mends his pace;   10
But, if the pointed javelin pierce his side,
The lordly beast returns with double pride:
He wrenches out the steel; he roars for pain;
His sides he lashes, and erects his mane:
So Turnus fares: his eyeballs flash with fire;   15
Through his wide nostrils clouds of smoke expire.
　Trembling with rage, around the court he ran;
At length approached the king, and thus began:
"No more excuses or delays: I stand
In arms prepared to combat, hand to hand,   20

5. *vulgar hate*: unpopularity.
16. This particular hyperbole is not Virgil's.

378

This base deserter of his native land.
The Trojan, by his word, is bound to take
The same conditions which himself did make.
Renew the truce; the solemn rites prepare,
And to my single virtue trust the war. 25
The Latians unconcerned shall see the fight:
This arm unaided shall assert your right:
Then, if my prostrate body press the plain,
To him the crown and beauteous bride remain."
    To whom the king sedately thus replied: 30
"Brave youth! the more your valor has been tried,
The more becomes it us, with due respect,
To weigh the chance of war, which you neglect.
You want not wealth, or a successive throne,
Or cities which your arms have made your own: 35
My towns and treasures are at your command;
And stored with blooming beauties is my land:
Laurentum more than one Lavinia sees,
Unmarried, fair, of noble families.
Now let me speak, and you with patience hear, 40
Things which perhaps may grate a lover's ear,
But sound advice, proceeding from a heart
Sincerely yours, and free from fraudful art.
The gods, by signs, have manifestly shown,
No prince, Italian born, should heir my throne: 45
Oft have our augurs, in prediction skilled,
And oft our priests, a foreign son revealed.
Yet, won by worth that cannot be withstood,
Bribed by my kindness to my kindred blood,
Urged by my wife, who would not be denied, 50
I promised my Lavinia for your bride:
Her from her plighted lord by force I took;
All ties of treaties, and of honor, broke:
On your account I waged an impious war—
With what success, 'tis needless to declare; 55
I and my subjects feel, and you have had your share.
Twice vanquished while in bloody fields we strive,
Scarce in our walls we keep our hopes alive:

The rolling flood runs warm with human gore;
The bones of Latians blanch the neighboring shore.   60
Why put I not an end to this debate,
Still unresolved, and still a slave to fate?
If Turnus' death a lasting peace can give,
Why should I not procure it whilst you live?
Should I to doubtful arms your youth betray,   65
What would my kinsmen, the Rutulians, say?
And, should you fall in fight (which Heaven defend!)
How curse the cause, which hastened to his end
The daughter's lover, and the father's friend?
Weigh in your mind the various chance of war;   70
Pity your parent's age, and ease his care."
    Such balmy words he poured, but all in vain:
The proffered med'cine but provoked the pain.
The wrathful youth, disdaining the relief,
With intermitting sobs thus vents his grief: 75
"The care, O best of fathers! which you take
For my concerns, at my desire forsake.
Permit me not to languish out my days,
But make the best exchange of life for praise.
This arm, this lance, can well dispute the prize;   80
And the blood follows where the weapon flies.
His goddess-mother is not near, to shroud
The flying coward with an empty cloud."
    But now the queen, who feared for Turnus' life,
And loathed the hard conditions of the strife,   85
Held him by force; and, dying in his death,
In these sad accents gave her sorrow breath:
"O Turnus! I adjure thee by these tears,
And whate'er price Amata's honor bears
Within thy breast, since thou art all my hope,   90
My sickly mind's repose, my sinking age's prop—
Since on the safety of thy life alone
Depends Latinus, and the Latian throne—
Refuse me not this one, this only prayer,
To waive the combat, and pursue the war.   95
Whatever chance attends this fatal strife,
Think it includes, in thine, Amata's life.

I cannot live a slave, or see my throne
Usurped by strangers, or a Trojan son."
　At this, a flood of tears Lavinia shed;   100
A crimson blush her beauteous face o'erspread,
Varying her cheeks by turns with white and red,
The driving colors, never at a stay,
Run here and there, and flush and fade away.
Delightful change! Thus Indian ivory shows,   105
Which with the bordering paint of purple glows;
Or lilies damasked by the neighboring rose.
The lover gazed, and, burning with desire,
The more he looked, the more he fed the fire:
Revenge, and jealous rage, and secret spite,   110
Roll in his breast, and rouse him to the fight.
　Then fixing on the queen his ardent eyes,
Firm to his first intent, he thus replies:
"O mother! do not by your tears prepare
Such boding omens, and prejudge the war: 115
Resolved on fight, I am no longer free
To shun my death, if heaven my death decree."
Then turning to the herald, thus pursues:
"Go, greet the Trojan with ungrateful news;
Denounce from me, that, when tomorrow's light   120
Shall gild the heavens, he need not urge the fight:
The Trojan and Rutulian troops no more
Shall dye, with mutual blood, the Latian shore:
Our single swords the quarrel shall decide,
And to the victor be the beauteous bride."   125
　He said, and striding on, with speedy pace,
He sought his coursers of the Thracian race.
At his approach, they toss their heads on high,
And, proudly neighing, promise victory.

100-7. Of Lavinia's preference for Turnus, Dryden wrote: "She had been
bred up with Turnus, and Aeneas was wholly a stranger to her. Turnus in proba-
bility was her first love; and favored by her mother, who had the ascendant over
her father. But I am much deceived if (besides what I have said) there be not a
secret satire against the sex, which is lurking under this description of Virgil, who
seldom speaks well of Women. . . . This fable of Lavinia includes a secret moral;
that women in their choice of husbands prefer the younger of their suitors to the
elder; are insensible of merit, fond of handsomeness; and generally speaking,
rather hurried away by their appetite than governed by their reason."

The sires of these Orithyia sent from far,   130
To grace Pilumnus, when he went to war.
The drifts of Thracian snows were scarce so white,
Nor northern winds in fleetness matched their flight.
Officious grooms stand ready by his side;
And some with combs their flowing manes divide,   135
And others stroke their chests, and gently soothe their pride.
   He sheathed his limbs in arms; a tempered mass
Of golden metal those, and mountain brass.
Then to his head his glittering helm he tied,
And girt his faithful falchion to his side.   140
In his Aetnaean forge, the god of fire
That falchion labored for the hero's sire,
Immortal keenness on the blade bestowed,
And plunged it hissing in the Stygian flood.
Propped on a pillar, which the ceiling bore,   145
Was placed the lance Auruncan Actor wore;
Which with such force he brandished in his hand,
The tough ash trembled like an osier wand:
Then cried: "O ponderous spoil of Actor slain,
And never yet by Turnus tossed in vain!   150
Fail not this day thy wonted force; but go,
Sent by this hand, to pierce the Trojan foe:
Give me to tear his corselet from his breast,
And from that eunuch head to rend the crest;
Dragged in the dust, his frizzled hair to soil,   155
Hot from the vexing iron, and smeared with fragrant oil."
   Thus while he raves, from his wide nostrils flies
A fiery steam, and sparkles from his eyes.
So fares the bull in his loved female's sight:
Proudly he bellows, and preludes the fight: 160
He tries his goring horns against a tree,
And meditates his absent enemy:
He pushes at the winds; he digs the strand
With his black hoofs, and spurns the yellow sand.

   146. *Auruncan Actor*: Actor appeared in Book IX, 665. His death at Turnus'
hands has not been mentioned before.
   154. *that eunuch head*: *semiviri Phrygis*, "the half-male Phrygian." This and
the following details accorded with later Phrygian reputation.

Nor less the Trojan, in his Lemnian arms, 165
To future fight his manly courage warms:
He whets his fury, and with joy prepares
To terminate at once the lingering wars;
To cheer his chiefs and tender son, relates
What heaven had promised, and expounds the fates. 170
Then to the Latian king he sends, to cease
The rage of arms, and ratify the peace.
  The morn ensuing, from the mountain's height,
Had scarcely spread the skies with rosy light;
The ethereal coursers, bounding from the sea, 175
From out their flaming nostrils breathed the day;
When now the Trojan and Rutulian guard,
In friendly labor joined, the list prepared.
Beneath the walls, they measure out the space;
Then sacred altars rear, on sods of grass, 180
Where, with religious rites, their common gods they place.
In purest white, the priests their heads attire,
And living waters bear, and holy fire;
And, o'er their linen hoods and shaded hair,
Long twisted wreaths of sacred vervain wear. 185
  In order issuing from the town, appears
The Latian legion, armed with pointed spears;
And from the fields, advancing on a line,
The Trojan and the Tuscan forces join:
Their various arms afford a pleasing sight: 190
A peaceful train they seem, in peace prepared for fight.
  Betwixt the ranks the proud commanders ride,
Glittering with gold, and vests in purple dyed—
Here Mnestheus, author of the Memmian line,
And there Messapus, born of seed divine. 195
The sign is given; and round the listed space,
Each man in order fills his proper place.
Reclining on their ample shields, they stand,
And fix their pointed lances in the sand.
Now, studious of the sight, a numerous throng 200
Of either sex promiscuous, old and young,
Swarm from the town: by those who rest behind,
The gates and walls, and houses' tops, are lined.

Meantime the queen of heaven beheld the sight,
With eyes unpleased, from mount Albano's height: 205
(Since called Albano by succeeding fame,
But then an empty hill, without a name.)
She thence surveyed the field, the Trojan powers,
The Latian squadrons, and Laurentine towers.
Then thus the goddess of the skies bespake,   210
With sighs and tears, the goddess of the lake,
King Turnus' sister, once a lovely maid,
Ere to the lust of lawless Jove betrayed—
Compressed by force, but, by the grateful god,
Now made the Naïs of the neighboring flood.   215
"O nymph, the pride of living lakes! (said she)
O most renowned, and most beloved by me!
Long hast thou known, nor need I to record,
The wanton sallies of my wandering lord.
Of every Latian fair, whom Jove misled   220
To mount by stealth my violated bed,
To thee alone I grudged not his embrace,
But gave a part of heaven, and an unenvied place.
Now learn from me thy near-approaching grief,
Nor think my wishes want to thy relief.   225
While Fortune favored, nor heaven's king denied
To lend my succor to the Latian side,
I saved thy brother, and the sinking state;
But now he struggles with unequal fate,
And goes, with gods averse, o'ermatched in might,   230
To meet inevitable death in fight;
Nor must I break the truce, nor can sustain the sight.
Thou, if thou dar'st, thy present aid supply:
It well becomes a sister's care to try."
  At this the lovely nymph, with grief oppressed,   235
Thrice tore her hair, and beat her comely breast.

---

214. *Compressed*: a Jovian act. Ruaeus explained *Marte gravis* in Book I as
a Marte compressa. Dryden had used the expression in *The Hind and the Panther*,
Book I, 352:

> A lion old, obscene, and furious made
> By lust, compressed her mother in a shade.

To whom Saturnia thus: "Thy tears are late:
Haste, snatch him, if he can be snatched, from fate:
New tumults kindle; violate the truce.
Who knows what changeful Fortune may produce?   240
'Tis not a crime to attempt what I decree;
Or, if it were, discharge the crime on me."
She said, and sailing on the wingèd wind,
Left the sad nymph suspended in her mind.

   And now in pomp the peaceful kings appear: 245
Four steeds the chariot of Latinus bear:
Twelve golden beams around his temples play,
To mark his lineage from the god of day.
Two snowy coursers Turnus' chariot yoke,
And in his hand two massy spears he shook.   250
Then, issued from the camp, in arms divine,
Aeneas, author of the Roman line;
And by his side Ascanius took his place,
The second hope of Rome's immortal race.
Adorned in white, a reverend priest appears,   255
And offerings to the flaming altars bears—
A porket, and a lamb that never suffered shears.
Then to the rising sun he turns his eyes,
And strews the beasts, designed for sacrifice,
With salt and meal: with like officious care   260
He marks their foreheads, and he clips their hair.
Betwixt their horns the purple wine he sheds;
With the same generous juice the flame he feeds.
Aeneas then unsheathed his shining sword,
And thus with pious prayers the gods adored: 265

   "All-seeing sun! and thou, Ausonian soil,
For which I have sustained so long a toil,
Thou, king of heaven! and thou, the queen of air,
Propitious now, and reconciled by prayer;
Thou, god of war, whose unresisted sway   270
The labors and events of arms obey!
Ye living fountains, and ye running floods!
All powers of ocean, all ethereal gods!
Hear, and bear record: if I fall in field,
Or, recreant in the fight, to Turnus yield,   275

My Trojans shall increase Evander's town;
Ascanius shall renounce the Ausonian crown:
All claims, all questions of debate, shall cease;
Nor he, nor they, with force infringe the peace.
But, if my juster arms prevail in fight   280
(As sure they shall, if I divine aright),
My Trojans shall not o'er the Italians reign;
Both equal, both unconquered, shall remain,
Joined in their laws, their lands, and their abodes:
I ask but altars for my weary gods.   285
The care of those religious rites be mine:
The crown to king Latinus I resign:
His be the sovereign sway. Nor will I share
His power in peace, or his command in war.
For me, my friends another town shall frame,   290
And bless the rising towers with fair Lavinia's name."
    Thus he. Then, with erected eyes and hands,
The Latian king before his altar stands.
"By the same heaven (said he), and earth, and main,
And all the powers that all the three contain;   295
By hell below, and by that upper god,
Whose thunder signs the peace, who seals it with his nod;
So let Latona's double offspring hear,
And double-fronted Janus, what I swear:
I touch the sacred altars, touch the flames,   300
And all those powers attest, and all their names:
Whatever chance befall on either side,
Nor term of time this union shall divide:
No force, no fortune, shall my vows unbind,
Or shake the steadfast tenor of my mind;   305
Not, though the circling seas should break their bound,
O'erflow the shores, and sap the solid ground;
Not, though the lamps of heaven their spheres forsake,
Hurled down, and hissing in the nether lake:
E'en as this royal scepter (for he bore   310
A scepter in his hand) shall never more
Shoot out in branches, or renew the birth—
An orphan now, cut from the mother earth

By the keen axe, dishonored of its hair,
And cased in brass, for Latian kings to bear." 315
   When thus in public view the peace was tied
With solemn vows, and sworn on either side,
All dues performed which holy rites require,
The victim beasts are slain before the fire,
The trembling entrails from their bodies torn, 320
And to the fattened flames in chargers borne.
   Already the Rutulians deemed their man
O'ermatched in arms, before the fight began.
First rising fears are whispered through the crowd;
Then, gathering sound, they murmur more aloud. 325
Now, side to side, they measure with their eyes
The champions' bulk, their sinews, and their size:
The nearer they approach, the more is known
The apparent disadvantage of their own.
Turnus himself appears in public sight 330
Conscious of fate, desponding of the fight.
Slowly he moves, and at his altar stands
With eyes dejected, and with trembling hands:
And, while he mutters undistinguished prayers,
A livid deadness in his cheeks appears. 335
   With anxious pleasure when Juturna viewed
The increasing fright of the mad multitude,
When their short sighs and thickening sobs she heard,
And found their ready minds for change prepared;
Dissembling her immortal form, she took 340
Camertes' mien, his habit, and his look—
A chief of ancient blood:—in arms well known
Was his great sire, and he his greater son.
His shape assumed, amid the ranks she ran,
And humoring their first motions, thus began: 345
"For shame, Rutulians! can you bear the sight
Of one exposed for all, in single fight?
Can we, before the face of Heaven, confess
Our courage colder, or our numbers less?

336. *Juturna*: the lake nymph, sister of Turnus.

View all the Trojan host, the Arcadian band,   350
And Tuscan army; count them as they stand:
Undaunted to the battle if we go,
Scarce every second man will share a foe.
Turnus, 'tis true, in this unequal strife,
Shall lose, with honor, his devoted life,   355
Or change it rather for immortal fame,
Succeeding to the gods, from whence he came:
But you, a servile and inglorious band,
For foreign lords shall sow your native land,
Those fruitful fields your fighting fathers gained,   360
Which have so long their lazy sons sustained."
    With words like these, she carried her design.
A rising murmur runs along the line.
Then e'en the city troops, and Latians, tired
With tedious war, seem with new souls inspired: 365
Their champion's fate with pity they lament,
And of the league, so lately sworn, repent.
    Nor fails the goddess to foment the rage
With lying wonders, and a false presage;
But adds a sign, which, present to their eyes,   370
Inspires new courage, and a glad surprise.
For, sudden, in the fiery tracts above,
Appears in pomp the imperial bird of Jove:
A plump of fowl he spies, that swim the lakes,
And o'er their heads his sounding pinions shakes;   375
Then, stooping on the fairest of the train,
In his strong talons trussed a silver swan.
The Italians wonder at the unusual sight:
But while he lags, and labors in his flight,
Behold the dastard fowl return anew,   380
And with united force the foe pursue:
Clamorous around the royal hawk they fly,
And, thickening in a cloud, o'ershade the sky.
They cuff, they scratch, they cross his airy course;
Nor can the encumbered bird sustain their force;   385
But, vexed, not vanquished, drops the pond'rous prey,
And, lightened of his burden, wings his way.

The Ausonian bands with shouts salute the sight,
Eager of action, and demand the fight.
Then king Tolumnius, versed in augurs' arts,   390
Cries out, and thus his boasted skill imparts:
"At length 'tis granted, what I long desired!
This, this is what my frequent vows required.
Ye gods! I take your omen, and obey.—
Advance, my friends, and charge! I lead the way.   395
These are the foreign foes, whose impious band,
Like that rapacious bird, infest our land:
But soon, like him, they shall be forced to sea
By strength united, and forego the prey.
Your timely succor to your country bring;   400
Haste to the rescue, and redeem your king."
    He said: and pressing onward through the crew,
Poised in his lifted arm, his lance he threw.
The wingèd weapon, whistling in the wind,
Came driving on, nor missed the mark designed.   405
At once the cornel rattled in the skies;
At once tumultuous shouts and clamors rise.
Nine brothers in a goodly band there stood,
Born of Arcadian mixed with Tuscan blood,
Gylippus' sons: the fatal javelin flew,   410
Aimed at the midmost of the friendly crew.
A passage through the jointed arms it found,
Just where the belt was to the body bound,
And struck the gentle youth extended on the ground.
Then, fired with pious rage, the generous train   415
Run madly forward to revenge the slain.
And some with eager haste their javelins throw;
And some with sword in hand assault the foe.
    The wished insult the Latine troops embrace,
And meet their ardor in the middle space.   420
The Trojans, Tuscans, and Arcadian line,
With equal courage obviate their design.
Peace leaves the violated fields; and hate
Both armies urges to their mutual fate:

With impious haste their altars are o'erturned,   425
The sacrifice half broiled, and half unburned.
Thick storms of steel from either army fly,
And clouds of clashing darts obscure the sky:
Brands from the fire are missive weapons made,
With chargers, bowls, and all the priestly trade.   430
Latinus, frighted, hastens from the fray,
And bears his unregarded gods away.
These on their horses vault; those yoke the car;
The rest, with swords on high, run headlong to the war.

   Messapus, eager to confound the peace,   435
Spurred his hot courser through the fighting press,
At king Aulestes, by his purple known
A Tuscan prince, and by his regal crown;
And, with a shock encountering, bore him down.
Backward he fell; and, as his fate designed,   440
The ruins of an altar were behind:
There pitching on his shoulders and his head,
Amid the scattering fires he lay supinely spread.
The beamy spear, descending from above,
His cuirass pierced, and through his body drove.   445
Then, with a scornful smile, the victor cries:
"The gods have found a fitter sacrifice."
Greedy of spoils, the Italians strip the dead
Of his rich armor, and uncrown his head.

   Priest Corynaeus armed his better hand,   450
From his own altar, with a blazing brand;
And, as Ebusus with a thundering pace
Advanced to battle, dashed it on his face:
His bristly beard shines out with sudden fires;
The crackling crop a noisome scent expires.   455
Following the blow, he seized his curling crown
With his left hand; his other cast him down.
The prostrate body with his knees he pressed,
And plunged his holy poinard in his breast.

   While Podalirius, with his sword, pursued   460
The shepherd Alsus through the flying crowd,
Swiftly he turns, and aims a deadly blow
Full on the front of his unwary foe.

The broad axe enters with a crashing sound,
And cleaves the chin with one continued wound;   465
Warm blood, and mingled brains, besmear his arms around;
And iron sleep his stupid eyes oppressed,
And sealed their heavy lids in endless rest.
But good Aeneas rushed amid the bands:
Bare was his head, and naked were his hands,   470
In sign of truce: then thus he cries aloud:
"What sudden rage, what new desire of blood,
Inflames your altered minds? O Trojans! cease
From impious arms, nor violate the peace.
By human sanctions, and by laws divine,   475
The terms are all agreed; the war is mine.
Dismiss your fears, and let the fight ensue;
This hand alone shall right the gods and you:
Our injured altars, and their broken vow,
To this avenging sword the faithless Turnus owe."   480
    Thus while he spoke, unmindful of defense,
A wingèd arrow struck the pious prince.
But, whether from some human hand it came,
Or hostile god, is left unknown by fame:
No human hand, or hostile god, was found,   485
To boast the triumph of so base a wound.
    When Turnus saw the Trojan quit the plain,
His chiefs dismayed, his troops a fainting train,
The unhoped event his heightened soul inspires:
At once his arms and coursers he requires;   490
Then, with a leap, his lofty chariot gains,
And with a ready hand assumes the reins.
He drives impetuous, and, where'er he goes,
He leaves behind a lane of slaughtered foes.
These his lance reaches; over those he rolls   495
His rapid car, and crushes out their souls.
In vain the vanquished fly: the victor sends
The dead men's weapons at their living friends.
    Thus, on the banks of Hebrus' freezing flood,
The god of battles, in his angry mood,   500
Clashing his sword against his brazen shield,
Lets loose the reins, and scours along the field;

Before the wind his fiery coursers fly;
Groans the sad earth, resounds the rattling sky.
Wrath, Terror, Treason, Tumult, and Despair   505
(Dire faces, and deformed), surround the car—
Friends of the god, and followers of the war.

　　With fury not unlike, nor less disdain,
Exulting Turnus flies along the plain;
His smoking horses, at their utmost speed,   510
He lashes on; and urges o'er the dead.
Their fetlocks run with blood; and, when they bound,
The gore and gathering dust are dashed around.
Thamyris and Pholus, masters of the war,
He killed at hand; but Sthenelus afar: 515
From far the sons of Imbrasus he slew,
Glaucus and Lades, of the Lycian crew—
Both taught to fight on foot, in battle joined,
Or mount the courser that outstrips the wind.

　　Meantime Eumedes, vaunting in the field,   520
New fired the Trojans, and their foes repelled,
This son of Dolon bore his grandsire's name,
But emulated more his father's fame—
His guileful father, sent a nightly spy,
The Grecian camp and order to descry—   525
Hard enterprise! and well he might require
Achilles' car and horses for his hire:
But, met upon the scout, the Aetolian prince
In death bestowed a juster recompense.

　　Fierce Turnus viewed the Trojan from afar,   530
And launched his javelin from his lofty car,
Then lightly leaping down, pursued the blow,
And, pressing with his foot his prostrate foe,
Wrenched from his feeble hold the shining sword,
And plunged it in the bosom of its lord.   535
"Possess (said he) the fruit of all thy pains,
And measure, at thy length, our Latian plains.

　　505–7. *circumque atrae Formidinis ora,/ Iraeque, Insidiaeque, dei comitatus,
aguntur*: Virgil and Dryden pay their respects to Mars.
　　528. *the Aetolian prince*: Diomede. The story is in the *Iliad*, Book X.

Thus are my foes rewarded by my hand;
Thus may they build their town, and thus enjoy the land!"
    Then Dares, Butes, Sybaris, he slew, 540
Whom o'er his neck the floundering courser threw.
As when loud Boreas, with his blustering train,
Stoops from above, incumbent on the main;
Where'er he flies, he drives the rack before,
And rolls the billows on the Aegean shore: 545
So, where resistless Turnus takes his course,
The scattered squadrons bend before his force:
His crest of horse's hair is blown behind
By adverse air, and rustles in the wind.
    This haughty Phegeus saw with high disdain, 550
And, as the chariot rolled along the plain,
Light from the ground he leapt, and seized the rein.
Thus hung in air, he still retained his hold,
The coursers frighted, and their force controlled.
The lance of Turnus reached him as he hung, 555
And pierced his plated arms, but passed along,
And only razed the skin. He turned, and held
Against his threatening foe his ample shield,
Then called for aid: but, while he cried in vain,
The chariot bore him backward on the plain. 560
He lies reversed; the victor king descends,
And strikes so justly where his helmet ends,
He lops the head. The Latian fields are drunk
With streams that issue from his bleeding trunk.
    While he triumphs, and while the Trojans yield, 565
The wounded prince is forced to leave the field:
Strong Mnestheus, and Achates often tried,
And young Ascanius, weeping by his side,
Conduct him to his tent. Scarce can he rear
His limbs from earth, supported on his spear. 570
Resolved in mind, regardless of the smart,
He tugs with both his hands, and breaks the dart.
The steel remains. No readier way he found
To draw the weapon, than t' enlarge the wound.

    563. *The Latian fields are drunk* . . . : All Dryden.

Eager of fight, impatient of delay,   575
He begs; and his unwilling friends obey.
   Iäpis was at hand to prove his art,
Whose blooming youth so fired Apollo's heart,
That, for his love, he proffered to bestow
His tuneful harp, and his unerring bow: 580
The pious youth, more studious how to save
His aged sire, now sinking to the grave,
Preferred the power of plants, and silent praise
Of healing arts, before Phoebean bays.
   Propped on his lance the pensive hero stood,   585
And heard and saw, unmoved, the mourning crowd.
The famed physician tucks his robes around
With ready hands, and hastens to the wound.
With gentle touches he performs his part,
This way and that, soliciting the dart,   590
And exercises all his heavenly art.
All softening simples, known of sovereign use,
He presses out, and pours their noble juice.
These first infused, to lenify the pain—
He tugs with pincers, but he tugs in vain.   595
Then to the patron of his art he prayed:
The patron of his art refused his aid.
   Meantime the war approaches to the tents:
The alarm grows hotter, and the noise augments:
The driving dust proclaims the danger near;   600
And first their friends and then their foes appear;
Their friends retreat; their foes pursue the rear.
The camp is filled with terror and affright:
The hissing shafts within the trench alight;
An undistinguished noise ascends the sky—   605
The shouts of those who kill, and groans of those who die.
   But now the goddess-mother, moved with grief,
And pierced with pity, hastens for relief.
A branch of healing dittany she brought,
Which in the Cretan fields with care she sought,   610

605. *undistinguished*: confused.
609. *dittany*: *dictamnus*. Aristotle (*Hist. An.* VI, 9. 1) reported that goats
ate the leaves of this plant to relieve themselves of arrows.

(Rough is the stem, which woolly leaves surround;
The leaves with flowers, the flowers with purple crowned),
Well known to wounded goats; a sure relief
To draw the pointed steel, and ease the grief.
This Venus brings, in clouds involved, and brews   615
The extracted liquor with ambrosian dews,
And odorous panacee. Unseen she stands,
Tempering the mixture with her heavenly hands,
And pours it in a bowl, already crowned
With juice of medic'nal herbs, prepared to bathe the wound.   620
The leech, unknowing of superior art
Which aids the cure, with this foments the part;
And in a moment ceased the raging smart.
Stanched is the blood, and in the bottom stands:
The steel, but scarcely touched with tender hands,   625
Moves up, and follows of its own accord,
And health and vigor are at once restored.
Iäpis first perceived the closing wound,
And first the footsteps of a god he found.
"Arms! arms! (he cries) the sword and shield prepare,   630
And send the willing chief, renewed, to war.
This is no mortal work, no cure of mine,
Nor art's effect, but done by hands divine.
Some god our general to the battle sends;
Some god preserves his life for greater ends."   635
    The hero arms in haste: his hands infold
His thighs with cuishes of refulgent gold:
Inflamed to fight, and rushing to the field,
That hand sustaining the celestial shield,
This gripes the lance, and with such vigor shakes,   640
That to the rest the beamy weapon quakes.
Then with a close embrace he strained his son,
And, kissing through his helmet, thus begun:
"My son! from my example learn the war,
In camps to suffer, and in fields to dare;   645
But happier chance than mine attend thy care!
This day my hand thy tender age shall shield,
And crown with honors of the conquered field:

617. *panacee*: plural of panacea.

Thou, when thy riper years shall send thee forth
To toils of war, be mindful of my worth: 650
Assert thy birthright; and in arms be known
For Hector's nephew, and Aeneas' son."
   He said; and, striding, issued on the plain.
Antheus and Mnestheus, and a numerous train,
Attend his steps: the rest their weapons take,   655
And, crowding to the field, the camp forsake.
A cloud of blinding dust is raised around;
Labors beneath their feet the trembling ground.
   Now Turnus, posted on a hill, from far
Beheld the progress of the moving war: 660
With him the Latins viewed the covered plains;
And the chill blood ran backward in their veins.
Juturna saw the advancing troops appear,
And heard the hostile sound, and fled for fear.
Aeneas leads; and draws a sweeping train,   665
Closed in their ranks, and pouring on the plain.
As when a whirlwind, rushing to the shore
From the mid ocean, drives the waves before;
The painful hind with heavy heart foresees
The flatted fields, and slaughter of the trees: 670
With such impetuous rage the prince appears,
Before his doubled front; nor less destruction bears.
And now both armies shock in open field:
Osiris, is by strong Thymbraeus killed.
Archetius, Ufens, Epulon, are slain,   675
(All famed in arms, and of the Latian train),
By Gyas', Mnestheus' and Achates' hand.
The fatal augur falls, by whose command
The truce was broken, and whose lance, embrued
With Trojan blood, the unhappy fight renewed.   680
Loud shouts and clamors rend the liquid sky;
And o'er the field the frighted Latins fly.

662. *gelidusque per ima cucurrit/ ossa tremor*: "a cold tremor ran through
them to the marrow." As Dryden sometimes translated one passage with another
in mind, he may have been thinking here of Book X, 452 (Latin text), *frigidus
. . . coit in praecordia sanguis*, "the chilled blood ran curdling to their hearts."
He had rendered this: "Pale horror sat on each Arcadian face" (Book X, 635).

The prince disdains the dastards to pursue,
Nor moves to meet in arms the fighting few.
Turnus alone, amid the dusky plain,   685
He seeks, and to the combat calls in vain.
Juturna heard, and, seized with mortal fear,
Forced from the beam her brother's charioteer;
Assumes his shape, his armor, and his mien,
And, like Metiscus, in his seat is seen.   690
    As the black swallow near the palace plies;
O'er empty courts, and under arches, flies;
Now hawks aloft, now skims along the flood,
To furnish her loquacious nest with food:
So drives the rapid goddess o'er the plains;   695
The smoking horses run with loosened reins.
She steers a various course among the foes;
Now here, now there, her conquering brother shows;
Now with a straight, now with a wheeling flight,
She turns and bends, but shuns the single fight.   700
Aeneas, fired with fury, breaks the crowd,
And seeks his foe, and calls by name aloud:
He runs within a narrower ring, and tries
To stop the chariot; but the chariot flies.
If he but gain a glimpse, Juturna fears,   705
And far away the Daunian hero bears.
    What should he do? Nor arts nor arms avail;
And various cares in vain his mind assail.
The great Messapus, thundering through the field,
In his left hand two pointed javelins held;   710
Encountering on the prince, one dart he drew,
And with unerring aim, and utmost vigor, threw.
Aeneas saw it come, and stooping low
Beneath his buckler, shunned the threatening blow.
The weapon hissed above his head, and tore   715
The waving plume, which on his helm he wore.
Forced by this hostile act, and fired with spite,
That flying Turnus still declined the fight,
The prince, whose piety had long repelled
His inborn ardor, now invades the field;   720

Invokes the powers of violated peace,
Their rites and injured altars to redress;
Then, to his rage abandoning the rein,
With blood and slaughtered bodies fills the plain.
    What god can tell, what numbers can display,   725
The various labors of that fatal day?
What chiefs and champions fell on either side,
In combat slain, or by what deaths they died?
Whom Turnus, whom the Trojan hero killed?
Who shared the fame and fortune of the field?   730
Jove! could'st thou view, and not avert thy sight,
Two jarring nations joined in cruel fight,
Whom leagues of lasting love so shortly shall unite?
    Aeneas first Rutulian Sucro found,
Whose valor made the Trojans quit their ground;   735
Betwixt his ribs the javelin drove so just,
It reached his heart, nor needs a second thrust.
Now Turnus, at two blows, two brethren slew:
First from his horse fierce Amycus he threw;
Then, leaping on the ground, on foot assailed   740
Diores, and in equal fight prevailed.
Their lifeless trunks he leaves upon the place;
Their heads, distilling gore, his chariot grace.
    Three cold on earth the Trojan hero threw,
Whom without respite at one charge he slew: 745
Cethegus, Tanaïs, Talus, fell oppressed,
And sad Onytes, added to the rest—
Of Theban blood, whom Peridia bore.
    Turnus two brothers from the Lycian shore,
And from Apollo's fane to battle sent,   750
O'erthrew; nor Phoebus could their fate prevent.
Peaceful Menoetes after these he killed,
Who long had shunned the dangers of the field:
On Lerna's lake a silent life he led,
And with his nets and angle earned his bread.   755
Nor pompous cares, nor palaces, he knew,
But wisely from the infectious world withdrew.

    743. *distilling*: dripping.

Poor was his house: his father's painful hand
Discharged his rent, and plowed another's land.
  As flames among the lofty woods are thrown   760
On different sides, and both by winds are blown;
The laurels crackle in the sputtering fire;
The frighted sylvans from their shades retire:
Or as two neighboring torrents fall from high,
Rapid they run; the foamy waters fry;   765
They roll to sea with unresisted force,
And down the rocks precipitate their course:
Not with less rage the rival heroes take
Their different ways; nor less destruction make.
With spears afar, with swords at hand, they strike;   770
And zeal of slaughter fires their souls alike.
Like them, their dauntless men maintain the field;
And hearts are pierced, unknowing how to yield:
They blow for blow return, and wound for wound;
And heaps of bodies raise the level ground.   775
  Murrhanus, boasting of his blood, that springs
From a long royal race of Latian kings,
Is by the Trojan from his chariot thrown,
Crushed with the weight of an unwieldy stone:
Betwixt the wheels he fell; the wheels, that bore   780
His living load, his dying body tore.
His starting steeds, to shun the glittering sword,
Paw down his trampled limbs, forgetful of their lord.
  Fierce Hyllus threatened high, and, face to face,
Affronted Turnus in the middle space: 785
The prince encountered him in full career,
And at his temples aimed the deadly spear;
So fatally the flying weapon sped,
That through his brazen helm it pierced his head.
Nor, Cisseus, could'st thou 'scape from Turnus' hand,   790
In vain the strongest of the Arcadian band:
Nor to Cupencus could his gods afford
Availing aid against the Aenean sword,
Which to his naked heart pursued the course;
Nor could his plated shield sustain the force.   795

Iölas fell, whom not the Grecian powers,
Nor great subverter of the Trojan towers,
Were doomed to kill, while Heaven prolonged his date:
But who can pass the bounds prefixed by Fate?
In high Lyrnessus, and in Troy, he held   800
Two palaces, and was from each expelled:
Of all the mighty man, the last remains
A little spot of foreign earth contains.
    And now both hosts their broken troops unite
In equal ranks, and mix in mortal fight.   805
Serestus and undaunted Mnestheus join
The Trojan, Tuscan, and Arcadian line:
Sea-born Messapus, with Atinas, heads
The Latin squadrons, and to battle leads.
They strike, they push, they throng the scanty space,   810
Resolved on death, impatient of disgrace;
And where one falls, another fills his place.
    The Cyprian goddess now inspires her son
To leave the unfinished fight, and storm the town;
For, while he rolls his eyes around the plain   815
In quest of Turnus, whom he seeks in vain,
He views the unguarded city from afar,
In careless quiet, and secure of war.
Occasion offers, and excites his mind
To dare beyond the task he first designed.   820
Resolved, he calls his chiefs; they leave the fight:
Attended thus, he takes a neighboring height:
The crowding troops about their general stand,
All under arms, and wait his high command.
Then thus the lofty prince: "Hear and obey,   825
Ye Trojan bands, without the least delay.
Jove is with us; and what I have decreed,
Requires our utmost vigor, and our speed.
Your instant arms against the town prepare,
The source of mischief, and the seat of war.   830
This day the Latian towers, that mate the sky,
Shall, level with the plain, in ashes lie:
The people shall be slaves, unless in time
They kneel for pardon, and repent their crime.

Twice have our foes been vanquished on the plain: 835
Then shall I wait till Turnus will be slain?
Your force against the perjured city bend;
There it began, and there the war shall end.
The peace profaned our rightful arms requires:
Cleanse the polluted place with purging fires."   840
    He finished; and—one soul inspiring all—
Formed in a wedge, the foot approach the wall.
Without the town, an unprovided train
Of gaping gazing citizens are slain.
Some firebrands, others scaling-ladders, bear;   845
And those they toss aloft, and these they rear:
The flames now launched, the feathered arrows fly;
And clouds of missive arms obscure the sky.
Advancing to the front, the hero stands,
And, stretching out to heaven his pious hands,   850
Attests the gods, asserts his innocence,
Upbraids with breach of faith the Ausonian prince;
Declares the royal honor doubly stained,
And twice the rites of holy peace profaned.
    Dissenting clamors in the town arise;   855
Each will be heard, and all at once advise.
One part for peace, and one for war, contends:
Some would exclude their foes, and some admit their friends.
The helpless king is hurried in the throng,
And (whate'er tide prevails) is borne along.   860
    Thus, when the swain, within a hollow rock,
Invades the bees with suffocating smoke,
They run around, or labor on their wings,
Disused to flight, and shoot their sleepy stings;
To shun the bitter fumes, in vain they try: 865
Black vapors, issuing from the vent, involve the sky.
    But Fate and envious Fortune now prepare
To plunge the Latins in the last despair.

---

   836. *till Turnus will be slain*: *libeat dum proelia Turno/ nostra pati,* "until
it please Turnus to stand up to us in combat."
   843–4. All from *primos trucidant,* "they slaughter the first met." The verb
implies that these citizens were "unprovided" with weapons, and this in turn
implies that they had come out to gaze and gape.

The queen, who saw the foes invade the town,
And brands on tops of burning houses thrown,   870
Cast round her eyes, distracted with her fear:—
No troops of Turnus in the field appear.
Once more she stares abroad, but still in vain,
And then concludes the royal youth is slain.
Mad with her anguish, impotent to bear   875
The mighty grief, she loathes the vital air.
She calls herself the cause of all this ill,
And owns the dire effects of her ungoverned will:
She raves against the gods; she beats her breast;
She tears with both her hands her purple vest: 880
Then round a beam a running noose she tied,
And, fastened by the neck, obscenely died.
    Soon as the fatal news by fame was blown,
And to her dames and to her daughter known,
The sad Lavinia rends her yellow hair,   885
And rosy cheeks: the rest her sorrow share:
With shrieks the palace rings, and madness of despair.
The spreading rumor fills the public place:
Confusion, fear, distraction, and disgrace,
And silent shame, are seen in every face.   890
Latinus tears his garments as he goes,
Both for his public and his private woes;
With filth his venerable beard besmears,
And sordid dust deforms his silver hairs.
And much he blames the softness of his mind,   895
Obnoxious to the charms of womankind,
And soon reduced to change what he so well designed—
To break the solemn league so long desired,
Nor finish what his fates, and those of Troy, required.
    Now Turnus rolls aloof, o'er empty plains,   900
And here and there some straggling foes he gleans.
His flying coursers please him less and less,
Ashamed of easy fight, and cheap success.
Thus half contented, anxious in his mind,
The distant cries come driving in the wind—   905

  896. *obnoxious*: subject. A Latinism not here suggested by the text.

Shouts from the walls, but shouts in murmurs drowned;
A jarring mixture, and a boding sound.
"Alas! (said he) what mean these dismal cries?
What doleful clamors from the town arise?"
Confused, he stops, and backward pulls the reins.   910
She, who the driver's office now sustains,
Replies, "Neglect, my lord, these new alarms:
Here fight, and urge the fortune of your arms:
There want not others to defend the wall.
If by your rival's hand the Italians fall,   915
So shall your fatal sword his friends oppress,
In honor equal, equal in success."
    To this, the prince: "O sister!—for I knew,
The peace infringed proceeded first from you:
I knew you, when you mingled first in fight: 920
And now in vain you would deceive my sight—
Why, goddess, this unprofitable care?
Who sent you down from heaven, involved in air,
Your share of mortal sorrows to sustain,
And see your brother bleeding on the plain?   925
For to what power can Turnus have recourse,
Or how resist his fate's prevailing force?
These eyes beheld Murrhanus bite the ground—
Mighty the man, and mighty was the wound.
I heard my dearest friend, with dying breath,   930
My name invoking to revenge his death.
Brave Ufens fell with honor on the place,
To shun the shameful sight of my disgrace.
On earth supine, a manly corpse he lies;
His vest and armor are the victor's prize.   935
Then, shall I see Laurentum in a flame,
Which only wanted, to complete my shame?
How will the Latins hoot their champion's flight!
How Drances will insult, and point them to the sight!
Is death so hard to bear?—Ye gods below!   940
(Since those above so small compassion show),
Receive a soul unsullied yet with shame,
Which not belies my great forefathers' name."

He said: and while he spoke, with flying speed
Came Saces urging on his foamy steed: 945
Fixed on his wounded face a shaft he bore,
And, seeking Turnus, sent his voice before:
"Turnus! on you, on you alone, depends
Our last relief;—compassionate your friends!
Like lightning, fierce Aeneas, rolling on,   950
With arms invests, with flames invades the town;
The brands are tossed on high; the winds conspire
To drive along the deluge of the fire.
All eyes are fixed on you: your foes rejoice;
E'en the king staggers, and suspends his choice—   955
Doubts to deliver or defend the town,
Whom to reject, or whom to call his son.
The queen, on whom your utmost hopes were placed,
Herself suborning death, has breathed her last.
'Tis true, Messapus, fearless of his fate,   960
With fierce Atinas' aid, defends the gate:
On every side surrounded by the foe,
The more they kill, the greater numbers grow;
An iron harvest mounts, and still remains to mow.
You, far aloof from your forsaken bands,   965
Your rolling chariot drive o'er empty sands."
    Stupid he sat, his eyes on earth declined,
And various cares revolving in his mind:
Rage, boiling from the bottom of his breast,
And sorrow mixed with shame, his soul oppressed;   970
And conscious worth lay laboring in his thought,
And love by jealousy to madness wrought.
By slow degrees his reason drove away
The mists of passion, and resumed her sway.
Then, rising on his car, he turned his look,   975
And saw the town involved in fire and smoke.
A wooden tower with flames already blazed,
Which his own hands on beams and rafters raised,
And bridges laid above to join the space,
And wheels below to roll from place to place.   980

977. A *wooden tower*: A movable defensive tower.

"Sister! the Fates have vanquished: let us go
The way which heaven and my hard fortune show.
The fight is fixed; nor shall the branded name
Of a base coward blot your brother's fame.
Death is my choice; but suffer me to try   985
My force, and vent my rage before I die."
He said: and leaping down without delay,
Through crowds of scattered foes he freed his way.
Striding he passed, impetuous as the wind,
And left the grieving goddess far behind.   990
    As when a fragment, from a mountain torn
By raging tempests, or by torrents borne,
Or sapped by time, or loosened from the roots—
Prone through the void the rocky ruin shoots,
Rolling from crag to crag, from steep to steep;   995
Down sink, at once, the shepherds and their sheep,
Involved alike, they rush to nether ground;
Stunned with the shock they fall, and stunned from earth
        rebound:
So Turnus, hasting headlong to the town,
Shouldering and shoving, bore the squadrons down.   1000
Still pressing onward, to the walls he drew,
Where shafts and spears and darts promiscuous flew,
And sanguine streams the slippery ground embrue.
First stretching out his arm, in sign of peace,
He cries aloud, to make the combat cease: 1005
"Rutulians, hold! and, Latin troops, retire!
The fight is mine; and me the gods require.
'Tis just that I should vindicate alone
The broken truce, or for the breach atone.
This day shall free from war the Ausonian state,   1010
Or finish my misfortunes in my fate."
    Both armies from their bloody work desist,
And, bearing backward, form a spacious list,
The Trojan hero, who received from fame
The welcome sound, and heard the champion's name,   1015
Soon leaves the taken works and mounted walls:
Greedy of war where greater glory calls,

He springs to fight, exulting in his force;
His jointed armor rattles in the course.
Like Eryx, or like Athos, great he shows,   1020
Or father Apennine, when, white with snows,
His head divine obscure in clouds he hides,
And shakes the sounding forests on his sides.
    The nations, overawed, surcease the fight;
Immovable their bodies, fixed their sight;   1025
E'en death stands still; nor from above they throw
Their darts, nor drive their battering-rams below.
In silent order either army stands,
And drop their swords, unknowing, from their hands.
The Ausonian king beholds, with wondering sight,   1030
Two mighty champions matched in single fight,
Born under climes remote, and brought by fate,
With sword to try their titles to the state.
    Now, in closed field, each other from afar
They view; and, rushing on, begin the war.   1035
They launch their spears; then hand to hand they meet:
The trembling soil resounds beneath their feet;
Their bucklers clash; thick blows descend from high,
And flakes of fire from their hard helmets fly.
Courage conspires with chance; and both engage   1040
With equal fortune yet, and mutual rage.
    As, when two bulls for their fair female fight
In Sila's shades, or on Taburnus' height,
With horns adverse they meet; the keeper flies;
Mute stands the herd; the heifers roll their eyes,   1045
And wait the event—which victor they shall bear,
And who shall be the lord, to rule the lusty year:
With rage of love the jealous rivals burn,
And push for push, and wound for wound, return;
Their dewlaps gored, their sides are laved in blood;   1050
Loud cries and roaring sounds rebellow through the wood:
Such was the combat in the listed ground;
So clash their swords, and so their shields resound,

    1020. *Eryx*: the height in west Sicily (Book V, 991). *Athos*: in Greece, later
the site of the famous monastery.
    1021. *father Apennine*: the main mountain range of Italy.

Jove sets the beam: in either scale he lays
The champion's fate, and each exactly weighs.   1055
On this side, life, and lucky chance, ascends;
Loaded with death, that other scale descends.
Raised on the stretch, young Turnus aims a blow
Full on the helm of his unguarded foe:
Shrill shouts and clamors ring on either side,   1060
As hopes and fears their panting hearts divide.
But all in pieces flies the traitor sword,
And, in the middle stroke, deserts his lord.
Now 'tis but death or flight: disarmed he flies,
When in his hand an unknown hilt he spies.   1065
Fame says that Turnus, when his steeds he joined,
Hurrying to war, disordered in his mind,
Snatched the first weapon which his haste could find.
'Twas not the fated sword his father bore,
But that his charioteer Metiscus wore.   1070
This, while the Trojans fled, the toughness held;
But, vain against the great Vulcanian shield,
The mortal-tempered steel deceived his hand:
The shivered fragments shone amid the sand.
    Surprised with fear, he fled along the field,   1075
And now forthright, and now in orbits wheeled:
For here the Trojan troops the list surround,
And there the pass is closed with pools and marshy ground.
Aeneas hastens, though with heavier pace—
His wound, so newly knit, retards the chase,   1080
And oft his trembling knees their aid refuse—
Yet, pressing foot by foot, his foe pursues.
    Thus, when a fearful stag is closed around
With crimson toils, or in a river found,
High on the bank the deep-mouthed hound appears,   1085
Still opening, following still, where'er he steers:
The persecuted creature, to and fro,
Turns here and there, to escape his Umbrian foe:
Steep is the ascent, and, if he gains the land,
The purple death is pitched along the strand: 1090
His eager foe, determined to the chase,
Stretched at his length, gains ground at every pace:

Now to his beamy head he makes his way,
And now he holds, or thinks he holds, his prey;
Just at the pinch, the stag springs out with fear,   1095
He bites the wind, and fills his sounding jaws with air:
The rocks, the lakes, the meadows, ring with cries;
The mortal tumult mounts, and thunders in the skies.
    Thus flies the Daunian prince, and, flying, blames
His tardy troops, and, calling by their names,   1100
Demands his trusty sword. The Trojan threats
The realm with ruin, and their ancient seats
To lay in ashes, if they dare supply,
With arms or aid, his vanquished enemy:
Thus menacing, he still pursues the course   1105
With vigor, though diminished of his force.
Ten times already, round the listed place,
One chief had fled, and t'other given the chase:
No trivial prize is played; for, on the life
Or death of Turnus, now depends the strife.   1110
    Within the space, an olive tree had stood,
A sacred shade, a venerable wood,
For vows to Faunus paid, the Latins' guardian god.
Here hung the vests, and tablets were engraved,
Of sinking mariners from shipwreck saved.   1115
With heedless hands the Trojans felled the tree,
To make the ground inclosed for combat, free.
Deep in the root, whether by fate, or chance,
Or erring haste, the Trojan drove his lance;
Then stooped, and tugged with force immense, to free   1120
The encumbered spear from the tenacious tree;
That, whom his fainting limbs pursued in vain,
His flying weapon might from far attain.
    Confused with fear, bereft of human aid,
Then Turnus to the gods, and first to Faunus, prayed: 1125
"O Faunus! pity! and thou, mother Earth,
Where I thy foster-son received my birth,
Hold fast the steel! If my religious hand
Your plant has honored, which your foes profaned,
Propitious hear my pious prayer!" He said,   1130
Nor with successless vows invoked their aid.

The incumbent hero wrenched and pulled and strained:
But still the stubborn earth the steel detained.
Juturna took her time; and, while in vain
He strove, assumed Metiscus' form again,   1135
And, in that imitated shape, restored
To the despairing prince his Daunian sword.
The queen of love—who, with disdain and grief,
Saw the bold nymph afford this prompt relief—
To assert her offspring with a greater deed,   1140
From the tough root the lingering weapon freed.
   Once more erect, the rival chiefs advance:
One trusts the sword, and one the pointed lance;
And both resolved alike, to try their fatal chance.
   Meantime imperial Jove to Juno spoke,   1145
Who from a shining cloud beheld the shock:
"What new arrest, O queen of heaven! is sent
To stop the Fates now laboring in the event?
What further hopes are left thee to pursue?
Divine Aeneas (and thou know'st it too),   1150
Foredoomed, to these celestial seats is due.
What more attempts for Turnus can be made,
That thus thou lingerest in this lonely shade?
Is it becoming of the due respect
And awful honor of a god elect,   1155
A wound unworthy of our state to feel,
Patient of human hands, and earthly steel?
Or seems it just, the sister should restore
A second sword, when one was lost before,
And arm a conquered wretch against his conqueror?   1160
For what, without thy knowledge and avow,
Nay more, thy dictate, durst Juturna do?
At last, in deference to my love, forbear
To lodge within thy soul this anxious care:
Reclined upon my breast, thy grief unload: 1165
Who should relieve the goddess, but the god?
Now all things to their utmost issue tend,
Pushed by the Fates to their appointed end.
While leave was given thee, and a lawful hour
For vengeance, wrath, and unresisted power,   1170

Tossed on the seas thou could'st thy foes distress,
And, driven ashore, with hostile arms oppress;
Deform the royal house; and, from the side
Of the just bridegroom, tear the plighted bride:—
Now cease at my command." The thunderer said;   1175
And, with dejected eyes, this answer Juno made:
"Because your dread decree too well I knew,
From Turnus and from earth unwilling I withdrew.
Else should you not behold me here, alone,
Involved in empty clouds, my friends bemoan,   1180
But, girt with vengeful flames, in open sight,
Engaged against my foes in mortal fight.
'Tis true, Juturna mingled in the strife
By my command, to save her brother's life,
At least to try; but (by the Stygian lake—   1185
The most religious oath the gods can take)
With this restriction, not to bend the bow,
Or toss the spear, or trembling dart to throw.
And now, resigned to your superior might,
And tired with fruitless toils, I loathe the fight.   1190
This let me beg (and this no fates withstand)
Both for myself and for your father's land,
That, when the nuptial bed shall bind the peace
(Which I, since you ordain, consent to bless),
The laws of either nation be the same;   1195
But let the Latins still retain their name,
Speak the same language which they spoke before,
Wear the same habits which their grandsires wore.
Call them not Trojans: perish the renown
And name of Troy, with that detested town.   1200
Latium be Latium still; let Alba reign,
And Rome's immortal majesty remain."
  Then thus the founder of mankind replies
(Unruffled was his front, serene his eyes):
"Can Saturn's issue, and heaven's other heir,   1205
Such endless anger in her bosom bear?
Be mistress, and your full desires obtain;
But quench the choler you foment in vain.

From ancient blood, the Ausonian people sprung,
Shall keep their name, their habit, and their tongue: 1210
The Trojans to their customs shall be tied:
I will, myself, their common rites provide:
The natives shall command, the foreigners subside.
All shall be Latium; Troy without a name;
And her lost sons forget from whence they came.   1215
From blood so mixed, a pious race shall flow,
Equal to gods, excelling all below.
No nation more respect to you shall pay,
Or greater offerings on your altars lay."
Juno consents, well pleased that her desires   1220
Had found success, and from the cloud retires.
    The peace thus made, the thunderer next prepares
To force the watery goddess from the wars.
Deep in the dismal regions void of light,
Three daughters, at a birth, were born to Night: 1225
These their brown mother, brooding on her care,
Indued with windy wings, to flit in air,
With serpents girt alike, and crowned with hissing hair.
In heaven the Dirae called, and still at hand,
Before the throne of angry Jove they stand,   1230
His ministers of wrath, and ready still
The minds of mortal men with fears to fill,
Whene'er the moody sire, to wreak his hate
On realms or towns deserving of their fate,
Hurls down diseases, death, and deadly care,   1235
And terrifies the guilty world with war.
One sister plague of these, from heaven he sent,
To fright Juturna with a dire portent.
The pest comes whirling down: by far more slow
Springs the swift arrow from the Parthian bow,   1240
Or Cydon yew, when, traversing the skies,
And drenched in poisonous juice, the sure destruction flies.
With such a sudden, and unseen a flight,
Shot through the clouds the daughter of the Night.

1240-41. Parthians and Cydonians (Cretans) were great archers.

Soon as the field inclosed she had in view,   1245
And from afar her destined quarry knew—
Contracted, to the boding bird she turns,
Which haunts the ruined piles and hallowed urns,
And beats about the tombs with nightly wings,
Where songs obscene on sepulchers she sings.   1250
Thus lessened in her form, with frightful cries
The Fury round unhappy Turnus flies,
Flaps on his shield, and flutters o'er his eyes.
     A lazy chillness crept along his blood;
Choked was his voice; his hair with horror stood.   1255
Juturna from afar beheld her fly,
And knew the ill omen, by her screaming cry,
And stridor of her wings. Amazed with fear,
Her beauteous breast she beat, and rent her flowing hair.
"Ah me! (she cries) in this unequal strife,   1260
What can thy sister more, to save thy life?
Weak as I am, can I, alas! contend
In arms with that inexorable fiend?
Now, now, I quit the field! forbear to fright
My tender soul, ye baleful birds of night!   1265
The lashing of your wings I know too well,
The sounding flight, and funeral screams of hell!
These are the gifts you bring from haughty Jove,
The worthy recompense of ravished love!
Did he for this, exempt my life from fate?   1270
O hard conditions of immortal state!
Though born to death, not privileged to die,
But forced to bear imposed eternity!
Take back your envious bribes, and let me go
Companion to my brother's ghost below!   1275
The joys are vanished: nothing now remains
Of life immortal, but immortal pains.
What earth will open her devouring womb,
To rest a weary goddess in the tomb?"
She drew a length of sighs; nor more she said,   1280
But in her azure mantle wrapped her head,

     1247. *the boding bird*: an owl.

Then plunged into her stream, with deep despair,
And her last sobs came bubbling up in air.
  Now stern Aeneas waves his weighty spear
Against his foe, and thus upbraids his fear: 1285
"What further subterfuge can Turnus find?
What empty hopes are harbored in his mind?
'Tis not thy swiftness can secure thy flight;
Not with their feet, but hands, the valiant fight.
Vary thy shape in thousand forms, and dare   1290
What skill and courage can attempt in war:
Wish for the wings of winds, to mount the sky;
Or hid within the hollow earth to lie!"
The champion shook his head, and made this short reply:
"No threats of thine my manly mind can move;   1295
'Tis hostile heaven I dread, and partial Jove."
He said no more, but, with a sigh, repressed
The mighty sorrow in his swelling breast.
Then, as he rolled his troubled eyes around,
An antique stone he saw, the common bound   1300
Of neighboring fields, and barrier of the ground—
So vast, that twelve strong men of modern days
The enormous weight from earth could hardly raise.
He heaved it at a lift, and, poised on high,
Ran staggering on against his enemy;   1305
But so disordered, that he scarcely knew
His way, or what unwieldy weight he threw.
His knocking knees are bent beneath the load;
And shivering cold congeals his vital blood.
The stone drops from his arms, and, falling short   1310
For want of vigor, mocks his vain effort.
And as, when heavy sleep has closed the sight,
The sickly fancy labors in the night;
We seem to run; and, destitute of force,
Our sinking limbs forsake us in the course: 1315

1283. Dryden's detail.
  1295. *non me tua fervida terrent/ dicta, ferox: di me terrent et Iuppiter hostis.*

In vain we heave for breath; in vain we cry:
The nerves, unbraced, their usual strength deny;
And on the tongue the faltering accents die:
So Turnus fared: whatever means he tried,
All force of arms, and points of art employed,   1320
The Fury flew athwart, and made the endeavor void.

A thousand various thoughts his soul confound:
He stared about, nor aid nor issue found:
His own men stop the pass, and his own walls surround.
Once more he pauses, and looks out again,   1325
And seeks the goddess charioteer in vain.
Trembling he views the thundering chief advance,
And brandishing aloft the deadly lance:
Amazed he cowers beneath his conquering foe,
Forgets to ward, and waits the coming blow.   1330
Astonished while he stands, and fixed with fear,
Aimed at his shield he sees the impending spear.

The hero measured first, with narrow view,
The destined mark; and, rising as he threw,
With its full swing the fatal weapon flew.   1335
Not with less rage the rattling thunder falls,
Or stones from battering engines break the walls:
Swift as a whirlwind, from an arm so strong,
The lance drove on, and bore the death along.
Nought could his sevenfold shield the prince avail,   1340
Nor aught, beneath his arms, the coat of mail;
It pierced through all, and with a grisly wound
Transfixed his thigh, and doubled him to ground.
With groans the Latins rend the vaulted sky:
Woods, hills, and valleys, to the voice reply.   1345

Now low on earth the lofty chief is laid,
With eyes cast upwards, and with arms displayed,
And, recreant, thus to the proud victor prayed:
"I know my death deserved, nor hope to live:
Use what the gods and thy good fortune give.   1350
Yet think, oh think! if mercy may be shown,
(Thou hadst a father once, and hast a son),
Pity my sire, now sinking to the grave;
And, for Anchises' sake, old Daunus save!

Or, if thy vowed revenge pursue my death,   1355
Give to my friends my body void of breath!
The Latian chiefs have seen me beg my life:
Thine is the conquest, thine the royal wife:
Against a yielded man, 'tis mean ignoble strife."
　　In deep suspense the Trojan seemed to stand,   1360
And, just prepared to strike, repressed his hand.
He rolled his eyes, and every moment felt
His manly soul with more compassion melt;
When, casting down a casual glance, he spied
The golden belt that glittered on his side,   1365
The fatal spoil which haughty Turnus tore
From dying Pallas, and in triumph wore.
Then, roused anew to wrath, he loudly cries
(Flames, while he spoke, came flashing from his eyes),
"Traitor! dost thou, dost thou to grace pretend,   1370
Clad, as thou art, in trophies of my friend?
To his sad soul a grateful offering go!
'Tis Pallas, Pallas gives this deadly blow."
He raised his arm aloft, and, at the word,
Deep in his bosom drove the shining sword.   1375
The streaming blood distained his arms around;
And the disdainful soul came rushing through the wound.

BIBLIOGRAPHY

1. *The Works of Virgil:* containing His Pastorals, Georgics, and Aeneis. Translated into English Verse; By Mr. Dryden. Adorn'd with a Hundred Sculptures / Sequiturque Patrem non Passibus Aequis. Virg. Aen. 2. / London, Printed for Jacob Tonson, at the Judges-Head in Fleetstreet, near the Inner-Temple-Gate, MDCXCVII.
2. *P. Virgili Maronis Opera:* Interpretatione et Notis Illustravit Carolus Ruaeus S. J. Ad Usum Serenissimi Delphini / Editio Secunda Veneta Auctior et Emendatior / Cui Accessit Index Accuratissimus, Omnibus Numeris et Concordantiis Absolutus / Juxta Editionem Tertiam Parisiensem Anni 1726 / Venetis MDCCLXXVI.
3. *John Dryden: Of Dramatic Poesy, and Other Critical Essays* / In Two Volumes / Edited with an Introduction by George Watson / London: J. M. Dent & Sons, Ltd., 1962.
4. *The Poems of John Dryden,* Edited by James Kinsley / In Four Volumes / Oxford, at the Clarendon Press, 1958.
5. *The Works of Virgil,* Translated by John Dryden. With an Introduction by James Kinsley. Oxford University Press, 1961. (The text followed, with some slight changes and corrections and Americanization of the spelling, in the present edition.)